THE ROAD MOVIE BOOK

The road is an enduring theme in American culture. The myth of the road has its origins in the nation's frontier ethos; in the twentieth century, technological advances brought motion pictures to mass audiences and the mass-produced automobile within the reach of the ordinary American. When Jean Baudrillard equated modern American culture with "space, speed, cinema, technology" he could just as easily have added that the road movie is its supreme emblem. *The Road Movie Book* is the first comprehensive study of this enduring but ever-changing Hollywood genre and its legacy to world cinema beyond the United States.

Movies discussed range from the classics such as *It Happened One Night*, *The Grapes of Wrath*, *The Wizard of Oz*, and the Bob Hope–Bing Crosby *Road to* films, through 1960s reworkings of the genre in *Easy Rider* and *Bonnie and Clyde*, to the road movie's contemporary flourishing with hits such as *Paris, Texas*, the *Mad Max* trilogy, *Rain Man*, *Thelma and Louise*, *Natural Born Killers* and *The Adventures of Priscilla, Queen of the Desert*.

The contributors explore how the road movie has confronted and represented issues of nationhood, sexuality, gender, class, and race. They map the generic terrain of the road movie, trace its evolution on American television as well as on the big screen from the 1930s through the 1990s, and, finally, consider road movies that go off the road, departing from the US landscape or travelling the margins of contemporary culture.

Contributors: Stuart C. Aitken, Mark Alvey, Steven Cohan, Corey K. Creekmur, Delia Falconer, Ina Rae Hark, Barbara Klinger, Robert Lang, Ian Leong, Christopher Lee Lukinbeal, Katie Mills, Angelo Restivo, Shari Roberts, Pamela Robertson, Bennet Schaber, Mike Sell, Julian Stringer, Kelly Thomas, Sharon Willis.

Editors: Steven Cohan is Professor of English at Syracuse University. He is co-author of *Telling Stories* and author of *Masked Men: Masculinity and the Movies in the Fifties*. Ina Rae Hark is Professor of English and Associate Dean of the College of Liberal Arts at the University of South Carolina. She is co-editor with Steven Cohan of *Screening the Male: Exploring Masculinities in Hollywood Cinema*.

THE ROAD MOVIE BOOK

Edited by
Steven Cohan and Ina Rae Hark

London and New York

First published 1997
by Routledge
11 New Fetter Lane, London EC4P 4EE

Simultaneously published in the USA and Canada
by Routledge
29 West 35th Street, New York, NY 10001

Typeset in Perpetua and Bell Gothic by
Keystroke, Jacaranda Lodge, Wolverhampton
Printed and bound in Great Britain by
Butler & Tanner, Frome and Somerset

British Library Cataloguing in Publication Data
A catalogue record for this book is available from the British Library

Library of Congress Cataloging in Publication Data
The road movie book / [edited by] Steven Cohan and Ina Rae Hark.
p. cm.
Includes bibliographical references and indexes.
1. Road films—History and criticism. I. Cohan, Steven.
II. Hark, Ina Rae.
PN1995.9.R63R63 1997
791.43′655—dc21 97–8924

ISBN 0–415–14936–3 (hbk)
0–415–14937–1 (pbk)

CONTENTS

CONTENTS

CONTENTS

PLATES

PLATES

CONTRIBUTORS

Stuart C. Aitken is Professor of Geography at San Diego State University. His books include *Putting Children in Their Place* (1994) and *Place, Power, Situation and Spectacle: A Geography of Film* (1994), as well as numerous articles. He is currently completing a book, *The Place of Families and the Power of Community*, for Rutgers University Press.

Mark Alvey received his Ph.D. from The University of Texas at Austin in 1995, completing a dissertation on television drama series of the early 1960s. His work has appeared in *The Revolution Wasn't Televised* (Routledge, 1996) and *The Encyclopedia of Television* (Fitzroy Dearborn, 1997). He is Director of Archives and Education at The Museum of Broadcast Communications in Chicago, just a few blocks from the eastern terminus of old Route 66.

Steven Cohan is Professor of English at Syracuse University, where he teaches film, gender studies, and narrative theory. He is co-author of *Telling Stories: A Theoretical Analysis of Narrative Fiction* and co-editor of *Screening the Male: Exploring Masculinities in Hollywood Cinema*; his articles on film have appeared in *Camera Obscura*, *Screen*, *The Masculine Masquerade*, and *Stud: Architectures of Masculinity*. His most recent book is *Masked Men: Masculinity and the Movies in the Fifties*, published by Indiana University Press in 1997.

Corey K. Creekmur has taught film and cultural studies courses at the University of Chicago, Wayne State University, and the University of Iowa. He is the co-editor, with Alexander Doty, of *Out in Culture: Gay, Lesbian, and Queer Essays on Popular Culture* (Duke University Press, 1995), and his current work examines the representation of gender and sexuality in the Western genre.

Delia Falconer received her Ph.D. from the University of Melbourne in 1996. Her thesis, *Vanishing Points: Mapping the Road in Postwar American Culture*, was undertaken in the Department of English, where she currently teaches.

Ina Rae Hark has, since 1975, taught film studies at the University of South Carolina, where she is Professor of English and Associate Dean of the College of Liberal Arts. Her articles on masculinity in film, Hitchcock, and film and politics have appeared in *Cinema Journal*, *Literature/Film Quarterly*, *The Journal of Popular Film*, *Film History*, *South Atlantic Quarterly*, *The New Orleans Review*, and the essay collection *Hitchcock's Re-Released Films*. She is co-editor with Steven Cohan of *Screening the Male* (Routledge, 1993).

Barbara Klinger is Director of the Film Studies program and Associate Professor of Comparative Literature at Indiana University in Bloomington, Indiana. She is the author of *Melodrama and Meaning: History, Culture, and the Films of Douglas Sirk*. She is currently working on a book entitled *Revolution Revisited: Cinema, Public Memory, and the 1960s*.

Robert Lang, who teaches film studies at the University of Hartford, recently spent a year at the University of Tunis as a Fulbright Scholar. He is the author of *American Film Melodrama: Griffith, Vidor, Minnelli* and the editor of *The Birth of a Nation: D.W. Griffith, Director*. He is currently completing a book on homosocial masculinity in Hollywood cinema.

Ian Leong is a doctoral student in literary theory and cultural studies in the Department of English at the University of Michigan.

Christopher Lee Lukinbeal received his Master of Arts in Geography from California State University at Hayward in 1995 and is presently in a joint Ph.D. program at San Diego State University and University of California, Santa Barbara. He is the author of articles in *California Geographer* and *APCG Yearbook*.

Katie Mills is completing her Ph.D. in English at the University of Southern California, and her thesis is on the road story since the Second World War. She has published articles in *The Spectator* and *Vanishing Point*.

Angelo Restivo is completing his Ph.D. in Critical Studies at the University of Southern California. He has articles forthcoming in *Film Quarterly* and *Quarterly Review of Film and Television*, and is editing a special issue of *The Spectator* on "The New Psychoanalysis."

Shari Roberts is Assistant Professor in the Department of Communications at Pennsylvania State University. She has published in *Cinema Journal* and is the author of *Seeing Stars: Spectacles of Difference in World War II Hollywood Musicals* (Duke University Press, 1998).

CONTRIBUTORS

Pamela Robertson is a Lecturer in Film Studies at the University of Newcastle, Australia. She is the author of *Guilty Pleasures: Feminist Camp From Mae West to Madonna* (Duke University Press, 1996).

Bennet Schaber is on the road three days a week, commuting to his job teaching in the English Department at the State University of New York at Oswego. He is co-editor (with the late Bill Readings) of *Postmodernism Across the Ages* (Syracuse University Press) and author of essays on literature, art, film, and television.

Mike Sell is a graduate student in the Department of English at the University of Michigan and has an article forthcoming in *Journal of Dramatic Theory and Criticism*.

Julian Stringer is a teaching assistant in the graduate film studies program at Indiana University. His articles appear in *Asian Cinema, CineAction! Popular Music,* and *Screen.*

Kelly Thomas is a doctoral student in American cultural studies in the Department of English at the University of Michigan.

Sharon Willis is Associate Professor in the Department of Modern Literatures and Cultures at the University of Rochester. She is co-editor of the journal *Camera Obscura*. Her many publications include chapters in *Boys* (1996), *The Ends of Theory* (forthcoming), *Film Theory Goes to the Movies* (1993), *Rethinking Translation* (1992), and *Seduction and Theory* (1989). She is co-editor of *Male Trouble* (University of Minnesota Press, 1989), author of *Marguerite Duras: Writing on the Body* (University of Illinois Press, 1987) and has completed a book on sexual and social difference in contemporary popular cinema.

INTRODUCTION

Steven Cohan and Ina Rae Hark

The mating of the road and the movies is as enduring as any of Hollywood's famous couples, and seemingly just as inevitable. The road has always been a persistent theme of American culture. Its significance, embedded in both popular mythology and social history, goes back to the nation's frontier ethos, but was transformed by the technological intersection of motion pictures and the automobile in the twentieth century. When Jean Baudrillard equates American culture with "space, speed, cinema, technology" (100) he could just as well be describing the characteristic features of a road movie. Forging a travel narrative out of a particular conjunction of plot and setting that sets the liberation of the road against the oppression of hegemonic norms, road movies project American Western mythology onto the landscape traversed and bound by the nation's highways: "The road defines the space between town and country. It is an empty expanse, a *tabula rasa*, the last true frontier" (Dargis: 16). The 1969 ad campaign for *Easy Rider* exclaimed, "A man went looking for America and couldn't find it anywhere," and this much-remembered sentiment condenses what is typically taken for granted as the ideological project of a road movie, regardless of what travel narrative it specifically recounts.

The ongoing popularity of the road for motion picture audiences in the United States owes much to its obvious potential for romanticizing alienation as well as for problematizing the uniform identity of the nation's culture:

> Road movies are too cool to address seriously socio-political issues. Instead, they express the fury and suffering at the extremities of civilised life, and give their restless protagonists the false hope of a one-way ticket to nowhere . . . road movies are cowled in lurking menace, spontaneous mayhem and dead-end fatalism, never more than few roadstops away from abject lawlessness and haphazard bloodletting . . . road movies have always been songs of the doomed, warnings that once you enter the open hinterlands between cities, you're on your own.
>
> (Atkinson: 16)

1

But much more significant is that a road movie provides a ready space for exploration of the tensions and crises of the historical moment during which it is produced. Key moments in the history of the road movie tend to come in periods of upheaval and dislocation, such as the Great Depression, or in periods whose dominant ideologies generate fantasies of escape and opposition, as in the late 1960s. Likewise, the three major cycles of outlaw-rebel road films – the subgenre that provokes the sentimental existentialism in the above quotation – have occurred in eras where the culture is reevaluating a just-closed period of national unity focused on positive, work-ethic goals: the *film noir* aftermath of the war (*Detour, They Live by Night*); the late 1960s challenge to the corporate conformism and anti-Communism of the Eisenhower era and the deepening involvement in Vietnam throughout the subsequent decade (*Bonnie and Clyde, Easy Rider*); and, most recently, in the early 1990s as the Reagan era's renewed offensive against the Communists lost its primary target and the masculinist heroics of the Gulf War gave way to closer scrutiny (*My Own Private Idaho, Thelma and Louise, Natural Born Killers*).

From the old studio system to the new Hollywood in short, the American road movie has measured the continuity of the US film industry throughout its various economic incarnations. The road movie is, in this regard, like the musical or the Western, a Hollywood genre that catches peculiarly American dreams, tensions, and anxieties, even when imported by the motion picture industries of other nations. However, despite the obvious popularity and significance of the road movie throughout the history of American cinema, there has not yet been much sustained inquiry into what precisely qualifies a film as a road movie, how the genre relates to the social and cultural history of the United States, or how its inflection alters when carried over to a non-American landscape such as Australia. As Timothy Corrigan has observed, "As a film genre, road movies are frequently bypassed by some of the best studies of genre" (143).

According to Corrigan, "the road movie is very much a postwar phenomenon" (143), and it finds its generic coherence, he explains, in the coalescence of four related features that connect the genre to the history of postwar US culture. A road narrative, first of all, responds to the breakdown of the family unit, "that Oedipal centerpiece of classical narrative" (145), and so witnesses the resulting destabilization of male subjectivity and masculine empowerment. Second, "in the road movie events act upon the characters: the historical world is always too much of a context, and objects along the road are usually menacing and materially assertive" (145). Third, the road protagonist readily identifies with the means of mechanized transportation, the automobile or motorcycle, which "becomes the only promise of self in a culture of mechanical reproduction" (146), to the point where it even becomes "transformed into a human or spiritual reality" (145). And fourth, as "a genre traditionally focused, almost exclusively, on men and the absence of women" (143), the road movie promotes a male escapist fantasy linking masculinity to technology and defining the road as a space that is at once resistant to while ultimately contained by the responsibilities of domesticity: home life, marriage, employment.

Corrigan's account of the road movie makes only partial sense of its generic continuity, however, which stretches back before the war to the 1930s. "Road movies are," as he observes, "by definition, movies about cars, trucks, motorcycles, or some other motoring self-descendant of the nineteenth-century train" (144). The significance of technology in the road movie, differentiating its quest narratives and wandering protagonists from those of the Western, has as much to do with representing modernity, its historical achievements as well as its social problems, as it does with reiterating masculinist fantasies of escape and liberation. One early shot in *Easy Rider*, which places Peter Fonda and Dennis Hopper in the background, fixing the flat tire on the former's motorcycle, while a rancher shoes his horse in the foreground, vividly captures how the genre repeatedly does not oppose so much as bring together the modernity of transportation on the twentieth-century road and the traditions still historically present in the settings that the road crosses.

The informing relation of modernity and tradition has repeatedly organized road narratives on film, leading David Laderman to conclude in a recent article that the genre is defined by its repeated positioning of conservative values and rebellious desires in an often uncomfortable, even depoliticized dialectic. As a result, the road movie genre has repeatedly worked, first, to set in opposition two contrasting myths central to American ideology, that of individualism and that of populism, and second, to use the road to imagine the nation's culture, that space between the western desert and the eastern seaboard, either as a utopian fantasy of homogeneity and national coherence, or as a dystopic nightmare of social difference and reactionary politics. The ad campaign for *Easy Rider* may confirm Wyatt's (Fonda) conclusion in the film that "We blew it," but these two travelers *do* find "America," even if it is not the one they initially set out in search of. As lawyer George Hanson (Jack Nicholson) concludes, when explaining why the two bikers represent so great a threat to the Southern rednecks who ultimately destroy them, it all has to do with the freedom they represent on their bikes. "Talking about it and being it, that's two different things," he comments. "I mean it's hard to be free, when you're bought and sold in the marketplace."

The irony here is that, while the bikers' being on the road testifies to their apparent freedom, visualized further in their counter-culture appearance and behavior, they themselves represent an incoherent conjunction of modernity and tradition (after all, the American flag is emblazoned on Wyatt's helmet and bike). More to the point, a plastic tube hidden inside the gas tank of Wyatt's bike is the evidence of this pair's own containment by the marketplace of US capital.

Plate I.1 Easy Rider. Dennis Hopper and Peter Fonda go in search of America and discover that "We blew it."

The tubing conceals the bankroll earned in the drug deal that opens the film, and Billy (Hopper) sees this money as their ticket to freedom, by which he means the same kind of economic security that drives corporate America on the two coasts that bound their road. Billy thus cannot understand why Wyatt thinks they "blew it": "We've done it. We're rich, Wyatt. Yeah, man. Yeah. . . . We'll retire in Florida now, mister. We're rich, man. . . . That's what it's all about, man. I mean, like you know, and then you do it for the big money, man, and then you're free. Dig?" As the film depicts it, though, what prevents these easy riders from achieving their counter-culture version of the American dream is the redneck Southern culture that they have to pass through on their quest for freedom, and this makes the road menacing once they leave the utopian promise of the desert and the hippie commune housed there. The dystopic view of America from the road they go on to travel, which sets the liberation of that desert wilderness against the oppression of the redneck culture beyond it, causing Wyatt to realize "we blew it," has dominated road movies since the release of *Easy Rider*, which, Lee Hill rightly asserts, "almost single-handedly created the road movie as a vital post-60s genre" (72).

The impact of *Easy Rider* is undeniable and important to any understanding of the genre, but it has also obscured the road movie's own history. Although the road has always functioned in movies as an alternative space where isolation from the mainstream permits various transformative experiences, the majority of road films made before the 1960s more successfully imagined an ultimate reintegration of road travelers into the dominant culture. Certain perpetual wanderers of the 1930s, most famously Tom Joad (Henry Fonda) in *The Grapes of Wrath*, might emerge in the genre, and other such defiers of the law might perish at the hands of an unforgiving society, as in the outlaw couple (Fonda and Sylvia Sidney) in *You Only Live Once*, but such cases were the exception rather than the rule. More paradigmatic of the "classic" road film is *It Happened One Night*, the big Academy Award winner of 1934. Its female protagonist, Ellie Andrews (Claudette Colbert) flees the oppression of her wealthy class background, and she finds her liberation in the "normality" of the people she meets on the road, most notably her unexpected companion, newsman Peter Warne (Clark Gable). The significance of their coupling is condensed when he teaches her how to dunk doughnuts: "Forty million dollars and you don't know how to dunk," he observes with scorn. "I'd change places with a plumber's daughter any day," she replies; and moments later, when her father's detectives come into their motel room to question them, she pretends that she is such common "folk," which allows her to escape their

Plate I.2 Gable and Colbert: the heterosexual couple on the road in *It Happened One Night*.

scrutiny. Ellie's road trip results in a change of character, which her father notices upon her return, allowing her to appreciate Peter's worth in contrast to her gigolo-husband, because it assimilates her to the culture that her wealth has isolated her from. Furthermore, while on the road she can be stripped of her luggage and money, subjected to chance meetings and detours, threatened with starvation and homelessness, and ultimately dependent on the hospitality and good will of strangers like Warne, but the precariousness of her situation still does not make the road a place of potential menace or danger.

Ultimately, the road traveled from Florida to New York State in *It Happened One Night* is a utopian space rather like the desert in *Easy Rider*, and it defines both the setting and agenda of road movies throughout the studio era. As Barbara Ching and Rita Barnard observe about this film: "The basic premise and source of laughter . . . is that all experience is mediated or filtered by class. This uncomfortably radical insight, however, is sanitized by the standard comic narrative, and finally distilled into the trite message that the rich are unlucky because they are sealed off from real people, real experience, and real community. However, the force of this ideological containment is balanced by the film presentation of communal experience," as evoked by Ellie's travels, as when she joins in a singalong on the bus (54). Romance and the reestablishment of a democratic consensus dominate the road in 1930s and 1940s Hollywood films such as *Love on the Run*, *Fugitive Lovers*, *Sullivan's Travels*, *Saboteur*, and *Without Reservations*, just as they do in the Frank Capra comedy.

The famous and influential example of *It Happened One Night* should remind us that Corrigan's account of the road movie, which emphasizes its "distinctly existential air" and the corresponding centrality of "male buddies, usually a pair whose questing will only be distracted or, at best, complemented by the women who intrude from time to time" (144), takes for granted a crucial paradigm shift in the genre that occurred in the decades following the Second World War, when the road and the road movie were both mediated by the publication of Jack Kerouac's *On the Road* in 1957. A recounting of journeys that occurred a decade prior to this date, the novel in fact chronicles a rethinking of the road myth that the cultural marginality of Kerouac's protagonists would later codify even before the release of *Easy Rider* in 1969.

The novel's famous pair of road buddies, Sal Paradise and Dean Moriarty, epitomize the road's prior and future connotations. Sal is in many ways a contrast to Dean, particularly in his middle-class origins and family safety nets; his long-suffering aunt is always bailing him out monetarily. He is the college boy who looks not only to live life on the road but to use it as raw material for his books. In an oft-cited example he envisions a trip that will promise to end just in time for him to return for the beginning of the next semester at school. Sal's adventures, moreover, resemble those in pre-1950s road films, where the unpredictability and chance occurrences of the road mean that getting to one's destination depends upon the kindness – and motor vehicles – of others. Most of Sal's road journeys without Dean combine hitch-hiking and bus trips. At one point Kerouac even cites a 1940s road film as an analogue of his adventure. Sal observes of the bus trip to Los Angeles where he meets the Mexican girl Terry: "In the gray, dirty dawn, like the dawn when Joel McCrea met Veronica Lake in a diner, in the picture *Sullivan's Travels*, she slept in my life" (82).

Sal's companion, Dean Moriarty, on the other hand, is an ex-convict and juvenile delinquent, whose drunken father is the never-realized goal of all his frantic motion. It is with Dean that the union of man and automobile becomes an integral part of the myth of the road. As Michael Herr (who has completed a screenplay of the novel for director Francis Ford Coppola) comments, Dean, like his real life alter-ego, Neal Cassady, "was like the Demon Driver. The guy could drive with his eyes closed. He just was born to drive." "It's Dean," Herr also comments, "who's the money character. He's the guy with the real juice" (Porter: 22). When Warner Bros. attempted to adapt the novel for the screen in the late 1950s, that unfilmed screenplay ended, unlike the novel, with Dean dying in a car crash "because he has to be chastised for his excessive sensibility" (14).

In *On the Road* Dean barrels both east and west in a 1949 Hudson and later takes a late 1930s Chevy on the climactic trip to Mexico. The pairing of the wild Dean with the more cerebral Sal is what announces the shift in thinking about America through the trope of the road and its future significance for postwar car culture. When, on his first trip west, Sal and his road-pal Eddie are offered the chance to take over one of two cars that a Montana cowboy needs driven home from Nebraska, Eddie is the one who takes the wheel, because urban easterner Sal doesn't even have a driver's license. By contrast, Dean's skills as a wild, speeding, yet masterful driver are celebrated throughout the novel, uncannily mirroring Hollywood's own personification of the liberation that speed represents, James Dean, who did, of course, die in a blazing car crash just like the one Warners wanted for the end of *On the Road*. Indeed, for Corrigan, Hollywood's speeding Dean is the quintessential road figure (though he did not make a road movie) and a prefiguration of Kerouac's Dean. Corrigan sees the image of James Dean haunting the genre's investment in masculinist fantasy: initially as symbolized by the imagery of the traveling pair's transcendental relation to their automobile, later by the "commodification of the image [itself] as vehicle," which eventually causes the road pair to lose "that James Dean-like innocence and [embrace], with increasing abandon, its own definition as material image" (148).

In redefining the road protagonist as marginal and unassimilable by mainstream culture, Kerouac's novel significantly reconfigured the road "personnel." Prior to *On the Road*, road movie protagonists were either heterosexual couples, as in *It Happened One Night*, *You Only Live Once*, *Sullivan's Travels*, *They Live by Night*, and *The*

Long, Long Trailer, or whole communities of displaced persons, as in *Wild Boys of the Road*, *The Grapes of Wrath*, or *Three Faces West*. After Kerouac, such pairs or groups of travelers were eclipsed by the male buddy pair. Here, too, *On the Road* appears to look forward as well as backward. For, although the shift in the gender of a traveling couple from a heterosexual pair to male buddies was clearly prompted by *On the Road*, ironically enough, Dean and Sal, even when Dean owns the car, are rarely alone. Various male friends and female lovers, or ride sharers from the travel bureaus, are usually passengers as well. Even the final expedition to Mexico, which reads most like a road movie script, brings mutual friend Stan Shepard along for the ride. That buddy-road movies of the late 1960s and 1970s so often center on two guys in a car or on bikes owes as much to the peripatetic Buz and Tod driving together in their Corvette on a seemingly endless road in the 1960s television series *Route 66* as to Kerouac. Previously male buddy teams had taken to the road primarily in comedies, most famously the Hope–Crosby *Road to* series. Post-Kerouac buddy-road movies take the male couple more seriously, while simultaneously problematizing it.

The couple is a dominant configuration in road movies just as it is in Hollywood movies in general. A road movie relies upon the couple for rather practical reasons of story-telling. Two people in the front seat of a vehicle make for easy classical framing and keep the dialogue going. The confined space of the car, the shared lodgings, booths in diners, and often hardship and desperation build intimacy and plot conflict quickly. While the Production Code was in effect, and before the sexual revolution happened, this intimacy created a sexual tension whose relief would have to be endlessly deferred. Road movies of the studio era thus frequently trace the spatial contours of a heterosexual courtship and its postponed consummation, most famously in *It Happened One Night* with its "Walls of Jericho" conceit for respecting the virtue of the couple while putting them in the same bedroom. Another Claudette Colbert road film, *Family Honeymoon*, well summarizes this convention while revealing, too, how the postwar domestic ideology of the late 1940s had already begun to pressure it. In this film, Colbert and her second husband, Fred MacMurray, end up having to take her three children along with them on their cross-country honeymoon, and the family, ironically enough, is what repeatedly thwarts the couple's efforts to consummate their union, which finally occurs only after they leave the road and return home.

The deferral of sexual intimacy in road films of the 1930s and 1940s allows for a closure that integrates the populist values of the road with the dominant culture through the trope of sexual consummation. By the 1970s, however, audiences would be more skeptical that a man and a woman who found passion on the road wouldn't simply act on it. And without the deferral of consummation much of the power of road intimacy and, eventually, the ameliorating closure enacted through consummation evaporated. Thereafter, heterosexual road movies had to derive their frisson instead from implicating the couple's sexual union in a wider tapestry of violence which became just another version of their relationship. Fireworks, sexual and ballistic, replaced romance, and the heterosexual couple became united through their criminality, like Bonnie and Clyde (Warren Beatty and Faye Dunaway) or Mickey and Mallory (Woody Harrelson and Juliette Lewis) in *Natural Born Killers*. The closures of such films are, as a corollary, also much more resistant to the liberation of the road, unable to imagine any form of synthesizing integration of individual freedom and the social order, of technology's movement and domesticity's stasis. With the couple's turn to outlawry, getting off the road is tantamount to going to jail if not worse, not to the marriage bed. Bonnie and Clyde's exultant "We rob banks!" is meant to signal the title characters' solidarity with those poor people whom Depression-era mortgage lenders have foreclosed upon. Yet when one robs banks and keeps the money instead of working to shut them down or destroy them, the politics get a little muddied, to say the least, and the outlaw couple's transgression necessitates their exclusion from the social order except as figures of mass-culture folklore: the poem about their exploits that Bonnie has published in the newspapers gives the couple their fame as figures of lore and, significantly enough, excites Clyde to the point where he overcomes his impotence and can consummate his relationship with Bonnie for the first time, a literal climax almost immediately followed by their execution. A similar if more blatant ambiguity surrounds Oliver Stone's pair of road criminals and media heroes, Mickey and Mallory, ironically pointed out by the seamless transformation of this outlaw couple into RV-driving family vacationers in the coda to *Natural Born Killers*.

Even more common than the transformation of romantic couples into outlaw lovers, at least until after the direct influence of *Easy Rider* had run its course, was the woman's removal from the road trip altogether. At the beginning of the decade 1969 to 1979, the tension between two men on the move, cut off from any emotional ties except to each other, could provide the same intimacy-without-sexual-union previously found in heterosexual screwball romances of the 1930s and 1940s, because the mainstream audience hardly expected two men to sleep with each other. While Corrigan sees the buddy-road movie as the archetype of the genre, generally speaking, it in fact had a relatively brief period of dominance. Many got made in the 1970s, Robin Wood reports, but in the early 1980s they had "virtually disappeared" (229). This is not to say that buddy-cops and other workplace sidekicks were not still in evidence, but the male buddy with whom a man travels, eats, and shares a room in the intimacy of the road quickly became a problematic figure. In buddy movies, as Wood notes, "the emotional center, the emotional charge, is in the male/male relationship, which is patently what the films are about" (228). By the end of the decade, partly through the increasing visibility of the gay liberation movement, and partly through the lessons taught by 1970s buddy movies themselves, audiences could no longer as easily ignore the possibilities that the intimacy of a same-sex road couple suggests, since such a queer subtext was by then widely acknowledged by the popular press, even when it was diegetically insisted to be "impossible."

Along with the United States' recentering of its economy from the east to the Sunbelt states, the increasingly problematic status of the buddy couple may help to explain the turn of road movies in the 1980s from existential narratives of rebellion to comedy and farce, usually set in the rural Southwest or South. Redneck chase farces like *Smokey and the Bandit* and its sequels persisted in the *Cannonball Run* films in 1981 and 1984. Willie Nelson chronicled the life of a touring country singer in *Honeysuckle Rose*, soon re-titled *On the Road Again* after the hit song on its soundtrack. Clint Eastwood, partial to the road genre from the *Outlaw Josey Wales* to *A Perfect World*, also played a country singer in the sentimental Depression-era film *Honkytonk Man* as well as the impresario of a traveling show in *Bronco Billy*. Other major studio road movies were played for broad laughs (*Bustin' Loose*, *Pee-wee's Big Adventure*, the *National Lampoon Vacation* series) or romance (*Back Roads*, *The Sure Thing*). Though there was a smattering of low-budget outlaw chase films like *Eddie Macon's Run* and *Running Hot*, from the late 1970s until the early 1990s the most interesting road films were being made outside mainstream Hollywood. Germany's Wim Wenders, who would name his production company Road Movies, pondered the genre's essential Americanness through European eyes in his powerful series of films that includes *Kings of the Road*, *Alice in the Cities*, *The American Friend*, *Paris, Texas*, and *Until the End of the World*. Other notable European road films of these years are *Leningrad Cowboys Go America*, *Landscape in the Mist*, and *Vagabond*, while at the same time the *Mad Max* films made their mark in Australia. The European road sensibility also influenced the road movies that independent film-maker Jim Jarmusch began making in the US in the mid-1980s.

The release of *Thelma and Louise* in 1991, significantly the same year in which Corrigan's chapter on the road movie genre appeared in his book *A Cinema Without Walls*, marked an important turning point in the popular and academic reception of the road film. Like the male protagonist who finds himself unexpectedly on the road with a fugitive or criminal in 1980s buddy films, Thelma (Geena Davis) discovers that she is more adept at being an outlaw than a housewife. Her skill is evident from the time she robs the convenience store to make up for inadvertently causing the theft of Louise's (Susan Sarandon) bankroll to the way she takes charge of the highway patrolman who stops them. "I know it's crazy," Thelma observes. "But I just feel like I got a knack for this shit." For all the disastrous violence that forever changes the lives of these two women, their road trip turns out to realize the temporary liberation from their oppressive, dissatisfying normality that they seek when they start out on their vacation. "Whatever happens," Thelma tells Louise as the police close in on them, "I'm glad I came with you."

Plate I.3 Women and cars: Geena Davis and Susan Sarandon in *Thelma and Louise.*

In many respects, *Thelma and Louise* performs on film the same critique of the road movie genre that Corrigan offers. Its female couple, who replace the male buddies or heterosexual lovers of earlier road movies, react to the failure of patriarchy to support their desires, just as they register the dynamic interaction of character and its road setting, identify their fantasies with their means of escape (Louise's green Thunderbird convertible) and, most of all, interrogate and, to some critics, overturn the masculinist bias of the road. The critical controversy surrounding *Thelma and Louise* as soon as it was released testifies to its impact in recodifying the genre (which, as *Los Angeles Times* critic Kenneth Turan commented, recounts "the classic American way of finding out who you were and what you were about"), in identifying the genre's complex history (see the critical perspectives on the film gathered together by *Film Quarterly* in "The Many Faces of *Thelma and Louise*"), and in generating a backlash to its feminist appropriation of the masculinist road fantasy, which the *Times*'s other film critics more disparagingly called a "high-toned 'Smokey and the Bandit' with a downbeat ending and a woman at the wheel" (Benson), and "a sort of post-feminist howl" (Rainer). As Sharon Willis points out, though, such dismissals of the film's female-revenge set-pieces (such as the immolation of the truck driver's rig) "recognize the fantasmatic drive of the film's pyrotechnic spectacle only to shut it down immediately in order to fixate on a stable, if imaginary, antagonism between men's anxieties and women's vicarious pleasures" (122). The apprehension that, as another *Times* writer put it, after seeing the film, "the women of America [will be moved] into flinging off their aprons, stowing the hubby's .38 in the diaper bag, pumping premium into the Country Squire and careening down the blue-line highways toward riot and mayhem, leaving behind a trail of dead men" (Morrison) ignores the basic fact that *Thelma and Louise* is, finally, "a story about women and cars" (Willis: 125), which draws its fantasy of road life from the television series *Route 66*. "Our cars and the roads we drive on are one of the few arenas where it is acceptable, and even anodyne, to act out aggression" (126). As Willis points out, this has always been accepted as a truism for men on the road, which is not to say that it does not determine the relation of women to their cars as well.

Not surprisingly, *Thelma and Louise* galvanized critical attention on the road movie as an identifiable Hollywood product and revived the genre, which by this point, Corrigan was arguing, had reached a point of traveling "in a culture where images of history now only recycle themselves. Now the representations that once secured a place are neurotically cut loose of any referent but themselves" (152). After *Thelma and Louise*, Hollywood films began to recognize again the increasing hospitality of the road to the marginalized and alienated – not only women (*Leaving Normal*), but also gays (*My Own Private Idaho*, *The Living End*, *To Wong Foo, Thanks for Everything! Julie Newmar*), lesbians (*Boys on the Side*, *Even Cowgirls Get the Blues*), and people of color (*Get on the Bus*, *Fled*, *Powwow Highway*) – and to renew the road's historical currency. "The law is some tricky shit, isn't it?" Thelma rhetorically asks after Louise explains why their explanation of self-defense will not excuse their criminality. Simply put, the road movie throughout its history has been wrestling with this question, and it continues to do so.

The essays in *The Road Movie Book* look at the genre from as many different perspectives as road movies themselves look at the consequences of adhering to or opposing laws, of freeing oneself from or seeking to rejoin the wider community. Using both historical and theoretical methodologies, they find the genre a productive ground for exploring issues of nationhood, economics, sexuality, gender, class, and race.

The first section, "Mapping Boundaries," sketches certain broad thematic and ideological tropes of the genre. Bennet Schaber delineates the discovery of "the people" as the true destination of mainstream Hollywood and European road classics of the 1930s and early 1940s and then cites as a significant generic transformation the ensuing impossibility of this project in postwar cinema. Shari Roberts uses the films of Clint Eastwood to explore the essential masculinism inscribed into road space, particularly as the road movie genre takes over the ideological burden of its close relation, the Western. Following these wide-ranging pieces, Ian Leong, Mike Sell, and Kelly Thomas turn to a historical discussion of the relationship between sexuality, consumer capitalism, and style in three classic outlaw couple films: *Gun Crazy*, *Bonnie and Clyde*, and *Natural Born Killers*. Corey Creekmur finds, in the mixture of fame and infamy, a surprising link between the careers of outlaw couples in such road movies as these and those of touring entertainers in musicals.

The next section of the book, "American Roads," further historicizes the issues raised by the volume's first group of essays, tracing the continual reinvention of the genre in Hollywood cinema from the early 1940s to the end of the 1980s. Steven Cohan examines the utopian association of the road and home, as achieved through the mediation of show business culture, in films of the 1940s and 1950s. Mark Alvey next studies the cultural, political, and industrial factors that combined to make the television series *Route 66* the emblematic road narrative between *On the Road* and *Easy Rider*; and Julian Stringer follows a parallel, but more culturally repressed, road also being traveled in the 1960s by Russ Meyer's low-budget, exploitation biker movies. Barbara Klinger then reconsiders the landmark impact of the release of *Easy Rider* by examining its complex placement in competing discourses of counter-culture politics and American nationalism. Finally, Ina Rae Hark charts the displacement of buddy-road movies from mainstream Hollywood at the end of the 1970s and their subsequent revival in the late 1980s as a Hollywood strategy for recuperating patriarchal capitalism from the yuppie excesses that had tarnished it during that "high-flying" decade.

The concluding section, "Alternative Routes," concentrates on road films that depart from the American landscape or that travel on its cultural margins. Angelo Restivo shows how the new Italian national highway system of the late 1950s and early 1960s broke down regional differences and created a new national subject. Delia Falconer next turns our attention from a European road to another nation with a powerful road mythology, examining how the *Mad Max* trilogy offered a means of renegotiating the economic connections between Australia's nationhood and its spatial history in the 1980s. Looking at the Australian road a decade later, Pamela Robertson explores the intersections of nationalist, sexual, and racial politics as organized through the trope of "home" in *The Adventures of Priscilla, Queen of the Desert*. Following somewhat similar terrain at the sexual margins of the American road, Sharon Willis analyzes the spectatorial position of fantasmic community, and its corresponding effacement of race and transgressive sexualities, in *To Wong Foo* and *Boys on the Side*. The next two essays then turn to the independent gay cinema movement of the 1990s, with Katie Mills and Robert Lang finding, in *The Living End* and *My Own Private Idaho*, respectively, a more genuinely alternative space for the representation of homosexual desire. Finally, Stuart Aitken and Christopher Lee Lukinbeal close the volume with an examination of the ways that masculinity is – and is not – liberated through the space and scale of the road movie's cultural geography.

As these final essays point out, the 1990s have once again revealed the endless permutations and combinations available on the road for the cinematic imagination. Even mainstream road films with heterosexual protagonists have changed markedly during this decade. The outlaw-couple film productively reinvented itself through the lens of postmodernism (*Wild at Heart*, *Kalifornia*, *True Romance*, *Natural Born Killers*). And, just when the buddy movie might seem to have exhausted its resources, late-1996 releases in the US feature a man–elephant buddy pair (*Larger than Life*) and feuding former presidents (*My Fellow Americans*), as well as a more familiar coupling of mismatched road men (*Good Luck*). The essays in *The Road Movie Book* remind us just how varied and adaptable the genre has always been and, we hope, will prevent in the future the ahistorical pronouncements that have too often underestimated the genre in the act of describing it.

Syracuse, New York
Columbia, South Carolina
December, 1996

Works Cited

Atkinson, Michael. "Crossing the Frontiers." *Sight and Sound* 1 (1994): 14–18.

Baudrillard, Jean. *America*, trans. Chris Turner. London: Verso, 1988.

Benson, Shelia. "True or False: Thelma and Louise Just Good Ol' Boys?" *Los Angeles Times* (May 13, 1991), Home Edition: F-1+. *Los Angeles Times* Online. August 9, 1996.

Ching, Barbara and Barnard, Rita. "From Screwballs to Cheeseballs: Comic Narrative and Ideology in Capra and Reiner." *New Orleans Review* 17.3 (1990): 52–9.

Corrigan, Timothy. *A Cinema Without Walls: Movies and Culture after Vietnam*. New Brunswick, NJ: Rutgers University Press, 1991.

Dargis, Manohla. "Roads to Freedom." *Sight and Sound* 3 (1991): 14–18.

Hill, Lee. *Easy Rider*. London: BFI, 1996.

Kerouac, Jack. *On the Road*. New York: Penguin, 1957.

Laderman, David. "What a Trip: The Road Film and American Culture." *Journal of Film and Video* 48.1–2 (1996): 41–57.

"The Many Faces of Thelma and Louise." *Film Quarterly* 45.2 (1991–2): 20–31.

Morrison, Patt. "Perspective on the Sexes; Get a Grip, Guys: This is Fantasy." *Los Angeles Times* (July 22, 1991), Home Edition: B5+. *Los Angeles Times* Online. August 9, 1996.

Porter, Mark. "Michael Herr on Jack Kerouac's On the Road." *Video Eyeball* 2.2 (1995): 14–15, 22.

Rainer, Peter. "True or False: Thelma and Louise Just Good Ol' Boys?" *Los Angeles Times*, (May 31, 1991), Home Edition: F-1+. *Los Angeles Times* Online. August 9, 1996.

Turan, Peter. "Smooth Ride For 'Thelma & Louise.'" *Los Angeles Times* (May 24, 1991), Home Edition: F-1+. *Los Angeles Times* Online. 1996.

Willis, Sharon. "Hardware and Hardbodies: What Do Women Want? A Reading of *Thelma and Louise*." *Film Theory Goes to the Movies*, eds. Jim Collins, Hilary Radner, and Ava Preacher Collins. New York: Routledge, 1993. 120–8.

Wood, Robin. *Hollywood from Vietnam to Reagan*. New York: Columbia University Press, 1986.

Part I

MAPPING BOUNDARIES

1

"HITLER CAN'T KEEP 'EM THAT LONG"
The road, the people

Bennet Schaber

> Hitler has a passion for movies – including the products of Hollywood.
> (Two of his favorites were *It Happened One Night* and *Gone with the Wind*.)
> William L. Shirer, *Berlin Diary*, Dec 1, 1940

> That was the first bad thing I'd heard about [*It Happened One Night*]. I was
> shocked and started to analyze it, but I gave it up. But I resent it like the
> devil.
> Frank Capra, 1941

In an entry from his diary for November 5, 1939, William Shirer makes the
following observations, worth quoting at some length.

> Hitler is a fiend for films, and on evenings when no important conferences
> are on or he is not overrunning a country, he spends a couple of hours seeing
> the latest movies in his private cinema room in the Chancellery. News-reels
> are a great favorite with him, and in the last weeks he has seen all those
> taken in the Polish war, including hundreds of thousands of feet which
> were filmed for the army archives and will never be seen by the public. He
> likes American films and many never publicly exhibited in Germany are
> shown him. A few years ago he insisted on having *It Happened One Night*
> run several times. Though he is supposed to have a passion for Wagnerian
> opera, he almost never attends the Opera here in Berlin. He likes the
> Metropol, which puts on tolerable musical comedies with an emphasis on
> pretty dancing girls. Recently he had one of the girls who struck his fancy
> to tea. But only to tea. In the evening, too, he likes to have in Dr. Todt, an
> imaginative engineer who built the great Autobahn network of two-lane
> motor roads and later the fortifications of the Westwall. Hitler, rushing to
> compensate what he thinks is an artistic side that was frustrated by non-
> recognition in his youthful days in Vienna, has a passion for architects'
> models and will spend hours fingering them with Dr. Todt. Lately, they say,

he has taken to designing new uniforms. Hitler stays up late, and sleeps badly, which I fear is the world's misfortune.

(244)

Shirer compiled these notes for "a picture of Hitler at work during war-time," to be broadcast on CBS radio. That picture is worked up through Shirer's rather wry humor, which traces a kind of fault-line on one side of which is Hitler-the-man (he "stays up late"), on the other, Hitler-the-political-leader ("the world's misfortune"). Film, however, runs directly down, or, at least, on both sides of that line. On the one side there is the man who loves the latest movies, on the other the Chancellor watching film from the army archives. Of course, this imaginary line was untenable and Shirer knew it. Capra seems to have known it as well and it irked him. Untenable and irksome because film here realizes the Führer as *both* contemplator *and* creator of images. Hence the repeated trajectories of Shirer's "portrait": from watching the news to making the news, from watching the girl to taking tea with the girl, from gazing to "fingering," etc.

Indeed, what one witnesses in this portrait is a small trace of the many ways in which National Socialism realized itself in competition with Hollywood. Capra himself was well aware of the struggle, and well before the making of *Why We Fight* and the revelation that *It Happened One Night* (1934) was one of Hitler's favorites. "I never cease to thrill at an audience seeing a picture. For two hours you've got 'em. Hitler can't keep 'em that long. You eventually reach even more people than Roosevelt does on the radio. Imagine what Shakespeare would have given for an audience like that!" (McBride: 432). One might detect in Capra's bombast something of Shirer's wryness. After all, Hitler's only watching movies when he's not "overrunning countries," as it were. But there is a hint here that between film and the most aggressive politics, there is less a relation of choice than of extension. Film belongs to its own overrunning. Film is extensive; it "reach[es] more people than Roosevelt," etc. Extensive and grasping, film not only reaches, it holds. It practices its own specific kinds of domestic and foreign policies. This is why it is essential to situate it not only within its contemporary political setting but within a nexus of political technologies: the metropolis, the *autobahn*, the newsreel, the lightning war, etc. The quotations from Shirer and Capra have the advantage (with their obvious differences) of doing just this. They invoke time and motion as political-cinematic questions.

The problem this essay sets for itself, then, has less to do with Hitler's personal filmic proclivities (it has more to do with Capra's recognition of them, and anyway, so what if the Führer secretly identified with Clark Gable?) than with the ways in which a seemingly innocent road film like *It Happened One Night* could get itself mixed up in and with a series of larger political questions. Hence the principal emphasis of this essay will be a consideration of the road movie as political in the broadest sense of the term. Capra's words, from which the essay's title is drawn, powerfully represent the director's sense of the massive political stakes of film-making (hence his resentment at finding out about Hitler's love of *It Happened One Night* strikes me as both appropriate and somewhat disingenuous). Indeed, it seems to me that Capra's prewar career is characterized by an increasing awareness of the interplay of populism, capitalism and fascism and the fact that film can represent these tendencies only at the risk of flirting with them (culminating in *Meet John Doe*, 1941).

What is at stake here is precisely "the people." And "the road" is very much the locus of the revelation of this people. In *It Happened One Night*, Gable will take on the weight of becoming the very image of the people, revealing them in the process of revealing himself to the upper-class Claudette Colbert and, later, her father. And seven years later, Capra returns to the road, when in *Meet John Doe* Gary Cooper and Walter Brennan, the two musical tramps, stage the meeting of the road with the image factory of the newspaper industry, with Barbara Stanwyck unwittingly furthering the fascist designs of Edward Arnold. Preston Sturges, more clever, wittier, smarter, and more cynical (but also and decisively less visionary) than Capra, would simply cut to the chase: in *Sullivan's Travels* (1941) Hollywood sets out explicitly to give the road and its people their definitive image as Joel McCrea's Sullivan sets out to make a film "like Capra."

The road, the people: this is the equation I wish to ponder. Who are these people? Are they a subject (of history, for example) or merely subjected? An image it is the duty of cinema to discover, or to invent? Obviously Capra is not the only prewar director to pose this question. We have already glimpsed it in Sturges, and it is there in Ford as well (to mention only the big three in the US). To be on the road is to be in the presence of the people, and this constitutes what Gilles Deleuze (216) has expressed as the "unanimism" of prewar American film. The people are present and real but also virtual and ideal: the summation of a real history which they unify, the seed, soul, or spirit (*anima*) of a greater people to come. The image of the people, then, is pregnant with its own political arrival. And this is where the Hitlerian threat makes itself most acutely felt, when the image through which the people finds itself and its freedom is reversed and becomes the instrument of its subjugation.

The burden of my essay is twofold. In the first section I hope to demonstrate some of the ways in which prewar films, predominately although not exclusively products of Hollywood studios, deployed the road as a cinematic vehicle for the coming-to-presence of the people. This coming-to-presence implied a specific practice of images the variety of which can be usefully cataloged according to the directors responsible for them. For example, John Ford films images relating a solitary, vertical figure to a vast horizon, or of simple exchanges of looks among ordinary people as they register and acknowledge an act of generosity. However, it is not my contention that the people become a single, unified image; rather, that they are given as simultaneously present and possible, a presence with both a being and a destiny.

In the second section I hope to demonstrate some of the ways in which post-war films, predominately although not exclusively products of independent American and European cinemas, deployed the road experimentally, as it were, with the result being various practices of images both of and in the absence of the people. For example, Jim Jarmusch films a forking road without an horizon, while Wim Wenders films a hand holding a photograph of a house that will not find its address. Unable to find a practice of images capable of bringing them to presence, the people discover their being-in-common through the various ways in which images communicate among themselves.

If we imagine, and no doubt we must, the people as a community, then the difference I am describing can be given as simply this. Before the war, on film, the road presents the community to itself, becomes a vehicle of self-presentation constitutive of the people, in two major modalities: dialectically, insofar as the relation of the one to the many becomes the unified being or oneness of the many; narratively, insofar as the deployment of redemptive scripts or texts enables the people to cross a boundary or obstacle and thus enter into its own fullness. After the war, the community progressively defies its own self-presentation; it literally cannot be presented, at least honestly, with its own proper image. Its presentation, then, is the channels of communication through which its members expose themselves one to another. These are the communities recent social theory has called unworking, unavowable, or arriving.[1]

Throughout my essay, which amounts to an extended meditation, I have tried to mark some of the salient differences between pre- and postwar road films by calling attention to their pervasive use of Biblical rhetoric – Exodus for the pre-war films, Apocalypse for the postwar. But this distinction is never hard and fast. In my last section I will turn my attention to a single image, the desert, at once the place of a gathering and the promise of a new homeland, but also the site of a new diaspora, a dispersion of the people and of the filmic image itself.

I

In his image of Hitler at the movies, Shirer made the connection between National Socialism and cinema. No doubt Capra had intuited this connection before reading those words; and he spent a good part of his career working through the relation of film to totalitarianism. Although this is hardly the place for an extended analysis, it is nevertheless crucial to point out just how strongly National Socialism was wed, not only to a specific repertoire of images, but to specific technologies of image production. One need only recall Leni Riefenstahl's *Triumph of the Will* to recognize the ways in which the camera not only insinuates itself into the advent of the Nazi event but realizes itself as an indispensable component in the very being of the event. Indeed, the camera grounds the dialectical play of being-with-the-people and the being-of-the-people, not only by juxtaposing the single face or figure with the massive phalanx, the single voice with the symphonic chorus (notably in the *Sprechchor* of the *Arbeitsdienst*), but by physically making available the one to the other. Now, this dialectic is procured through a relation of motions to a series of returns to rest (all in the service of making perfectly clear a series of hierarchical equivalences: the Führer is the people is the land is the nation, *etcetera ad infinitum*). The camera encounters Nuremberg through the clouds, in flight aboard a plane; it comes to rest outside the plane to witness Hitler's dis-embarkation. It encounters the people on the road, in a moving car through the city streets, and comes to rest outside the Deutscher Hof, Hitler's hotel, newly remodeled with the Führer's name in lights, recalling a Broadway or Hollywood marquee (the Nazi–Hollywood competition that haunts the film). The people, at march or at play, encounter the camera in ceaseless motion: it either penetrates their ranks or they parade past it. They encounter themselves when the camera comes to rest with the Führer, aligns itself with his gaze (which is also a gaze that gazes upon itself). This is Nazi "unanimism": *Ein Volk, ein Führer, eine Kamera*. It is not precisely that the camera manufactures events (propaganda in the simplest sense) but that the events themselves are conceivable only in the presence of the camera (given its outward and objectified double in the famous nighttime rally, the sea of flags in an architecture of light, the latter phrase at least a partial designation of cinema, of political life affirming itself in the presence of and as film).

The year 1934, the date of the fourth Nazi Party Rally at Nuremberg, the subject of Riefenstahl's film, brings us full circle, back to Capra and *It Happened One Night*, also made that same year. And, like Riefenstahl's film, Capra's too means to think through the emergence of the people in the presence of the camera. But it does so in a completely different way, on the road, as it were, which requires of the camera not a coming to rest but a certain restlessness.[2] And this is sometimes literalized, for example near the film's conclusion, with a shot of the cameramen pursuing Claudette Colbert across the lawn of her father's estate. This is important to notice. Unlike Riefenstahl, Capra does not so much set the camera in motion as set it the task of discovering and recording a relation of cameras and motions. Indeed, the only really interesting shot-in-motion occurs as Gable watches, from his car, the entourage of vehicles carrying Colbert off toward the horizon. But this is the only point at which Capra encounters the road in one of its essential visual/filmic modalities – its vanishing[3] (Ford is the great American master of this image/insight, and this no doubt because of the experience of the Western).

Capra might be said to have inaugurated the road film with *It Happened One Night*. The film seemed to sketch the contours of a remarkably open, fluid genre which could nevertheless maintain its conditions of recognizability even across a series of finely layered wagers (what the film, finally, would be about: love, class, travel, communication, nation, sex, technology, etc.). The film includes a visual account of nearly every possible means of transportation: from walking to boats, buses, cars, motorcycles, planes, autogyros, and trains, even swimming). Horses are metaphorically included when Gable refers to the entire caprice as a "buggy ride." Only bicycles seem neglected. The list can be expanded if one adds to it the transport of communication: phone, telegraph, mail, newspaper, newsreel, radio, intercom, all points bulletin. This is Capra's restless nation, and the camera casts about (and sometimes tags along) for as many of these images as it can possibly find, only coming to rest, generally, only at motor camps, rest stops for the restless. The film throws down the gauntlet, so to speak, so that, by the time Sturges inherits it, the rather simple halts of Capra's buses (by the police or by the elements) have been transformed into full-scale, catastrophic and slapstick motions (sometimes accompanied by special effects, notably slow motion) in "land yachts" and "whippet tanks." And Sturges opens *Sullivan's Travels* with film footage of a gunfight atop a moving train on a bridge over a rushing river. Hence for the road movie, as originally conceived and constructed, any political wager finds its primary condition in an analysis of film and motion.

Bodies at rest, bodies in motion: the road film could be likened to an entire physics. And it is the road film itself that perhaps provides the vocabulary, the periodic table or thermodynamics, that makes possible both its analysis and its analytical work. In short, far from designating a genre merely, the phrase "road movie" can be taken to express a cinematic concept.[4] To inquire into this concept is to inquire immediately into just what we mean when we say or write the words "road movie." Now the road, as theme or metaphor, has exercised a powerful grasp upon the narrative imagination for a very long time. Its hold extends far beyond the borders of Western film-making, even as the road movie belongs to the global extension of the West.[5] It may be fair to say then, that the hybrid nature of the genre, the vast differences that traverse it and constitute it, belongs in a number of important ways to a social and historical mode of being with difference. On the road there are, inevitably, encounters, which have to do with precisely how men, women, things, and places will be with one another.

For the road movie, even those of limited ambition, there is a relation, a belonging together of "what happens" and "happiness" (here using precisely the vocabulary provided by Capra's film). This is what makes the stakes of the road movie so often and so explicitly ethical or political: the road enacts a symbolic circulation so that the traffic of events comes to bear a meaning far in excess of itself. As Jacques Lacan observes, "*Happiness* is after all *happen*; it, too, is an

Plate 1.1 It Happened One Night. Traveling with the people.

encounter, even if one does not feel the need to add the prefix, which strictly speaking indicates the happy character of the thing" (12). His comment elaborates on the relation of happiness to what happens, that is, the conditions under which seemingly random events come to fulfill a kind of symbolic destiny.[6]

The "It Happened . . . " of Capra's film has to perform, therefore, the double task of letting happen both a love affair and "the people" themselves. Gable and Colbert are the instrument, their liaison giving birth, so to speak, not to the people as such, but to their image. And what becomes clear, not only in Capra's film but in a number of prewar road films, is that this letting happen of the image of the people amounts to the people's liberation. In fact, for the prewar road film, this dialectic is given explicitly within the rhetoric of the Biblical Exodus: the Walls of Jericho tumble in *It Happened One Night*, the Colorado River is transformed into the Jordan when the Joads cross into Canaan–California in *The Grapes of Wrath*, the congregation of the Negro church sings "Let My People Go," the story of Israel's Exodus from Egypt, as Joel McCrea and his fellow shackled convicts enter the homemade cinema in *Sullivan's Travels*. Hence the story, the fable of a few finite lives to and for whom "it happened . . . ," links itself to the infinity of the people, the universal project of its emancipation ("we'll go on forever, 'cause we're the

Plate 1.2   The Grapes of Wrath.
The Okies pack their truck for their journey to the promised land of California.

people" says Ma Joad); and film itself, a specific practice of images, is called upon
to perform this miracle. Sturges, again, having inherited a genre that already
included Capra's and Ford's masterpieces (McCrea's Sullivan wants not only to
make a film "like Capra," but to film a novel, *Oh Brother, Where Art Thou?*, which
might have been written by, if not Steinbeck, then at least Sinclair Lewis),[7] was in
a position to be explicit about the whole thing: his images of the people are themselves illuminated by the light of the movie screen, so that the people begin to find
themselves and their freedom at the movies (in an early scene at a triple feature,
three melodramas, in which Sturges shoots only the audience, eating, coughing,
and variously registering the effects of the films on their faces; later in the bayou
church, where a Disney cartoon liberates the convicts into laughter).

So far I have been invoking the images produced principally by prewar films of
major ambition. My aim has been simply to establish a relation between the genre,
road movie, and a specific kind of imagistic (or, if you like, imaginary) destiny.
This relation, between a specific kind of narrative itinerary (the road) and a
specific kind of image production (film) is what I have called the road movie as
concept. It is as if the narrative and the filmic suddenly find themselves in one
another's grasp precisely at the end of the road. That is, while the road constitutes

itself as a specific (if sometimes aimless) narrative trajectory, an extended metaphor of discovery and invention, the filmic (the second term of the designation "road movie") constitutes itself as a specific mode of encountering this metaphorics. So for example, even in a film like *The Wizard of Oz* (1939), concerned with establishing the direct link between the inside and the outside of the dream (Oz and Kansas), the narrative road leads directly to the Wizard as image-producer, as movie-maker, who reveals to the people's representatives (Kansas farm hands become the new ruling junta of Oz) that they already are what they had only dreamed themselves of becoming (the people set free into its already existing essence: hence not so much that there is no place *like* home, but no place *but* home!). Here we encounter the road film as the story of the people's becoming what essentially they already are and always have been. An updated and politically impoverished version of this would be *Forrest Gump*, in which the road is reduced to first-person narration at the road side, but for which there is still no place but home (complete with rainbows and magic shoes). But even this sentimental fable consistently encounters the filmic through the splicing of Tom Hanks's Gump into file footage of televisual political events. Here the people's political history becomes nothing but a series of punctual images supplied by the nightly news. "Where were you when . . . ?" the film repeatedly asks. Even to answer it is to submit to an empty logic.

The road movie, then, takes as its specific project the aligning of event and meaning within the image of and as political geography. This is nowhere so powerfully signified as in the genre scene, prevalent in so many road films, of the cut between the map and its territory. Indeed, the road film forges an explicit connection between the map as political representation (say, in the hands of the police as they track the progress of bodies in flight, or in the hands of hapless voyagers, trying to find, say, Pismo Beach) and place as the being of territory. In general, the two elude each other, usually to the benefit of the latter, but with widely differing results. Hence, we see in Ford the difference between the marking out of territory by the ubiquitous US 66 signs and the hands that grasp the dirt; or in Capra, between the flags on Edward Arnold's map which draws the nation into his fascist web of John Doe clubs and Cooper and Brennan fishing under a bridge, beneath the road and out of sight; or the unmappable position of the lost horizon, Shangri-la.

But if the map or road sign stamps territory or earth with an imposed, even official meaning, the territory-event can find a meaning equally powerful but in another direction. In this direction road events are linked to memories, knowledges, or discourses which events awaken and from which they draw meaning. Gable lifts Colbert onto his shoulder in order to cross a stream. She then recalls the piggyback rides her father gave her as a child. Gable responds that she (and probably her father) knows nothing about piggybacking. The scene ends when

Gable gives Colbert a playful spanking. This is repeated in the more famous scene in which Gable discourses on the proper way in which to dunk a doughnut. By the time their journey is finally concluded, then, Gable and Colbert will have been childhood sweethearts, journeying as they do into one another's pasts through hitch-hiking, doughnut dunking, piggybacking, eating carrots, and playing at marriage.[8] Road events here take on meaning because they always go in two directions at once: to go forward (Colbert goes from spoiled brat to mature woman, Gable from drunken braggart to responsible man) is to go backwards (the consummation of their wedding requires a toy trumpet, so that the truth of events, the truth of love and love-making, is their childhood, their perpetually initiatory status). In *Sullivan's Travels* this dual directionality or forking of the road is rendered as a kind of unconscious automatism: no matter in what direction he goes or with what means of transportation, McCrea keeps winding up back in Hollywood (with Veronica Lake).[9] All of these modalities conjoin with the burial of Grampa in *The Grapes of Wrath*. The body is buried along with a written account of its death, a kind of memory, in order to secure it a meaning over and against the suspicions of the state (which "cares more about a man dead than when he's alive").[10]

The road film builds up its conceptual vocabulary by linking territory and memory, terrain and time, event and meaning, initiation and representation, narration and image. Clearly this vocabulary extended itself well beyond the pre-war films upon which I have so far concentrated. My concern has been to look generally at how in these prewar films, those that, after all, established the genre, film was capable or willing to encounter the metaphorics of the road as well as how the road physically injects itself, as image, into film. For these early films, the road metaphor oscillates between abandonment and promise, desperation and a new resourcefulness. Joel McCrea's Sullivan says: "I'm going out on the road to find out what it's like to be poor and needy and to make a picture about it." But he is followed by his studio crew in the land yacht (a 1940s motor home) which immediately converts the road into modern living space. Or, as Muley in *The Grapes of Wrath* complains: "One hundred folks and no place to live but on the road . . . they just threw us into the road." Indeed for nearly all the Okies (except Tom) the road can mean only the disintegration of life. And yet Ford's road is the very condition of the gathering up again of a nation of displaced persons: migrants, Indians, truckers, roadside workers (gas jockeys to waitresses, etc.) who assert the persistence of honest and generous life against the police, border guards and Pinkertons. And of course in Capra, for whom the dream of a "real life" is the dream of travel (the Pacific island to which Gable wants to take Colbert, but doesn't every Capra hero mean to be going someplace, so that the very dream of motion secures the wonder of living?), the road is the very matrix of America, the restless nation.

Two other road movies of this era strike me as both essential and germinal, Hitchcock's *The 39 Steps* (1935, UK) and Vigo's *L'Atalante* (1934, France). The first established the fugitive character of the heterosexual couple and the road/map relation as the tracing of the paranoiac web of power and official intrigue (hence the road is both route of escape and entry into the demi-monde of political/sexual power, culminating for Hitchcock in *North By Northwest*, 1959); the second, the Surrealist possibilities of the road couple as *vases communicants*, to use Breton's famous phrase. These films share many of the characteristics of their American friends but exploit them in different, remarkable, and no less influential ways.

Like the road films of Capra and Sturges, Hitchcock's *The 39 Steps* is committed to a fairly elegant and formal brand of comedy emerging from the wit, which in general means the talk, of the heterosexual couple at the film's center. Indeed Robert Donat and Madeleine Carroll are dead ringers for Gable and Colbert. And as in Capra's film, they play at being a married couple, first when Donat kisses Carroll in a train compartment, later when they pose as a runaway couple in order to get a room at a remote inn in Scotland. And, as in Capra's film, this play leads to the fact of their relationship (although they do not get married in Hitchcock's film). But unlike Capra's film, the means of transportation tend to be more private – train compartment, back seat of a car, on foot through the Scottish hills. The couple pursued by the police and murderous foreign agents clearly take a differ-ent tack from the couple pursued by patriarchy and the press (Colbert the fugitive socialite versus Donat the fugitive murder suspect). Nevertheless, the couple's initial meeting remains a matter of happenstance, and their commitment to remain together remains a matter of justice. This justice is private for Capra, public for Hitchcock. Hence Gable and Colbert move from private moments (Gable is first shown to us in a phone booth, Colbert in a stateroom) through the people (principally on the bus of salesmen, sailors, mothers and children, migrants, etc.) and return to the privacy of a motel room. Hitchcock's trajectory is the inverse: from the music hall through a series of private compartments (apartments, homes, automobiles, police interrogation rooms) and a return to the music hall. The entire itinerary is bisected by Donat's *tour de force*, impersonating a candidate for Parliament at a political meeting.

As is the case in the other films touched on here, Hitchcock's too revolves around a certain labor of memory, of which there are essentially two kinds: the first a memory which possesses one, the tune you just can't get out of your head (Donat whistles it throughout the film, to the interminable chagrin of Carroll), and which properly belongs to the people as to their popular culture (hence the music hall as the source and resource of popular memory); the second a private and purloined memory, a kind of information storage that ultimately puts the people in jeopardy (the spy ring has "stolen" the plan for a silent plane engine, this silence posed precisely against music and the people). Mr Memory, vaudeville performer and unwitting spy, is the link between these two memories, and the stage is the site at which political intrigue is called to account before the public (both *Stage Fright* and *The Man Who Knew Too Much*, 1956, play with this same dynamics of stage, music, memory). The people, then, remain a real presence. Hitchcock's heroes will be recruited, forcibly and inevitably by mistake, from their ranks. Manipulable and even stampedeable (as when Annabella Smith's gunshot causes a riot in the first music hall scene), traversed by a series of coercions, the people give rise to a series of powerful counterimages: fighters and popular criminals (hence the first questions Mr Memory answers are about prize fights and the deaths of famous sex criminals). Donat's Hannay is linked precisely with the category, popular sex criminal, and he is not above playing the role to the hilt when he is physically linked, by handcuffs, to Carroll. Hence the Hitchcockian image of the people arises out of the linking of law and transgression and a fairly complex analysis of the popular as constituted by the sum total of its perversions, which appear at those edges where different forces link up and come to bear on one another (fleshed out most chillingly in the violence of the older husband against his young wife, the woman whose kindness Donat promises "never to forget"). The handcuffs, which in the film's final image give way to the couple's clasped hands, shot from behind so through them we witness the final actions of the police, give the image of this linkage, a Boolean logic whose overlapping brings perversion into contact with love while putting the nation-state into contact with the people.

Of all the films examined so far, Jean Vigo's is bound to seem to occupy the most atypical position, this no doubt because its mode of travel is the barge canal rather than the road as such. Nevertheless it shares many characteristics with the other road films. Like most of them, it is centrally concerned with a heterosexual couple and their vicissitudes in transit. But, unlike those other films, this couple is already married. Like Ford's film, Vigo's is very much committed to a realist account of a specific class condition, and, also like Ford's film, *L'Atalante* has affinities with the documentary (Vigo's *A Propos de Nice*, 1930, is of course a documentary of the vacationing bourgeoisie). But unlike *The Grapes of Wrath*, where realism finds a counterpart in a powerful and luminous expressionism, Vigo's realism turns toward a spectral Surrealism. This is in part an effect of Ford's affinity with the earth, the desert, the plains, the mine, and Vigo's affinity with the water, the canal, the seaside, and swimming. Where Ford can balance and counterpoise the horizon and the vista with the darkly lit close-up, Vigo's bodies find themselves locked in fog or submerged in their watery element. Where Fordian desire belongs to the earth and its horizonal fading, Vigo's belongs to a submersion, a blinding separation out of which arise ghostly images. Indeed the film's title evokes less a lost horizon (to paraphrase Capra rather than Ford) than a sunken continent.

Vigo's film, then, takes its impetus from a series of separations, beginning with the young bride's separation from her family and village (during the wedding parade, the couple of Dita Parlo and Jean Dasté are filmed in near solitude), followed by her separation from the earth and her entry onto the barge (punctuated by the strewing of flowers upon the water). The film's main drama derives from the separation of the couple from one another, Parlo's Juliette struggling to make ends meet in Paris, Dasté's Jean sinking into drunken apathy aboard the barge. Out of their disappearance to one another the film's most beautiful and erotic images arise. Thus Juliette and Jean, each alone, she in her room in the city, he in his cabin on the barge, lie in bed as their hands caress their progressively convulsive bodies. Images arise from fantasy, so that the blind, tactile tracing of the body's contours becomes the primary source of visuality.

Where for Hitchcock the visual belongs to a certain way of linking bodies (handcuffs), for Vigo it belongs to their separation (Père Jules shows Juliette a pair of severed hands in a bottle, once again associating separation and the liquid, submerging element). Vigo's canals become progressively arterial, tracing lines on the body of the globe, refiguring its surfaces, and doubled by the tattooed body of Père Jules, sublimely amorphous: he places a cigarette in his navel and his belly becomes a face, Boris Kaufman's camera analyzes his twisting motions over the barge's deck in slow motion, and he becomes a crab. It is Michel Simon's Père Jules, like the camera itself, who makes possible the presence to one another of separated elements: the primitive tattoo to the mechanical victrola, the city to the country, the land to the water, bosses to workers, woman to man, animal to human, children to adults. His cabin, a veritable junkyard, bears witness less to a visual tourism than the way in which things testify to a practice of life.

With Vigo the road film is introduced to the possibility of a certain slowness, of certain difficult and almost imperceptible motions, emotions, and communications within the image as opposed to the impulse to get from one place (and one image) to the next. Capra flirts with this when he shoots between Gable and Colbert in their separate beds, the "Walls of Jericho" between them. In this way Vigo's film anticipates much of what will happen in the postwar period, where the road will take on a number of visionary possibilities only briefly explored in the prewar films. Hence at the conclusion of *L'Atalante*, when the camera rises into the air, no doubt on board a helicopter or autogyro, the road has ceased to be a way from one place to another, one image to another, but has become a dermal tracing in which the image becomes the volume through which variable times and perspectives overlap.

In a way, Vigo's film, lifting us into the clouds, brings us back full circle to the ascending-descending Führer-camera of Riefenstahl. The difference is in the way the latter submits these visual flights to a controlling and unitary point of view, while Vigo gives them over to something more automatic, foreign, and inhuman.

The differences Vigo's camera must trace and traverse, even caress, demand a certain responsibility to the grotesque, the unhealthy, the frankly libidinal or instinctual. One recognizes here the "degenerate" face of modernity with which National Socialism would take issue. But if Hitler could never have stomached the work of Vigo, we know he did enjoy *It Happened One Night*, and this was no doubt in part an effect of the way the film corroborates a sense of the reality of the people (Vigo's people is haunted by its own unreality) and its essential unity. The Hitlerian project is to take this people and give it its life in the camera, in the image; Capra resisted this project through a refusal to submerge the people within the camera-image and instead to film their restless motions, the camera being among the people and not above them, as it were.

Vigo–Riefenstahl–Capra, then, represent a certain choice – a difficult one, no doubt – that the road film would inherit. For Riefenstahl, the end of the road is the coming to rest of the camera and the coming into its being of the people (as gaze). For Vigo, this same coming to rest of the camera leads to a convulsion of the image, the concussive movements of the Paris café and its working-class clientele or of the junkman and his wares on the teetering bicycle. For Capra, the camera takes a breather as it follows the endless, restless stirrings of the melting pot. By the end of the prewar era, the road-image had been given in three of its fundamental modalities: totalitarian, avant-garde, democratic. Obviously it would be the second of the three that would inspire the ambitious road films of the post-war era, in part because it would make possible a dialectics of mainstream and marginality so crucial to an emerging politics and image-making.

II

Pre-Second-World-War road films, across their many differences, are in general united within a specific concern, the presentation of the people – specifically, the *image* of the people. Indeed, many postwar road films attempted to revive the image of the people in tandem with an optimistic narrative of technology and modernity (for example, *The Great Race*, 1965 and *Those Magnificent Men in their Flying Machines*, 1965) or within more or less hackneyed discourses of authenticity (the newly naturalized peoples of *Road Scholar*, 1993, for example). But more often than not, these later films found only images of the *absence* of the people, of the people as memory or yet to come.

Over and against the great images of liberation, the coming of the people into their own through the figure of the Biblical Exodus, were suddenly a series of catastrophic, even apocalyptic images: the conglomerate of flag, fire, and motor-cycle in *Easy Rider* (1969), the suspended convertible above the Grand Canyon of *Thelma and Louise* (1991), the "cool" and "hot" explosions of *Zabriskie Point* (1970), or, to invoke the truly sublime, Ethel Merman slipping on a banana peel so that justice might finally keep its appointment with pleasure at the close of *It's a Mad, Mad, Mad, Mad World* (1963). As in the classic films already discussed, these later films weave together the narrative and the filmic, but more and more inevitably they produce visionary images in place of the absent image of the people. Increasingly, the road movie makes certain demands upon the camera (which, as we have already seen, were there, only less so, in the earlier films) to think its way through time and space (neither of these being any longer univocal): trees reveal themselves as hieroglyphics (*It's a Mad . . .*), or the desert oscillates between strata of geological time that eclipse or defeat anything human and the mineral element through which bodies rediscover their manifold flesh (*Zabriskie Point*), or the ghost of Elvis materializes in a motel room (*Mystery Train*, 1989), or the bringing of eyesight to the blind in Wim Wenders' most ambitious road film, *Until the End of the World* (1991). And in Sluizer's *The Vanishing* (1988), the camera must enter the grave itself in order to reveal a truth the horror of which is less death than its incommunicability.

When death can be posited but not communicated (the exact inverse of Grampa's death in *The Grapes of Wrath*), it is the people who experience their vanishing. Godard's *autoroutes* landscapes (in, say, *Weekend*, 1967), strewn with human and auto wreckage, call into being as their response not the people but the terrorists, the cannibals. And this landscape finds itself perfected in George Miller's *Mad Max* films (1979–85), where Max, simultaneously "maggot" and "honorable man," "feeds off the corpse of the world" (*The Road Warrior*, 1981). And finally, to end this list, the *Trois Couleurs* trilogy (1993–5) of Krzysztof Kieslowski begins with a car wreck and ends with his main characters, brought together by chance, being plucked from a capsized Channel ferry, viewed on a television screen by a man who spends his time eavesdropping on his neighbors. This filmic exposition of a newly arrived European unity tracks the movements of bodies, capital, goods, and information in a series of inhuman (or at least post-humanist) love stories. What is implied by Kieslowski's effort is the possibility of the road film without the unity of characters that usually stabilizes and centers it. The landscape becomes a series of gradients or borders to be crossed or skirted or overleapt. Thus *White* poses the seemingly simple question: how to get from France to Poland? The answers generate very different kinds of stories from those traditionally supported by the road.

The postwar road films, then, turn in two directions, sometimes simultaneously: on the one hand towards new political images or figures in the absence of the people as such, and on the other back towards a history of film. For this second movement, the road emerges from or injects itself into film from the very beginning – the *chemin de fer* of Lumière's *L'Arivée d'un Train en Gare* (1895), for instance – as a very specific revelation of "motion pictures." The road reveals, at least in principle, something very specific about the fact of film, at the very least about time and recorded movements, at the extreme about the variable presence of time in the depth of the image itself. This revelation of the alterity of the image, its inability to come to be quite itself, then leads back to the new political demand of making images in the absence of the people. One can detect something of this in the films already discussed. For example, in *It Happened One Night*, Capra records the presence of a helicopter, the autogyro, as a commentary on travel and human relations. The autogyro is associated with King Westley, the effete playboy who means to marry Colbert (ostensibly for her fortune). King is posed against Gable, who first appears in the film crowned the carnivalesque King of the Road ("make way for the king," shout his fellow reporters after he hangs up on his boss and exits a public phone booth). However, when Vigo takes his camera aloft in a helicopter, its result is not a polarization of two images – as in Capra, one of the people, another of the elite – but a polarization of the image itself, a kind of vertigo of land, water and air.[11]

For the serious road films of the postwar era, it is this second polarization that predominates. For example, when Vogler, writer and photographer and hero of Wenders's road trilogy, decides to sell his car at the conclusion of the American leg of his journey (*Alice in the Cities*, 1974), the sale, under an elevated railway in Queens, takes place in view of and open to Shea Stadium. The image juxtaposes the sound of the stadium organ and the clatter of train and street, the spectacle of American sport and the griminess of the sale itself, the pastoral and the urban. The list could go on, but what is at stake here is the myriad passages through the image itself. And since Vogler will take a Polaroid of the very same image, the image itself relates to its own fading, disappearance as lived and reappearance as memory. The loss of the image, the becoming past of the present, is related less to a successor image than to memory and time themselves. The road here is not so much a narrative device (although it is that, to a degree) as an aleatory sequence of images, punctuated by the photos Vogler takes, and later by those shown to him by Alice. Metonymy, we might say, belongs to the image as much as it belongs to the relation of successive images.

Wenders is the master of the postwar road film, or at least of a certain type of road film. Although he occasionally films action sequences (the kind which have preoccupied so many makers of road movies – here the master is surely *Mad Max*'s George Miller), what characterizes these films is Wenders's insistence upon vision as their central concern. Vogler, of the early films, is a writer turned photographer; *Paris, Texas* (1984) situates Nastassja Kinski in a peep show; *Until the End of the World* (1991) follows William Hurt as he photographs portions of the globe in order to bring images to his blind mother. Throughout these films one witnesses an oscillation between the spectacular organization of images within modern economies and a strain of resistant images, no doubt smaller, sometimes primitive, sometimes sophisticated. If Wenders's films become increasingly paranoid (beginning most fully with *Paris, Texas*, but already in *Alice*, when Vogler kicks his foot through a television set), it is because this oscillation relates itself to another: that between seeing and being seen, watching and being watched. These oscillations are not simple binarisms, however. They simply link every appearance to a disappearance (hence Wenders's fondness for shadows, especially those of large objects like planes, which literally detach themselves from their sources, or his fondness for points of view which imperceptibly shift without the viewer moving, as when Harry Dean Stanton sits on a hill and watches landing aircraft move from above to below), every present to a past and a new becoming present.

Two images from *Alice in the Cities* make fine examples. The film is pervaded by the presence of American pop music, often grating and insipid on the car radio (Vogler continually turns the dial), energizing as it resounds from a jukebox (especially Canned Heat), convulsing and rocking in the film of an aging Chuck Berry in concert. The music, like the film's protagonists, traverses two continents; but we are witnessing not only the Americanization of postwar Europe, but also the way in which the music, already partially lost to Americans, finds itself again at home in a foreign land. In another striking image, Vogler and Alice use a binocular viewer to look around New York from atop the Empire State Building. The camera surrenders its gaze to the sweeps, ascents and descents of the machine, sometimes in the hands of Vogler, sometimes in those of the little girl. It is as if one were entering the visual field for the first time, so that big and small, up and down, far and near continually shift and trade places. The gaze descends along the flight of a bird, hits the street just in time to witness Alice's mother enter a taxi. From flight to flight, what is biggest and smallest, closest and farthest away, undulate. In resisting the panoramic, the inclusive or unifying view, the spectacle gives way to an initiation of the visible, not a representation of but an exposure to other people's lives and the little differences that give them shape. This is nowhere so poignant as when Alice, who has watched Vogler continually take photos, shows him her own family snapshots. Exposure, then, in its various meanings, might be understood to be Wenders's major theme. Here the visual, or even the visionary, is not revelation, but a being exposed to and hence initiated into another person and his or her existence.

Alice in the Cities ends very much in the style of Vigo. A close-up of Vogler and Alice, their heads out a train window, hair blowing in the wind, gives way to the camera's rise into the air, giving to view the train, the Rhine, the sky and an entire, striated landscape, turning with the camera, a *Vogel(er)schau*, as it were.[12] But this bird's-eye view is not a revelation. It simply recalls its opposite, its own coming from and returning to the ground. What Wenders discovers on the road is not the people but mortals in the absence of the people, interrelated lives, relations of opposite and oscillating predicates, which resist their becoming subject even as Wenders's images resist their becoming spectacle (in Debord's sense). With

Wenders, or at least the early Wenders, the road movie becomes resolutely little, minor.

The postwar road film finds itself situated in a vastly changed landscape (or autoscape). In the United States, the major difference between pre- and postwar road films revolves around the massive interstate highway projects of the 1950s and 1960s so that the great migratory routes of the Depression years become transformed into the great tourist routes of the 1960s "See America First" and "America's Most Scenic Highways" campaigns.[13] Getting your kicks on Route 66 is not quite what the Joads had in mind.[14] It is precisely within the spectacular commodification of the American landscape as such that the majority of road movies will take place after the war. Behind every billboard a highway patrolman potentially lurks, lies in wait for any expression beyond the boundaries of the law (the pervasive, even if contradictory logic of American ideology: consumption and renunciation). Hence the highway system (an entire semiotics) provides: the spectacle of law and transgression without community so that both remain essentially abstract and empty of real content (*Vanishing Point*, 1971, or the *Smokey and the Bandit* trilogy, 1977, 1980, 1983); a representation of the hierarchies of age, race, and class but in the absence of real social practice (*Gumball Rally*, 1976; *Eat My Dust*, 1976); marginality reduced to a case of mistaken identity (*Macon County Line*, 1974); freedom as the spectacle of consumption and speed in the absence of production (*Slither*, 1973; *Deathrace 2000*, 1975). The list could go on, but is finally very much summed up in *Lost in America* (1985) when Albert Brooks proposes to Julie Hagerty that they hit the road "just like Easy Rider." Here the entrance to the road and the entrance to the cinema have finally joined (in a reprise of Sturges but without the possibility of a redemptive rhetoric). With Brooks, the end of the road can be only cynical capitulation: the two erstwhile yuppies, having squandered their "nest egg," return to the corporate fold. Not the police but simple economic coercion rules the day.[15]

What all these films would seem to have in common is a phrasing of simple being in the world as a kind of capitulation to a blind necessity. Freedom, which all of the protagonists of these films demand, is reduced to a right of which one feels deprived. Hence the seemingly "marginal" position of these denizens of the road. But this marginality, like the freedom toward which it grasps, is abstract and without content. It is, in the long run, only the freedom guaranteed by the highway lobby and the gas companies, the freedom to drive. Hence it capitulates, in the long run, to those same mainstream automobile advertisements against which it ostensibly revolts. Brooks, of course, is more canny than most, placing his protagonists in a motor home rather than a Galaxie 500. But the result is just as sterile.

The disappearance of the people yields an image of the road as marginal territory, as a perpetual in-between. The best road films of the postwar era take it upon themselves to trace the content of this liminal terrain, to refuse abstract freedom in favor of generally open-ended passages through series of concrete experiences. Thus *Thelma and Louise* moves from vacation to criminal flight to political-libidinal choice, and the convertible converts itself from abstract symbol of leisure into the vehicle of a blinding and impossible choice between love and death. And so the stakes of the road film have been displaced from a politics of the people towards a politics of the absence of the people (which may or may not be what is sometimes called "identity politics").

Dennis Hopper's *Easy Rider*, certainly the most famous, perhaps the most important, of the postwar road films, staked out once and for all this marginal geography. Fonda, called "Captain America" because of his American-flag helmet, Hopper decked out as some kind of Buffalo Bill, the two set out in search of "the real America." The film is a celebration of marginal culture: drugs, bikers, desert communes, alcoholism, free love. The two chart a course into the heart of the old Confederacy, tracing a path into the traumatic kernel of the "birth of a nation." This clearly aligned their project with the civil rights movement in general, although the film never examines this connection in any serious way (Antonioni tried to do this in *Zabriskie Point*, dividing the film in half, the first part about race and American leftism, the second about a more visionary liberation). What the film discovers is not the people but a kind of memory: "this used to be one hell of a country" says Jack Nicholson, the film's drunken-philosophical voice. He is

Plate 1.3 Crossing the desert in *Easy Rider*.

murdered by what amount to his own neighbors. Like *Thelma and Louise* and others that followed, what *Easy Rider* recognizes is not the people so much as the searing sacrificial order of the social itself, so that the road leads to nothing short of blood sacrifice, sacrifice of the excessive, exorbitant, perverse. In this one feels the profound influence of 1950s films like *The Wild One* or *Rebel Without a Cause*. But Hopper's heroes have broken the links with straight society in ways these 1950s characters could only dream of. The 1960s road is therefore both revolutionary and utopian in inspiration. Unable, however, to find the people and unable to travel the roads being walked by Martin Luther King (Fonda, Hopper, and Nicholson also do time in Southern jails), these inspirations spirit themselves away in clouds of black smoke. Nevertheless, the freedom riders and civil-rights marchers were pointing the way; bent on equal rights, armed with the liberatory rhetoric of Exodus, the result would be neither one people nor separate but equal. The new politics would be that of minorities, of emerging peoples, who, in order to keep faith with the concrete, material conditions of their lives, could not settle for abstract freedoms.

In short, for the prewar road films, the people constitute a real presence and a political struggle is waged for the soul of the people *qua* image. For the postwar road films, the people progressively appear only within the conditions of their unrepresentability, that is, as we have already glimpsed, as cynical spectacle or sublime emergence. For the best neo-road films, in fact, the image explores the very conditions of communicability that fissure it. For example, the road films of Jarmusch and Kaurismaki both play on the polyglot condition of the image. Their roads always fork, and the question is no longer to where the road leads but how various singular and fluctuating conduits can communicate across their differences. *Down By Law* (1986) brings Roberto Benigni, its Italian-speaking hero, into a jail cell where his attempt to learn English precipitates a great moment of jailhouse solidarity as the prisoners parade in their cells chanting: "I scream, you scream, we all scream for ice cream." In this new (but also very old) vernacular declension/conjugation, modernity's *lingua franca* – *amo*, *amas*, *amat* – is no longer current. The people does not rise to its imperial tongue; in the people's absence there is only the sovereignty of communication (inflecting the noun "cream," conjugating the verb "scream").

Down By Law opens with a series of extended shots (in black-and-white) of New Orleans filmed from a moving car. The camera traces, at road level, the various arteries of the city's demi-monde and *banlieus*, the underworlds and no-man's-lands of the modern city. Each sequence leads to an interior, to a body upon a bed, its eyes just opening. It is as if vision were everywhere in search of its body. But this embodying is balanced by a becoming abstract of what the camera in fact sees. Aided by black-and-white photography and chiaroscuro lighting effects, interiors resolve into a play of geometrical shapes, pools of

Plate 1.4 Jailhouse solidarity in *Down by Law*.

water become complex interference patterns reflected on concave surfaces. Here the road forks between the concrete, materially singular condition of the body and its visionary being in light. "It is a sad and beautiful world" says Benigni to Tom Waits ("Zack," the out-of-work disc jockey whose radio patter gives flesh to the night), reading from his self-compiled notebook of American phrases. And the film will resonate with this found poetry, coming back to its mother tongue from the foreigner who reads Whitman and "Bob" Frost.

The film ends with a forking road (photographed by Robbie Muller, also responsible for so many of Wenders's images), Jack and Zack at the crossroads. But it is exactly the difference between the initial phonemes of the two names, a difference over which Benigni incessantly stumbles as he struggles to name his two new "friends," that names the decisive fork in the film's road. Where the road divides is precisely where it communicates, and Jarmusch is at pains to catalogue this communication, as monologue, dialogue, and communal chant. The crossroads in the woods defeats, architecturally as it were, the dialectics of both center and periphery as well as the dialectics of margin and mainstream (through a virtual eclipse of the horizon: there is no vanishing point but instead an interior dehiscence, a kind of splitting along a sutured line, of the frame itself). Jarmusch had experimented with a similar scenario in *Stranger than Paradise* (1984), in which another foreigner comes to America, and in which foreignness signifies neither marginality nor alienation but provokes the convulsions, ecstasies, and chances of communication. Kaurismaki's *Leningrad Cowboys Go America* (1989) plays the same arena, with his expatriate band of musical Lapps encountering America not through the universality of music but precisely through recognition of its irreducible singularities (not so-called "world music").

Like the prewar road films, the postwar too seem to have come to the condition of a choice, this time, it seems to me, between marginality and minority. In the former, lost, disaffected, and wandering souls still hold out hope for their salvation and just reunification with the people. Here the people are absent precisely insofar as they are phrased as "mainstream." But any representative of this so-called mainstream invariably appears as marginal. The utopian hope of these films is that, in tracing a single, marginal path, one might discover so compelling an image that margin and mainstream, preriphery and center, would once more cohere. This is why these films travel between a nostalgia for a lost people and a hope for a future one. Their inevitable dead end reveals that the dialectics of marginal and mainstream issues not in a new unity but only in an open series of duplicated and repeated individual alonenesses. We are all marginal, as it were. In this first case, then, the people are either lost or futural. For this reason, *Easy Rider* leads not to a politics but to a lifestyle.

For the films I have designated as minor, those for which Wenders and Jarmusch have been my main examples, the absence of the people is, perhaps paradoxically so, its very condition. The figures of these films travel not between a lost unity and its future reparation, not within the fragmented wasteland of a broken fullness, but within a kind of general agonistics. Where for the "marginal" films images exist in time and the road stretches between two points, for the "minor" films time is in the image and the road exposes various facets, figures, or elements one to another. Where the first aim for a certain largeness of vision, the latter trace and analyze series of very concrete differences. For example, when Wenders's Alice lights matches in a darkened bathroom, the effect is not that given in the firelight effects of *Easy Rider* and certainly not those of *The Grapes of Wrath*. In both of those the fire lights a face to give it both its unity and solitariness and in order to link it, as image, to a rising class or insurgent marginal project. But Alice lights matches because of, as she says, "the stink." Light and dark, face and buttocks, eye and nose, child and adult, speech and waste are exposed to one another, illuminated in the image. When, in *Wild at Heart* (1990), Lynch films lighted matches in close-up, seemingly illuminating the entire desert, the image is striking, but insofar as it rejoins a general metaphorics of "burning desire," less demanding (despite its violence) than the small metonymies of Wenders's childhood of the toilet. The minor road links more than it leads, connects, assembles, and exposes more than it issues, unifies, and reveals.

III

In part one I tried to show some of the ways prewar road films made use of Biblical texts in order to produce their political effects as images. Capra, Ford, and Sturges all invoked Exodus in order to suggest the coming of the people into its promised land. But, if the thrust of the prewar films was to bring the people across and out of the desert, to shepherd them across the Jordan into the fulness of their meaning/identity, the later films return to the desert as the scene of wandering. It is almost as if the postwar films, deprived of their people, literalized the metaphors of their great precursors and so cast themselves back into Sinai in the hope of one more burning bush, one more revelation of the Law. Thus Spencer Tracy, the aging, lonely, alienated cop of *It's a Mad, Mad, Mad, Mad World* returns to the desert to find justice beyond the law in the form of buried treasure. His quest an outright failure, he finds himself joined in solidarity with a band of misfits (once again, the dialectics of marginality) with Ethel Merman (the stereotyped and scapegoated mother-in-law) humiliated as the sacrifical token of that bond.

In a way, *Easy Rider* is only a more violent version of this same scenario; except this time we follow the victims through the desert to the scene of their immolation. Neither Fonda and Hopper nor Merman can play the role of the Moses whose death in the desert guarantees the vision of Canaan beyond the river. Exodus, then, gives way to Apocalypse: Thelma and Louise will not cross the Grand Canyon, Bonnie and Clyde come to the end of the road in a dance of death, the tune played by the gunfire of G-Men. Hymns to marginality, these films ask us to identify with the sacrificial victims but also with the policeman-profiler who attempts to give meaning to the sacrifice he cannot prevent (Harvey Keitel's role in *Thelma and Louise*).

"They tore up the countryside with a vengeance right out of the Bible," says the voice of a newscaster as we watch Mickey and Mallory drive RTE 666. And indeed Stone's *Natural Born Killers* (1994) invokes Apocalypse rather than Exodus. But, while Stone's protagonists wander the desert, his camera wanders through a frame that continuously divides itself. Televisual images fill window frames in motel rooms, subtitles are projected upon bodies, color images become black-and-white. In a film dedicated to the proposition that mass media finally equals mass murder, all of these technologies "make sense," as it were. But more interesting is the camera's response to and search for an engendering of images that is at once technological and organic. Drops of blood fall from hands through the air, into water, become the entwining helices of genetic strands, resolve into snakes and disperse to locate themselves in rings or tattoos or as the actual snakes and lizards of the desert. It is as if Chaucer had opened his road trip to Canterbury with X and Y chromosomes rather than March and April, and thus also in the absence of his pilgrims.

Stone's film, then, bears violent witness to the dissolution of the image of the people under the weight of its own constitutive technology as well as a certain dissolution of the person in the presence of its own engendering codes. That we experience this primarily as violence is no wonder. No wonder too that one of the features of the desert is precisely the presence of native or aboriginal people charged with either healing or reconfiguring this violence. This return need not be simply mythical or romantic. And can indeed be a return to the origin precisely as insurmountable difficulty.

No mainstream director has brought the road film closer to these aboriginal conditions than George Miller, whose *Mad Max* trilogy explores a road that winds only through the possibility of a world. By the conclusion (*Beyond Thunderdome*, 1985) Miller has told not the story of a newly emergent people (the children who return to Sydney) but has discovered story-telling as the condition of emergence of life. In place of the narrative of the people's coming into their own being we have story-telling in the absence of a people. In all of the films, the directed narrativity of the road is balanced by the senseless repe-tition of the LP record (wild children repeating French lessons, etc.). But it is this senseless kernel, a sacrifice of meaning, that deflects the violence of desert and Bartertown. And indeed, despite the massive violence contained in these films, the very same *bricolage* that gives rise to violent assemblages (weapons, armor, vehicles) gives rise to a primary generosity, of meaningless exchanges constitutive of sociality. Miller consistently holds out the hope that there may be a people convened in the absence of its meaning, a being-in-common without a common being.

With the return to the desert the road film returns to the scene of the origins of the people. For what I have been calling the best or most ambitious of these films, the desert is the place of a people always already in exile, constitutively diasporic. To communicate something of these origins means filming original instances of communication. The image of the road disperses into the multiform images of arteries that traverse and put into communication the earth, bodies, and even the sky. In *The Adventures of Priscilla, Queen of the Desert* (1994) for example, the colors and shapes of the clothes and head-dresses of the drag queens commu-nicate with lizards, dunes, the sky, and brush fires. Progressively, the image of the people gives way to the images of the earth's inhabitants. If I have been using the word 'minor' in relation to these films it is because they demand of themselves, as practice, and of us, as viewing, a willingness to wander within the image with-out the expectation that we will eventually, in time, recognize ourselves as the subject of that image. That subject, the people, cannot quite be shown; they must be sought, traced, pursued across a series of small, often nearly imperceptible differences. Big or little, white or red, straight or gay, alive or dead. . . . No longer simply the attributes of a common human substance, the minor road films acknowledge and engage these signs as predicates without a subject. The camera is made into the condition of a nomadism without, strictly speaking, nomads.

As a final example, and by way of a conclusion, let us return to Kieslowski's *Trois Couleurs* trilogy. The three colors, blue, white, and red, from which the three films draw their titles, are the colors of the French flag. What Kieslowski does is this: he separates the colors from their support, the flag. Hence blue is a candy wrapper, but also a window, water, or a coat; white is a wedding veil, but also pigeon droppings, marble, and snow; and red is a dress, but also blood and the hull of a ship. The people, but also the things and animals, drawn along with the colors, are by virtue of these multi-supported trajectories, these roads, brought into communication, indeed into community, but precisely in the absence of identity. They emerge from their journeys not as French or Polish or English or even quite European, nor even as the sum total of all their filmic attributes. They will have been just the drawing into communication of colors linked and assembled by and in the film's images. It is not clear, politically, where this road gets us. But it is clear that it keeps faith with the difficult political wagers that have characterized, historically, the very best road films.

Notes

1   Although I will not address this work directly, I want simply to acknowledge the texts of Jean-Luc Nancy, Maurice Blanchot, and Giorgio Agamben. They are central to my meditations on film, image, and community. I would like also to acknowledge that the entirety of this essay represents, to my mind at least, an extension of the conversations opened up by the work of Stanley Cavell and Gilles Deleuze. Indeed, my ruminations on time and motion as well as my particular use of the word "image" derive directly from Deleuze.

2   Restlessness is, of course, one of Capra's major and recurring themes. Indeed, all of his films, it seems to me, might be analyzed in terms of a dialectic of restlessness and coming to rest. Just think of how fidgety Gary Cooper and James Stewart are in every Capra film. This dialectic is given its most concrete and full treatment in *You Can't Take It With You* (1938), in which Jean Arthur's entire family is in constant motion (and this despite Barrymore's broken foot!). But what motivates the film's action is that same family's refusal to move from its old house. Hence what is at play here is the desire to stay put traversed by the inability to sit still (even in jail). In Capra, music often signifies just this restlessness: the singing of "The Daring Young Man on the Flying Trapeze" in *It Happened One Night*, or the harmonica playing of both *Meet John Doe* and *You Can't Take It With You*. Ford's relation to music, as would be expected, is just the opposite: music belongs to horizons, to the night and rest, and especially to memory (hence the importance of "Red River Valley" and its mnemonic work in *The Grapes of Wrath*).

3   Later I will have occasion to compare Capra's film with Vigo's *L'Atalante*, another road film, made the same year, and for which questions of vanishing, separation, disappearance are essential. Indeed, for Vigo, separation, the vanishing of one body to or from another, becomes an element of visuality itself. This finds its high point in

the intercut shots of the separated newlyweds, eyes closed, miles apart in separate beds, and yet bound to one another in a strangely hetero-autoerotic circuit.

4   Deleuze, once again: "A theory of cinema is not 'about' cinema, but about the concepts that cinema gives rise to and which are themselves related to other concepts corresponding to other practices, the practice of concepts in general having no privilege over others, any more than one object has over others. It is at the level of the interference of many practices that things happen, beings, images, concepts, all the kinds of events. The theory of cinema does not bear on the cinema, but on the concepts of the cinema, which are no less practical, effective or existent than cinema itself" (280). My hope is to demonstrate how the road movie might be considered one such concept or practice of concepts.

5   In this respect one should note the adjacency of the road film and adventure film. Clearly the line between the two is shifty, but it clarifies itself in those films dealing with specifically "foreign" or exotic locations. In this respect the road film is closer to tourism than actual adventure, a kind of second wave of colonialism (of and in images, of course). Capra's *Lost Horizon* (1937), then, might be taken as a kind of limit towards or from which the road extends (extension, limit, border: these belong within the conceptual apparatus of the road movie). And I would add that even in Shangri-la we once again encounter Capra's restless beings. The Hope–Crosby films probably belong within this context.

6   The full quotation is as follows: "That the unconscious is structured as a function of the symbolic, that it is the return of a sign that the pleasure principle makes man seek out, that the pleasurable element is that which directs man in his behavior without his knowledge (namely, that which gives him pleasure, because it is a form of euphony), that that which one seeks and finds again is the trace rather than the trail – one has to appreciate the great importance of this in Freud's thought, if one is to understand the function of reality.

"Certainly Freud leaves no doubt, any more than Aristotle, that what man is seeking, his goal, is happiness. It's odd that in almost all languages happiness offers itself in terms of a meeting – *tuché*. Except in English and even there it's very close. A kind of favorable divinity is involved. *Bonheur* in French suggests to us *augurum*, a good sign and a fortunate encounter. *Glück* is the same as *gelück*. *Happiness* is after all *happen*; it, too, is an encounter, even if one does not feel the need to add the prefix, which strictly speaking indicates the happy character of the thing" (Lacan: 12). In the relation of what Lacan calls "the trail" and "the trace" we could find precisely the over- lapping of symbolic (unconscious) economies in a kind of Boolean web that constitutes the best road films. For example, the handcuffs yoking Madeleine Carroll to Robert Donat in *The 39 Steps* (1935) produce an image of a kind of Venn diagram; when they are finally removed, the couple, in the film's final image, join hands, so that an inaugural clasp that happens by chance (in fact by chance twice, once on a train, again at a political rally) gives way to the willed clasp of happiness. Here, as in *It Happened One Night*, it is by first pretending to be married, by playing or tracing a symbolic condition, that the couples bring themselves towards the actual condition. A more complicated scenario presents itself in *The Grapes of Wrath*, when Grandma, despite the fact she is dead, brings the family across the state line into "the land of milk and honey, California." Indeed, more than anyone, it was Ford who knew how to film the road and the horizon or the enfolding of the trail and the trace. His figures are invariably accompanied by their shadows, or glow in a borrowed light (in any number of close-ups). Or, in the scene of Grampa's burial, the camera shows Fonda literally tracing the letters of the words which will accompany the dead body into the earth.

7 Indeed, Sturges combines in the film both Capra's exquisite formal mechanics of comedy and something of Ford's realism. This oscillation between the two directors and their styles allows Sturges to give substance to a real people even as he infinitizes them through film and laughter. Every viewer of this film has recognized, in one way or another, the immensity of this achievment.

8 Stanley Cavell was the first to comment on the centrality of food in the film. My readings are indebted to him.

9 And while I'm invoking unconscious automatism: is it an accident that the appearance of Lake in the film sets off a series of aquatic misadventures in swimming pools, tubs, showers, and the bayou?

10 Whatever one takes its shortcomings to be, *How Green Was My Valley* (1941), which followed soon after *The Grapes of Wrath*, takes up many of that film's themes and images within the explicit framing of memory. Here one wanders through time, and the road (the street leading to and then into the mine) cuts a sinuous path through the earth and memory. The road, path, or lane become ways of exploring the multi-layeredness of the image. In *How Green Was My Valley*, this relation between road and memory, road and image, is directly related to the filmic gaze through a series of continual re-framings, through doorways, windows or the box bed to which Huw is confined, as well as the caged window through which the miners receive their pay. This relation of frame, enclosure, motion, road, and gaze traverses Ford's work, from the initial and irridescent appearance of John Wayne in *Stagecoach* (1939) to the recollections and narratives linked by the stagecoach railroad nexus in *The Man who Shot Liberty Valence* (1962). Many of these relations are foreclosed in *The Grapes of Wrath*, where the windows and doorways seem turned in toward the Joads, always under surveillance. The Okies cower in the darkness, taking cover from Capital and its paid lackeys. Here the people and its memories are given as either tactile (hands sifting through soil, the clutch of folk dancers, etc.) or as suffusing the darkness (as in Fonda's last and most famous monologue).

11 I am, quite obviously, playing on Deleuze's distinction between the movement-image and the time-image. Deleuze associates the first with the classic cinema, the second with the postwar cinema inaugurated by the neo-realists. On the surface this distinction would seem to coincide with Bazin's, between the presence and absence of deep focus, and in many ways it does. But Deleuze's project is not an ontology of cinema as such, but a serious inquiry into the relation of time and movement, and the liberation of the former from the latter, which has been a consistent subject of philosophical thought since the pre-Socratics.

12 All of these elements, exposure, initiation, the relation of near to far and large to small, of the sky to the earth, ascent to descent, are given very full treatment in the two Berlin films: *Wings of Desire* (1988) and *Faraway, So Close!* (1993).

13 The PBS "P.O.V." documentary, *Taken for a Ride* (1995), although not technically a road movie, is must viewing for anyone interested in the US highway system as the incarnation of monopoly capital. In this case capital profits both directly and indirectly from the production of its own circulatory system, which in turn becomes an image (the cloverleaf, for example) punctuated by images (billboards, etc.). What Hausmann did for Paris at the dawn of the modern spectacle, General Motors, Dow Chemical, and the rest of the highway lobby did for the US.

14 And while we're on the subject of popular song (so many of them about the road, some even transformed into films and television shows, *Convoy* (1978) being my personal favorite), it is interesting to note how Bob Dylan's "Highway 61" attempted to restore the Biblical rhetoric of the road so pervasive in prewar films. Highway 61, of course, was the route the Blues took from the Delta to Chicago. Dylan would be a central figure in an extended examination of the culture of the road, as would be his antetype, Woody Guthrie. Hal Ashby's *Bound for Glory* (1976) is therefore both biography (of Guthrie) and road film. In general, however, the road film's insistence upon east–west routes has been complicitous (along with the Western) in the complete failure to come to grips with race as an (perhaps the) American condition. Even the 'minor' films presently under discussion suffer from this oversight (which amounts to nearly complete suppression). The major exception to this rule would be *The Bingo Long Traveling All Stars and Motor Kings* (1976), a story based loosely on the lives of Satchel Paige, Josh Gibson, and Jackie Robinson and the days of barnstorming, razzle-dazzle baseball. But the film can never delve too deeply into the bitter pill of success within the confines of racism: entrance into white baseball.

15 Brooks would, more successfully I think, return to an exploration of the consumption/renunciation dialectic in *Defending Your Life* (1991). Like Wenders, he turns from the road to the afterlife. Unlike Wenders, Brooks imagines mortality as a form of failure.

Works Cited

Agamben, Georgio. *The Coming Community*, trans. Michael Hardt. Minneapolis: University of Minnesota Press, 1993.

Blanchot, Maurice. *The Unavowable Community*, trans. Pierre Joris. Barrytown, NY: Station Hill Press, 1988.

Cavell, Stanley. *Pursuits of Happiness: The Hollywood Comedy of Remarriage*. Cambridge, MA: Harvard University Press, 1981.

Deleuze, Gilles. *Cinema 2*, trans. Hugh Tomlinson and Robert Galeta. Minneapolis: University of Minnesota Press, 1989.

Lacan, Jacques. *Seminar VII, The Ethics of Psychoanalysis (1959–1960)*, trans. Dennis Porter. New York: Norton, 1992.

McBride, Joseph. *Frank Capra, The Catastrophe of Success*. New York: Simon & Schuster, 1992.

Nancy, Jean-Luc. *The Inoperative Community*, trans. Peter Connor. Minneapolis: University of Minnesota Press, 1991.

Shirer, William L. *Berlin Diary*. New York: Alfred A. Knopf, 1941.

2

WESTERN MEETS EASTWOOD
Genre and gender on the road

Shari Roberts

They tell me everything isn't black and white. . . . Well I say, why the hell not?

> John Wayne ("John Wayne as the Last Hero": 55)

I like simple things, yet I'm obviously more complex than I appear on the surface.

> Clint Eastwood (Thompson: 121)

Introduction

As portrayed in the Western and alluded to in the road movie, frontier symbolism is propelled by masculinity and a particular conception of American national identity that revolves around individualism and aggression. During the height of the studio system, this symbolic core codified into the Western film as an iconography evoking already nostalgic ideas about the frontier. As the Western condensed further into what we now refer to as the genre of the road film, these characteristics become concentrated and codified, in part through the insistence on the extremely linear narrative structure of the road film. What ultimately links the road movie to the Western is this ideal of masculinity inherent in certain underlying conceptualizations of American national identity that have persisted, if only through continual ideological struggle.

Eastwood provides the touchstone for my analysis of the road film, its relationship to the Western, and the gendered assumptions that inform both genres.[1] This essay contextualizes Eastwood within the genres, and then uses his star text as an example through which to explore them.[2] A consideration of recent "feminine" road films, that is, road films featuring female protagonists and feminine issues, further highlights the inherent masculinity of the road movie.

Westerns, Road Narratives, and Masculinity

The films of director and actor Clint Eastwood include Westerns, road films, and some films that fit both categories, thereby straddling these two genres. Eastwood reached international fame as the Man with No Name in the Sergio Leone Western trilogy, *A Fistful of Dollars* (1964), *For a Few Dollars More* (1965), and *The Good, the Bad, and the Ugly* (1966), produced after the genre of the film Western has been established for fifty years. Subsequently, Eastwood starred in many Hollywood films, including Westerns, some of which he also directed (*Hang 'Em High*, 1967, *High Plains Drifter*, 1973, *Pale Rider*, 1985, and *Unforgiven*, 1992), and road movies, some of which he also directed (*Two Mules for Sister Sara*, 1970, *The Outlaw Josey Wales*, 1976, *Every Which Way But Loose*, 1978, *Bronco Billy*, 1980, *Honkytonk Man*, 1982, and *A Perfect World*, 1993), and all of which either fall within or allude to the Western genre.[3] Even his television series, *Rawhide* (1959–66), organized around an extended cattle drive, constitutes a road narrative.

The generic logic that helps to produce Eastwood, who crosses back and forth between Western and road film, results in a star who enunciates a macho, jingoistic brutality at one with the earlier John Wayne Western cowboy, and takes advantage of the underlying masculinist tendencies of both genres. That Eastwood straddles the Western and road film makes generic sense, and, although this study focuses on one star in particular, it has implications for the genre as a whole.

The Western has been popular with the American public across changing media as well as shifting historical context, starting with literary frontier narratives, such as James Fenimore Cooper's Leatherstocking tales (e.g., *The Pioneers*, 1823), and including Western novels by authors such as Zane Grey and Louis L'Amour. Westerns have been part of Hollywood since its inception, with serials in the 1920s and 1930s, and hundreds of nationally distributed feature films produced from the 1920s through today, starring the likes of Roy Rogers, Gene Autry, John Wayne, and Eastwood. Western radio shows of the 1930s and 1940s gave way to television Western programs in the 1950s and 1960s (Tompkins: 5; Cawelti: 3, 89–119; Buscombe: 48). Such consistent popularity demonstrates how this "quintessential American genre" (Smith: 3) persistently speaks to the American public. As Virginia Wright Wexman notes, "the venerable Hollywood formula articulates a view of America that has dominated the popular imagination throughout the greater part of the twentieth century. The classic Western – defined in part by its association with the images of John Wayne and stars like him – participates in a . . . discourse on American history and American identity that uses the myth of the frontier to contain . . . inconsistency in American nationalist ideology" (71).[4] The Western continues to resonate as symbolic of a particular version of US national identity.

Many have noted the masculinist character of the Western.[5] Jane Tompkins argues that, in the twentieth century, secular, masculine, male-authored novels and films replaced nineteenth-century Christian, domestic, female-authored sentimental novels. According to Tompkins, "the Western *answers* the domestic novel" as "the antithesis of the cult of domesticity that dominated American Victorian culture" in a "gender war" over both "literary landscape" and the "national scene" (39, 42). She argues that the Western is "about men's fear of losing their mastery, and hence their identity, both of which the Western tirelessly reinvents" (45). The Western film continues this masculinist tradition, and during the studio era ranked among women's least favorite film genres (Handel: 124). Not only did the Western become popular because of male readers, who, in Tompkins's argument, may have fantasized a refurbished, masterly gender identity, but it also has continued to be popular in part because of Americans who desire to re-create a revitalized, and particularly masculinist, national identity through popular culture. The road genre further emphasizes this cultural function.

A brief consideration of John Wayne's star text demonstrates the masculinist, nationalist ideology enunciated by both the Western, precursor to the road film and Eastwood's own road films. In 1963, "God and Man in Hollywood" appeared in *Esquire*. In this article, the author calls Wayne a "superpatriot" and relates how when Wayne was once asked in a nightclub if he would like to have his favorite tune played, Wayne replied, "No, if you played my favorite tune, everybody would have to stand up" (Morgan: 74). Wayne's extra-filmic life coalesces with his filmic Western persona, consistently presenting a masculinist, chauvinistic ideal. He started adult life with a college football scholarship; he was a staunch and public supporter of the US government even for controversial domestic and foreign policies, such as the 1950s "red scare" and the 1960s involvement in the Vietnam War,[6] and he heroically battled his last enemy, cancer, which he called "the big C" in the pages of the popular press. Sample articles among many include "John Wayne Rides Again," or "Big John," which begins, "John Wayne, the big boy, the Duke, . . . had licked 'the big C.' . . . He threw a couple of ascorbic-acid pills into his mouth and washed them down with a slug out of a half-gallon jug of mezcal – which is 120 proof and called *la gasolina* by the locals. 'Goddam!' bellowed Duke, 'I'm the stuff that men are made of!'" Another typical Wayne statement is this self-conscious articulation of his "macho" perspective on the film industry: "There's a lot of yella bastards in the country who would like to call patriotism old-fashioned. . . . My main object in making a motion picture is entertainment. . . . If at the same time I can strike a blow for liberty, then I'll stick one in" ("John Wayne": 55). Wayne's metaphor for the nationalistic function of the mass media – "strike a blow" and "stick one in" – may be mixed, but they are also singularly coded as masculine.

Stagecoach (1939) and *The Searchers* (1956), directed by John Ford and starring Wayne, are Westerns structured by road narratives. As such, an analysis of these films provides a contrast to Eastwood road films with Western allusions. *Stagecoach*, a relatively early, traditional Western, uses a road journey to redefine community. The stagecoach, whose path structures the film, is peopled by a miniature community, including both representatives and misfits of society, from the doctor and the banker to the prostitute and the outlaw. The hero, Ringo (Wayne), is on a quest for vengeance against those who have murdered his family. He also serves as a catalyst to articulate a particular definition of the Western and, metonymically, the American community, based on communal values and against the exclusionary practices of the East and South. The final shoot-out, in which the hero avenges his family through vigilante killings, demonstrates how might sides with right in the black-and-white world of the Western. The marshal's acquittal supports Ringo's stand for a "natural" justice that supersedes society's unfair laws.

The film concludes with Ringo and Dallas (Claire Trevor) riding together into the sunset, with the promise of their own nuclear family, home, and land on the horizon. This resolution demonstrates that even Ringo and Dallas, a fugitive and a prostitute, may create new identities, a new community, and a new start in the open spaces, "safe from the blessings of civilization." The East – represented by the town and the "Ladies of the Law and Order League" – signifies the feminine – domestication, corruption, class stratification. By contrast, the film privileges the West and equates it with the masculine – nature, open spaces, heroism, vitality, and justice. The images of Monument Valley symbolize Westward expansion and the opportunity promised by America's wide open spaces. Ford/Wayne films conflate the East and the old, defeated South, which together connote regressive values, decay, decadence, effeminacy, and foppishness. Ford/Wayne films create a new Western world that stands in for an ideal version of America in which the masculine acts as the standard for all that is valuable.

The Road Rises to Meet the Decline of the Western

Genres maintain their vitality by combining difference and familiarity. For instance, although Wayne and Eastwood both play macho Hollywood cowboys, their star texts are quite different, emerging as they do from different historical contexts. As Wayne himself points out in a 1960 interview, "'I like to play *men* – be they good guys or bad,' . . . lighting a cigarette. 'I don't mind being brutal, or tough, or cruel. . . . The day film companies think that a Western is a place for weaklings, I'll go'" ("John Wayne's Ordeal": 107). Wayne adds that the Western film should not "get the audience involved in thinking," and, still speculating on his new-media rivals, he continues, "On TV, the cowboy is introverted and oversensitive. The cowboy loved, hated, had fun, was lusty. He didn't have mental problems. . . . " Wayne distinguishes himself from the "TV cowboys" – including Eastwood, who had begun his seven-year *Rawhide* stint – who threaten to replace him.

The Searchers, a later, revisionist Western, simultaneously works within the genre and throws all it stands for open to question. Many critics, popular and academic, have discussed *The Searchers*, released almost twenty years after *Stagecoach*, as a problematic Western: as a detestable excuse for violence, racism, and misogyny, as an indictment of such, and as a work of art that exceeds the boundaries of the genre.[7] Superficially, *Stagecoach* and *The Searchers* resemble each other. In both, the bugle signals the arrival of the cavalry, cowboys and Indians fight, the men with white hats draw faster than those with black, the women either need to be rescued or remain at home, and in the end some sort of justice is served. However, in *The Searchers*, the cavalry is not heroic, but comic; the women are raped, murdered, and kidnapped. Moreover, as Ethan (Wayne) rejects the goal of rescuing the kidnapped woman and instead rushes to kill her, the viewer must grapple with the difficulty of accepting a pathologically racist and murderous protagonist, and realizing that the basis for the film title entails issues that were never "black and white." The conflict between civilization and savagery becomes muddy and confused, as Ethan and Scar (Henry Brandon), the Comanche chief, mirror each other, hero and enemy sharing the same space. No simple rescue or vengeance ensues, and, although the film closes with the promise of a wedding and a reuniting of some semblance of family, this home-coming does not resolve the search that structures the film. As Brian Henderson notes, the theme song overlaps with the closing images of the settlers entering the house as Ethan turns away: "A man will search in heart and soul. . . . His peace of mind he knows he'll find, but where, O Lord, O where? Ride away, ride away, ride away" (11). The film ends without answering these questions or fulfilling the title search, leaving the "hero" on the road, wandering. The relentless linear thrust of the search takes on its own life and power, and overwhelms all other values.

While some contemporary viewers might have been unimpressed with *The Searchers* – *Variety*, for instance, calls it "disappointing" and "overlong and repetitious" – Stuart Byron notes the wide-reaching influence of *The Searchers* on American film-makers, suggesting "that . . . it can be said that all recent American cinema derives from . . . *The Searchers*," and lists among those influenced Paul Schrader, John Milius, Martin Scorsese, Steven Spielberg, George Lucas, and Michael Cimino (45). Byron argues that, in particular, films showing the mark of *The Searchers* have a structure identical to the 1956 film, including *Taxi Driver* (1976), *Close Encounters* (1977), *The Deer Hunter* (1978), and *Hardcore* (1979). It may seem impossible to explain – beyond the statement of its qualities as an "artistic masterpiece," as Godard has called it – that one studio film could affect so many different directors in the "new Hollywood" and result in such different films, none of which would be classified as Westerns. However, if viewed as part of the establishment of the road film, *The Searchers'* uniqueness as a Western may be owed to its straddling of cultural and generic shifts.

It is no coincidence that *The Searchers* was created toward the end of the film Western's heyday. Feature Westerns were popular until the 1960s, when production gradually declined. For instance, 27 percent of all films produced in 1953 were Westerns, but only 9 percent produced in 1963 were, and production continues to drop through the present. By the 1970s, Westerns were seen by the industry as a liability, and in 1979 the genre lost its greatest and most consistent advocate, Wayne (Smith: 45–6).[8] Beginning with *The Searchers*, the focus changed from a hero traveling across the frontier to the searcher hitting the road.

Robert Ray discusses how fundamental structures and tropes of a genre can be "disguised," a Western structure being used, for instance, in a Second World War film or a space odyssey.[9] However, it's not simply the case that the Western disguises itself in road clothing; instead, a distillation takes place in which certain elements from the Western help to form a new genre of the road genre. What was at first a theme becomes a recognized genre in its own right. Of course, the road has existed as a theme or structuring device since the beginning of film and before. At some level, all narratives incorporate the theme of the road. One might call Homer's *Odyssey* a proto-road-narrative, and point out the similarities between it and Hollywood road movies. However, the road does not constitute a genre until a body of films become recognizable as separate and distinct for audiences.

We think of Francis Parkman Jr's *The Oregon Trail* and L'Amour novels as part of the Western tradition, even though *The Oregon Trail* would not have been understood as a Western at the time it was published in 1849. In the same way, while contemporary viewers would have recognized films, from *The Great Train Robbery* (1903) to *Stagecoach*, as versions of the Western, neither of these films nor non-Western road narratives such as *The Grapes of Wrath* (1939) or *They Live By Night* (1949) would have been understood as part of a road genre at the time of their release. While critics and viewers may have discussed travel or a quest in relationship to *Stagecoach*, it would have been recognized and described as a Western, and still would be labeled as such today. Retrospectively, elements of *Stagecoach* structure it as a road movie as well as a Western; however, this is an understanding obtained only by reading American film history backwards. To call *Stagecoach* a road movie would be meaningless without the publication of books such as *On the Road* (1957) and *Zen and the Art of Motorcycle Maintenance* (1974), and the release of films such as *Easy Rider* (1969) and *Stranger than Paradise* (1984).

Road Films, Western Allusions, and Masculinity

The road film did not exist as a recognizable genre until, roughly, the release of *Easy Rider* in 1969.[10] Social upheavals helped to define this period in America, including the women's liberation, civil rights, and youth movements, but of particular note is the gradual increase in American involvement in the Vietnam War. US involvement began in 1955, the year that the French left and Vietnam was partitioned into North and South. Between 1955 and 1964, American troops in Vietnam increased from the hundreds to a hundred thousand. By the end of 1965, 188,000 American troops were stationed in Vietnam, and protests, mostly among youth groups, began.[11] To put the two genres in context, by 1956, the year *The Searchers* was released, Americans had already experienced the stalemate of the Korean conflict, and feelings of certainty about foreign involvement seemed as distant as "the last good war"[12] over a decade earlier. Domestic racial unrest and civil rights activism had been building since the time of the Second World War, and desegregation began to come to an end with *Brown* vs. *Board of Education of Topeka* in 1954, only two years previously.[13] By 1968, the year that Lyndon Baines Johnson chose not to run for re-election, partly owing to the Vietnam issue, the tide had turned and the public generally demanded withdrawal from the war. And in 1969 the independent film *Easy Rider*, Cannes Film Festival award-winner, was embraced by a generation as a statement of youth, rebellion, and counter-culture.

A linear, yet almost non-narrative film, *Easy Rider* set the standard for the road genre. The advertising describes it with an economy of words: "A man went looking for America and couldn't find it anywhere." The film features protagonists Wyatt (Peter Fonda), who wears a helmet emblazoned with the American flag, and Billy (Dennis Hopper), who wears a pioneer-styled, leather fringe outfit, who are named after legendary Wild West figures Wyatt Earp and Billy the Kid. Their names and costumes emphasize the link between a genre that would enunciate an American dream, and one that represents the absence of clear-cut ideals. Although the characters travel to New Orleans, this literal road only gives structure to a parallel, spiritual quest for freedom for life and art, and freedom from restrictive traditions, mores, and social norms. Wyatt literally reads the writing on the wall: "If God did not exist, it would be necessary to invent him." The main characters search for a new spiritual place for themselves appropriate to their counter-culture and the modern world. The film experiments with editing, camera movement, angles, and film stock, while the characters simultaneously experiment with sex and drugs in an attempt to break through old boundaries and create a revitalized set of values. The physical journey to Mardi Gras structures the process of self-discovery, the search for new personal and national identities. *Variety* states: "Film does not force parallels but they resemble men looking for some sort of new frontier, giving an ironic cast in a land now populated from sea to shining sea. The bikes, while part of them, are also a means of giving them movement and freedom. No dwelling on reasons, didactics or explanation of why they are what they are but filling it in on their long hegira." This contemporary review recognizes the aspects of the Western inherent in what can only be called a road film. The link between the Western and this constitutive road film proves informative throughout the genre.

In my undergraduate Road Movie course, one of the small group projects performed is a discussion of images and words that connote America, an exercise through which the concept of national identity is investigated as an "imagined community" (Anderson). Students regularly create provocative lists, merging such concrete items as cars, McDonald's, guns, and "The Brady Bunch" with abstract concepts such as democracy, individualism, and freedom.[14] Sergio Leone himself remembers feeling that "America was like a religion. . . . I dreamed of the wide open spaces . . . the great expanses of desert, the extraordinary melting pot. . . . The long, straight roads . . . which begin nowhere, and end nowhere" (Frayling: 65). In a recent editorial concerning terrorism, the author sums up what he thinks "America" means to those included in and excluded by "American culture . . . : our blend of individualism, 'Baywatch,' hamburgers, capitalism and Beach Boys. It has the power to supplant any culture on the planet. To us, it's Route 66; to the medievally inclined, it's the road to hell, paved with 'Good Vibrations'" (Lileks: 20). This casual description of America indicates how "the road" is of a piece with some of the goals, such as individualism, of the American Dream. These examples demonstrate how the mere mention or image of the road has commonly come to symbolize a conceptualization of America.

In the Eastwood films, and, by extension, the road film in general, the frontier, the wide open spaces of the Ford/Wayne films, transforms into the road, a more current icon. American geography and history play much the same role here as in the Western, so that the image of the white dotted line becomes a visual short-hand indicating a new start, endless possibility, and equal opportunity – the American Dream. Western imagery was already nostalgic when the genre was established, and now the Western itself seems dated. The road stands in for the frontier, but, instead of symbolizing a romanticized America in which the American Dream will come true, it simply asks over and over, as each mile marker is passed, what does America mean today? Are dreams even possible? While the traditional Western often works to resolve and contain disturbances, as in *Stagecoach*, the road tends to reveal the illusory nature of these terms.

Rather than setting these films in the iconic Western frontier, road films are characterized by an absence of civilization, law, and domesticity, marked instead by primitivism or post-apocalyptic space. With a more global understanding of the frontier *qua* road, the journey may move along a highway (*Bronco Billy*), a river (*Apocalypse Now*, 1979), or through space and time (*Star Trek VI: The Undiscovered Country*, 1991). While other elements of the Western remain important to the road film, the transformation of the frontier into an often metaphorical road introduces the crucial, structuring device of the road – the dual journey, the interdependent physical and spiritual journeys. The road as theme may appear in any film, regardless of historical context, whereas, in the road film genre, the metaphor of the road becomes the main structuring device through this interdependence of the physical and spiritual journeys.

The protagonist – sometimes with a "buddy," as in *A Perfect World*, or a hodge-podge, *ad hoc* family, as in *The Outlaw Josey Wales* or *Bronco Billy* – moves through the film on a physical journey that parallels a spiritual quest. Often escaping a threat, the law, and/or an unwanted lifestyle (*Bonnie and Clyde*, 1967, *A Perfect World*, or *Thelma and Louise*, 1991), the hero also usually begins a quest, often unbeknownst to her/himself, for a better life, a new social order, or fulfillment. For instance, in *The Searchers*, as opposed to the earlier, more traditional *Stagecoach*, the goal of the search remains as ambiguous as in many road films. The road protagonist searches for a concrete goal: Ethan follows Debbie (Natalie Wood) for years in *The Searchers*; Wyatt and Billy travel to Mardi Gras in *Easy Rider*; Red (Eastwood) tries to make it to Nashville for an audition in *Honkytonk Man*; and Butch (Kevin Costner) in *A Perfect World* escapes prison and so is on the run towards Alaska. However, in these road movies, as opposed to Westerns, internal journeys fuel the physical wanderings. Moreover, while one might suggest that in *Stagecoach* Ringo Kid takes the road to Lordsburg to avenge his family, the film's simple journey, traditional goal, and closure seldom occur for the protagonists of road films. Ethan perhaps searches for an elusive peace, Billy and Wyatt search for something like enlightenment, Red and Butch search for immortality – in each of these the spiritual journey parallels but always overshadows the physical journey.

In part because Eastwood's road films conform to this extremely linear structure, actions may seem to speak louder than words. This masculinist hierarchy is common to both the Western and the road genre, although it functions differently within each. Regarding the Western, Tompkins notes that the "interdiction masculinity imposes on speech arises from the desire for complete objectivization. And this means being conscious of nothing, not knowing that one has a self. . . . Not fissured by self-consciousness, nature is what the hero aspires to emulate: perfect being-in-itself" (55–7). Smith corroborates this observation in his analysis of Eastwood's performance in the Leone films, noting "close-ups of faces, costumes, and gestures . . . do not so much signify the internal qualities of the classic cowboy, . . . as construct instead a mere exterior, a purely physical demeanor that stands in for masculinity itself" (11). Leone says of Eastwood,

"I looked at him and I didn't see any character . . . just a physical figure" (Cumbow: 154). Tompkins suggests that the silence of the male Western informs the Western genre in all its permutations, suppressing "inner life" in men (66). Smith further reads Eastwood's silence as particular to the Man with No Name, suggesting that it implies the "emptying out of the moral codes of the western hero . . . openly insulting to the American tradition," whereby this subaltern production resists American domination and hegemony (13–14). The laconic hero works as an element in transit from Western to Eastwood, notable in the Leone Westerns in which Eastwood's character, instead of history, has a richness of surface, all actions and attitude, using an economy of performance that points toward an anticipated generic unfolding in a manner consistent with a revisionist product. That is, Eastwood's Western persona appears when the over-saturated genre anticipates its audience, for whom the merest gestures towards the conventions suffice, and the resulting film may even be read as camp by some viewers. In contrast to the traditional Western, in which the silent male hero is privileged through an assumed association with nature, in the road movie action *becomes* the inner life. For the crossover Eastwood hero, in late Westerns and in road films, silence signifies neither the death of the inner life, as in Tompkins, nor the emptying out of morality, as in Smith, but instead the *literalization* of the inner journey. The road movie involves a dual journey, physical and spiritual. It is not the case that the external journey replaces the internal quest, but rather that the two are instead interdependent.

Violence and death, also associated with the masculine, permeate both the Western and the road film. Tompkins takes the title of her book, *West of Everything*, from a L'Amour passage in *Hondo*: "hero of a Washington romance, dead now in the long grass on a lonely hill, west of everything" (56). She argues that "To go west, . . . west of everything, is to die. Death is everywhere in this genre" (24). Tompkins argues that death and violence help to define the masculinist genre (24–5). Violence and stoicism, in other words, are the means by which the men of the Western demonstrate their heroism, and death is the means by which they gain glory. At a recent tribute to Eastwood, the master of ceremonies, Jim Carrey, attributed Eastwood's popularity to male fantasies of control and natural justice fulfilled by the image of Eastwood, who always beats into submission the specter of the viewer's "school yard bully."[15]

In the traditional Western, violence and death are the means by which to test the unquestioned ideal of masculinity; in the Eastwood road film violence becomes hyper-real, ritualistic, a spectacle that alludes to the old codes of the Western in the pastiche of this postmodern genre. Neale has noted that, in Eastwood's Leone trilogy, the violence becomes spectacle in that its denouement comes without suspense. This is not to suggest that the violence becomes meaningless, or that, by implication, audiences do not register violence and its consequences, but rather that, owing to genre over-saturation and audience expectations, the moments of violence unfold without suspense, so that audiences wonder not if or when violence will occur, but how. Death similarly becomes an underlying assumption as the films begin and end with death. Films that begin with death – often the motivation for the hero to go on the road in vengeance – include *The Searchers*, *The Outlaw Josey Wales*, and *Mad Max*; films that end with death (not the death of the "bad guys" of *Stagecoach*, but the death of the hero) – include *Easy Rider*, *Honkytonk Man*, and *A Perfect World*. Ethan's actions typify those of the road hero, whose journey is often motivated by death, and who never reaches any goal or satisfaction, and instead remains on a road that never ends. If something like "love" is denied Ethan at the start of *The Searchers*, urging him on, these dreams forever elude him, and the last shot frames the door closing on what might have been a home. *Easy Rider* ends with both Wyatt and the flag lying bloodied and burning, the American Dream a corpse along with the hero, left on the side of the road as the credits roll over them.

It's not so much death *per se*, but life that characters both escape and seek in the road movie. Death seems self-evident, not something necessarily either avoided or pursued in this genre. Road narratives are constituted by a search for life, the characters running from death which always threatens at either end of the road. A romantic notion, death here may work to give meaning to life, much as form gives shape to art, and darkness gives definition to light.

The characters' desires to get on the road indicates a longing for a self-transformation, as well as a revitalized belief in the nation, or at least in the American Dream. Although the search often aborts or remains unfulfilled at the end of the movie, the characters search for a secular moral code and a renewed belief in self, and by extension, in the nation. The frontier is the Western leveler that allows equal opportunity to misfits like Ringo. The old values are superseded by the vitality of the West. The road, the new symbol for opportunity and freedom, offers the same possibilities, but in the postmodern world of the road film, no order *per se* exists to be replaced; instead, the only straw man available is nostalgia for past beliefs, represented by the Western itself.

Honkytonk Man links itself to the Western partly through the presence of Eastwood himself, who plays an aspiring country singer, Red, wearing a cowboy hat. Red's motivation to go on the road is an invitation to audition at the Grand Ol' Opry. Because he is dying of tuberculosis, Red sees the audition as his last chance for fame. Although he is unable to make it through a song without convulsing in coughing, he receives a recording contract in time to sing painfully, yet manfully, giving up his life to effect a vinyl immortality. Red's road trip to Nashville parallels his desire for, and posthumous achievement of, a new identity. A community forms around Red, reminiscent of Ringo and his group in *Stagecoach*, that includes Red's nephew, Whit (Kyle, Eastwood's son), Grandpa

Plate 2.1 Honkytonk Man. Red (Clint Eastwood) links the pioneer and
Depression generations.

(John McIntire), and Emmy (Verna Bloom). Grandpa's recollection of his youthful
road trip from Tennessee on a mule makes the Western connection at the heart
of this road movie explicit. Grandpa describes "the run" of 1893, when "they
opened the Cherokee strip to white settlers. . . . It was the greatest horse race for
the greatest prize." He explains the meaning of the trip and "the prize": "It wasn't
just the dirt, just land. It was the promised land. . . . it wasn't just the land – it
was the *dream*. We wasn't just land chasers, we was dream chasers." Simply by
participating in the run, by going on the road, Grandpa transforms himself into
a "dream chaser," at once an individual pursuing a dream, and a part of a vital
community of settlers. Even though Grandpa loses the literal goal of the journey,
the "dirt" means much less than the alchemic properties of the road. Whit's dream
to do better than his sharecropper parents aligns him with Grandpa and Red. Red,
raises his surrogate son in a masculinist tradition, by teaching him to become a
miniature version of himself. He encourages him to write songs, such as the title
track, "Honkytonk Man," drink whisky, have sex with prostitutes, and to follow
his dreams. In the film's final scene, Emmy, the stand-in mother, complaining
of morning sickness, and Red's spiritual son, Whit, wearing Red's cowboy hat
and guitar, walk together away from his funeral; his song symbolically plays over
a car radio. These two "dream chasers" continue on their now joint quest to keep
traveling and "be somebody" in the spirit of Red and Grandpa. *Honkytonk Man* is
set during the Depression, thus bridging the era of the Western and of the

contemporary road movie. It neatly exhibits how the Western articulation of the American Dream continues to beckon in this new genre, and how the over-determined referent of the frontier has been translated into the road.

Bronco Billy, another example of a Western-cum-road-film, also uses Eastwood both to locate the Western in a contemporary setting and incorporate a road structure. Bronco Billy (Eastwood), the self-proclaimed "head ramrod" of a traveling Western show, leads a hodgepodge group of misfits across the country. Dressed as a parody of his Western persona, wearing cowboy hat, rodeo shirt, and pearl-handled six-shooters, he is toasted by his cohort as "the fastest gun in the West." Hackneyed Western references abound, from the spectacle of the bucking broncs, smoking guns, hooting Indians, and squealing, starry-eyed women of the road show to verbal clichés such as "Just tell 'em I died with my boots on" and "Looks like it's the end of the trail." More interesting than these superficial gestures toward the Western is the mutation of crucial elements from one to the other genre. The film presents Billy initially through the eyes of Miss Lily (Sondra Locke). From her point of view, this Western champion appears as an anachronistic cliché, a buffoonish sham of the cowboy hero. When a redneck sheriff forces him to grovel and admit, with downcast eyes, that his is not the fastest draw it seems to confirm her initial impressions of this shadow of the masculine ideal. The viewer also sees the show from a backstage point-of-view, watching the backs of the performers as they do their routines, which emphasizes the illusory, performative nature of the Western and thereby deflates it.

However, when Lily calls Bronco Billy "nothing but an illiterate cowboy," he responds, "No one talks like that about a cowboy." The viewer learns that Billy promulgates the standards of the macho Western hero by playing surrogate father to his followers and performing charity acts, so that even the doubting Lily finally agrees with the words, "Anything you say, Bronco Billy." Moreover, he teaches his values not only to his "family," but to an endlessly growing group of "little pardners" through the medium of the show. As did Ringo in *Stagecoach*, Bronco Billy creates a community out of the misfits of society. Yet, located within a contemporary and deflated setting, Eastwood's character can achieve only a mock-heroic stance.

In fact, the film explicitly points to the need for a cowboy hero in modern times, even if the need is filled only through illusion. For instance, when he discovers that his war-deserter colleague has been jailed, his concern extends to the children who come to the Western show, and who need their positive masculine images: "What about those little pardners that look up to you?" The film nondiegetically supports and mimics Billy's sentiment, that we need to fabricate a hero, by ending the film with the following words of the theme song, addressed ostensibly to the children watching Billy's Western show, but also to the watching film audience: "I've got a message for you li'l pardners out there, finish your

Plate 2.2 Bronco Billy.
Eastwood reconstructs the American cowboy as heroic ideal.

oatmeal, listen to your parents, don't tell a lie, say your prayers before you go to bed. . . . " The theme song, sung by a paternal voice, infantalizes the viewer and offers reassuringly direct, old-fashioned advice. The film further connects the father figure to the American ideal of the Western hero. As the "Bronco Billy" theme song speaks to all the "li'l pardners" in the audience, the final crane-out reveals the show's new tent, rising like a nylon phoenix from the ashes, sewn from hundreds of American flags. This reconstruction symbolizes the re-creation of the American Dream out of the ideological materials of the Western.

In *A Perfect World*, another Eastwood-directed film that addresses the role of the hero in the modern period, the protagonist, Butch (Costner), again plays surrogate father to a boy, Phillip (T. J. Lowther), whose father is absent. The film equates the fatherless boy with an orphan. Even though his mother is present, she is inadequate on her own, unable to protect herself or her child, as demonstrated through her molestation and Phil's kidnapping in the first scene. As opposed to *Honkytonk Man* and *Bronco Billy*, films which emphasize the successful discovery of the heroic father figure in the protagonist, *A Perfect World* explores the repercussions of missing and inadequate biological fathers. Butch tries to teach Phil, who he calls "son," all the lessons a father might share with a son in a lifetime. For instance, upon discovering that Phil's Jehovah's Witness mother does not let him celebrate Halloween, Butch lets him wear a stolen Casper trick-or-treat outfit for much of their journey together, asking in dismay, "No Christmas? Birthdays? You ain't never been to the carnival? Cotton candy? Roller coasters?" Having received a negative answer to all these questions, Butch exclaims, "You know, Phillip, you have a god-damned red-white-and-blue right to eat cotton candy and ride roller coasters." The scene cuts from the two characters in the interior of the car to a long shot of Phil, joyfully sitting with his legs hooked through the luggage rack and his arms above his head, yelling "Faster, Butch, faster!" Butch also tries to teach others the importance of fatherhood. Wielding his gun, he tries to teach child-rearing techniques to a terrified grandfather, ordering him to "hold that boy . . . tell him you love him. . . . say it like you mean it." Butch ties them up while, in the meantime, the horrified Phil shoots Butch in the stomach.

That Phil must shoot Butch, who in this scene proves that he, too, is an inadequate father, demonstrates how wide-reaching is the problem of deficient fathering for this film. The viewer learns that the violence is attributable to a cycle of fatherless children, including Butch, on the road to Alaska to find his missing father. Butch carries with him a raggedy picture postcard from his father that reads, "Someday you can come and visit and we can maybe get to know each other." This tattered reminder is the only thing his father has ever given him, a signifier of his broken promise – "we can maybe get to know each other" – and of his absence. The film suggests that being without a father is at the bottom of all Butch's problems, and that the consequences of being fatherless, for Butch, are either to be on the road, or to be dead.

During his terrorization of the family, Butch says, in a moment of self-assessment, "No, I ain't a good man; I ain't the worst, neither." Similarly, after Butch's death the Texas ranger (Eastwood) is reassured, "You know, you did everything you could." He replies, "I don't know nothin', not one damn thing." Butch's corpse fills the first and last shots in this film, emphasizing the failure of the father. In the final shot, the camera cranes out to reveal that the point of view belongs to Phil, who now holds the symbolic postcard, signifier of the absent father, the only thing that Butch can give him. The road trip in *A Perfect World* is a quest for the missing hero that Phil and Butch take together – for Phil to gain a father, and for Butch and the Texas Ranger to become fathers. All of these journeys result in failure, except, perhaps, for the viewer, who learns the value of fatherhood and of heroes in this clearly imperfect world.

Butch describes Alaska, the home of his father, to Phil as "The last of the wild frontiers" and "wild and woolly," indicating that the missing father remains in the romantic American Dream of the frontier. Red performs here in the other father figure role, attempting to guide Butch to a better life. Eastwood's character, too, is linked with the Western, with his tough-guy, Texas ranger persona, his

Western garb, and his Western motif office. He watches helplessly as Butch runs and, finally, dies. The father, the masculine hero who seems self-evident in the romantic Western, is missing from this world, and all that remains is the search for this hero.

The Ford/Wayne Westerns already express the need for heroes. For instance, in *Fort Apache* (1948), the viewer suffers along with the regiment through the unbearable treatment of York (Wayne) by Thursday (Henry Fonda), the belligerent superior officer, only to watch Thursday killed, along with most of the soldiers, through his own foolish command. The film's coda adds insult to injury when Thursday, not York, goes down in history as a legendary warrior. York tells newspaper reporters that Thursday was a great hero, and that his example was such as to "make them [the regiment] better men." Ford echoes these sentiments in an interview with Peter Bogdanovich. Bogdanovich asks, "The end of *Fort Apache* anticipates the newspaper editor's line in [*The Man Who Shot*] *Liberty Valance*, 'When the legend becomes a fact, print the legend.' Do you agree with that?" Ford answers, "Yes. . . . We've had a lot of people who were supposed to be great heroes, and you know damn well they weren't. But it's good for the country to have heroes to look up to" (86). The Western creates for us the authentic, if unacknowledged, hero, Wayne, whose heroic qualities permeate his star text so fully that he became equated with his Western hero performances. In contrast, the road film offers us only the illusion of and the unfulfilled desire for heroes.

While Wayne's heroic characters all ride horses, Eastwood's would-be heroes all drive cars, as in *Honkytonk Man*, *Bronco Billy*, and *A Perfect World*. Tompkins suggests that, in the Western, horses "fulfill a longing for a different *kind* of existence. Anti-modern, anti-urban, and anti-technological, they stand for an existence without cars and telephones and electricity." (93). The hero and the horse are one with nature in the Western. In the road film, the hero still needs a means of transportation s/he can control, because the ability to control one's own destiny is at the base of the road film. Americans' love affair with the car is fueled by ideology that upholds our individualism, and the car has become a symbol for our rights to freedom, and our belief in technological progress.[16] In *A Perfect World*, at one point Butch asks Phil, "You ever been in a time machine before? . . . Ahead is the future. Behind us is the past. If life's going too slowly, press the gas. If you want it to slow down, press the brake." Butch's description convinces Phil of the car's fantastic ability to take him anywhere, unlimited by space, time, or imagination. Later, Butch again teaches Phil lessons on the importance of free choice, saying, "There's lots and lots of stuff you can do. . . . Make up a list of everything you ever wanted to do . . . like cotton candy." A moment passes before Phil asks, "Butch, how do you spell rocket ship?" The bird's-eye view of the car in the middle of a corn field, with Butch's paternal laughter echoing through the night, seems surreal, and the car might be a rocket ship blasting off.

In the Western, the horse and frontier symbolize the struggle between man and nature, a nostalgic signifier of the nineteenth century. In the road film, the car and road, contrivances of man, connote technological progress as a sign of the twentieth century. However, they also indicate restrictions because, while the horse can go anywhere, the car needs a road. Therefore, while the horse connotes freedom, the car indicates limitations and the end of the wild West, which has been paved.

In the concluding scene of *A Perfect World*, Phil encourages Butch to run to escape the police, but Butch replies, "No, I need me a time machine with a live radio to take me where I'm going. Walking's for squares." Without his car – his roller coaster, his rocket ship, his time machine, his means to control his own destiny – his future is gone. Not surprisingly, in moments, the police kill Butch. The physical journey – the car moving down the highway – is of a piece with the spiritual journey, so that when Butch's freedom – his American privilege – is taken from him, symbolized by his loss of a car, he simply ceases to live. His last words are, "Bye, Phillip, it's been one hell of a ride," and the road, the journey, and his life end simultaneously.

The road movie's linear structure and the metaphorical road's connotations of individualism, aggression, independence, and control, combine the Western's ideal conceptions of the American and the masculine. Masculine superiority links itself with racial hierarchies, manifest destiny, and closure through heterosexual romance and marriage. This is not to suggest that either the Western or the road movie are simply masculinist, nor is it a reduction of these genres to a monolithic formula. Instead, this analysis points to an underlying residual, American, masculinist ideal which informs both genres despite their seeming differences both in content and historical context. This masculinism causes tension in the postmodern road film. The Western, born from an earlier period and out of a nostalgia for a mythic American past, more clearly privileges male protagonists and masculine settings. Even late, revisionist Westerns, such as *The Searchers* or *Unforgiven*, are informed by the concept of the male cowboy hero and the masculine frontier, if only as structuring absences. In contrast, the road film is less prescribed and more open, fueled by quests for missing values, often simply indicated by a blank marker. The road movie transforms the frontier into a metaphorical road, the horse into a car, and the cowboy into an illusory and elusive metaphor. All of these generic elements are man-made products, perhaps suggesting the genre's recognition that the masculine, American ideal, enunciated by the Western, is a social construction.

Starting with *Easy Rider*, the road film concerns not just journeys and searches, but notably alternative paths and choices. The more fluid genre of the road film has ample room for protagonists of any nationality, gender, sexual orientation, or race. For instance, popular road films have included *Mad Max* (1979), *The*

Adventures of Priscilla, Queen of the Desert (1994), and *Boys on the Side* (1995). This small sampling includes films produced in Australia and the US, centering on not only heterosexual, white male protagonists, but also homosexual, transsexual, black, and female protagonists. These films serve to indicate how road films may veer from a male-centered, homophobic, racist, pro-US Western. Therefore, although the road genre is informed by residual conceptions of the American and the masculine, the uneasy and self-reflexive genre of the road film simultaneously calls their hegemonic equation into question.

Femininity on the Road

Another way to understand the gendered construction of road films is to examine how women figure in them. In the traditional Western, women often figure as helpless, parasitic embellishments to a masculine genre. In addition, in Westerns with road narratives such as *Stagecoach*, the hero flees decay, corruption, and cloying domesticity to forge a new, revitalized world. In the Eastwood road vehicles, the recurring figure of the talkative, modern, independent, urban woman is positioned as a foil to the laconic, macho, male actor. For instance, with Lily and Billy, in *Bronco Billy*, and with the novice detective (Laura Dern) and Red, the experienced ranger, in *A Perfect World*, the woman relies on superficial facts whereas the man is imbued with spiritual knowledge. This dichotomy persists throughout the Eastwood films. These films teach the viewer that an illusion, performed by the Eastwood hero and by the movie, stands in for the transcendental truth. In road films, male heroes are still the norm, and masculine privileging prevails. Women continue to be nonexistent or peripheral in buddy-road movies, from the Bing Crosby/Bob Hope *Road to* series to *Midnight Run* (1988). Even in films featuring female stars, such as *Bonnie and Clyde* and *Badlands* (1973), the actresses play integral halves of the heterosexual, anti-heroic couple, yet they remain bound up in the limitations of a male-oriented and -dominated fantasy. Fleeing the law-abiding sphere of family, child-raising, and community to escape onto a road that ends violently, these women are crucial to the films, yet still act as appendages to masculinist fantasies.

The inherent masculinity of the road movie is demonstrated by recent "feminine" road films. While male protagonists use the road to flee femininity, women cannot similarly flee the masculine because of the gendered assumptions of the genre. In the last few years, beginning with Ridley Scott's *Thelma and Louise*, and including such films as *Leaving Normal* (1992) and *Boys on the Side*, a few road films have featured female main characters and feminist issues, targeting a primarily female audience. *Thelma and Louise* caused a great deal of public debate in the popular and academic press over issues including feminism, patriarchy, male-bashing, and female bonding. In *Thelma and Louise*, women take on roles coded as masculine in a masculinist genre, and therein lies part of the controversy that still surrounds this film. Not only do these films upset audience expectations concerning content and protagonist, they also disrupt formal genre norms.

At the peak of the 1991 high public discourse on the film, some argued that *Thelma and Louise* was a simple case of role reversal. In this argument, a savvy male director used the buddy movie genre to please the males in the audience by having attractive actresses accentuate their sexiness with their gun-wielding, fast-driving shenanigans, and simultaneously pacify female viewers as the characters shoot male chauvinist characters. However, the *Thelma and Louise* trend cannot be so easily explained. The trend serves to open up the issue of a new type of women's film, a subgenre which targets a female audience. The most substantive generic alternation is not that actresses are substituted for male stars, but that the protagonists take to the road not to escape socially coded notions of the feminine, but rather to flee patriarchy and its effects on their lives. The trend, therefore, works to bring concerns associated with women and feminism into the public discourse. For instance, *Thelma and Louise* helped encourage people to discuss wife-abuse, rape, self-defense by women, violence against women in films and in our society, suicide, and the patriarchal character of our society. *Boys on the Side* raises the issues of lesbianism, AIDS, single motherhood, mixed-race relationships, and mother–daughter relationships, and

Plate 2.3 Thelma and Louise take femininity on the road.

Leaving Normal focuses on domestic abuse, child abandonment, and female heads of households. That conversations on such topics could be sparked by Hollywood films in the 1990s is noteworthy in itself.

Questions raised by the conjunction of a male-centric genre and female-focused topics include the following: Do women "need" the kind of heterosexual pairing symptomatic of most established Hollywood films, including road movies? If the female characters in these films are escaping from society, why do they cling to society's structures, such as the family and the romantic couple? If they don't need these structures "on the road," do they ever need them? Where do same-sex bonding rituals adopted from men's stories break down with women? For instance, in *Leaving Normal*, the two women begin playing a "one up" game to prove who is more badly behaved, and Darly (Christine Lahti) stops the game playing cold when she suddenly admits to abandoning her child eighteen years before. How do women's friendships work out under the pressure, not only of the road, away from society, but also of their former immersion in patriarchal society, and that society's omnipresence? The women's pasts set events into motion and determine the actual physical course of their journey, as well as its emotional momentum. For instance, the aversion Louise (Susan Sarandon) has to Texas, where she purportedly was raped, determines the women's route. Because Marianne (Meg Tilly) dislikes decision-making, the women in *Leaving Normal* choose their route through tossing coins, picking cigarettes, and waiting for birds to excrete on their map. If men go on the road to escape feminine civilization, can women ever in their turn effectively escape patriarchal society?

Inserting female protagonists into this male-oriented genre neither simply subverts nor subsumes its masculinist tendencies. In traditional Westerns, and in road films that clearly derive from this genre's Western origin, such as the Eastwood films, men often flee the feminine figure which stands for that which is limiting, cloying, and degrading. In the female-protagonist road films, the women more clearly flee real men and the abuses of patriarchy. Men physically beat Thelma (Geena Davis), Holly (Drew Barrymore), and Marianne, prompting them to go on the road. From the truckers making lewd comments to the women in *Thelma and Louise* and *Leaving Normal* to the unsympathetic prosecutor in *Boys on the Side* who cross-examines the women on the stand on every aspect of love between women, these female protagonists go on the road to avoid what is pictured as a male-dominated, anti-woman society. They gain temporary escape into single-sex freedom that can end only in death, compromise, or fantasy.

As with the Westerns and the road films discussed here, the women end up creating new communities on the road. All three of the films offer the escapist image of a euphoric car ride, although it is figured as a still-domestic flight in which these women take a last chance at building alternative families. However, the traditional, nuclear family that they have been raised to expect for themselves and which society still anticipates for them remains in stark contrast throughout the films. For instance, the wedding bands and married names of the women who have fled their married identities are repeatedly stressed in the films through lingering close-ups. In addition, Robin (Mary-Louise Parker), in *Boys on the Side*, explains that what she really wants is an employed husband, two kids, a boy and a girl, in that order, and a house with white banisters and a convertible den – a banal description of herself integrated into a family structure centering *on* a woman's traditional wife and mother roles. Robin's flashbacks to black-and-white memories of her childhood, which flesh out this description, serve only to demonstrate to the viewer how impossible, and often unwanted, are these retrograde dreams for the female film characters who – arrested for murder, single and pregnant, HIV-positive, black, and gay – cannot fit themselves into this all-American, exclusive prescription for feminine social roles.

For instance, Robin, Jane (Whoopi Goldberg), and Robin's mother (Anita Gillette) watch *The Way We Were* (1973) and *An Officer and a Gentleman* (1982). The viewer is allowed to watch along with them the Hollywood romantic leads in the concluding moments of these love stories, which enforces the fantasy status of their traditional male–female role-playing in contrast to the very different paths being taken by the characters in *Boys on the Side*. Jane compares Robin's gender-identity fantasies to Donna Reed, and Robin's mother even offers Katharine Hepburn, as quoted in the woman's magazine *Redbook*, to Robin as a female model: "Never complain, never explain." *Leaving Normal* similarly contrasts Marianne and Darly, who hitch-hike, steal, and semi-prostitute themselves, with Marianne's sister and her more traditional lifestyle. Marianne also shares her desire, similar to Robin's, for "a home . . . big noisy holidays, coats on the bed, happy faces – a family." The film begins with a prologue of Marianne's childhood; she imagines her family van leaving the highway and taking off for the stars. Later, as Marianne and Darly begin their spontaneous trip together, the camera draws back to show that a rainbow touches down where their road meets the horizon.

Only in their fantasies, only over the rainbow, somewhere beyond the material world, are these women able to achieve their dreams of negotiation with, or escape from, media depictions of women, outdated prescriptions for social roles, changing expectations for gender identities, and their personal goals, hopes, and fears for themselves, born out of a male-dominated society. The escape to the road indicates avoidance of the material conditions which these characters, and presumably audience members, must face every day. These feminine films add up to a criticism of our society and of a genre that maintains dominant, patriarchal ideology, in that the only solution for these women seems to be to escape patriarchy by leaving behind their relationships with men for fantastical journeys that would move "outside" society on the road. However, because they attempt to escape patriarchy within a masculinist genre, these female protagonists are unable to avoid cultural constructions of femininity. For instance, on the road of their choosing, stars of their show, Thelma and Louise are nonetheless interpellated within the film by sexist labels, including beaver, peach, Kewpie doll, baby, girl, and bitch; the equivalent of such continual undermining of the male hero and his quest would be unthinkable in an Eastwood film. At one point, while already on the road, driving through the desert, Thelma and Louise watch the sun rise, and are framed against a classic Western landscape (Putnam: 300). However, the soundtrack disables this attempted cooption of a masculinist generic moment by the women, as Marianne Faithfull sings of a woman's unaccomplished, and unachievable dreams: "At the age of 37 she realized she'd never ride through Paris in a sports car with the warm wind in her hair."[17] Faithfull's words contradict the promise the "open" road is supposed to hold. In the end, Thelma and Louise refuse the Western trope of the final shoot-out, choosing instead a bittersweet freedom from patriarchy through their suicidal acceleration into the Grand Canyon. In sum, although the feminine road films critique dominant ideology, because of their attempted escape specifically into a masculinist genre, these films tend metaphorically to raise their hands in "feminine" despair.

The masculinist genre of the road film works to limit the solutions for the female protagonists. Attempting to flee men and patriarchy, the femal protagonists go on the supposedly open road only to discover that escape from the effects of patriarchy is impossible. These "feminine" road films demonstrate that the road does not provide, or even allow for, a female space for escape or revitalization because of the cultural codes that make up the masculinist road film, which reinscribe women into regressive social prescriptions of femininity. The women bring masculinist concepts of gender identities for women, and their roles in society, with them on the road, even as they recognize the artificiality of these prescriptions. While Eastwood's characters successfully flee the limitations of "feminine" civilization by creating a revitalized, masculine world on the road, these female characters attempt to flee not just men, but patriarchy, which is omnipresent and which in part defines the road and the genre, and so are ultimately unsuccessful.

Conclusions

In the transference from the Western to the road film, the frontier becomes the road, the horse becomes the car, and the hero becomes a desire, perhaps Quixotic, for heroism. The road itself at once incorporates the two most striking aspects of the Western, its American and masculine qualities. In standing in for the frontier, it captures the essence of the American Dream by incorporating all that which the frontier has symbolized for the history of the United States' development, and the masculine brand of heroism that the Western has equated with the frontier. In addition, the linear structure that the road movie offers – such as directness, aggression, independence, control, all linked to American ideals and privileges of choice – all remain masculinely codified traits. Given the proliferation of new media, such as the World Wide Web, and new media formatting, such as the multiplication of cable channels and the rapid editing of media products, such as MTV or Nickelodeon commercials, the linear structure of the road film may prove to be a genre as nostalgic as the Western. The Western expresses a romantic desire for an ideal America, a fantasy version of the frontier which never existed. The road film exhibits a similar nostalgia for a time when the world seemed, if not marked by black-and-white hats, at least informed by a straightforward motion, like time, going in just one direction. In other words, the road film, with its linear structure, may seem appealing in part owing to the increasing non-linearity of today's world, with all its seemingly new possibilities and diversity, such as expanding forms of communication and travel. The simplicity of getting in a Ford and pushing a pedal to accelerate in one direction down one road may seem reassuringly inviting.

Acknowledgments

Thanks to Steve Cohan and Ina Rae Hark for advice in the writing of this essay. Thanks also to Pam Robertson, Priscilla Barlow, Chris Anderson, Ruth Feingold, and my original PSU Comm 451 Road Movie class of Fall 1995 for all the discussions on gender, genre, and the road.

Notes

1 My analysis of Eastwood's character indicates that he, like Wayne before him, provides a consistently patriotic and masculine figure throughout his films and related publicity. A different perspective comes from Bingham, who asserts that Eastwood's image gets less violent and less masculine with each film, and that in fact "his career . . . has illustrated a twelve-step withdrawal program from masculinism" (243). Also note Knee's article on Eastwood in his directorial debut, a "passing moment of progressive questioning of traditional constructions of male identity prior to the conservative reaction which launched him to greater macho stardom" (101).

2 See Dyer's work on star texts for a delineation of this methodology.

3 Louis L'Amour offers a literary counterpart to Eastwood's straddling of the Western and the road genre. His last novel (*The Last of the Breed* (1986)), structured arguably as a road narrative, is his only non-Western book which, as Tompkins notes, contains most of the elements of the Western, only removed in space and time (206).

4 See Wexman for a discussion of Wayne's star text and the Western, nationalism, and race.

5 See, for instance, Mulvey; Neale ("Masculinity"); and Wexman.

6 Wayne notoriously directed and starred in 1968's *The Green Berets*, a glorification of

US Special forces and one of the only films made in support of the Vietnam War in which, ironically, the sun sets in the East in the closing scene.

7 See, for instance, Byron, Henderson, and the *Screen Education* special issue.
8 Smith notes how Hollywood's declining interest in the Western left room for Italy's "Spaghetti Westerns" (4–5).
9 See Schatz for an articulation of "evolution" and genre.
10 Discussed in this volume by Barbara Klinger.
11 For one source on the war and American public response to it, among other things, see Shapely.
12 As Studs Terkel has termed it.
13 See Henderson on contemporary race issues and *The Searchers* (19–21).
14 For instance, one list included: "'I have a dream'; 'Ask not what your country can do for you'; 'Let me make this perfectly clear'; Levi's; Harley-Davidson; flannel; Superman; Las Vegas/Atlantic City; corn; porn; Elvis/Graceland; Springsteen; Regis & Kathie Lee; MTV; M. Monroe/Madonna; N. Rockwell; Hellenic Diners; Nittany Lion; Bill Cosby; James Dean; Roseanne; Coke; farms; B-B-que; Buick Roadmaster; K-Mart; McDonald's; Hollywood; Statue of Liberty; Oprah; Yankees/N.Y.; Holiday Inn; Clark Gable; Lucy; Archie and Edith Bunker; Jason, Michael Myers & Freddy Kruger; Rush Limbaugh" (18 Sept. 1995).
15 American Film Institute Life Achievement Award, Feb. 1996.
16 On America's love affair with the car see Flink: 140–90.
17 "The Ballad of Lucy Jordan," written by Shel Silverstein.

Works Cited

Anderson, Benedict. *Imagined Communities: Reflections on the Origins and Spread of Nationalism*. London: Verso, 1983.

"Big John." *Newsweek* (March 1, 1965): 86.

Bingham, Dennis. *Acting Male: Masculinities in the Films of James Stewart, Jack Nicholson, and Clint Eastwood*. New Brunswick: Rutgers University Press, 1994.

Bogdanovich, Peter. *John Ford*. Berkeley: University of California Press, 1978.

Buscombe, Edward. *The BFI Companion to the Western*. New York: Atheneum, 1988.

Byron, Stuart. "*The Searchers*: Cult Movie of the New Hollywood." *New York Magazine* (March 5, 1979): 45–8.

Canby, Vincent. "*Easy Rider*." *The New York Times* (July 15, 1969).

Cawelti, John G. *The Six-Gun Mystique*. Bowling Green: Bowling Green University Popular Press, 1971.

Cooper, James Fenimore. *The Pioneers*. 1823.

Cumbow, Robert C. *Once Upon a Time: The Films of Sergio Leone*. Metuchen: Scarecrow, 1987.

Dyer, Richard. *Heavenly Bodies: Film Stars and Society*. New York: St Martin's Press, 1986.
—— *Stars*. London: BFI, 1979.

"*Easy Rider*." *Variety* (May 14, 1969).

Flink, James J. *The Car Culture*. Minnesota: MIT, 1975.

Frayling, Christopher. *Spaghetti Westerns*. London: Routledge, 1981.

Handel, Leo. *Hollywood Looks at Its Audience: A Report on Film Audience Research*. Champaign: University of Illinois Press, 1950.

Henderson, Brian. "*The Searchers*: An American Dilemma." *Film Quarterly* (Winter 1980–1): 9–23.

"John Wayne as the Last Hero." *Time* (August 8, 1969): 53–6.

"John Wayne Rides Again." *Life* (May 7, 1965): 69–75.

"John Wayne's Ordeal." *Newsweek* (July 25, 1960): 107.

Kerouac, Jack. *On the Road*. New York: Penguin, 1957.

Knee, Adam. "The Dialectic of Female Power and Male Hysteria in *Play Misty For Me*." *Screening the Male: Exploring Masculinities in Hollywood Cinema*, ed. Steven Cohan and Ina Rae Hark. New York: Routledge, 1993. 87–102.

L'Amour, Louis. *Hondo*. New York: Bantam, 1953.

Lileks, James. "Battle Lines Along the Home Front." *Omaha World Herald* (August 2, 1996): 20.

Morgan, Thomas B. "God and Man in Hollywood." *Esquire* (May, 1963): 74–5, 123.

Mulvey, Laura. *Visual and Other Pleasures*. Bloomington: Indiana University Press, 1989.

Neale, Steve. "Masculinity as Spectacle: Reflections on Men and Mainstream Cinema." *Screen* 24. 6 (1983). Rpt in *Screening the Male: Exploring Masculinities in Hollywood Cinema*, ed. Steven Cohan and Ina Rae Hark. New York: Routledge, 1993. 9–20.

—— "Questions of Genre." *Screen* 31.1 (1990): 45–66.

Parkman Jr, Francis. *The Oregon Trail* (1849). New York: Library of America, 1991.

Pirsig, Robert. *Zen and the Art of Motorcycle Maintenance*. New York: William Morrow, 1974.

Putnam, Ann. "The Bearer of the Gaze in Ridley Scott's *Thelma and Louise*." *Western American Literature* 27.4 (1993): 291–302.

Ray, Robert. *A Certain Tendency in Hollywood Cinema*. Princeton: Princeton University Press, 1985.

Schatz, Thomas. *Hollywood Genres*. New York: Random, 1981.

Screen Education 17, Special Issue on *The Searchers*. Autumn 1975.

"*The Searchers*." *Variety* (March 14, 1956).

Shapely, Deborah. *Promise and Power: The Life and Times of Robert McNamara*. Boston: Little, Brown & Co., 1993.

Smith, Paul. *Clint Eastwood: A Cultural Production*. Minneapolis: University of Minnesota Press, 1993.

Thompson, Douglas. *Clint Eastwood: Riding High*. Chicago: Contemporary Books, 1992.

Tompkins, Jane. *West of Everything: The Inner Life of Westerns*. New York: Oxford University Press, 1992.

Wexman, Virginia Wright. *Creating the Couple: Love, Marriage, and Hollywood Performance*. Princeton: Princeton University Press, 1993.

3

MAD LOVE, MOBILE HOMES, AND DYSFUNCTIONAL DICKS
On the road with Bonnie and Clyde

Ian Leong, Mike Sell, and Kelly Thomas

Natural Born Killers (1994) boasts a body count – twelve and climbing – linking it to more copycat killings than any other film. Two years after its debut, the film was still making headlines via the lawsuit filed by attorney-turned-Hollywood-player John Grisham against Oliver Stone for product liability in connection with the murder of a cotton-gin worker from Hernando, Mississippi.[1] Grisham's suit is just one component of a larger conservative mobilization against what Presidential candidate Robert Dole has called the "mainstreaming of deviancy" by the Hollywood culture industry. Dole's May, 1995, address to Los Angeles Republicans and Hollywood bigwigs seemed to recognize the interrelated tensions of violence, mass culture, and the crisis of "family values" – and specifically took aim at two postmodern variants on the familiar theme of young, tragic love in "The Story of Bonnie and Clyde."[2] On the first leg of a tour whose goal was the congealing of an increasingly fractured Republican constituency, Dole exhorted his audience to retool the culture industry and return to the "Combining-Good-Citizenship-with-Good-Picture-Making" days when the Disney studios daubed their merry little toy-citizens on the noses of B-52's and Warner Bros. beefed up public confidence in the police. "Ours is not a crusade for censorship," Dole comforted us, "it is a call for good citizenship."

Good citizenship is certainly lacking in the two films Dole specifically targeted, *True Romance* (1993) and *Natural Born Killers*. But there is an irony to Dole's attack. Dole endorsed the moral rectitude of *The Lion King* (1994), *Forrest Gump* (1994), and fellow Republican Arnold Schwarzenegger's ultra-violent revision of high-tech patriarchy, *True Lies* (1994), even as he demanded an interdiction of "mindless violence and loveless sex." Dole's choice of films suggests that violence in defense of the nation and the nuclear family is not only appropriate but good family fun. Indeed, it seems that Dole singled out *True Romance* and *Natural Born Killers* for criticism because they posit heterosexual desire as anti-family, crime and violence as pleasurable, and the road as a fracturing (rather than a consolidation) of nation and community. Nonetheless, a more profound disruption may lie at the heart of the conservative agenda. As we will demonstrate, the Bonnie-and-Clyde genre purposely fragments certain narrative conventions of classic Hollywood cinema but at the same time shares certain assumptions with popular notions of conservatism, namely that love is good and affluence is right. As the candidate correctly surmised, these "nightmares of depravity" erode the cornerstones of American "family values," particularly apple-pie fantasies concerning the domestic sphere and the social regulation of consumption, reproduction, and patriotism through the home.

Profoundly aware of the cultural dilemmas posed by free-market capitalism, Dole warned the entertainment industry that "those who cultivate moral confusion for profit should understand this: we will name their names and shame them as they deserve to be shamed." His nostalgia for the studio system and vilification of corporate greed exhibited deep anxieties about the effects of the late-1960s deregulation of Hollywood production. Dole countered these fears by pitting ethics against profit: "There is a difference between the description of evil through art, and the marketing of evil through commerce." Yet, soon after delivering this speech, Dole played a key role in obtaining legislation deregulating telecommunications, paving the way for even more corporate mergers and monopolies among the entertainment giants. But Dole's seemingly contradictory actions shouldn't surprise us; the conservative cultural agenda which attempts to revivify an older sense of community is tortuously entwined with the rupturing dynamics of an expanding economy. In the final analysis, mobility and its threat to the stability of home and community is the same tension that both plagues the conservative agenda and propels Bonnies and Clydes. After all, the means of alleviating that volatility is the same: cultivate the spectacle, retain the attention of the masses, and, by all means, keep the show on the road.

The conservative mobilization against "deviancy" is primarily concerned with the ways in which property, propriety, and bodies are produced, distributed, and consumed in American culture. The road as both cultural signifier and economic infrastructure is a crucial component of this police action – as is the continuing democratic appeal of upward mobility. The regulation of the movements of people, goods, and values exerts a profound influence upon the ways in which the road functions as, in Lévi-Strauss's term, an "imaginary solution" to the paradoxes of America's stratified democracy.[3] These insecurities surrounding mobility, however, do not originate in the context of twentieth-century life; new forms of mobility and their accompanying tensions have long been recognized as central to capitalism's employment of technology and popular desire – what Marx and Engels called the "unconscionable freedom" of free trade (15–16).[4] The road's old, old age, its inherent suggestiveness, and its evocation of horizon and liberty seem to guarantee it as an effective symbolic container for American culture's most cherished and most volatile ideals. But the road's seductive speed disguises its reality, particularly in an era in which speed plays a significant role in social control.[5] The road is the Möbius strip of American capitalism: despite the thrill of acceleration, escape is illusory, and the drive into the sunset takes you right back where you started.

The road's ambivalence is exemplified by a particular subgenre of the road movie, the Bonnie-and-Clyde film. This genre typically features two young people who fall in love, speed away from home in a stolen car, shoot guns, make love, and get caught. While this group of films has been variously named (couple on the run, outlaw couple, bad couple, criminal couple), we feel that the term "Bonnie-and-Clyde film" maintains a deep focus on the referential or real-life Bonnie Parker and Clyde Barrow and the implicit moralism of Parker's published poem, "The Story of Bonnie and Clyde." In fact, Parker and Barrow's ghosts haunt the genre and its surrounding discourses; these movies always threaten to succumb to the conservative narrative arc of the poem which ends with punishment and death. Despite this implicit threat, Parker and Barrow's flight through the Southwest became a popular myth because it articulated the anxieties, conflicts, and crises of a particular moment in the history of US capitalism, without necessarily displacing antipathy toward crime.[6] Parker and Barrow's revolt against middle-class values and the modernizing state as well as their canonization in the mass media signaled a new form of mobility that outstripped earlier notions of family, production, and desire without wholly abandoning them. Bonnie-and-Clyde films replay this ambivalence by expressing in narrative form the pressures placed on the domestic sphere in a century of chronic economic crisis, media saturation, and inconstant forms of pleasure and consumption. In fact, these films do more than just express these pressures; they aspire to incite such changes, blurring the line between superstar bandits and copycat crazies.

Films as incontiguous as *Gun Crazy* (1949), *Bonnie and Clyde* (1967), and *Natural Born Killers* serve as representational solutions to the dilemmas of popular political and cultural expression by working- and middle-class people who desire liberation but are not willing to abandon their faith in family, upward mobility, and nation. The imaginary solutions generated by the Bonnie-and-Clyde genre are: first, heterosexual desire as potentially spawning a perversely portable domestic sphere; second, cinematic crime and violence as a narrative and stylistic strategy that disrupts the flow of the traditional romance and amplifies its intensity; and, third, the road as a liminal site where the promises of twentieth-century capitalism and the fantasies of prosperity it engenders are temporarily realized.[7] As we shall see, the Bonnie-and-Clyde film is a highly self-conscious example of the road movie, always seeking a cinematic vocabulary capable of articulating a promise it can never fully keep.

We are particularly interested by the resurgence of the Bonnie-and-Clyde genre in the 1990s and why these films are simultaneously so threatening and popular at this historical, political moment. We will approach this question by examining three defining films of the genre: Joseph Lewis's *Gun Crazy* and its appeal to the Surrealists; Arthur Penn's *Bonnie and Clyde* and its efforts to articulate a revolutionary style that is both popular and historicized; and Oliver Stone's *Natural Born Killers* and its desire to break the conventions of the genre while maintaining a troubled kinship with Dole's cultural politics. Exemplifying the genre's "mad love" for money, marriage, mobility, and travel, these movies simultaneously tell a history of film as popular art, industry, and the negotiations of everyday life under twentieth-century captitalism. *Gun Crazy*, *Bonnie and Clyde*, and *Natural Born Killers* cultivate the postwar branch of a road-film family tree: Bonnies and Clydes are the bad children of mobilized homes and the proliferation of sexualized objects compelled by an affluent, mobile, and deeply stratified consumer society.

Long Shots, Fetishes, and the Birth of a Cult Audience

Joseph H. Lewis's B-movie masterpiece *Gun Crazy* (a.k.a. *Deadly Is the Female*) is perhaps most notable for its original cult fans, the Surrealists. For this revolutionary artistic collective, the film's titillating blend of middle-class normalcy and audacious criminality symbolized the sort of revolutionary thrill that they invested in their anti-bourgeois poems, performances, and paintings. Delighted at the sight of this exquisitely "detourned"[8] vision of bourgeois marriage and "upward mobility," Surrealists Raymond Borde and Eugene Chaumeton described *Gun Crazy* as "one of the rarest [post-Second-World-War] illustrations of *l'amour fou* (in every sense of the term) . . . a sort of *L'Age d'Or* of the American film noir" (quoted in Naremore: 20). The "mad love" of Bart (John Dall) and Laurie (Peggy Cummins), the star-crossed lovers of Lewis's film, struggles to transcend the constraints of its time and place, seeking an intensity that cannot prosper in the desiccated suburbs of the bourgeois landscape. Assembling a filmic vocabulary to express this intensity, *Gun Crazy* elaborates on the paradoxes of desire, love, and liberation in an era of mass media, patriotism, and free-market capitalism. However, this vocabulary was developed within the constraints of the Production Code, which prohibited open displays of sex and criminal violence. As a result, Parker and Barrow's crimes and the popular fantasies of liberation they invoked were incapable of being explicitly represented within those constraints. Hollywood's claustrophobic conventions compelled Lewis to rely upon powerful images of commodity fetishism, particularly fetishism of guns, money, and female sexuality, in order to represent love's potential for madness. These narrative techniques afford *Gun Crazy* a high degree of irony that radically reworks the symbolic structures of a certain kind of conservative, domestically oriented capitalism while at the same time relying on those structures to fulfill the Production Code's requirement that criminal activity in films be punished.

The doomed romance of Bart and Laurie is the tragedy of mad love trapped within conservative efforts to regulate consumption and reproduction, the building blocks of the domestic sphere. As Bart and Laurie's lifestyle makes clear, efforts to maintain political and economic control through responsible consumer behavior often conflict with the vicissitudes of desire, the accidents of repro-duction, and the domestic's penetration by media and market. *Gun Crazy* is of particular historical significance because it transposes the violence and passion of "The Story of Bonnie and Clyde" into the post-Second-World-War dreamscape of spectacular affluence, accelerated consumption, and good housekeeping. If the post-Second-World-War household was compelled to consume on a level previously unimaginable by the American working and middle classes, then Bart and Laurie's mad love represents that compulsion's extremity and perversion – a state of explosive consumption. After the honeymoon trip to Las Vegas leaves them short of cash, Laurie makes it clear to Bart that she will not settle for the quotidian, declaring "I want it all." Yearning for all the comforts of home and family but craving Laurie's transgressive, gun-toting sexuality, Bart capitulates, and they embark on a life of crime. Their love of the road marks the paradoxical effects of a regime of affluence and mobility founded upon discourses of domesticity, accelerated consumption, and heterosexual monogamy. Bart and Laurie's mad love and bad domesticity, then, mediate the demands of the postwar economy.[9] They're honeymooners who don't want the honeymoon to end.

Bart and Laurie's mad love is perversely determined by their uncanny adoration of one of the first great products of industrial capitalism (the gun) and one of its last (wealth and conspicuous consumption), and finds visual repre-sentation in scenes of honest and purposeful fetishization of romance, labor, and heterosexual desire. Just prior to their first robbery, Bart is seen cleaning his prized set of English dueling pistols as Laurie comes out of the shower com-plaining about the lack of hot water. In response to Laurie's frustrated demand for affluence, Bart volunteers to sell his cherished guns as he vigorously reams one of them out. Meanwhile, Laurie slips into stockings and garters and lights a cigarette. But selling the guns isn't enough for Laurie, who threatens to leave him unless he consents to a life of banditry, the only possible means to ensure them the leisure and excitement they both crave. The scene establishes a crucial dynamic. While Bart and Laurie's mad love for one another deviates only slightly from traditional romance narratives, the diffusion of that mad love into the objects and events that surround them is something altogether different. The scene is as profoundly sexual as it is "perverse": Bart and Laurie make love to space and objects, not each to other. In this manner, Lewis's film portrays the sacred space of the domestic sphere as a carnival of fetishes.

Fetishism and perversity, however, exact the high cost of unsettling the fantasies of home and stable subjectivities associated with the domestic. Bart's discomfort with the myriad disguises they wear to elude the law and fool their victims portends his and Laurie's ultimate doom. Feeling his identity crumbling under the stress of violence, speed, and homelessness, Bart complains, "Everything's happening so fast. It's all in such high gear that sometimes it just doesn't feel like me." After a series of daring daylight robberies and audacious costumes, Bart and Laurie decide to rob the Albuquerque Armour meat-packing plant.[10] Posing as employees, they steal the payroll and attempt to hide at the home of Bart's sister. Clearly exhausted from the labor of raising four children and unsympathetic to her brother's predicament, Bart's sister reveals his painfully maudlin vision of home. As often happens in Bonnie-and-Clyde films, the return home marks the beginning of the end for Bart and Laurie, the first step toward their final entrapment in the shrouding mists of the hills above town. A strategic disaster, the lovers' unwillingness to escape in separate cars and their return to Cashville is compelled by Bart's inability to accept the domestic as a matrix of contradictions, banality, and back-breaking labor. Moreover, in contrast to Bart's rose-colored view of the domestic, Laurie's fatal mistake stems from her inability to imagine herself without a man, to escape hetero-normative discourse.

Despite this flaw, Laurie's previous life as a highly disciplined performer and her visceral disgust with housework and motherhood allow her to be more comfortable with the shifting identities of the road. Her power, after all, is as much due to her seductive looks and words as it is to her deadly aim. When she is introduced as a stage performer in a traveling carnival, Laurie's insatiable greed, chameleon-like changes of costume, and astonishing skill with a pistol guarantee her a paycheck. Although she fires a blank pistol into his leering grin when Bart first sees her, the threat is real. Laurie's transformation from trick-shooting performer to sharpshooting criminal is realized as she and her lover flee their first bank robbery. Turning around to see if anyone is following them, Laurie shoots the camera an exquisite look of thrilled and lascivious delight, betraying her mad love for objects – her unbridled consumption. Like representative Bonnie-types – Mallory (Juliette Lewis) in *Natural Born Killers*, Thelma (Geena Davis) in *Thelma and Louise* (1991), or Alabama (Patricia Arquette) in *True Romance* – Laurie is dangerous because she desires, and she's not afraid to kill to get what she wants.

If Bart and Laurie's mad love inspires their road trip and Bart's sentimentalization of the domestic brings about its tragic conclusion, the couple's first major crime functions as an anti-narratival spectacle that momentarily defers the inevitable tragedy by introducing an alternative sense of cinematic temporality. What this stylistic gesture accomplishes is, first, a brief suspension of the narrative's movement toward punishment and death, and, second, a momentary disruption of the film's narrative pace. The thrill of the genre – and its proximity to the action film – is its ability to suspend, at least briefly, the conservative narrative structure which always destroys the bad couple. This deferral is accomplished by way of intense representations of sex, violence, and the flow of action. As if trying to represent the possibility that Bonnies and Clydes might escape the fate of Barrow and Parker, the action sequences are distinguished by their stylistically different use of film stock, lighting, and editing. This break in style is the filmic equivalent of mad love, a warping of time that exceeds conventional narrative. In *Gun Crazy* this discontinuity takes the form of an extended, unedited shot with a hand-held camera that blurs the boundaries between cinematic time and real time, catapulting the audience into the action. This noticeably long sequence, clocking in at over three and a half minutes, works to maintain the crime as an event temporally dissociated from the main flow of the narrative. However, the experience of mad love, like the scene itself, comes to an end. Although the genre fetishizes crime as much as it fetishizes love, it fails, finally, to overcome history, the Production Code, and the fate of Parker and Barrow. While both crime and mad love promise an escape from politics, history, and economy, motion pictures can provide only flights of fancy.

Plate 3.1 Loaded with cash, Bart (John Dall) holds back a gun-crazed Laurie (Peggy Cummins) in *Gun Crazy*.

Style as History, Style as Revolt

If Laurie Starr's flirtatious gaze through the rear window of a getaway car signified the hijacking of heterosexuality in a nascent mass-media society, then the extreme close-up of Bonnie Parker's (Faye Dunaway) open mouth in the first scene of Arthur Penn's *Bonnie and Clyde* signaled the shotgun marriage of cinematic sex and violence, gangster capitalism, and the counter-culture. While *Gun Crazy* languished in B-movie limbo, adored only by the most cultish of cult audiences (Surrealists and film scholars), *Bonnie and Clyde* garnered both castigating notoriety and critical praise for its explosive and bloody evocation of the political and social turmoil of the late 1960s.[11]

Self-consciously building upon its filmic forerunners, Penn's version of the well-worn story of Bonnie and Clyde nostalgically recalls populist responses to the Great Depression. Featuring detailed sets and costumes that deploy the iconography of the Depression, the 1967 film purposefully attempted to consolidate popular political and cultural fantasy after the immobilization of the New Left. Discussing the scene where Bonnie and Clyde (Warren Beatty) are aided by a community of Okies, Penn noted, "Socially, the people were paralyzed by the Depression, for example, the scene in the camp near the end is nearly stylized in its immobility. . . . At least Bonnie and Clyde were mobile and functioning – sometimes in behalf of foolish things, sometimes self-destructively – but at least they functioned" (15–16). Penn sees this encounter not just as a meeting of bandits and labor but as the convergence of counter-cultural rhetoric of the 1960s and populist political discourses of the 1930s.

The intended effect of this encounter was the unification of class oppression and racial oppression under the signs of a revised and decidedly "Pop" populism that utilized the vocabulary of love, sex, violence, and mobility. Indeed, Penn was particularly proud of the film's potential to galvanize a counter-culture splintered by difference:

> It's very interesting that during a screening of *Bonnie and Clyde* one evening, five Negros present there completely identified with Bonnie and Clyde. They were delighted. They said: "This is the way; that's the way to go, baby. Those cats were all right." They really understood, because in a certain sense the American Negro has the same kind of attitude of "I have nothing more to lose" that was true during the Depression for Bonnie and Clyde. It is true now of the American Negro. He is really at the point of revolution – it's rebellion, not riot.
>
> (Penn: 19)

Thus, Penn's revision of Parker and Barrow's rampage against banks and lawmen – the pillars supporting state capitalism – represented the disenfranchisement of the new social movements of the 1960s and suggested alternative patterns of action and political fantasy. Penn's visually stunning film speaks to both the crisis of production and reproduction of capital and to the rise of new American social identities – women, teens, ethnic and racial minorities – whose relations to hegemonic capitalist culture and the male-dominated counter-culture were complex and contradictory.[12]

Though lauded for its politicized sensibilities, the film would draw its harshest criticisms for its morally nebulous "romanticization" of Parker and Barrow. Countering rage and disempowerment with glee and the aestheticization of bloodshed, Penn's mixture of comedy and gore made for an unholy brew of criminality, spectacle, and bad taste. As Bosley Crowther wrote in a famous *New York Times* review, "This blending of farce with brutal killings is as pointless as it is lacking in taste, since it makes no valid commentary on the already travestied truth" (23). In addition, numerous criticisms of the film highlighted its historical inaccuracies, amassing a prodigious list of Penn's deviations from Parker and Barrow's exploits. Among the most egregious of these mistakes was the casting of the charming and beautiful Warren Beatty and Faye Dunaway as the shiftless, lumpen lovers, a far cry from the original, rather homely, white-trash duo. Yet it is precisely this deviation, the spectacularization of the "real" young star-crossed killers, that remains the film's most intriguing achievement.

From the moment of its release, *Bonnie and Clyde* spilled over its celluloid edges, becoming much more than just a film. Embraced internationally, the film spawned a litter of related products and media stories that included books about the historical figures, an album-length recording made by the sister of Bonnie Parker, hit singles by Mel Tormé, Brigitte Bardot, and British pop sensation Georgie Fame, and a global fan club sporting berets and doffing gangland-style fedoras. The film's aesthetic sensibility – especially Theodora Van Runkle's Oscar-winning design of Faye Dunaway's draping, unconstricting wardrobe – has even been apocryphally credited with singlehandedly reviving the urban boutique market, altering the postwar face of women's high fashion.[13] Moreover, the popularity of the film manifested itself during the events of May, 1968, as graffiti scrawled on the wall of the Sorbonne signed by "Bonnot and Clyde": "Yes to organizing! No to party authority!" (Viénet: 73).

The variety of responses to *Bonnie and Clyde* reveal a paradoxical dynamic of post-1960s capitalism. Both a challenge to and a reflection of the state of capitalism, the tsunami of commodities generated by the movie's success may be attributed to its reformation of taste canons and its creation of a style of revolt that recalled a long history of popular dissent. As Robert Steele noted, "Youngsters imitate Warren Beatty's mannerisms and Faye Dunaway's look. Bonnie is on the covers of *Life* and *Time*, and models aping her are on fashion-magazine covers" (119). Indeed, the film itself thematizes this imitation. C. W.

Moss (Michael J. Pollard) is ultimately responsible for Bonnie and Clyde's deaths; his desire to imitate the young lovers by joining in their crime spree infuriates his father, who arranges the final ambush in what might be considered an attempt to wipe out Bonnie and Clyde's infectious style. Situated on the cusp of the world economic crisis of the 1970s, the gangster styles worn by the film's beautiful American stars heralded the precarious future of the United States' dominance of global capital and suggested an imaginary solution to the impact of that crisis on everyday life.[14] Inasmuch as this economic crisis threatened the ability of American capitalism to reconstitute and expand its domain, *Bonnie and Clyde* made it possible to imagine new styles of consumption, new forms of mobility, and potential reconfigurations of class, racial, and sexual boundaries.

The paradoxically liberatory and conservative nature of the genre becomes obvious in the youthful appropriation and celebration of *Bonnie and Clyde*. Robert Steele's concern about the film's impact on youth and their relations to state, school, and familial authority is vividly realized in a letter to the *New York Times Magazine* dated April 21, 1968. Nancy Fisher of Oklahoma City writes, "A Bonnie and Clyde fever has taken over the minds of teens the world over, especially in my high school" (142). Cast in a school pageant celebrating the coronation of the yearbook king and queen, Fisher worries that she doesn't resemble Faye Dunaway as much as she does the historical Bonnie Parker. But her concern about her appearance pales in comparison to that of the school administrators (one of whom had an uncle who was murdered by Parker and Barrow). Reflecting these anxieties, Fisher asks, "Wouldn't it be awful if there was a rash of teens who thought they were modern-day versions of the real Bonnie and Clyde?" (142). The administration's answer to Fisher's question isn't difficult to imagine, but the solution is worth noting. Fisher writes:

> I was told that when we use Bonnie and Clyde for our assembly that we must make it clear that we do not respect or idolize the real Bonnie and Clyde, for they were cold-hearted killers, but we would be imitating the Warren Beatty and Faye Dunaway characters, with many lines patterned after their movie's script.
>
> There will be posters of the Beatty and Dunaway Bonnie and Clyde used in the assembly to clearly define that we are portraying their styles and influence.
>
> (142)

Clearly among the brightest and the best in their class, Fisher and her boyfriend seem like nothing so much as a prototypical yuppie couple – stylish, admired, and strangely enamored with the gangster ethos.[15] More significantly, Fisher and her schoolmates were instructed to demarcate style from history and performance from real life.

Fisher's anxieties reveal *Bonnie and Clyde* as both an articulation of counter-cultural desires and a fantastic image of capitalist reformation, united under the aegis of a generational shift in personal consumer style, the attendant shattering of family tradition by the youth market, new forms of class mobility, and a new way of dealing with the tense relationship between domestic heterosexuality and free love. The radicalism of Penn's film lies in its use of history for starting a dialogue between the counter-culture and the traditions of radicalism from which it deviated. However, Penn's radical gesture couldn't have anticipated the cooption by a new generation of young capitalists in love. As Oliver Stone's lawsuit proves, enthusiastic movie-goers have the unwholesome habit of breaking the boundaries between cinema and real life and dismissing history as one more lame explanation for their boring lives.

The populist politics of *Bonnie and Clyde* are destabilized by this uneasy relationship between style politics and historical knowledge. Penn's deployment of migrant-worker types, folk music, political campaign posters, and antiqued automobiles flattens and simulates history in order to lend Bonnie and Clyde's road trip the illusion of escaping politics, economy, and domesticity. The simultaneous familiarity of the film's antique image and its revisionist history of Parker and Barrow are what drew crowds to the theaters. Penn's effort to free Bonnie and Clyde from the prison house of labor, domesticity, and social immobility reflected, and possibly abetted, shifts in the market. As a result, this fantasy of flight spawned an oppositional taste culture for a generation of young, voracious consumers who saw history not as a burden or a responsibility but as a source of lifestyles, fashion tips, and vicarious adventure.

One should not, however, underestimate the potential power of style and its tendency to erode dominant assumptions about politics and history. This potential is seen nowhere better than in the famous death scene, the moment of tragic narrative closure and Penn's most noted artistic gesture. As if gambling on the possibility of escaping Parker and Barrow's legacy and the narratives of social control it has inspired, Penn utilizes slow motion and fast cutting to ignite temporal, stylistic, and narratival dissociation. This rupture is set off by an intensely private exchange of glances between the lovers acknowledging their imminent demise. This charged moment echoes the first scene of the film in which Bonnie and Clyde make eye contact through the window of her mother's stifling house; Bonnie smiles the same excited smile at the possibility of escape. Therefore, the last vision of love imaginatively returns us to the moment of love at first sight, seeming to work against the gradual embourgeoisement that their mad love has suffered at the hand of Clyde's insufferable relatives. Immediately following this intimate glance, their murders are shown through rapid cuts and slow motion, shot with a variety of cameras equipped with different lenses and running at different speeds. This simultaneous acceleration and deceleration attempts to challenge narrative closure through a moment of paradoxical temporal intensity. Penn slows it down, presenting their demise as a lyrical moment that, as he says, "[makes] their deaths more legendary than real" (17). Penn also speeds it up, decentering the audience's point of view and, significantly, altering the time and speed of filmic violence. Like the real-time bank heist of *Gun Crazy*, Penn's destabilization of narrative temporality creates a filmic vocabulary for representing speed, violent action, and mad love. This disruption of narrative time defines the formal difference of the Bonnie-and-Clyde genre as a whole. Yet despite the discontinuity, the ending is ambiguous: on the one hand the film celebrates the punishment of Bonnie and Clyde; on the other, the way that moment is filmed defers narrative closure by canonizing their deaths.

Superstars, Mass Murder, and Surfing the Mediascape

Seen through the lens of contemporary action-adventure blockbusters, the twenty-four seconds of slow motion, multiple camera angles, and shifting film speeds that recorded Bonnie and Clyde's spectacular deaths seem rather timid and sentimental. This stylistic intensification of violence in recent cinema is epitomized by *Natural Born Killers*, where the discontinuity that characterizes the death scene in *Bonnie and Clyde* dominates Stone's film in its entirety, as if the fragmented quality of the death scene is being obsessively rehearsed. For Penn, this formal disruption invokes legendary time, the timelessness of the ballad or the epic, and allows him to reclaim love and history from the conservative fate of Parker and Barrow. Stone, however, is concerned less with romance and history — concepts too sentimental for him — than with the power of superstars and the possibility of escaping what Guy Debord calls "the society of the spectacle."

Skeptical about the possibility of truth, justice, and the American way in a culture dominated by the media, Stone focuses upon an often neglected aspect of "The Story of Bonnie and Clyde." The poem, it should be remembered, was written by Parker herself and sent to newspapers as a gesture of self-aggrandizement. Like Parker and Barrow, Mickey (Woody Harrelson) and Mallory Knox's popularity is inconceivable outside their parasitic relationship with the mass media, specifically the tabloid television show *American Maniacs* and its smarmy Australian host Wayne Gale (Robert Downey, Jr). Gale's own celebrity allows him to engineer a prison interview with Mickey on Super Bowl Sunday, setting the stage for the couple's escape. Reinforcing the diegetic connection of media and violence, Stone also relies on a relentless montage of different film stocks, sampled images from B-movies, and a collage of hackneyed and melodramatic story lines to undercut the film's own sensationalism. These fractured, multiple realities reflect Stone's belief that "the power in this country

Plate 3.2 Buck's (Gene Hackman) shadowy visage threatens to spoil the fun of the lovers' road trip in *Bonnie and Clyde*.

to conceal our own history is becoming more apparent. Everything has been poisoned by TV in our lifetime" ("Making").

Framed in the context of media overload, mad love appears to be emptied of its encrypted conservatism and sentimentality. Indeed, Stone's version of "The Story of Bonnie and Clyde" seems closer to trash television than bad poetry. Reflecting the mediated quality of their revolt, Mickey and Mallory's road trip rarely leaves the sound studio; they travel through a shifting back-projected geography of highways, dirt roads, and newspaper headlines. Lacking depth, motivation, and history, their violence seems all the more awful. Furthermore, *Natural Born Killers'* supersonic montage of pop iconography is complemented by a deluge of inane pop psychology that disables the viewer's ability to determine the cause of Mickey and Mallory's psychosis. In this manner, Stone undercuts the ways in which domestic dysfunction is popularly used to explain away violence. Mickey and Mallory's childhood traumas are as clichéd as they are horrifying. These allusions to incest, abuse, and parental neglect – what Mickey calls "some awful, secret thang" – are undermined by contradictory evidence or blatant parody. Nor does the Bonnie-and-Clyde genre's habitual recourse to love at first sight escape Stone's scrutiny: rather than seeing each other through a bedroom window, Mickey and Mallory meet on the imaginary sound stage of the perverse family sitcom *I Love Mallory*. Just like Lucy, Mallory wants to get out of the house and into the spotlight. As both the star of her own memories and the victim of family pathology, Mallory gets her big break into showbiz and celebrity after being discovered by Mickey the meat man. By deconstructing the boundaries between television, the family, romance, and mass murder, Stone ensures that Mickey and Mallory will appear both utterly familiar and disturbingly alien – the serial killers next door.

This uncanny blend of star quality and grotesquely detourned "family values" deeply upsets conservative visions of American progress. Rather than being trapped by their abusive families, Mickey and Mallory exploit their traumas, becoming international media darlings. On their way into court, they are surrounded by a cheering throng of adoring fans and paparazzi. As one of their slacker groupies suggests in an *American Maniacs* interview, "I'm not saying I believe in mass murder and that shit . . . but, if I was a mass murderer, I'd be Mickey and Mallory." If Penn's Bonnie and Clyde are at once historical legends and fashion models, they are still good folk in bad circumstances. But by making Mickey and Mallory celebrity superstars rather than working-class legends, Stone foregrounds the ambiguous politics of the genre as a whole. Not one to quote Karl Marx, Mallory-as-starlet tells her adoring fans, "I never had so much fun in my life." Mickey and Mallory are muscle-bound superheroes in their own demented cartoons; they are beyond history, beyond politics, beyond good and evil. We don't love them because they're beautiful, and we don't sympathize with them. We watch them – as we watched O. J. Simpson – simply because they're stars.

Emphasizing the cult of superstardom enables Stone to criticize the negative effects of the mass media on our collective sense of right and wrong. Mickey and Mallory's revolt, romantic as it may seem, is inextricable from contemporary telecommunications. Mickey and Mallory don't travel down freeways and back roads – that's all back-projected – they surf the mediascape. However, in a gesture we consider highly problematic, the media is ultimately rejected at the end of the film in favor of privacy, tourism, and the mobile home. At the center of Stone's critique is Wayne Gale, who, unfortunately, makes the fatal mistake of thinking that Mickey and Mallory must have the media to maintain their mad love. Unlike Clyde, who thanks Bonnie for telling his story in the newspapers and celebrates his stardom by making love with her, Mickey doesn't need to have his story told to get it up. Thus, after aiding and abetting Mickey and Mallory's prison break and realizing his true calling as a natural born killer, Gale is surprised to discover that three's a crowd. Mickey and Mallory reclaim their privacy by killing Gale and leaving his live-feed camera behind to "tell the tale" as its battery pack slowly dies.

Once again, the end of a Bonnie-and-Clyde film problematizes the very conditions of escape. In the case of *Natural Born Killers*, after making their getaway from the state penitentiary, Mickey and Mallory become eternal tourists. We last see them traveling down the road in a mobile home with two kids in tow and Mallory in labor. Their travels are nestled in a montage of B-movie images; footage of pop killers like O. J. Simpson and the Menendez brothers and "angry women" like Tonya Harding and Lorena Bobbitt; time-lapse shots of blossoming flowers; hydra-headed monsters; and madly multiplying march hares. In effect, Mickey and Mallory simply escape into more of the same. Eschewing safe and happy closure and re-establishing the road as a kind of Möbius strip, the end of *Natural Born Killers* disables the viewer's ability to determine if Stone is affirming the possibility of escape or demolishing it altogether. The polyvalent quality of this last sequence demonstrates Stone's troubled liberalism and his obsession with producing a radical critique within the formal and economic constraints of Hollywood. In this sense, Stone is much like Dole and his cronies: they all agree that Hollywood doesn't make the kinds of films it should. Dole may champion family-friendly blockbusters as a bulwark against a slough of obscene and naughty products, but Stone, no less a champion, defends his own films as unromantic representations of "family values" under attack from evil capitalists like *Wall Street*'s (1987) Gordon Gekko, *JFK*'s (1991) Clay Shaw, and sleaze-peddler Wayne Gale. Capitalism, finally, is not an issue for Dole and Stone, only what it sells.

Plate 3.3 Media superstars Mickey and Mallory (Woody Harrelson and Juliette Lewis) in *Natural Born Killers*.

Liberating the Road Movie

The three films we have discussed disrupt concerns that are fundamental to American culture: marriage and family, the proper uses of violence, and dreams of upward mobility. *Gun Crazy*, *Bonnie and Clyde*, and *Natural Born Killers* articulate the potentially explosive contradictions of domesticity, mobility, and desire within their respective historical moments. And while these films maintain critical attitudes toward capitalism and conventional romance, they sustain an ardent belief in true love. This conviction, however, can be rendered only through formal innovations such as stylized violence and time-warping editing procedures that stretch the boundaries of the traditional Hollywood love story and subsequently enkindle the genre's particular brand of mad love. In order to accomplish this, Lewis employs the commodity fetish and documentary techniques to foster alternative forms of desire and temporality. Penn flattens and aestheticizes history, inspiring a mass culture of resistance and a revolutionary style of love. And Stone builds upon his forerunners by utilizing the fractured narrative forms popularized by MTV in the hope of articulating a critique of American culture itself and, in his words, its relentless destruction of "compassion and love" ("Oliver": 11). In all three films, the disruption of narrative frees love from outmoded notions of morality and social conduct even though the films ultimately solidify heterosexual monogamy, domestic tranquillity, and the pleasures of travel.

Despite its ambivalence toward "family values," the Bonnie-and-Clyde genre constantly seeks to escape its own ideological boundaries, challenging canons of taste and good behavior. The allure of such flight is evident in the various and occasionally deadly consumer strategies practiced by the Surrealists, Oklahoma beauty queen Nancy Fisher, and day-tripping copycat killers Sarah Edmondson and Ben Darras. What we have tried to establish is that these kinds of challenges are always related to shifts in the relationship between capitalism and the domestic sphere. In a capitalist culture, these kinds of changes allow for the generation of new markets, taste cultures, and product lines. However, while these shifts may allow for economic growth, they often introduce pernicious dynamics into the family fold. Such hazards are made clear in *Gun Crazy*, where Laurie's greed and aversion to hard work fatally clashes with Bart's longing for home. Similarly, the greed of all "good" Americans, while sustaining a vibrant economy, may lead to the erosion of domestic tranquillity. Thus, Grisham, Dole, and other conservatives are right to be concerned. Bonnie-and-Clyde movies articulate exactly what people want to do with capitalism – and, conversely, what capitalism wants to do with them. Like capital, film fans want to be mobile, and the genre's glamour lies in its promise of flight.

When Bonnies and Clydes take to the road they fulfill the worst and best dreams of capitalism; they imagine new ways of moving, loving, and consuming.

In this sense, the Bonnie-and-Clyde film maps the intersection of capitalism and desire. The genre's perennial success at the box office indicates the persistent appeal of these films as action-packed imaginary solutions to the contradictions inherent to domestic stability and economic growth. The radical possibility promised by the Bonnie-and-Clyde film is that, despite the historical manner in which love has been disciplined and marketed, love still retains its excitement, its air of rebellion, and its potential for madness. The genre's scandalous violence and sexy style lure couples who hope their attraction to one another is not merely convention or the result of slick advertising but something real and pure. If sitting in the dark feels like speeding down the road, the Bonnie-and-Clyde genre epitomizes this experience for the couple in love, making their love feel revolutionary, even if they still have to go to work in the morning. Therefore, Bonnies and Clydes mobilize domesticity. Such mobile homes resist – if only momentarily – privatization and restraint by the demands of both biological and social reproduction. And, in this way, the genre in some sense liberates the road movie, perhaps film itself, by threatening to displace this imaginary mobility and intense desire onto real-life highways.

Notes

1   Grisham became embroiled in this controversy in an attempt to seek justice and, it seems, to defend the sanctity of locality and community for the Mississippi town where he once worked after his friend William Savage was murdered on March 7, 1995, by Ben Darras and Sarah Edmondson. Edmondson admitted that she and her boyfriend were fond of consuming great quantities of hallucinogens while repeatedly watching Stone's film. We would, however, contend that the fuss about copy-cat killings is symptomatic of a larger concern: the diffusion of culture industry commodities into local communities and the attendant "liberation" of formerly subservient populations (particularly youth) via the appropriation of alternative styles of commodity consumption. For example, a similar concern has been shown regarding the appropriation of the "gangsta" styles of disenfranchised urban youths by middle-class teenagers in suburban and rural areas. For an overview of the murders allegedly linked to the film see Shnayerson.

2   "The Story of Bonnie and Clyde" refers to the poem (written by Bonnie Parker in 1934 and published in numerous newspapers) which established the tragic legend of the pair. We should clarify that when we refer to "Parker and Barrow," we are referring to the historical figures. We reserve the names "Bonnie and Clyde" for discussing the characters in Arthur Penn's 1967 film.

3   Fredric Jameson also uses the term "imaginary solution" in *The Political Unconscious* to describe the ways in which the realist novel resolves the deep contradictions of ideology. Moreover, members of the Birmingham School of Cultural Studies employ the term to describe the significance of such things as skinhead culture and mugging.

4   The first pages of *The Manifesto of the Communist Party* are devoted to the profoundly (and ambivalent) revolutionary nature of the bourgeoisie and the opportunities and dilemmas that the bourgeois class poses for socialist development. As Marx and Engels

demonstrate, despite its willing support of the system of wage slavery, the bourgeoisie was responsible for sundering earlier "all feudal, patriarchal, idyllic relations" (15). As they put it, "[F]or exploitation, veiled by religious and political illusions, it has substituted naked, shameless, direct, brutal exploitation" (15).

5 Paul Virilio argues that speed, not simply a measure of time and space, is inextricable from social and economic development. Amongst his many books, see *Speed and Politics*.

6 Jonathan Crary has identified the year 1927 as marking the birth of "spectacular" capitalism. In that year, the technological perfection of television (and the attendant interlocking of corporate, military, and state control of television) and the advent of synchronized sound film (and the system of distribution it necessitated) marked the birth of the modern American culture industry (Crary: 101–2). While Crary does not discuss it, 1927 also brought about the drafting of the Motion Picture Production Code in response to the widespread public scandals of Hollywood and the perceived threat of dissolute youth made giddy by the economic boom of the 1920s (Cook: 282). Historically, the American culture industry has always had to contend with the practical effects, the "moral crises," and, in particular, the "deviant" appropriations of its liberatory promises. The canonization of Parker and Barrow marks the recognition (in mythic form) of capitalism as an inherently unstable system that profoundly impacts selves, families, and communities. Parker and Barrow embody the systemic crises of American capitalism; they are the prodigal progeny of capitalist reform. As such, they constantly challenge the kinds of moral boundaries established by cultural police such as the MPAA, the Catholic Legion of Decency, and, more recently, Bob Dole.

7 The most notable variations on this theme include: *Persons in Hiding* (1939), *They Live by Night* (1948), *Gun Crazy* (1949), *The Bonnie Parker Stor* (1958), *Machine Gun Kelly* (1958), *The Getaway* (1972), *Badlands* (1973), *Thieves Like Us* (1974), *Drugstore Cowboy* (1989), *Wild at Heart* (1990), *Kalifornia* (1993), *Guncrazy* (1992), *True Romance* (1993), *The Getaway* (1994), and *Natural Born Killers* (1994).

In addition, there are a number of movies which seem to problematize the resolutely heterosexual bias of the genre by placing queer couples behind the wheel. The best-known of these variations, *Thelma and Louise* (1991), tells the tale of two women who go on the road after an inadvertent murder. *The Living End* (1992) features a gay couple infected with the HIV virus. *Josh and S.A.M.* (1993) stars two young boys, one of whom is a robot. *Johnny and Clyde* (1995) adds a twist to the familiar tale by featuring a boy and his dog. While the genre has incorporated the highway high jinks of lesbians, gay couples, children, pets, and even androids, our suspicion is that these queer couples on the lam still mimic heterosexuality by portraying potentially resistant forms of sexuality as somehow "dysfunctional." It seems clear that these films are deeply concerned with the tensions of love, home, and a type of mobility that was formerly available only to white, heterosexual couples. The 1990s rash of Bonnie-and-Clyde movies may be a hysterical response to a crisis within white heterosexuality and "family values." Moreover, it is interesting to speculate on the relative absence of people of color in the genre. Perhaps the notion of a black couple racing through the Southwest in a stolen car still pushes the suspension of disbelief a bit too far.

8 The term "détournement" has been translated as "diversion" or "subversion." Greil Marcus defines it as "the theft of aesthetic artifacts from their contexts and their

diversion into contexts of one's own devise" (168). Sadie Plant calls it "a turning around and a reclamation of lost meaning: a way of putting the stasis of the spectacle in motion. It is plagiaristic, because its materials are those which already appear within the spectacle" (86). While best known for its application to comic strips, it is a tactic applicable to all forms of popular culture. For a discussion of détournement and its function within cultural struggle as well as its utility as a form of resistant historiography, see Marcus, particularly 398–410.

9 The domestic sphere experienced profound and troubling changes after the Second World War. These changes can be traced to the war's achievement of the utopian dreams of labor left unfulfilled by the New Deal. The war enabled a resolution of the dilemmas of increased productivity that caused the world economic crisis of the 1930s. But the invigorated consumerism and economic security of American labor (whose beneficiaries also included certain women and teenagers) was founded on sexism, apartheid, the realization of a global market propelled by the Cold War "military industrial complex," and the reorganization of military and economic power in favor of the United States.

10 The magnitude of Bart and Laurie's crime is less apparent today. Before its dismantling, Armour was one of the largest corporations in the world. The first edition of the *Fortune 500* placed it among the top ten largest American industrial companies. See Loomis.

11 For an informative summary of the torrent of critical responses to *Bonnie and Clyde*, see Cawelti: 1–6; see also McCarty: 124–5.

12 Not known for turning down markets ready to be penetrated, American capitalist culture has often embraced the very identities it oppresses, promising political progress and social reformation through entrance into the market and the workforce. As Tom Frank writes, "When business leaders cast their gaze onto the youth culture bubbling around them, they saw both a reflection of their own struggle against the stifling bureaucratic methods of the past and an affirmation of a new dynamic consumerism that must replace the old" (quoted in Perlstein: 37).

13 Of note: according to industry legend, beret production and consumption sky-rocketed in 1967 and 1968.

14 US dominance of world finance was facilitated through the postwar reconstruction of the economies of Germany, Japan, and other "friendly" nations, marking one of the more significant trends that led to the "crisis" of over-accumulation and the slowing of the American economy in the late 1960s. All dressed up with nowhere to go, surplus capital was rerouted into expanded domestic and overseas markets and centers of production. America's lucrative experience of the Cold War's bipolar power structure thus resulted from tapping unexpected veins of capitalist desire and fetishism – both inside and outside American borders. For an enlightening history of the world economic crisis of the 1970s, see David Harvey's *The Condition of Postmodernity* and Giovanni Arrighi's *The Long Twentieth Century*.

15 Noted for its decadent and often profligate sense of style and consumption, the gangster in American culture codes for both the viciousness of consumer desire and the unruly potential of capitalism itself. The gangster, like the stereotypical yuppie, practices a capitalism without reserve.

Works Cited

Arrighi, Giovanni. *The Long Twentieth Century: Money, Power, and the Origins of Our Times.* New York: Verso, 1994.

Cawelti, John G., ed. *Focus on Bonnie and Clyde.* Englewood Cliffs, NJ: Prentice-Hall, Inc., 1973.

Cook, David A. *A History of Narrative Film.* 3rd ed. New York: Norton, 1996.

Crary, Jonathan. "Spectacle, Attention, Counter Memory." *October* 50 (Fall 1989): 97–107.

Crowther, Bosley. Rev. of *Bonnie and Clyde.* In Cawelti: 22–3.

Debord, Guy. *The Society of the Spectacle.* Detroit: Black and Red, 1977.

Dole, Robert. Address. Los Angeles, May 31, 1995.

Fisher, Nancy. Letter. *New York Times Magazine* (April 21, 1968): 21+.

Harvey, David. *The Condition of Postmodernity.* Cambridge, MA: Blackwell, 1989.

Jameson, Fredric. *The Political Unconscious: Narrative as a Socially Symbolic Act.* Ithaca: Cornell University Press, 1981.

Lévi-Strauss, Claude. "The Structural Study of Myth." *Critical Theory Since 1965*, eds. Hazard Adams and Leroy Searle. Tallahassee: University Presses of Florida, 1986. 809–22.

Loomis, Carole J. "Forty Years of the Fortune 500." *Fortune* 131.9 (May 15, 1995): 182–8.

Marcus, Greil. *Lipstick Traces: A Secret History of the Twentieth Century.* Cambridge, MA: Harvard University Press, 1989.

Marx, Karl and Engels, Frederick. *The Manifesto of the Communist Party*, trans. Samuel Moore. Chicago: Charles H. Kerr Publishing Co., 1947.

McCarty, John. *Hollywood Gangland: The Movies' Love Affair with the Mob.* New York: St Martin's Press, 1993.

Naremore, James. "American Film Noir: The History of an Idea." *Film Quarterly* 49.2 (Winter 1995–6): 12–28.

Penn, Arthur. "*Bonnie and Clyde*: An Interview with Arthur Penn." By Jean-Louis Commolli and André S. Labarthe. In Cawelti: 15–19.

Perlstein, Rick. "Who Owns the Sixties?: The Opening of a Scholarly Generation Gap." *Lingua Franca* 6.4 (May/June 1996): 30–7.

Plant, Sadie. *The Most Radical Gesture: The Situationist International in a Postmodern Age.* New York: Routledge, 1992.

Shnayerson, Michael. "Natural Born Opponents." *Vanity Fair* (July, 1996): 98+.

Steele, Robert. "The Good-Bad and Bad-Good in Movies: *Bonnie and Clyde* and *In Cold Blood*." In Cawelti: 115–21.

Stone, Oliver. "Making Movies Matter." University of Michigan Ann Arbor, March 20, 1996.

—— "Oliver Stone: Why Do I Have to Provoke?" By Gavin Smith. *Sight and Sound* (December, 1994): 8–12.

Viénet, René. *Enragés and Situationists in the Occupation Movement, France, May '68* (1968). New York: Autonomedia, 1992.

Virilio, Paul. *Speed and Politics: An Essay on Dromology.* New York: Semiotext(e), 1977.

4

ON THE RUN AND ON THE ROAD

Fame and the outlaw couple in American cinema

Corey K. Creekmur

Outlaws On the Lam (that perennial fave with filmgoers everywhere, closet criminals of every age and gender). . . . Cars, guns, blood, and explosions. Let the camera weave its charm.

(Wright: 100)

The freeway was my show, my arena. It's always been home to me . . . I was born and bred for it. I'm an American. I love the freeway.

(Johnson: 41)

In twentieth-century American popular culture, there are really only two reasons to go on the road: to become famous or to hide. Born too late for the pioneer projects of blazing trails, extending natural frontiers, or just lighting out for the territory, modern Americans hit a road not only already taken, but paved, ramped, mapped, and marked by the commercial sites of mobile mass culture: the motel, the roadside diner, the filling station, and the drive-in movie theater. For those traversing this ground for purposes other than leisurely sight-seeing, the road points towards a promising future or leads away from a dead-end past: the slightest redefinition of perspective shifts the purpose of a road trip from seeking a desired goal into flight from a desperate origin. In fact, despite the strong emphasis given to departures and arrivals, the road trip is largely defined by its extended middle; as Jack Kerouac's terse title affirms, being "on the road," rather than starting or stopping, defines the postwar American experience. As the narrator of Bayard Johnson's road novel *Damned Right* insists: "That's why they're called freeways. It's on stretches like that you can be free in America . . . After all, it's a free country" (9). No matter how many actual lanes a modern superhighway expands into laterally, the American road is always metaphorically a two-way street generating either exploration (the panoramic view ahead through the windshield) or escape (the furtive backward glance in the rear-view mirror), and, perhaps, the sudden reversibility of destiny and destination promised by the possibility of making a – legal or illegal – u-turn. Every American who knows "there's no place like home" – the mantra of America's most famous road movie – also remembers that "you can't go home again."

This essay attempts to demonstrate that, after the frontier-exploration narratives of conquest produced in the nineteenth and early twentieth centuries, the cultural oppositions generated by the modern American road are most effectively narrativized in two apparently dissimilar though unusually self-reflexive film forms: the Hollywood musical and the distinct cycle or subgenre of classical and contemporary "road films" centered on the flight of a fugitive pair, or outlaw couple.[1] In fact, this essay's principal claim is that *"outlaw couple" road films are inverted musicals*, mirror forms that reflect a number of fundamental structural and thematic concerns despite their superficially opposed moods and styles; at the very least they are the two film forms that most insistently associate liberation with motion, whether automotive or terpsichorean. While I think the musical and outlaw couple road film intersect on a number of formal and thematic levels, I will especially emphasize how the two forms are essentially interrelated through their shared but differently expressed obsession with the cultural construction and maintenance of modern celebrity and fame, or, in their inverted terms, notoriety and infamy. Although both "kinds" of films are most commonly understood as examples of Hollywood genres – the musical and the more loosely defined road film, *film noir*, or crime genres – it might also be revealing to locate the examples discussed in this essay within the broader context of the twentieth century's mass-mediated "culture of celebrity," where personal "star" qualities like charisma and personality potentially lead to public fame and celebrity, a larger frame that might subsume more specific narrative patterns and generic meanings previously associated with these forms.[2]

Although we don't commonly think of them as "road" films, a significant number of Hollywood musicals, especially those set "backstage" in the entertainment world, or which Rick Altman subcategorizes as "show musicals," are structured whole or in part by taking their "shows" – the show within the show – on the road. Here *The Band Wagon* (1953) might serve as a model: all of the narrative's "problems," whether personal or professional, romantic or commercial, are repaired by "taking the show on the road." In fact, the road is apparently the only cohesive glue binding together what look like wildly discontinuous musical numbers in *The Band Wagon*'s finally successful show; repeated stock shots of trains with superimposed titles introduce and link the otherwise unrelated performances of: "Philadelphia" – Cyd Charisse's balletic "New Sun in the Sky"; "Boston" – Fred Astaire and Jack Buchanan's soft-shoe "I Guess I'll Have to Change My Plan"; and "Washington" – Nanette Fabray's folksy "Louisiana Hayride." *The Band Wagon* furthermore usefully highlights the musical's most commonly identified structural underpinnings: like the American cinema generally according to Raymond Bellour, but perhaps in its most consistent and emphatic elaboration, the musical's motive is to create a heterosexual couple through romantic, musical, and ideological harmony.[3] This function of the genre is most fully defined by Altman, who insists that "in the musical *the couple is the plot*" (35). In other words, in the musical "the formation of the couple is linked either causally or through parallelism to success in the ventures which constitute the plot. . . . Time and again, to solve the couple's problems becomes synonymous with, and thus a figure for, a solution of the plot's other enterprises" (108–9).

The couple is of course *the plot* in "outlaw couple" films as well, but instead of creating or forming a couple, the general pressure of these films is towards finally destroying or "de-forming" the couple. Although many recent films (*The Getaway*, 1972 and 1994; *Wild at Heart*, 1990; *The Living End*, 1992; *True Romance*, 1993; *Natural Born Killers*, 1994; *Love and a .45*, 1994) allow their outlaw couples to live, most classic examples (*You Only Live Once*, 1937; *They Live By Night*, 1949; *Gun Crazy*, 1949) as well as many later films (*A bout de souffle*, 1959; *Pierrot le Fou*, 1965; *Bonnie and Clyde*, 1967; *Thieves Like Us*, 1974; *Badlands*, 1973; *Thelma and Louise*, 1991; *Guncrazy*, 1992; *Kalifornia*, 1993) tear the outlaw couple violently apart. Perhaps the main reason that musicals and outlaw couple road films are not commonly linked is because the ideological goals of each form seem so antithetical. Thomas Schatz's well-known distinction between "genres of indeterminate, civilized space" (including musicals) and "genres of determinate, contested space" (including gangster and detective films), for instance, would apparently oppose musicals, which "tend to celebrate the values of *social integration*," to "outlaw couple" films, which, especially in the classic examples produced under Hollywood's Production Code, "uphold the values of *social order*" (*Hollywood Genres*: 29). Outlaw couple films, however, consistently challenge Schatz's distinctions by dramatizing the typical "musical" or "comic" activity of coupling within the contested spaces and through the social conflicts usually associated with crime stories. But before they end up professionally teamed, married, incarcerated, or dead, the couples in both forms frequently meet one another and develop their relationships in surprising similar ways. The cocky Fred Astaire repeatedly irritates Ginger Rogers into submission – a pattern Gerald Mast calls "Fred's invitation and Ginger's initiation" (150) – until their first "challenge dances" clear the ground for the romantic and thus more conventionally gender-coded waltzes to follow. In *Gun Crazy*, the two main characters, who "go together . . . like guns and ammunition," form as a couple immediately after firing bullets at each other's heads in a carnival shooting competition that, Jim Kitses notes, "quickly develops ritualistic and symbolic dimensions that collapse combat and courtship" (29). Bonnie and Clyde become attached after the braggart Clyde robs a bank to impress Bonnie, and their attachment grows after he teaches her how to fire a gun so that they can rob banks *together*. (*Annie Get Your Gun*, 1950, is perhaps the only example that directly forms its couple around sharing guns *and* music, a link condensed by the shooting/singing competition of the duet "Anything You Can Do, I Can Do Better.") In short, the appeal of both musicals and outlaw couple films is in large measure fueled by our desire to see two individuals – who often dance, sing, rob, or kill quite effectively on their own – *team up and perform as a couple*; as David Laderman recognizes, although emphasizing male "buddy" pairs, "the road was destined to be traveled by a couple," and in terms consistent with Altman's "dual focus" pattern for the musical, he adds that "most often the road film couple is divided along these lines: one is more wild, the other more straight" (45).

Although it's tempting to contrast musical and outlaw couple films by claiming that the creation of musical couples is basically *romantic*, and the destructive passion of outlaw couples essentially *erotic*, the European Romantic tradition certainly provides the models of *l'amour fou* and *liebestod* still motivating most road films, as Godard recognized when he identified his characters in *Pierrot le Fou* as "the last romantic couple,"[4] or perhaps when Carlos Clarens called *They Live By Night*'s doomed lovers a "Romeo and Juliet of the sticks" (227). Besides this deep continuity, I might also at least note here that the backstage or show musical and the outlaw couple genres in their dominant American forms emerge out of the same historical context of the American Depression: the 1930s romantic musical star couples – Dick Powell and Ruby Keeler, Fred Astaire and Ginger Rogers, and Nelson Eddy and Jeanette MacDonald – are all perhaps shadowed by the contemporary notoriety of outlaw couple Bonnie Parker and Clyde Barrow.[5] Eric Mottram has suggested that even earlier "film, car, and jazz grew together as a key twentieth century triad," and by the Depression this triad might be more specified: film musicals (the only major sound film genre without silent precedents), getaway cars ("cars as wheels for guns," in Mottram's phrase), and radio (most obviously car radios) all revise and update the technologies of the previous decades, although at least through the 1950s the musical will persistently represent travel through the "public" transportation of the train, which always appears more communal than the "private" automobile. If the trains in musicals often retain their symbolic role, most explicit in the Western, as the vehicle for the expansion of American space, then cars replace the individual cowboy's horse, as their names (Mustang, Pinto) and measurement in "horsepower" often suggest. The train also, in musicals as late as *A Hard Day's Night* (1964), conveniently provides the necessary space for spontaneous musical performances. While the car radio certainly invites singing along, the automobile's restricted space encourages few other musical activities.

As many cultural historians have noted, the role of the motion picture as America's principal leisure activity in the early twentieth century continually competes with the automobile's similar function "as a release," in the telling phrase of the authors of *Middletown*. (Eventually, of course, the development of the drive-in movie theater would explicitly address this competition between visual and automotive diversions.) By 1929, Robert and Helen Merrell Lynd recognized that "The threat which the automobile presents to some anxious parents is suggested by the fact that of thirty girls brought before the juvenile court in the twelve months preceding September 1, 1924, charged with 'sex crimes,' for whom the place where the offense occurred was given in the records, nineteen were listed as having committed the offense in an automobile." According to a local newspaper "'The desire of youth to step on the gas when it has no machine of its own . . . is considered responsible for the theft of the greater part of the (154) automobiles stolen from [Middletown] during the past year'" (258). Movies, and especially luxurious musicals set among the fantasy elite, remained popular throughout the Depression because, it is often assumed, they provided an "escape" from everyday misery; it's also worth recalling, as Mottram does, that "Even in the Depression decade, thirty-eight million cars were sold in America, ten million more than in the previous decade" (51).

As a late "non-integrated" musical, in which many songs don't clearly advance the plot or function to convey character feelings, *The Band Wagon* exhibits the structural tension between "narrative" and "number" frequently noted in discussions of musicals, wherein the performances that define the "musical" as such threaten to disrupt the narrative line linking the non-musical scenes together. Although the musical segments are the *raison d'être* for musicals, they commonly delay, detour, or completely derail the narrative's drive toward completion, as in Busby Berkeley's *The Gang's All Here* (1943), in which a thin narrative remains completely unrecovered after the final, typically surreal musical number. We might also recall that some musicals in the genre's history have been structured by a variety or revue format of narratively unrelated musical numbers, abandoning plot in the usual sense altogether: for example, consider *The King of Jazz* (1930), *Ziegfeld Follies* (1946), *Invitation to the Dance* (1957), and the "greatest hits" format of the *That's Entertainment!* series (1974, 1976, 1994), which treats musical numbers from narrative films as fully isolatable segments. While rarely canonized among the "great" musicals, such examples nevertheless emphasize the potential escape from linear narrative in the musical's deep structure, and suggest an analogy with the notably loose or episodic plot lines of many recent road films, which may be products, as Michael Atkinson suggests, "of a generation raised on television and the open-ended, road-like format of the weekly serial" (14).

In their tension between narrative and number, or in the alternating pattern between "rhymed" segments Altman emphasizes, musicals bear an uncanny resemblance to many road films, which are also typically structured by a regular pattern of forward motion and more static "set-pieces," or stretches of driving and regular rest stops. Whereas musical performers on a circuit of one-night stands stop at hotels, boarding houses, and theaters to sing and dance before getting back on the road, outlaw couples on the lam pull into motels, roadside diners, gas stations, and, increasingly, convenience stores, to steal and kill before resuming running for their lives. (*The Harvey Girls*, 1946, is perhaps worth recalling here, given its cross-generic status as a musical Western largely set in a [rail]roadside diner.) Moreover, the spectacle of musical numbers finds its evil twin in the road film's scenes of action and violence. It's now common for critics to describe Astaire and Rogers's intimate dance numbers as sublimated acts of sexual intercourse, as in Jim Collins's claim that "the actions of the dances themselves strongly suggest the sexual nature of the dance," and that a "total freeze in the action" of the "Cheek to Cheek" number from *The Gay Divorcee* (1934) "creates a symbolic or metaphoric orgasm" (144); similarly, Robin Wood observes that "Bonnie robs with Clyde as a substitute for intercourse: it is at least *one* exciting thing they can do together" (85), and Carlos Clarens recognizes that, in the shooting-match courtship of *Gun Crazy*, "gunplay substitutes for foreplay" (229). Just as big musical numbers are often preceded by brief rehearsal numbers (Mast: 125), the mayhem of armed robberies is frequently delineated in planning sessions: in *Gun Crazy*, robberies are outlined like stage blocking, and the characters even wear theatrical Western costumes for their crime spree suggesting a community theater production of *Annie Get Your Gun*. In *Thelma and Louise*, Thelma's lines and behavior during a videotaped hold-up are a reenactment of J.D.'s earlier coaching of the scene. Frequently, both musicals and outlaw couple films then proceed by a pattern of *escalation*, building from relatively intimate numbers like a duet or from "small" crimes, to lengthy scenes of mass musical spectacle or action-packed slaughter. As Mast points out, the numbers in Berkeley's films at Warner Bros. "grow as the cycle progresses," ranging from five to eventually eleven choruses which therefore demand a corresponding visual elaboration (128). The thirteen-minute "Broadway Melody" from *Singin' in the Rain* (1952) and the seventeen-minute *An American in Paris* (1951) ballet demonstrate the similar tendency for MGM's Freed Unit to build their musical segments into increasingly complex numbers two decades later.

In a nightmarish reversal of this pattern, outlaw couple films like *Gun Crazy* or *Bonnie and Clyde* grow from armed robbery to murder, and from efficient little capers to messy bloodbaths. More recent examples like *Natural Born Killers* and *True Romance* weave their way toward long, bloody shoot-outs (a prison break and a complex drug bust) that yank in all the film's narrative threads. There are of course musicals like *Guys and Dolls* (1955), *West Side Story* (1961), and *The Cotton Club* (1984), or musical numbers like Astaire's *film noir* parody "The Girl Hunt" ballet in *The Band Wagon*, that suggest the musical's own awareness of its affinity with popular crime narratives, and I will later suggest that contemporary outlaw couple films are often aware of their own ability to mutate into musicals. As Carol Clover (738) has recently pointed out with respect to the Hollywood musical's racial guilt, the police who often oversee and even "arrest" musical numbers like Kelly's "Singin' in the Rain" and both "Pettin' in the Park" and "Remember My Forgotten Man" from *Gold Diggers of 1933* imply that bursting into song or dance might need as much legal supervision as characters recklessly waving guns around.[6]

When the road doesn't provide an overall structure to musicals (like *Show Boat*, in which the road is, as it was for Huck Finn, the river), it is commonly represented through time-collapsing montage sequences that summarize the process of "paying one's dues" before achieving success, or which briefly outline the "rise to fame" of musical stars. Frequently such sequences demonstrate the expansion of "local" celebrity into national or "mass" recognition: in *The Story of Vernon and Irene Castle* (1939), a long montage sequence detailing the commercial exploitation of products featuring the Castle name or image concludes with a high-angle shot of Astaire and Rogers dancing across North America, summarizing both the Castles' "whirlwind country-wide tour" of "35 cities in 28 days" as well as their commercial saturation of the American marketplace. This is a fantastic elaboration of the nondiegetic road maps commonly featured in outlaw couple films like *They Live By Night*, which clarify spatial shifts in the narrative and often suggest some of the tedium of unrelenting flight. (Graham Greene, reviewing the Bonnie-and-Clyde-influenced *Persons in Hiding*, could note only that "the story opens, as it were, in the middle . . . and after that it's all speeding cars and montage" [210]). An even more elaborate montage sequence from *Lady Be Good* (1941) follows the title song through its composition, transcription, publication, sheet-music sales, recording, record sales, and popular dissemination through a range of regional and ethnic interpretations. This "success montage" not only carries the film's central songwriting-team couple to greater fame, but secures their once-threatened romantic coupling, even as it links the stages of romance to the key commercial processes of the popular music industry. As a final example, consider the temporally and spatially mind-boggling "Born in a Trunk" sequence from *A Star Is Born* (1954), which traces the fictional metamorphosis of Esther Blodgett into Vicki Lester as well as the perhaps even more dramatic "real life" evolution of Frances Gumm into Judy Garland. In addition to these rather complex sequences, many musicals represent the performer's rise to fame with the speed and efficiency characteristic of classic Hollywood film-making generally; a brief segment from *The Jolson Story* (1946) represents the unknown boy singer Asa Yoelson's transformation into the young adult star Al Jolson – equating commercial success with cultural and ethnic assimilation – through a montage of picture postcards home, and a later scene summarizes Jolson's career through the montage-simulating collage of the show biz scrapbook as its pages are flipped and newspapers from across the country re-create a tour itinerary. All of these examples, like the "road show" version of a Broadway musical or mass media technologies generally, extend the commercial range of a performer, show, or song beyond their limited local, "live" success on Broadway to address and profit from a mass audience. In the more jaded vaudeville tradition commonly reiterated in Hollywood musicals, "overnight success" is a myth: stars "pay their dues," "hone their skills," and "develop a following" through their years on the road.

One common range of terms to designate the achievement of fame by an entertainer revolves around the performer's *name* – not only are "given" names changed into "stage names" for commercial purposes, but the goal of the performer is "making a name for oneself," "seeing one's name in lights," or "getting one's name in the papers." Recalling the summary effect of the montage sequence, the musical can quickly show a performer's name travel from the bottom of a bill up to the position of headliner, or trace a beginning singer's recording up the charts of the national hit parade. Outlaw couple road films, inversely, are haunted by the public use of names. In classical examples like *You Only Live Once*, *Detour* (1945), *They Live By Night*, and *Gun Crazy*, the central couples are terrified of being "named," or identified by their real names. In both *They Live By Night* and *A Star is Born*, the couples are hesitant about using their names at small-town wedding ceremonies: Bowie and Keechie want to hide the infamy attached to their real names, while Norman Maine and Vicki Lester wish to obscure the fame advertised by their stage names. In *Detour*, Al and Vera rent their squalid "newlywed" apartment as "Mr and Mrs Charles Haskell" (after the car owner-corpse who links them) and, in *You Only Live Once*, Eddie and Jo, just married after his release from prison, are thrown out of their honeymoon room because they sign their real names – which the motel operator has seen along with a mug shot of Eddie in a popular detective magazine. If the alias is the outlaw's inverted version of the musical star's stage name, the mug shot is the publicity photo's anti-glamorous double.[7] In a well-known example from *You Only Live Once*, three newspaper headlines prepared in anticipation of Eddie's conviction, acquittal, or a hung jury are linked to three different photographs of Henry Fonda: if convicted, a glowering mug shot will accompany the story; if acquitted, a smiling publicity photo will be used (the hung-jury photo is of Fonda with a blank expression).

Once again, the interchangeable and transient "rest stops" in road films such as diners, filling stations, and motels offer anonymity to travelers in general, and especially to those on the run. Cynthia Kadohata's Japanese-American road novel *The Floating World* takes its title from this contradictory effect of life on the road: "We were traveling through what she [the narrator's grandmother] called ukiyo, the floating world. The floating world was the gas station attendants, restaurants, and jobs we depended on, the motel towns floating in the middle of fields and mountains. In old Japan, ukiyo meant the districts full of brothels, teahouses, and

Plates 4.1 and 4.2   Fame and infamy versus the couple's desire for anonymity in
They Live by Night and *A Star Is Born*.

public baths, but it also referred to change and the pleasures and loneliness change brings" (2–3). In Pagan Kennedy's road novel *Spinsters*, a character claims "'There's nothing lonelier than the highway – after a while, you don't even have yourself anymore'," causing the narrator to think: "I knew what she meant. With each motel, each diner, I felt more anonymous, wiped clean" (58). And the end of the road in Marc Behm's obsessive cross-country *roman noir The Eye of the Beholder* is announced by these terse lines: "No more motels. No more cars. No more money. No more airports" (149). All of these examples, as well as a folk song tradition running from Woody Guthrie through Hank Williams to Bruce Springsteen, emphasize the commercialized road's undifferentiated and lonely spaces, and might be contrasted to the giddy celebration of "the Functional Motel – clean, neat, safe nooks, ideal places for sleep, argument, reconciliation, insatiable illicit love" – that begins "outlaw couple" Humbert and Lolita's "extensive travels all over the States" in the second half of Nabokov's *Lolita* (145).[8]

But the outlaw couple's anonymity, their desire to be publicly unnamed, is commonly thwarted by the sort of publicity campaigns musical stars can't even buy. Wanted posters, mug shots, police radio descriptions, and especially newspaper reports or television reports in later films, all combine to threaten the outlaw couple with public recognition. Like scandal stories about movie stars, newspaper reports in *They Live By Night* or *Bonnie and Clyde* quickly escalate into descriptions of overlapping crimes in multiple states, building reputations for the criminals that they can't possibly support. Jo's sister in *You Only Live Once* complains that the couple "are being blamed for every crime committed in the country." In *Gun Crazy*, another typical montage sequence juxtaposes generic shots of police cars and roadblocks with newspaper headlines that come closer and closer to *naming* the outlaw couple: the sequence ends with their names being printed on a police Teletype, the crime film's version of the show business press release. Again, the outlaw couple's doom is secured by their achieving exactly what the ambitious musical star most desires: name recognition. (The fact that the female character in the film is named "Starr" perhaps insures her eventual public identification.) The inverted form of Hollywood's list of top box office stars is of course the FBI's "Most Wanted" list, a form of "publicity" that the Bureau in fact resisted until public demand and fascination with "celebrity criminals" forced the informal list to be codified.[9]

However, even early outlaw couple films betray an ambivalence about the ultimate desirability of complete anonymity: in *They Live By Night*, Chickamaw, Bowie's older partner-in-crime, resents the minimal attention the gang's early crimes receive from the local papers, and he's eventually incensed that "Bowie the kid" receives "top billing" (to use the obvious showbiz term) in later newspaper accounts. This is a concern motivated by brief lines in the film's source, Edward

Anderson's 1937 novel *Thieves Like Us*; "Just don't do anything to get your name in the paper. . . . That is the thing," Keechie reminds Bowie after he has told her "Why, Keechie, there's guys that will put on acts and do anything just to get their names big in the newspapers" (257–8). Anderson's "thieves" frequently read newspaper accounts of their exploits, and the novel ends with a newspaper report of the killing of Bowie and Keechie, although Keechie survives in both films adapted from the book. In later films, outlaw couples openly seek and generate publicity. In both *Bonnie and Clyde* and *Natural Born Killers* the criminals take the time to introduce themselves at crime scenes and leave victims "to tell their tale," and in *Kalifornia* the outlaw couple attach themselves to another couple producing a coffee-table photography book on American serial killers, who in effect serve as the outlaw couple's publicity agents. Bonnie and Clyde also produce self-staged "publicity" photographs, and delight in the publication of Bonnie's heroic ballad about the couple in a newspaper, a public memorial ("You made me somebody they're gonna remember," Clyde recognizes) which apparently cures Clyde's "private" problem of impotence.[10] In *Guncrazy*'s electronic update of this moment, the equally impotent Howard Hickok can perform sexually with Anita only after the outlaw couple watch their story on television and thereby become fully aware of their notoriety: "Hell, we're celebrities – people will be asking for our autographs." In *Love and a .45*, a kid *does* ask the outlaw hero for his autograph as they stand in front of a wall of television sets tuned to the fictional Crime Channel's 24-hour coverage of the couple's crime spree.

In self-reflexive modernist and even more allusion-saturated postmodernist outlaw couple films, characters explicitly affiliate themselves with popular celebrities like Humphrey Bogart (*A bout de souffle*), James Dean (*Badlands*), Jerry Lee Lewis (*Breathless*, 1983) and Elvis Presley (both *Wild at Heart* and *True Romance*) as role models or spiritual advisers. In *Boys on the Side* (1995), a slight variation on the form following *Thelma and Louise* and *The Living End*, since it expands the couple to a same-sex, part-queer trio, the characters knowingly link themselves to the already mythic American figures of Thelma and Louise, and Amy tells Watty in *Love and a .45* that "we're movie stars, desperados and outlaws on the road to freedom. I swear to God we remind me of Faye Dunaway and Warren Beatty. . . . Thank God we brought the Polaroid." *Natural Born Killers*, despite its wildly inventive style, finally seems an ineffective satire of the now commonplace idea that the modern media make celebrities out of society's monsters. Unlike the less indignant but possibly more revealing models of the form, it never clearly recognizes or admits to its own complicity in the culture of celebrity and the indulgence in violent spectacle that it wishes to attack.[11] *Cover Girl* (1944) provides a rather odd, but almost equally sadistic, musical comparison by consistently equating its female character's (Rita Hayworth) desire for fame with disloyalty to the male lead (Gene Kelly) and eventually, given the film's wartime context, with a disturbing lack of patriotic, democratic values; but like *Natural Born Killers*, and to some degree almost all outlaw couple films, *Cover Girl* can't ever figure out how to make fame, however achieved, completely unattractive or undesirable.

While the obvious point to make about more recent outlaw couple films is that they acknowledge and perhaps satirize a society in which fame and infamy are finally indistinguishable, and in which celebrity culture includes serial killers as well as pop stars – a culture in which even popular sports figures might be murder suspects or professional figure skaters could contract hit men – it might be more interesting to redraw attention to the tendency of recent outlaw couple films to veer back frequently into the explicit style of the musical. It's worth noting that many classic outlaw couple road films contain nightclub musical numbers featuring song lyrics that bluntly comment upon the situations of the couples: Claudia Drake performs "I Can't Believe That You're in Love With Me" in *Detour*, Frances Irvin sings "I'm Mad About You" in *Gun Crazy*, and Marie Bryant provides "Your Red Wagon" in *They Live By Night*. However, the contemporary road film seems especially suited to the now dominant mode of constructing and marketing film soundtracks through a selection of semi-autonomous, nostalgic hits or newly recorded pop songs. In films which contain no explicit musical sequences, perhaps a dozen or more musical "numbers" link as well as sonically replicate the episodic stop-and-start structure of the road trip. Michel Chion briefly refers to this musical structuration in his analysis of *Wild at Heart*, noting that David Lynch "uses a contrasting mosaic of themes from hard rock, classical music, old-fashioned jazz and crooner songs," and adding that "this characteristic musical treatment for a road movie was encouraged by the novel [by Barry Gifford], which was already full of allusions to the car radio and bar music which accompany the protagonists" (134). While I am wary of identifying them as the first soundtracks to be constructed and marketed in this way, the nondiegetic pop songs by Simon and Garfunkel on the hit soundtrack of *The Graduate* (1967) and especially the multiple-artist soundtrack of the influential road film *Easy Rider* (1969) seem to have encouraged this construction for later films; by *Nashville* (1975), a film's opening credits could explicitly introduce the entire narrative film to follow as a kind of pop music compilation album. Modeled perhaps on the autonomous selections picked up by radio reception while driving – the explicit model for the soundtracks of films like *Thieves Like Us* or *American Graffiti* (1973), which have no nondiegetic musical scores – or heard on the radios and jukeboxes in motels (*A Star is Born*) and diners (*Detour*, *Natural Born Killers*) along the way, this dominant technique now allows films that no one would typically identify as "musicals" to nevertheless commonly contain more *songs* than many "proper" musicals. For example, *Gold Diggers of 1933* contains five songs to *Thelma and Louise*'s seven. The Astaire–Rogers RKO films contain from four to seven songs each, whereas the soundtracks of most contemporary "non-musical" road films, such as *The Doom Generation* (1995) (twenty-six songs) or *Love and a .45* (twenty-one songs) are constructed out of dozens of whole or, more often, fragmented pop songs.[12]

American Graffiti's construction of its musical soundtrack out of the approximately forty "nostalgic" rock and roll songs heard on the characters' car radios suggests the historical origins of this practice while the film itself paved the way for future organizations of the soundtrack. Although early television's challenge to the motion picture studio system is well known, television's virtually complete appropriation of radio's successful narrative formats, including soap operas, Westerns, sitcoms, and crime dramas, also led to commercial radio's massive reorganization around pop music formats like Top 40 defined in 1955, the year of the teenage cultural milestones *The Blackboard Jungle* and *Rebel Without a Cause*, and, increasingly, the narrowing of most pop music consumption to the postwar youth audience. Whereas radio dramas and comedies encouraged audiences to gather around the home set in rapt attention to unfolding narratives, the restructuring of programming around short, autonomous "singles," played in repeating cycles, seemed immediately ideal for providing "soundtracks" for both quick car trips and long cross-country drives. More than any other previous musical style, rock and roll also incorporated the language and imagery of automobile travel into its lyric content, as the key work of Chuck Berry and The Beach Boys, among many others, easily demonstrates.

Defined, once again, by generation as much as stylistically by "youth music," the popular appeal of rock and roll, with its structural origins (an eight-bar refrain) in African-American blues, also played a significant role in the simultaneous decline of the traditional Hollywood musical, since that genre had largely relied upon and perpetuated the more melodic and less rhythm-based musical form (the thirty-two-bar refrain) defined early in the century by Tin Pan Alley and Broadway composers such as George and Ira Gershwin, Cole Porter, and Irving Berlin. Road films, which increase in number steadily after the rise of rock and roll, might therefore provide cultural compensation for the general absence of Hollywood film musicals in the same period. Musically saturated, and commercially successful at generating and promoting hit songs and soundtracks, road films may now replace narrativized musical spectacle for contemporary audiences that find the fantastic conventions of the traditional musical genre old-fashioned, undesirably unrealistic, or simply unfamiliar; road films thus participate directly in what Thomas Schatz has identified as "the shift from the traditional Hollywood musical to the 'music movie,' a dominant eighties form, and . . . an obvious precursor to MTV" ("The New Hollywood": 22)

Finally, the road films that center on outlaw couples preserve a romance plot, once the explicit base of Hollywood musicals, as the core structure of American popular cinema generally, whether dramatized through song and dance or theft and murder. In the middle of Gregg Araki's nihilistic "heterosexual movie" *The Doom Generation*, Jordan tells Amy, "I hope we die simultaneously, like in a fiery car wreck, or a nuclear bomb blast or something." When she responds, "You are so romantic," the line plays like the typical punk irony that characterizes the film, as if her response actually demonstrates how unromantic these contemporary amoral and affectless youth have become. But of course her response is actually more aware of the romantic tradition than she or even the film-maker may know, relocating the couple's desire for unifying oblivion, once available in the transcendent dance or song sequence, into the ever-present possibility of the road film's lethal car crash.

Recent outlaw couple films also frequently shift into fragmentary *performances* of song and dance, a distinction that often distinguishes "musicals" from otherwise musically saturated films. This genre-crossing occurs quite explicitly in *Pierrot le Fou* when Marianne sings "Jamais je ne t'ai dit que je t'aimerai toujours" ("I never told you that I would love you forever") and later when she and Ferdinand pause in their flight to sing "Ma ligne de chance" ("My luck-line") and dance for an extended scene, or more realistically in *Bonnie and Clyde* when Bonnie's fascination with watching Busby Berkeley's "We're in the Money" from *Gold Diggers of 1933* is continued into the next scene through her own "performance" of the song before a mirror. Godard may be the most influential source (perhaps before Dennis Potter) for such jarring genre-shifting, but outdoor dances in *Badlands* (briefly to Mickey and Sylvia's "Love is Strange" and more elaborately to Nat "King" Cole's "A Blossom Fell"), manic dance scenes along the highway and in a nightclub in *Wild at Heart*, an impromptu transformation of a house trailer into a disco in *Guncrazy*, or a pre-credits murder spree and romantic waltz (as well as Mallory's solitary-confinement dancing and singing of "Born Bad") in *Natural Born Killers* all reinforce the sense that a tell-tale musical heart beats underneath the killing floor of the American crime story.

Despite earlier origins, both rock and roll music and the outlaw couple film achieve their greatest cultural impact in their adolescent phases, in the decade following the Second World War; now that rock and roll music defines the film soundtrack for almost all popular cinema, the teenager's fundamental evaluative judgment of the commercial pop song applies just as well to the contemporary outlaw couple film: it has a good beat and you can dance to it. As a compelling model for representing the road to twentieth-century fame, the Hollywood musical may now only survive with blood on its hands; mutated and inverted into the outlaw couple road film, the musical nonetheless sustains its core ideological belief that the road to fame is best traveled with a partner, someone who can carry a tune, complete a step, take the wheel, or reload a gun when you get tired.

Acknowledgments

Thanks to Steve Cohan, Cynthia Erb, Ina Rae Hark, Pamela Robertson, and audiences at the 1995 Society for Cinema Studies Conference and at Wayne State University for helpful advice along the road. Thanks to Caryl Flinn for especially insightful travel tips.

Notes

1 The musical has of course been commonly understood as a genre, and most fully defined as such by Altman, but I shall not attempt to clearly define "outlaw couple" films as a genre in this essay. For my purposes, Krutnik's summary is sufficient: "these films are concerned with a heterosexual couple who find themselves branded as criminals, and who are consequently forced into an 'outsider' lifestyle, on the road" (213–14) (although the restriction to "heterosexual" couples now needs serious qualification.) Even the larger categories to which these films are commonly linked or subsumed – the road film (see Atkinson; Corrigan: 137–60; Kinder; and Laderman) and *film noir* (see Krutnik: 213–26; Silver and Brookover; and Silver and Ward: 419–20) – have proven especially resistant to stable definition as genres. Moreover, Corrigan's claim that "as a genre traditionally focused, almost exclusively, on men and the absence of women, the road movie self-consciously displays the crisis of gender" (143), or his reference to "the mostly token appearance of women" (148) in these films makes me question whether previous definitions of the road movie help us to understand more than three dozen "outlaw couple" films. Dargis's similar claim that "The road trip is always a male trip and the road movie makes literal the rite of passage that Oedipally-driven narratives demand of their male heroes" seems equally overstated, although she recognizes the consistent presence of women in the films, noting however that "If a woman hops a ride with a man, the journey, perfumed with a female sexuality, breeds danger and violence rather than pleasure" (16).

2 General studies of fame, celebrity culture, and "personality" that provide a backdrop for this essay include Braudy; Gamson: 15–39; James; Schickel; and Susman. More specific studies of the Hollywood star system and individual stars are also relevant but now far too numerous to mention here.

3 Bellour's (in)famously sweeping claim that "the creation of the couple . . . organizes, indeed constitutes, the classical Hollywood cinema as a whole" (88) is most fully developed and historically grounded by Wexman, in addition to Altman. Dyer's essay on heterosexuality and dance is also illuminating in this regard.

4 I justify the inclusion of Godard's *A bout de souffle* and *Pierrot le fou* in this study of "American" films and culture because of their obvious dialogue with the American tradition; Godard's "outlaw couple" films are clearly influenced by, and of course themselves influence, other films in my discussion. A larger segment of Godard's quotation is worth citing here: "I thought about *You Only Live Once*; and instead of the *Lolita* or *La Chienne* kind of couple, I wanted to tell the story of the last romantic couple, the last descendants of *La Nouvelle Heloise*, *Werther* and *Hermann and Dorothea*" (5).

5 On the "celebrity" of gangsters like Al Capone and John Dillinger and their symbolic intersections with the early careers of movie stars like James Cagney and Edward G.

Robinson, see Ruth; and the superficial analysis in Prassel: 264–85. By emphasizing the "resolutely urban" (2) character of the gangster in the period of his study, Ruth points only toward the "outlaw's return to the countryside" (146) – or "the road" – around 1934, after "the media coronation of J. Edgar Hoover and his G-Men as the nation's crime busters" (145). Despite, therefore, an illuminating chapter on gangsters and their "molls," Ruth does not discuss outlaw couples such as Bonnie and Clyde. On Bonnie and Clyde see Treherne; Milner; and Prassel: 297–303. Keyssar, discussing *Thieves Like Us*, makes another point about the impact of the 1930s: "Since its colonial origins, physical mobility, across the land and toward new frontiers, has been uniquely conjoined in American culture with economic "upward mobility. . . . The mobility of the thirties was of a different order, a fleeing from as much or more than an adventure toward a particular way of life, an attempt to sustain the illusion of economic mobility through the literal movement so aptly emblematized by automobiles and the proliferation of highways to accommodate these machines" (114). On highways and cinema, see the brilliant analysis by Dimendberg.

6 According to Clover, "The venue, at least, of the 'Singin' in the Rain' sequence and the figure of the policeman conjure up the 'school of the street' in which black tappers learned their trade in the shadow of the law. . . . If we in the nineties do not know the racial resonances of the trope of the street-dance-interrupted-by-policeman, Kelly and his colleagues surely did" (737–78). This dance-stopping cop has hardly gone unnoticed by the film's critics: in Peter Wollen's description of the same moment, "the cop comes into frame and Kelly stops dead, freezes, and then turns and steps back sheepishly on to the sidewalk. He has not done anything really wrong, but the cop acts as a censor who has caught him in the act, bringing his infantile behavior to an abrupt halt" (27). Jim Collins notes that "the suspicious glance of the policeman who enters at the end of the scene suggests how close the convention [of the musical] comes to a clinical violation of the law and how close Kelly may truly be to Alex in *A Clockwork Orange* (1971)" (141). The police presence in *Gold Diggers of 1933* also reinforces Pamela Robertson's reading of the film, which emphasizes the gold digger's links to prostitution; the musical performances of the film's working-class female characters continually imply other questionable professional activities (57–84).

7 On early photography and the development of criminology, see: Tagg; Lalvani; Pultz; and Thomas. On the mug shot as a form of celebrity portrait, recall Marcel Duchamp's 1923 photo-collage self-portrait "Wanted, $2,000 Reward," and Andy Warhol's 1964 silkscreen series "Thirteen Most Wanted Men," first installed at the New York State Pavilion, New York World's Fair, a series which combined the concerns of his earlier celebrity images (of Troy Donahue, Elvis Presley, Warren Beatty, Natalie Wood, Elizabeth Taylor, Jackie Kennedy, and Marilyn Monroe, among others, from 1962 to 1964), and his death and disaster series (1962–4), all illustrated in McShine. The "novelty" collections which followed the arrests, and tie-ins like mug-shot-photo T-shirts, of O. J. Simpson and Hugh Grant provide more recent examples; see Seminara; and *Famous Mugs*.

8 According to Richard Corliss, Nabokov's *Lolita* is "a road movie in embryo; it is as curious about motel architecture and diner menus as it is about the mismatched man and girl who have sex in those beds and get sick on that food . . . Most of the book is set in 1947, the year of *Out of the Past*, the year after *Detour*, the year before *They Live By Night*, two years before *Gun Crazy*. Moviegoers, if not readers, were used to the picture of two people, in the front seat of a car, staring ahead, nothing to say, anticipating a crash" (77).

9 According to Richard Gid Powers, the Chicago Crime Commission's "most famous contribution to law enforcement lore was the Public Enemies List, begun in April, 1923, with Al Capone holding top billing" (23). A sequence in the 1935 Warner Bros. film *G-Men* "has the movie's FBI director set up a public enemies list to dramatize his attack on gangsters. . . . Throughout the thirties the public believed that there was a public enemies list, although [Attorney General Homer] Cummings and [FBI director J. Edgar] Hoover, sensitive to charges that they were ignoring the vast majority of criminals to concentrate on a few celebrities, steadfastly denied that there was a scoreboard. All '10,000 Public Enemies,' they insisted, were being chased just as hard as Dillinger. The public enemies list does seem to have been a creation of Justice Department reporters, who borrowed the idea from the Chicago Crime Commission's famous list, because not until the fifties did the bureau begin its own 'Most Wanted Fugitive Program.' By showing the FBI director himself with the public enemies list, the film made the FBI conform, not to reality, but to the image created by the extravagant stories of the era's flamboyant crime reporters" (59–60). Hoover's most explicit attempt to challenge the celebrity status of criminals was his 1938 book *Persons in Hiding* (written in fact by crime reporter Courtney Ryley Cooper); a series of four films based on the summarized cases in the book was produced in 1939–40 by Paramount (following MGM's *Crime Does Not Pay* series from 1935 to 1947), although the first film, also entitled *Persons in Hiding*, was based on Bonnie and Clyde, who are not treated in the book. "Nevertheless," according to Carlos Clarens, "this little B-film . . . could not quite suppress the romantic aspect of an outlaw couple meeting by the roadside or hiding out in shabby rented rooms" (135).

10 The complete version of Bonnie Parker's "The Story of Bonnie and Clyde" is reprinted in Treherne: 192–4; Milner: 136–8; and Prassel: 342–4. Both of these studies briefly discuss the film versions of the story, reinforcing the common notion that Barrow and Parker are the historical models for most cinematic outlaw couples, at least until Charles Starkweather and Caril Ann Fugate's 1958 crime spree. On the 1967 film, which generated a great deal of commentary, see: Cawelti; Clarens: 259–69; Wake and Hayden (which includes the screenplay by David Newman and Robert Benton); and Wood: 72–91. On Starkweather and Fugate, and their cinematic influence, see Sargeant, who provides a brief and sloppy, but perhaps appropriately lurid account that discusses *Badlands*, *Wild at Heart*, *True Romance*, *Kalifornia*, and *Natural Born Killers*, and briefly identifies *Murder in the Heartland* (Robert Markowitz, 1993, made for television), *The Sadists* (a.k.a. *Profile of Terror*) (James Landis, 1963), and *Fingered* (Richard Kern, 1986) as indebted to the case, while noting that films like *Thelma and Louise* and *Heathers* "make oblique references to the Starkweather and Fugate case" without engaging in "the love-on-the-run thematic" (143–4).

11 In Tarantino's original screenplay for *Natural Born Killers*, the critique of the media celebration of criminals is explicit, but allusions to Westerns are more frequent than references to the musical (Mickey's final line, delivered in a John Wayne voice quoting *Rio Bravo*, is "Let's make a little music, Colorada": 119); however, in the script Mallory does dance (alone) and, when isolated from Mickey in the first half of the film, will communicate only by singing numerous pop songs like "He's a Rebel," "Leader of the Pack," and "I Only Want to Be With You"; in Stone's film this musical element is largely displaced onto the dense and highly fragmented soundtrack designed by Trent Reznor of Nine Inch Nails. Other recent parodies of the celebrity of criminals focus almost exclusively on the female killer/star who simply uses or

deceives male partners: see *Serial Mom* (John Waters, 1994) and *To Die For* (Gus Van Sant, 1995), based on Joyce Maynard' s novel.

12   The construction of so many contemporary soundtracks out of pre-existing "nostalgia" hits, new pop songs, or, more often, a mix of old and new pop songs, or new remakes of older songs, hasn't been adequately explored by scholars of film sound and music (or of the recent film industry, since the links created by entertainment conglomerates are often at the heart of this construction), especially given the ubiquity of the practice; see, however, the useful essays and especially many of the artists' statements in Romney and Wootton.

Works Cited

Altman, Rick. *The American Film Musical*. Bloomington: Indiana University Press, 1987.

Anderson, Edward. *Thieves Like Us* (1937). Rpt Norman: University of Oklahoma Press, 1993.

Atkinson, Michael. "Crossing the Frontiers." *Sight and Sound* 4.1 (January 1994): 14–17.

Behm, Marc. *The Eye of the Beholder* (1980). Rpt in *3 Novels*. London: Zomba Books, 1983.

Bellour, Raymond. "Alternation, Segmentation, Hypnosis: Interview with Raymond Bellour." Conducted by Janet Bergstrom. *Feminism and Film Theory*, ed. Constance Penley. New York: Routledge, 1988. 186–95.

Braudy, Leo. *The Frenzy of Renown: Fame and Its History*. New York: Oxford University Press, 1986.

Cawelti, John G., ed. *Focus on Bonnie and Clyde*. Englewood Cliffs, NJ: Prentice-Hall, 1973.

Chion, Michel. *David Lynch*, trans. Robert Julian. London: BFI, 1995.

Clarens, Carlos. *Crime Movies: From Griffith to The Godfather and Beyond*. New York: Norton, 1980.

Clover, Carol J. "Dancin' in the Rain." *Critical Inquiry* 21 (Summer 1995): 722–47.

Collins, Jim. "Toward Defining a Matrix of the Musical Comedy: The Place of the Spectator Within the Textual Mechanisms." *Genre: The Musical*, ed. Rick Altman. London: Routledge/BFI, 1981. 134–46.

Corliss, Richard. *Lolita*. London: BFI, 1994.

Corrigan, Timothy. *A Cinema Without Walls: Movies and Culture after Vietnam*. New Brunswick, NJ: Rutgers University Press, 1991.

Dargis, Manohla. "Roads to Freedom." *Sight and Sound* 1:3 (July 1991): 15–18.

Dimendberg, Edward. "The Will to Motorization: Cinema, Highways, and Modernity." *October* 73 (Summer 1995): 91–137.

Dyer, Richard. "'I Seem to Find the Happiness I Seek': Heterosexuality and Dance in the Musical." *Dance, Gender and Culture*, ed. Helen Thomas. New York: St Martin's, 1993. 49–65.

Famous Mugs: Arresting Photos and Felonious Facts for Hundreds of Stars Behind Bars. New York: Cader Books, 1996.

Gamson, Joshua. *Claims to Fame: Celebrity in Contemporary America*. Berkeley: University of California Press, 1994.

Godard, Jean-Luc. *Pierrot le Fou*, trans. Peter Whitehead. New York: Frederick Ungar Publishing, 1984 (transcription of 1965 film, including "Let's Talk About *Pierrot*: Interview with Jean-Luc Godard").

Greene, Graham. *Graham Greene on Film: Collected Film Criticism 1935–1940*, ed. John

Russell Taylor. New York: Simon & Schuster, 1972.

Hoover, J. Edgar. *Persons in Hiding*. Boston: Little, Brown & Co., 1938.

James, Clive. *Fame in the 20th Century*. New York: Random House, 1993.

Johnson, Bayard. *Damned Right*. Boulder: Fiction Collective Two, 1994.

Kadohata, Cynthia. *The Floating World*, New York: Ballantine, 1989.

Kennedy, Pagan. *Spinsters*. New York: High Risk Books/Serpent's Tail, 1995.

Keyssar, Helene. *Robert Altman's America*. New York: Oxford University Press, 1991.

Kinder, Marsha. "The Return of the Outlaw Couple." *Film Quarterly* 27.4 (Summer 1974): 2–10.

Kitses, Jim. *Gun Crazy*. London: BFI, 1996.

Krutnik, Frank. *In a Lonely Street: Film Noir, Genre, Masculinity*. New York: Routledge, 1991.

Laderman, David. "What a Trip: The Road Film and American Culture." *Journal of Film and Video* 48.1–2 (Spring–Summer 1996): 41–57.

Lalvani, Suren. *Photography, Vision, and the Production of Modern Bodies*. Albany: State University of New York Press, 1996.

Lynd, Robert S. and Lynd, Helen Merrell. *Middletown: A Study in American Culture*. New York: Harcourt Brace Jovanovich, 1929.

Mast, Gerald. *Can't Help Singin': The American Musical on Stage and Screen*. Woodstock: Overlook Press, 1987.

Maynard, Joyce. *To Die For*. New York: Dutton, 1992.

McShine, Kynaston, ed. *Andy Warhol: A Retrospective*. New York and Boston: The Museum of Modern Art and Bullfinch Press/Little, Brown & Co., 1989.

Milner, E. R. *The Lives and Times of Bonnie and Clyde*. Carbondale: Southern Illinois University Press, 1996.

Mottram, Eric. "'That Dark Instrument': the American Automobile," and "Blood on the Nash Ambassador: Cars in American Films," in *Blood on the Nash Ambassador: Investigations in American Culture*. London: Hutchinson, 1983. 39–89.

Nabokov, Vladimir. *The Annotated Lolita*. Revised and updated edition. Edited, with preface, introduction, and notes by Alfred Appel, Jr. New York: Vintage Books, 1995 (*Lolita* originally published 1955).

Powers, Richard Gid. *G-Men: Hoover's FBI in American Popular Culture*. Carbondale: Southern Illinois University Press, 1983.

Prassel, Frank Richard. *The Great American Outlaw: A Legacy of Fact and Fiction*. Norman: University of Oklahoma Press, 1993.

Pultz, John. *The Body and the Lens: Photography 1839 to the Present*. New York: Harry N. Abrams, 1995.

Robertson, Pamela. *Guilty Pleasures: Feminist Camp from Mae West to Madonna*. Durham, NC: Duke University Press, 1996.

Romney, Jonathan and Wootton, Adrian, eds. *Celluloid Jukebox: Popular Music and the Movies Since the 50s*. London: BFI, 1995.

Ruth, David E. *Inventing the Public Enemy: The Gangster in American Culture, 1918–1934*. Chicago: University of Chicago Press, 1996.

Sargeant, Jack. *Born Bad*. London: Creation Books, 1996.

Schatz, Thomas. *Hollywood Genres: Formulas, Filmmaking and the Studio System*. Philadelphia: Temple University Press, 1981.

—— "The New Hollywood." *Film Theory Goes to the Movies*, ed. Jim Collins, Hilary Radner, and Ava Preacher Collins. New York: Routledge, 1993. 8–36.

Schickel, Richard. *Intimate Strangers: The Culture of Celebrity*. New York: Fromm International, 1985.

Seminara, George, compiler. *Mug Shots: Celebrities Under Arrest*. New York: St Martin's Griffin, 1996.

Silver, Alain and Linda Brookover. "What is This Thing Called *Noir?*" *Film Noir Reader*, ed. Alain Silver and James Ursini. New York: Limelight, 1996. 261–73.

Silver, Alain and Ward, Elizabeth, eds. *Film Noir: An Encyclopedic Reference to the American Style*. 3rd ed. Woodstock: Overlook Press, 1992.

Susman, Warren I. "'Personality' and the Making of Twentieth-Century Culture." *Culture as History: The Transformation of American Society in the Twentieth Century*. New York: Pantheon, 1984. 271–85.

Tagg, John. *The Burden of Representation: Essays on Photographies and Histories*. Amherst: University of Massachusetts Press, 1988.

Tarantino, Quentin. *Natural Born Killers*. London: Faber & Faber, 1995.

Thomas, Ronald R. "Making Darkness Visible: Capturing the Criminal and Observing the Law in Victorian Photography and Detective Fiction." *Victorian Literature and the Victorian Visual Imagination*, ed. Carol T. Christ and John O. Jordan. Berkeley: University of California Press, 1995. 134–68.

Treherne, John. *The Strange History of Bonnie and Clyde*. New York: Stein & Day, 1984.

Wake, Sandra and Nicola Hayden, eds. *Bonnie & Clyde*. New York: Frederick Ungar Publishing, 1972 (includes the screenplay by David Newman and Robert Benton).

Wexman, Virginia Wright. *Creating the Couple: Love, Marriage, and Hollywood Performance*. Princeton: Princeton University Press, 1993.

Wollen, Peter. *Singin' in the Rain*. London: BFI, 1992.

Wood, Robin. *Arthur Penn*. New York: Praeger, 1969.

Wright, Stephen. *Going Native*. New York: Delta, 1994.

Part II

AMERICAN ROADS

5

ALMOST LIKE BEING AT HOME
Showbiz culture and Hollywood road trips in the 1940s and 1950s

Steven Cohan

Beginning with the Second World War years of the 1940s and extending through the 1950s, "home" stood for the utopian myth of a coherent, homogeneous popular culture. Road films made in these two decades thus project a different set of values for the road than one finds during the Great Depression or, more dramatically, after *Easy Rider* (1969). Films from this era equate "America" with popular entertainment, the nation's traveling showbiz culture that brought "home" to the road, as best exemplified by the USO shows during the war.

A comment made by John Hersey while reporting on a military campaign for *Life* in 1942 is emblematic of the value that "home" had for the wartime imagination of soldiers who were, in effect, forcibly put on the road. "Perhaps this sounds selfish," Hersey remarks. "It certainly sounds less dynamic than the Axis slogans. But home seems to most marines a pretty good thing to be fighting for. Home is where the good things are – the generosity, the good pay, the comforts, the democracy, the pie" (60). Variations of this exaggerated appreciation of "home" were inserted into many American films made during the war years.[1] *Since You Went Away* (1944), for instance, begins by declaring in a title card: "This is the story of the Unconquerable Fortress: the American Home." Of course, today that movie cliché is significant for its irony. While "home" may have been where all the good things were, the war itself – fought to preserve "home" in whatever material incarnation a soldier fondly remembered it – actually caused a radical disruption of US society. The extensive relocation of American men and women both domestically and abroad during the 1940s because of the war helped to efface what had previously been strong regional identities and values regarding family life and gender roles. Furthermore, it began the process of broadening the national culture toward that homogeneous image of "America" taken for granted during the 1950s and splintered in the late 1960s.

In the 1940s, the road readily served the movies as a symbolic route for tracing a unified national identity in the face of the regional, racial, ethnic, and class differences that the war made apparent, and, even more pointedly, for showing how popular culture gave the United States its coherence as "America," everyone's "home." For while representing what GIs had left behind, as Hersey points out, "home" also reminded them that, along with all the other hardships and sacrifices of wartime, they were geographically excluded from the nation's popular culture – excluded, this is to say, from "the hundreds and the thousands of little and big things, tragic, funny, profound, silly, vital, unimportant, American things" that had occurred throughout the duration of the war, "those years from the spring of '42 to the summer of '45," Paul Gallico observed, addressing the returning soldier, "while you were gone." Writing for a collection of essays summarizing those missing years for veterans, Gallico reviews "things you would have talked about, shuddered or marveled at, laughed about, repeated, or discussed with your friends": not just the obvious topics like catastrophes, scandals, and murders, but also "new customs, fads and fashions, popular songs, books, plays, movies, radio shows and the people who made them" (28). Other essays in the volume fill in these blanks, focusing separate chapters on newspapers, broadcasting, advertising, publishing, the stage, comic strips, and film to give popular culture parity with the book's accounts of the nation's governance and social upheaval during the war years.

The "little and big things" characterizing the Americannness of the home front in the GI's absence served to project a utopian representation of national unity that effaced the various divisions of US society. As a central element in this patriotic ideology of "home," popular entertainment was especially meaningful in displacing the war as the nation's common ground. Movies were imported for exhibition in makeshift cinemas erected at army bases, often months before their theatrical release in the states, and each unit had its own local radio station, transmitting shows like *Mail Call*, *Command Performance*, and *Jubilee* from V-discs – 106 radio programs were recorded on long-playing records and shipped abroad each week – that were explicitly represented as bringing "a touch of home" to American soldiers. The intent of these programs, as Lena Horne told her listeners on *Jubilee* (an all-African-American program), was to "send you week after week the kind of entertainment that you used to look for back home" (Mugge). In a documentary about entertainment in the war years, Dorothy Lamour remembers that, when soldiers on leave visited the Hollywood Canteen, the stars "made them feel at home." She says the same about the armed forces radio shows: "it was almost like they were home," she recalls in one interview (Mugge); "it was like someone from home entertaining them," she concludes in another ("Bob").

Army camps could even imitate Hollywood barnyard musicals by putting on a show for themselves. The Special Services Branch supplied so-called "blueprint specials," handbooks instructing soldiers how "to reproduce within the military a version of the civilian theatre world" (Bérubé: 69). The most famous – because most professionalized – of such military revues was *This is the Army* with songs by Irving Berlin. It played four months on Broadway in 1942 before going on the road in the US, Europe, North Africa, the Pacific and, ultimately, Burbank, where Warners turned it into a movie in 1943 (69–70). That the quintessential military road show *This is the Army* concluded its international tour on a studio backlot was in perfect accord with the movies' project of defining home through show business. Flag-waving musicals like Paramount's *Star Spangled Rhythm* (1942), Warners' *Thank Your Lucky Stars* (1943), MGM's *Thousands Cheer* (1943), and Universal's *Follow the Boys* (1944) offer a thin narrative excuse for putting on what is virtually an all-star revue for a diegetic audience of GIs. As Gerald Mast points out about *Follow the Boys*, the show within that film, as in other wartime musicals like it, mixes styles of entertainment and integrates its cast of performers (though segregating their appearances) in order "[to assure] us that we *are* all alike, different but the same, one nation, one people of peoples, divisible but indivisible, in contrast to enemies perceived as racial and racist" (227). Fixing show culture (the revue) and the road (the GIs in the diegetic audience) to home (Holly-wood as the locus for authenticating the distinct American idiom of US popular entertainment), these musicals reproduce the ameliorating logic of the USO.

Formed in 1941 after the US had initiated a peace-time draft, the USO was "established to become the G.I.'s 'Home Away From Home" ("Proud"), whether in local communities or, increasingly throughout the war, in touring shows at the front. As promotional literature from 1944 depicted it, "The story of USO camp shows belongs to the American people, for it was their contribution that made it possible. It is an important part in the life of your sons, your brothers, your husbands, your sweethearts. When they marched off to war it helped them to take with them something of home that wasn't GI." More to the point, the USO amounted to "the biggest enterprise American show business has ever tackled. The audience was millions of American fighting men, the theatre's location: the world, the producer: USO camp shows" ("Our Story"). Through its various activi-ties the USO brought show business to the theaters of war and addressed soldiers as consumers of the popular culture that represented their absence from America and "home," thereby making Americanness synonymous with show business. Speaking to the Hollywood Victory Committee at the start of the war, George Raft established the comparison right away: "Now it's going to be up to us to send to the men here and abroad real, living entertainment, the songs, the dances, and the laughs they had back home" (Mugge). One of the first activities of the committee in its support of the USO was the formation of the Victory Caravan in 1942, fifty major Hollywood stars in a cross-country railroad tour selling war bonds.

Most of all, though, it was the touring acts that, in taking home on the road, equated the nation with showbiz. USO camp shows were "designed in their export to remind soldiers of home" (Tynes), nurturing in troops a sense of patriotic identification with America through popular entertainment. As *Look* magazine put it at the time: "For the little time the show lasts, the men are taken straight to the familiar Main Street that is the goal of every fighting American far away from home" (*Movie Lot*: 82). Reflecting on the war, Maxene Andrews remembers about the tours and radio broadcasts: "The entertainers brought home to the boys. Their home" (Mugge). In their appreciative letters to entertainers, GIs apparently felt the same way. "It really brought to us, home," one solider wrote of Bob Hope's show, "right there in the middle of a damn big ocean." Another wrote after watching Hope's show in Algiers: "for a few seconds, I was back home" ("Letters"). In 1944 Hope published (with Carroll Carroll's assistance) an account of his European tour and entitled it *I Never Left Home*, explaining: "everywhere I went, I met people from places I knew or had played vaudeville or had lived. And I kept running into people I knew who were now in uniform. So it was like I never left home" (Marx: 189).

Like the war, road movies, of course, are all about men and women leaving home – but then so is show business, particularly as represented by the many backstage musicals that celebrate the formation of a community of performers while on the road, stress the importance of self-sacrifice for the good of the show, and follow the route to success and fame in Hollywood or on Broadway. Musicals have discernible road elements – so that, as Corey Creekmur argues elsewhere in this book, they can usefully be understood as inversions of the outlaw-couple road movie – but not many actually make the road itself central to their narratives. Rather, they invoke the road in a montage of showbiz labor (as in backstage musicals) or as a means of transportation to another setting (as when Jane Powell travels to Brazil in *Luxury Liner*, 1948, and *Nancy Goes to Rio*, 1950). Calling attention to the way that road films of the 1940s and 1950s invariably travel across the US either to or from Hollywood, this essay examines how the road and show business interact differently in films produced during these two decades to represent America as a utopian space in which the nation's citizens – comprising what Bennet Schaber terms, in another of this volume's essays, "the people" – feel "at home" on the road by discovering, through their travels, the popular culture they all share. Simply put, whereas the 1940s road film associates the road with the production of popular entertainment to ensure its utopian ethos, the 1950s road film achieves the same end by associating the road *and* entertainment with consumption. The deployment of show business as a trope of national unity in this era's road movies thus traces an important shift in cultural value for "home" and "showbiz" as well as for the road itself.

Star Treks: Hope and Crosby's Road Show

Road movies of the 1940s cite show business to represent how America cohered through the popular culture which USO acts, armed forces radio, and amateur revues exemplified for troops who, serving in Europe, the Pacific, and North Africa, were far away from home. Centered in Hollywood's various entertainment industries (the movies, broadcasting, records, vaudeville), show business mediated the distance between being "over here" and "over there." This premise informs the enormously successful Hope and Crosby *Road to* series, which in many respects defines the utopian value system of the studio-era road movie although, unlike most American road films made before or afterwards, none of the Hope and Crosby jaunts traverses the continental United States, and none follows the narrative syntax of the classic road movie form. Nevertheless, if the *Road to* series did not actually give a name to that discernible type of Hollywood product called "a road picture," it surely popularized the label.

Bob Hope's mobility as an entertainer during the 1940s exemplifies the wartime correspondence of showbiz and the road. At the same time that he was a major movie star for Paramount, he toured extensively in vaudeville, appearing on stage shows with his films, and he had his own weekly radio program on NBC. He often did his radio show on the road, first leaving the studio in Hollywood to perform in California service bases in 1941. He MC'd the Victory Caravan, and then began doing his USO tours with Frances Langford and Jerry Colonna, regulars on his radio show at that point, throughout the US in 1942, Europe in 1943, and, with dancer Patty Clark added to the cast, the Pacific in 1944. After the war he kept on broadcasting his popular weekly show from army camps even though "his radio audience was becoming tired of service jokes" (Marx: 205), critics complained that "playing Army camps had made him lazy about trying anything new" (211), and his original sponsor, Pepsodent, dropped his contract because it was too expensive to continue broadcasting outside of the studio.

In the six *Road to* films produced between 1940 and 1953, Hope's partnership with Bing Crosby brings the vaudeville style of his radio show, with its homey connotations of popular American entertainment, to colonial outposts (Singapore, Zanzibar, Morocco, Rio, the Klondike in the "utopian" days of the Gold Rush, Bali) just as his USO shows did during the Second World War.[2] Hope and Crosby, in fact, first performed together on a vaudeville stage – New York's Capitol theater – in 1932. Unlike other comedy teams, whenever they appeared together on radio and in army camp shows as well as in Paramount's all-star musicals or the *Road to* series, Hope and Crosby establish their camaraderie before an audience through a repartee more typical of live performance than film. The self-referentiality of their patter – from affectionate to competitive to outright put-downs – emphasizes their star personae as famous entertainers over any diegetic characterizations. Even the gags built on Crosby's frequent guest appearances in Hope's solo films during this period, far from testifying to their off-screen closeness (one star doing a favor for the other), remind audiences of the *Road to* pictures and, more importantly, acknowledge that the series motivates their traveling and teamwork alike in show business.[3] Remembering his European tour in a recent television special, Hope goes so far as to mention that his life as a USO performer imitated his road pictures with Crosby. After touring in Britain, Hope remarks, he then literally went on the road to Morocco, moving next to North Africa for his first USO performances in a combat zone ("Bob").

Road to Morocco is the only one of the series to acknowledge even remotely its setting in contemporary world events. This film opens with a ship exploding at sea (a result, it turns out, of Hope lighting a cigarette near the space where ammo is stored) and then cuts to various radio news commentators – two in Asia (supposedly of Chinese and Japanese origin), one in the USSR, one in the UK – speculating on its likely cause. However, *Road to Morocco* soon leaves a world at war behind once Hope and Crosby travel to an exotic land whose mise-en-scène evokes the Orientalized atmospheric movie palaces of the 1920s more than anything else. As *Morocco* typifies, the entire series seems a throwback to the colonial narratives of Kipling and Conrad as filtered through jingoistic American eyes. (The first film, *Road to Singapore*, in fact, resulted from Paramount's attempt to salvage such a script entitled "Road to Mandalay" earmarked for Fred MacMurray and Jack Oakie.) One of the series' writers, Don Hartman, explained: "You take a piece of used chewing gum and flip it at a map. Wherever it sticks you can lay a *Road* picture, so long as the people there are jokers who cook and eat strangers. If they're nasty and menacing, it'll be a good *Road* picture. The key to the thing is menace offsetting the humor" (Hope: 139). With Hope and Crosby playing cocky Westerners encountering "primitive" native cultures, it appears to follow that one location can readily replace another in the series' formula, proving that "you don't have to know the language," as Crosby and the Andrews Sisters sing in *Road to Rio*, or appreciate cultural difference. Show business, these films assume, is the universal language. When in Rio, Hope and Crosby get a job in a nightclub by claiming they have an American band; since they don't have other musicians, they hire local talent, the three Wiere Brothers, who speak no English. So Hope and Crosby teach each one a different Yankee expression – "hep talk," they call it – connoting the idiom of American popular culture: "You're telling me," "You're in the grove, Jackson," "This is murder."

What establishes the Americanness of these two famous road men, then, is not the "otherness" of the foreign culture they encounter while on the road, since the films render their exotic locales and adventure plots cartoonish enough to make the condescending stereotypes ideologically transparent, but the stars' identification with show business, which uses the road trip to display the global hegemony of US entertainment. The *Road to* pictures thus repeatedly disrupt their jingoistic parodies of imperial adventure stories with show business "shtick" that draws its humor from the recognizable personae of Hope, Crosby, and their co-star Dorothy Lamour. "If she looks like Lamour, she can sing like Lamour," Crosby explains to Hope in *Rio*, when featuring her character, whose resemblance to Lamour has not been previously noted, as the singer of the bogus American band. This type of extradiegetic awareness characterizes the entire series, underscoring each film's coherence as a show in contrast to its exaggerated incoherence as a narrative. The most obvious example occurs as the signature "patty-cake" routine gets used from film to film within the series, since the gag it provokes, by failing to work in the expected way set up in the first film, *Road to Singapore*, is the realization that the villains have already learned about it from the movies. By the time Hope and Crosby take their road to Rio, Gale Sondergaard's two henchmen fall for the routine precisely because they haven't been paying close enough attention: "That's what they get for not seeing our pictures," Hope cracks. Indeed, at one point in *Road to Rio*, Crosby and Lamour watch a ballroom dance number from a film within the film, and he tells her to look closely at two of the musicians performing in the background, none other than Hope and Crosby themselves. Crosby explains: "We stopped off in Hollywood for a few days and stole a couple of dollars doing extra work."

Road to Utopia (produced before Hope began his Pacific USO tour in 1944 but not released until 1946 because of Paramount's backlog) even begins with a pre-title segment in which well-known humorist and sometimes-actor Robert Benchley directly addresses the audience to foreground the film's status as an object of popular entertainment:

> For those of you who don't go to the movies, let me introduce myself. I'm Robert Benchley. (*Pause.*) No matter. For one reason or another the motion picture you are about to see is not very clear in many spots. As a matter of fact, it was made to demonstrate how not to make a motion picture and at the same time win an Academy Award. Now some one in what is known as the front office has thought that an occasional word from me might help to clarify the plot and other vague portions of the film. Personally, I doubt it. Shall we go?

After inviting the spectator to join in the road trip, as it were ("Shall we go?"), Bentley repeatedly interrupts the narrative, his head appearing in a corner of the screen to provide a running commentary about the fictiveness of the diegesis. He explains the use of a flashback, for instance, points out the insertion of a crowd scene in post-production, remarks that the villains want only to see Dorothy

Lamour in a sarong, and so on. Finally, as the villains chase Hope and Crosby through the snow, Benchley's visage pops up and he remarks: "Exciting, isn't it?" Then he ponders the situation, and his language shifts attention to the two stars' personae once he realizes: "If Hope and Crosby are caught, they'll be killed, they won't be able to tell any more of those jokes. . . . Mush!" he shouts, to encourage the villains' dog sled.

Benchley's extradiegetic narration sets the tone for the film's continuing allusions to showbiz as its primary referential field. *Road to Utopia* opens in the present day, with Hope and Lamour an old-married couple; when Crosby appears on the scene, the comic faces the camera and mutters: "And I thought this was going to be an A picture." At one point in the extended flashback to the 1910 Gold Rush narrative, as Hope and Crosby stoke the furnace of a ship, a magician walks by, prompting Crosby to ask: "Are you in this picture?" "No," the interloper replies, "I'm taking a shortcut to Stage Ten." When Hope and Crosby fail to win an amateur night contest aboard the ship, the former pouts (anachronistically, of course), "Next time I'll bring Sinatra." When he gets to kiss Lamour relatively early in the plot, Hope turns to the audience and says, "As far as I'm concerned this picture is over now." At another point. Hope hears an orchestra playing as Lamour sings to him out of doors. As the couple walks away, he turns around and complains, "Aw, c'mon folks, quit following us, will you?" Similar recognition that

Plate 5.1 Bing Crosby and Bob Hope admire the Alaskan scenery in *Road to Utopia*, and the mountain they see reminds Hope of his "bread and butter," the Paramount logo.

the stars are acting in a film occurs when Hope curses their bad luck, and his voice is blanked out on the soundtrack. "I told you they wouldn't let you say that," Crosby reminds him. Right before they begin their "buddy" number ("Put It There, Pal"), Crosby announces, "Well, here we are, off on another road." Hope pushes the self-referentiality of this observation even further, exclaiming: "And look at that mountain!" When his partner does not react, Hope continues: "It may be a mountain to you, but it's bread and butter to me," and the Paramount logo appears over the snow-capped peak.

As traditionally used in a musical, Jane Feuer explains, direct address in the numbers violates the realistic codes of classical Hollywood narrative, breaking the diegetic illusion with a regularity that most other genres do not, in order to "signify the intimacy of live entertainment" (39) and to remystify the stardom of performers (113). Comedian comedy similarly relies upon "a direct performance situation," as Frank Krutnik points out, to find its generic mechanism for incorporating the star personae of stage comics and for then drawing upon that extra-cinematic theatrical history with gags arising from the resulting disruption of the diegesis ("Clown": 52).[4] The *Road to* series obviously draws upon conventions of both genres. However, disruptions of the diegesis in a *Road to* film are not confined to the musical numbers or to sight gags but define the entire road trip as a utopian adventure, rendering in non-narrative terms how, by way of its association with show business, the road represents the nation cohering around its popular entertainment as exemplified by Hope and Crosby.

According to Richard Dyer, entertainment is utopian because it "offers the image of 'something better' to escape into, or something we want deeply that our day-to-day lives don't provide. . . . Entertainment does not, however, present models of utopian worlds. . . . It presents . . . what utopia would feel like rather than how it would be organized" (18). Musicals typically conflate the show and the dream in order to project this utopian dimension of entertainment. The result, in Feuer's view, is a "solipsistic" vision of freedom, foreclosing "a desire to translate that vision into reality" because of the genre's "endless reflexivity," which ultimately "can offer only itself, only entertainment as its picture of Utopia" (84). Musicals, she continues, thus confuse the production and consumption of entertainment, just as they blur the distinctions between professional and amateur performances, giving mass art the value of folk art and disguising both the labor that goes into the product and the differences between the consumers of showbiz, its performers, and the economic institutions supporting it (22). This is no doubt why, in order to preserve their vision of cultural homogeneity as represented by the diverse talents working together to put on a show, when the wartime musical revues bring the spirit of the USO home to the US in a showbiz setting, they take it *off* the road by locating the show in a confined space – a studio backlot, a theatre, a canteen.

In the aptly titled *Road to Utopia* Hope and Crosby travel to "utopia" in two very different senses. On one hand, the Gold Rush narrative defines "utopia" as a place. Hope wants to leave San Francisco and return to New York City, but Crosby tricks him into going north to the Klondike instead. "It's utopia there. Everybody's getting some of that gold." And indeed, this proves true, since *Utopia* is the only film in the series which allows at least one of the two travelers (Hope) to get the pot of gold at the end of the rainbow. On the other hand, the film's self-referentiality equates utopia with showbiz, displacing the desire for capital onto the pleasure of performing for an audience, which in its turn achieves the mutual identification of spectator and performer with America as their common "home." Crosby's two solos assert this utopian logic and register the contradiction motivating it. "It's Anybody's Spring," sung in the amateur show aboard ship as an attempt to earn some money for his and Hope's passage, maintains in its lyrics, in contradistinction to the narrative context, that money is not important because the best things in life are free; while "Welcome to My Dream" invites Lamour into a dream world of romance, overlooking the fact that Crosby has a map to a gold mine rightfully hers, which she is scheming to get back. Crosby's opening number with Hope, set on a diegetic stage, works similarly. Their celebration of "Good Time Charlie" is the prelude to the confidence game ("Ghost-O") that attempts to bilk the audience of their cash.

The Hope and Crosby films use the road to characterize popular entertainment as distinctly American, whatever its geographic setting.[5] Their road is utopian insofar as it perpetuates the illusion that the producers of showbiz are no different from the consumers of their product, and the series imagines this comparability by affiliating the road with the values of home through showbiz, thereby historicizing it in the 1940s' valorization of entertainment as the condensation of American popular culture. However, the two entertainers' apparent freedom from diegetic constraints in these films also points to the more complex economic relation of showbiz performance, the industrial conditions making it possible, and the nationalist ideology it serves. Hope's reference to Paramount as his "bread and butter" in *Utopia* is in fact double-edged as an allusion to his labor as America's most traveled entertainer. While he and Crosby were well-paid employees associated with the studio as their top star attractions, their popularity gave them the power to renegotiate their contact, and they were part-owners with Paramount of the *Road to* films that followed *Utopia* in the series (Marx: 223). Beneath the trappings of "home," what their road trip ultimately confirms is Hope and Crosby's status as producers of popular entertainment, quite literally so, as it turned out.

The Road to Utopia: Tours, Saboteurs, and Detours

The *Road to* series does not narrativize its projection of home onto the road but instead reproduces the effects of their condensation through ongoing extradiegetic references to showbiz, which take for granted the entertainment industry's position as the mediator of American culture. The series, moreover, illuminates the utopian value of show business in the era's more straightforward road narratives. For when the more classically structured road films of the 1940s show more directly — that is, through their actual plotting of transcontinental travel — how all US roads followed Route 66 in leading straight to or from Hollywood, they condense America with its popular culture by evoking the same trope of showbiz that characterizes the Hope and Crosby road pictures.

Made right before the United States' entrance into the war, *Sullivan's Travels* (1941) similarly glosses the road through a mythology of national coherence that draws on popular entertainment for its rationale. A film director seeking first-hand knowledge of "real" American life that will allow his new film to overcome the escapism connoted by Hollywood entertainment, John L. Sullivan (Joel McCrea) tours the road in disguise as a hobo only to discover right away that he cannot escape Hollywood, his own home town. "It's a funny thing," he observes midway through the film:

> How everything keeps shoving me back to Hollywood and Beverly Hills. . . . Almost like, like gravity. As if some force were saying, get back where you belong. You don't belong out here in the real world, you phony you. . . . Maybe there's a universal law that says, stay put. As you are so shall you remain. Maybe that's why tramps are always in so much trouble.

That Hollywood keeps pulling him back appears to oppose the safety of home, its "gravity" arising from the economic power of show business, which supports the materiality of Sullivan's home life in Beverly Hills, and the danger of the road, which may be more "real" but only promises "trouble." Thus, when Sullivan finally does confront the "real world" of the road — economic privation and transience — he finds "trouble" enough. He loses his identity and is presumed dead, is arrested, convicted, and sentenced to six years on a chain-gang for vagrancy and assault, and returns home only through Hollywood's intervention.

Sullivan's road trip through America moves him to embrace popular entertainment, its value exemplified for him when he witnesses the laughter of fellow convicts and African-Americans as they watch a Walt Disney cartoon together. If a metaphoric death is the end of the "real" road for him, that road also validates Hollywood, not as a dead weight, but as a genuine force of culture, a healing mechanism uniting and giving coherence to the disparate, unempowered sectors of US society. After his rescue, Sullivan refuses to do the serious film he had originally wanted to research and instead returns to Hollywood to make the kind of comedy that propels a Hope and Crosby picture.[6] "There's a lot to be said for making people laugh," Sullivan tells the startled studio heads on the plane back to Hollywood. "Did you know that's all some people have? It isn't much. But it's better than nothing in this cockeyed caravan. Boy!"

Ultimately, then, *Sullivan's Travels* does not oppose home and the road. Sullivan's final remark indicates their conflation, since he describes the lives of ordinary Americans everywhere as a road journey, "this cockeyed caravan." In his own effort to leave what appears to be the hermetically sealed world of Hollywood and join that caravan, Sullivan's travels demonstrate how home over-takes the road; the director can never escape the presence of Hollywood since its product – which he helps to manufacture – permeates the culture. Initially, since the studio does not want to jeopardize its investment in the director, Sullivan's producers try to prevent him from leaving but finally relent on condition that a well-furnished land-yacht follow him, with a doctor, cook, secretary, PR man, and the like. Sullivan sabotages the entourage to show the folly of their expedition, makes an agreement to meet them in Las Vegas some time later, and returns to the road alone. He picks up work as a handy man at the home of two middle-aged sisters, goes to the movies with them after they give him supper, and, when one of the women indicates her lascivious interest in him, flees from their house in the middle of the night. Hitching a ride from the first vehicle that comes along, it turns out the truck is going west, not east, right back to Hollywood. Stopping for breakfast, he meets a girl (Veronica Lake), an unsuccessful actress who herself has trouble leaving Hollywood, and the two eventually set out to tramp by train only to welcome the studio's rescue when hunger gets the best of them and they discover the lucky coincidence that the land-yacht is parked nearby. Refreshed, Sullivan and the girl start out again, and a montage recounts their successful integration in tramp life this time – sleeping on floors, taking public showers, eating in missions – until hunger once more drives them back to the comforts of studio-financed shelter in a Kansas City hotel. Finally, in a show of gratitude and patronage, Sullivan returns to the city's skid row to pass out five-dollar bills and is mugged by a greedy hobo, who is then hit by an oncoming train while trying to get away. The thief's death causes the series of events bringing Sullivan's tour of the nation's road life to an unexpected destination: a prison camp in the backwaters of Missouri.

Taken together, these journeys identify two different trajectories for the road, although both in fact acquire their meaning via reference to Hollywood. Sullivan's inability to escape the movie capital indicates that it follows and defines him wherever he goes. This road is the utopian path linking popular culture and the nation through Hollywood, which provides the comforts of home, literally so in the land-yacht that follows the director on the road when he first sets out. And to be sure, Preston Sturges's screenplay takes care to expose the class privilege that ensures this comforting view of America. Sullivan's valet and butler, for instance, not only have to teach the director and the Girl how to catch a free ride on a freight train, they themselves don't know and must telephone the railroad company to learn how it is done!

On the other hand, freed from that protective support when he loses his identity, Sullivan ends up traveling the more dystopic road of privation and alienation. Once he forgets who he is and cannot speak in his own defense at his trial, Sullivan loses his social privilege along with his famous name; nevertheless, the director is rightfully convicted of breaking the law since he has in fact committed a crime, striking a railroad official, a point the film somewhat glosses over. When he discovers how to signal his presence by getting his photograph in the papers to show that he is still alive, Hollywood quickly rushes to his rescue, and the film refrains from depicting exactly how the studio arranges for his freedom to bring him back home. More importantly, Sullivan's cathartic revelation while watching the Disney cartoon proves how Hollywood also redeems this more "real" road through popular entertainment, which, as Dyer observes, substitutes a utopian feeling (laughter) for a dystopic place (the prison camp and the otherwise segregated church of an African-American community in the South). Rather than recognize the irresolvable difference between these two different routes across America — which manifest themselves in the screwball comedy of the first hour and the sobering melodrama of the second – the closure of *Sullivan's Travels* reconciles its protagonist to the ideological value of Hollywood product, leading him to see how the popular entertainment he will continue to produce has value for the entire culture because it ensures that every stop on the "cockeyed caravan" of life can seem like home. But while the utopian road paves over the dystopic road it cannot efface its presence entirely, as a final montage of the laughing faces recognizes, resulting in the film's ambivalence about American culture: for, despite Hollywood's mediation, tramps not only get into trouble, and represent the nation's socio-economic troubles, they *cause* trouble, too. After all, it is a tramp who greedily steals the wad of bills that Sullivan, in his gesture of beneficence to America's homeless, is doling out in Kansas City's skid row district. Clearly, making movies is less condescending – and less risky.

The two versions of the road in *Sullivan's Travels* mark out the territory of the 1940s road narrative: on one hand, the utopian road across the nation from Los Angeles to New York that Barry Kane (Robert Cummings) follows in *Saboteur* (1942), respecting the wartime urgency to imagine the nation as a unified and comforting homeland, and on the other, the dystopic road that Al Roberts (Tom Stern) travels in *Detour* (1945), which turns that earlier film's wartime ideology of home inside out, just as it reverses the direction of Kane's road trip. What is

Plate 5.2 Joel McCrea and Veronica Lake pose as tramps in *Sullivan's Travels*
and meet the real thing.

worth noting about these two very different road films, though, is the comparable
significance of popular entertainment in texturing their representations of the
nation through such diametrically opposed journeys.

Saboteur puts Kane on the road when he is falsely accused of setting fire to a
defense plant. As he follows the trail of this conspiracy across the continent, he
also discovers how the road reveals the nation's unity as a homeland. As the blind
man Philip Martin points out about hitch-hiking when helping Kane: "I've always
thought that was the best way to learn about this country, and the surest test of
the American heart." The head spy, Charles Tobin (Otto Kruger), by contrast,
calls Americans "small, anonymous, soft," deriding "the great masses, the moronic
millions" who "live small, complacent lives." In a speech that does not need to be
underscored by "The Star Spangled Banner" to make its point, Kane challenges
Tobin's fascist politics by summarizing what he has learned while on the road: "I've
met guys like you and others – people that are helpful and eager to do the right
thing. People that get a kick out of helping each other fight the bad guys. . . . We'll
win if it takes from now until the cows come home."

Though he hails from Los Angeles, Kane is himself not affiliated with showbiz,
but his partner on the road is. Patricia Martin (Priscilla Lane) is a model – indeed,

her face instantly catches Kane's eye as soon as he takes to the road – and the bill-boards she adorns, her uncle Philip comments, "would reach across the continent if placed end to end", mapping a path across the nation just as the spy ring does. The centerpiece of the film's ideological agenda also occurs in a setting associated with showbiz, when a group of six sideshow freaks temporarily shelter Kane and Pat Martin in a circus caravan. The entertainers themselves disagree about allowing the couple to remain, so the leader takes an unofficial vote because he believes their differences parallel "the world situation," and they must, as in any democracy, stand by "the will of the majority." Other references to entertainment culture appear as a seeming matter of course when the film depicts the uniform Americanness of the people Kane and Martin encounter, from a trucker who complains about his wife spending money on "moving pictures and hats," to one of the spies, who hopes the planned sabotage of the Brooklyn Navy Yard will go on schedule, because "I promised to take my sister to the Philharmonic." The spies themselves use a truck bearing the sign "American Newsreel, Inc." as their cover to get onto the dock; and the famous climax of the film at the top of the Statue of Liberty, the icon of America as everybody's home in the 1940s, actually begins with a chase through Rockefeller Center, disrupting the screening of the film showing at Radio City Music Hall. Such references to America establish the nation's unity as a people through their relation to popular entertainment, all the while (this is Hitchcock, after all) registering an unmistakable sense of menace – of hidden political subversion – lurking beneath ordinary, normal American life. Entertainment offers the same utopian pleasure to patriots and spies alike, giving a more sinister twist to the road than appears on the surface.

In *Detour*, contrary to the optimism that Philip Martin expresses and that Barry Kane confirms, hitch-hiking turns out to be the worst possible way to travel. Thumbing his way from New York to Hollywood to rejoin his fiancée, Sue (Claudia Drake), who has gone there hoping to make a career as a singer, pianist Roberts is picked up in Arizona by Charles Haskell, who dies unexpect-edly while on the road. Panicked, Roberts assumes that the police would never believe it was not foul play because of the circumstances, so he takes Haskell's name, car, and money, puts his own identification papers on the corpse, and dri-ves on, only to pick up, in turn, the one hitch-hiker who knows the deceased: Vera (Ann Savage). Vera blackmails Roberts into staying with her until they can sell the car, then ups the ante of their scheme by insisting that he pose as Haskell in order to get the dead man's inheritance. Roberts refuses but also cannot get away from Vera and, in a quarrel heated by her drinking, he accidentally kills her. Again circumstances seem to be pushing him towards the gas chamber, and he flees, a nameless, homeless fugitive caught on a road with no beginning or end, since he cannot return to New York, where Al Roberts is presumed dead, or to Los Angeles, where Charles Haskell is wanted for Vera's murder. The road in this film traces the fatal wrong turn – or as Roberts puts it, "Fate sticks out its foot and trips you." The only possible means of bringing such as circuitous road to closure is through the Production Code Administration's enforced ending: arrest the piano player.

Detour marks the absence of home on the road for Roberts through references to showbiz. In the opening scene, a popular song playing on the jukebox, "I Can't Believe That You're in Love With Me," prompts his voice-over account of his road trip, locating his origin in show culture: he remembers not only that Sue sang this song but also that he played it at the Break O'Dawn club in New York City. "That tune, that tune," he moans, "why is it always that rotten tune, following me around, beating me up?" The flashback narrative begins with Sue and him temporarily breaking up so that she can try her luck in Hollywood, and from this point on "I Can't Believe . . . " alternates with "I'm Always Chasing Rainbows" on the film's soundtrack as haunting traces of what forever eludes Roberts – Hollywood – in effect inverting the recuperative function of popular music in a USO show, where such songs comforted the audience as reminders of home. When Roberts finally arrives in Hollywood, it is with Vera, and he can see only the irony: "Far from being the end of my trip there was greater distance between me and Sue than when I started out." He never gets back to Sue and he never achieves the musical career he aspired to in the opening of the flash-back; all the same, while the film gives the impression that he fails to reach his intended destination because of fate's "detour," Hollywood envelopes this dystopic road and *film noir* story. Roberts and Vera go out looking for a used-car dealer in order to sell Haskell's convertible, and, while her dialogue indicates they are driving away from Hollywood Boulevard ("Look, after the deal's closed, let go back to that place on Hollywood Boulevard where I saw that fur jacket"), the rear projection footage shows the boulevard still behind them. The marquee of the old Iris movie theatre at the Wilcox Avenue intersection stands out quite visibly in the background, so Vera's remark seems oddly incongruent. In a reversal of Sullivan's appreciation of Hollywood as a source of comfort for the spiritually homeless, the full dystopic effect of Roberts's road trip in *Detour* is that he *can* reach Los Angeles but not see it *as* "Hollywood."

Hollywood on the Road: No Reservations Needed

Much more so than the Hope and Crosby films, *Sullivan's Travels*, *Saboteur*, and *Detour* each place 1940s showbiz culture on the road to hold utopian and dystopic views of America in discomfiting tension. By comparison, *Without Reservations* (1946) more optimistically depicts how the road centers the nation in the populist values of Hollywood entertainment. At the same time, this film begins to record a shift in cultural attitudes toward the road that would become even more apparent in the following decade. *Without Reservations* is thus a somewhat neglected road film of the 1940s that deserves a closer look.

Claudette Colbert, the female star most identified with Hollywood road movies, plays Christopher "Kit" Madden, a writer whose best-selling novel, *Here Is Tomorrow*, which seems to be modeled on Ayn Rand's *The Fountainhead*, has become a national bestseller because, in the words of the newsreel that opens the film, its vision of postwar America offers "a blueprint of the future." "People in every walk of life have been influenced by this book," the newsreel solemnly declares when announcing its sale to the movies. On her way to Hollywood to adapt her novel into a film starring Cary Grant and Lana Turner, Kit encounters the popular culture that has taken her book so closely to its heart and mind. At the train station she finds that the studio could not arrange for a drawing room, just an upper berth until Chicago, where she will transfer to the Super Chief, but she doesn't care: "I like traveling on a Pullman. You meet the people." Then she gets worse news. Turner is set for the film but Grant is out, and she rejects the studio's new plan of casting an unknown as Mark Winston, the lead male role. Settled into her seat with "the people," she begins an angry telegram to Hollywood, but, before finishing, she meets two Marine fliers, one of whom – Rusty Williams (John Wayne) – looks remarkably like the imaginary portrait of Mark Winston featured on her novel's dustjacket. Deciding that Rusty will be perfect casting in the film version of *Here Is*

Plate 5.3 Claudette Colbert meets "the people" (John Wayne and Don DeFore) while traveling coach in *Without Reservations*.

Tomorrow, she cancels the telegram and assumes the alias of "Kitty Klotch" in order to keep close to the marine as he and pal Deke Thomas (Don DeFore) make their way west to a San Diego base. Kit therefore changes to their train in Chicago, giving up her comfortable drawing room on the Chief for an unreserved coach seat on the Sunrise Limited, and is eventually kicked off that train in Colorado for unruly behavior inspired by the two men, who leave with her. As the trio continues traveling cross-country by foot and then automobile – after Kit purchases an Italian touring car formerly owned by a Hollywood actor – they end up on Route 66 and in Albuquerque, New Mexico, where "Kitty Klotch" is arrested for impersonating the famous Christopher Madden, forcing her to reveal her true identity and her intentions to Rusty, much to his anger, and the couple temporarily breaks up.

Somewhat reminiscent of Colbert's famous road trips in *It Happened One Night* (1934), *Midnight* (1939), and *The Palm Beach Story* (1942), the romantic plot of *Without Reservations* most obviously works to reestablish the traditional gender roles upset by wartime America. Not knowing that Kit has written this bestseller, Rusty has nothing but criticism for *Here Is Tomorrow*, which he read out of boredom while laid up in a military hospital. He thinks its plot of a woman chasing a man makes no sense whatsoever, and cannot understand why Cary Grant would ever agree to play Mark Winston, since Grant "always seemed like a pretty sharp fellow." In response, Kit, speaking as one of the novel's readers and not its author, tries to explain its thematic goal, but Rusty does not buy her description of the ideas being dramatized by the sexual relation of Mark Winston and the anonymous girl, the role planned for Lana Turner.

> *Rusty*: This pilot is a progressive and Lana Turner, according to this book, is a reactionary?
> *Kit*: The characters are symbols. He is the future and she is the past. The clash between them is purely ideological.

According to Rusty, sex transcends ideology. "She's a woman and he's a man," he points out. ". . . If I were Mark Winston, I'd behave like Lana Turner were a woman, and argue afterwards." The more politically minded Kit then asks him: "Suppose you were a pilot and you just came back from the war and were tired." "Honey," he replies, with a common sense obviously meant to get a big laugh from the audience, "no pilot gets *that* tired!"

In love with Rusty, Kit comes to accept his conservative viewpoint, which reduces the problems facing postwar American society to the sexual relation. "I don't want a woman to tell the world what to do," Rusty exclaims when leaving Kit in Albuquerque. "I don't want a woman to tell me what to do. I want a woman who's helpless." She does not win Rusty back until she acquiesces to what he says, identifying with the heroine of her novel and not its hero to find the appropriately feminine perspective that does not challenge the male ego – and that significantly revises Colbert's feisty, independent persona from her earlier road films. As she dresses for Rusty's return, Kit happily tells her maid: "You gotta keep a fellow on his toes. You gotta keep him worried and upset – you gotta make him jealous."

If *Without Reservations* were interested only in restoring traditional gender roles, it would not need to be a road narrative, and the film is certainly that, using the road to teach Kit about the America whose social problems she wants to solve. "I don't think [this society] will change as much as people think," Rusty tells her after she describes what *Here Is Tomorrow* is trying to do. "But it must," she replies. Kit's plan for curing postwar America in *Here Is Tomorrow* is entirely invested in her hero, a visionary who is at once an emblem of progressive post-New-Deal politics and her imaginative construction of an idealized masculinity; she herself is outspoken, free-thinking, and aggressive in a way that connects her to the independent women of wartime. As she herself says, the characters in her book are symbols and their clash is ideological, and her comment applies equally well to this film. *Without Reservations*, however, does not propose a solution for postwar America in the manner that Kit's novel is reported to do. As she travels cross-country from New York to Hollywood, the road liberalizes Kit's politics by educating her in the values of "the people," leading her to rethink her vision of America's future in *Here Is Tomorrow*.

Aside from developing her romance with the marine and conforming her femininity to his conservative understanding of the sexual relation, what the road reveals to Kit is her novel's impact on the culture. As Rusty himself notes, "that book sure gets around." "The people," furthermore, may be reading her book wherever she goes, but they all do not look or sound the same. The appeal of *Here Is Tomorrow* crosses gender and class lines, from New York City (where "the people" on coach are all reading it) to Chicago (where Kit uses a liquor store owner's admiration for the novel to get more Scotch than rationing will allow), to Albuquerque (where her novel's popularity with a women's book club causes the commotion that pulls off her cloak of anonymity). At the same time, *Without Reservations* uses the road to contrast Kit's imaginary construction of America in her book with a new, more "authentic" understanding based on her road trip to Hollywood. After finally reaching her destination, as well as plotting to win Rusty back by making him jealous, Kit also quarrels with the studio over changes she wants to make in her screenplay, since they insist she keep to the novel. As Louella Parsons tells a nationwide radio audience, Kit now "thinks she had a lot of nerve trying to tell the world how to cure itself."

The road Kit travels across the US, in short, amounts to a series of detours from her original conception of America as well as her ticketed seat in a private drawing room on the Super Chief; and this road is not the homogeneous one usually portrayed in films of the studio era since it is crisscrossed by racial and class differences. For example, after the three travelers depart the Sunrise at La Junta, Colorado – and Kit has to teach Deke and Rusty how to pronounce the town's Spanish name correctly – they end up at the Ortega ranch in New Mexico. On one hand, the Spanish-speaking Ortega family – an old-fashioned patriarchy dominated by a middle-aged father and lacking a mother – supports the film's apparent alignment with Rusty's sexual conservatism. The males, young and old alike, are ardent patriots of America, despite their Mexican heritage, while the teenage female shamelessly flirts with Rusty, making Kit jealous. On the other hand, while the Hispanic family is depicted through a Hollywood stereotype, Kit's encounter with them highlights the ethnic heterogeneity of American culture, introducing a dimension to the road that one does not find in *Sullivan's Travels* or *Saboteur*.

Even earlier in her travels, Kit strikes up an acquaintance with a working woman, Consuela "Connie" Calhoun, also going to California on the Sunrise. The two marines dismiss Connie as just another dame ("a beetle"), in contrast to the more classy Kitty Klotch, but Kit takes her much more seriously. Connie's viewpoint considerably differs from Kit's. While Connie adopts the traditional gender roles advocated by Rusty (she is the one who advises Kit to make a man jealous as a means of keeping him in line), her background as a waitress dating a union organizer – albeit alluded to elliptically in dialogue meant to make her character humorous – situates gender relations in the much more precise social context of class labor. To get Rusty into her bedroom (the setting of the film's final scene), Kit has to come down from the upper class toward his more working-class viewpoint, if not in economic fact then in ideological perspective. She lives quite well in Beverly Hills, and Rusty seems to have no objection to her income, just her opinions. Connie's presence in the film reminds us how the romance plot works to get around confronting the economic differences between the politically mismatched couple, focusing attention solely on their sexual frisson and not their asymmetrical incomes.

Toward the end of *Without Reservations*, at the moment when Rusty decides to forgive Kit, Connie unexpectedly turns up again in San Diego. She declares to the two marines that, inspired by the no-name Kitty Klotch – who, in Connie's mind, has apparently turned herself into that big-time author and Hollywood celebrity Christopher Madden only after their encounter on the train – she is quitting her waitress job because she too has decided to become rich and famous by writing a book. Connie is comically right about how to measure the impact of Kit's success. *Without Reservations* uses the road trip to prove that, as the newsreel at the start of the film predicts, Kit's real influence on her public will ultimately come about through Hollywood's ability to connect the producer of popular entertainment with its consumers. During the road trip, as Deke watches Kit and Rusty falling in love, he happily hums "I'll Buy that Dream." The song supplies the background musical theme throughout the film. Deke's bringing it into the diegesis at this point underscores the condensation of the road and showbiz while connecting it to Kit and Rusty's romance, suggesting how and why the entertainment industry will be the means of bringing the couple together despite their political differences. For, while reworking her novel into a film, Kit makes full use of Hollywood to mediate her estrangement from Rusty. She not only corresponds to Deke about all the men she dates, knowing he will share the letters with Rusty and make the latter jealous, but invites Deke up to LA to enjoy the perks of her labor, arranging a double date that gives him his dream for free, as it were, and Kit's too: he dances with his favorite star, Dolores Moran, and Kit with Cary Grant, the star originally meant to play Mark Winston.

From her new reluctance to tell the world what she thinks and from the film's own concentration on reforming her progressive sexual politics, it seems clear that, when writing her screenplay, Kit has no reservations whatsoever about conforming her novel's social vision of America and allegorical narrative of Mark Winston to the depoliticized conventions of Hollywood product. To be sure, when she tempers her didacticism upon reaching Hollywood and decides to make changes in the film adaptation of *Here Is Tomorrow*, she appears to be remembering what Senor Ortega advises when she tells him about her novel: "It's better to live and *then* write the book." What her road trip dramatizes, however – first by introducing her to "the people," then by revealing to her how the popularity of her book threads their diverse culture together, and finally by sending her to the movie capital to turn that book into a film for an even larger audience – is how Hollywood comes to displace her social philosophy as the organizing principle of her utopian vision for America. As this happens, the heterogeneous culture of "the people" that she encounters on the road becomes more homogenized as mass culture, as the consumable Hollywood product that she herself manufactures when turning her novel into a screenplay. Indeed, when Rusty teaches her about the importance of sex over politics in his synopsis of the book's plot, he in effect instructs Kit how to write a classic Hollywood film like *Without Reservations* itself, and this, even more than his speech on the proper sexual relations of a man and woman, appears to be the lesson she takes to heart when revising *Here Is Tomorrow* for its mass audience. Her road trip across America to undertake this task consequently leads Kit to the same appreciation of entertainment that Sullivan finds at the end of his travels, or that Hope and Crosby display through the self-referentiality of their series, reiterating the value of showbiz in ensuring the continuity of home and the road. More importantly, *Without Reservations* recognizes how the road itself has begun to change in its relation to show business: from a site traveled by producers of entertainment making contact with their audience to one traversed by those consumers.

Consuming Showbiz: "I'll Buy that Dream"

Travelers in the handful of road films produced during the 1950s also make a journey across the US, and they likewise encounter a culture marked by a show business ethos. However, when protagonists go on the road in the 1950s, in contrast to their 1940s counterparts, more often than not they are now characterized like Deke in *Without Reservations*: as fans of popular entertainment, not its performers (Hope and Crosby), directors (John L. Sullivan), or writers (Kit Madden). I don't think it is an oversimplification to say that, when viewed from this perspective, 1950s road films indirectly register the impact of the United States' postwar transformation from a nation based in production to one increasingly geared towards consuming. This dramatic shift in the nation's economy coincided with its achievement of global hegemony in the years between 1945 and 1958 (McCormick: 238–9) *and* its consumption, beginning in 1955, of more energy than it could produce (Oakley: 230).

The history of Route 66, stretching across the country from Chicago to New Mexico to Santa Monica Pier (via Sunset Boulevard in Hollywood), is itself emblematic of the resulting transformation of the road's utopian connection to the nation. Opened in 1926, the famous "Mother Road" of Depression migrants like the Joads in *The Grapes of Wrath* (1939) was also the route traveled by "all the song writers, all the movie makers, all the writers who came from the Algonquin Hotel in New York to the Garden of Allah in Hollywood" (Dean, "Still"). In 1946, Bobby Troup turned it into a famous popular song, and, in 1960, Stirling Silliphant made it the setting of a popular television series. Eventually, "The Main Street of America," as Route 66 was also nicknamed, was replaced by the nondescript, high-speed interstates, and then officially decertified and shut down for good in 1984. By 1993, in celebration of its sixty-sixth anniversary, the mythic highway, a nostalgic memento of a bygone populist America – "those days when people gave everyone the time of day and urgent travelers didn't have to buy gasoline to use the restroom" (Dean, "Still") – was now being merchandised as "a $195 wristwatch with a revolving dial showing each town mentioned [by Troup's song]" (Dean, "100 Classic").

The shift in the road's meaning in the 1950s is apparent when *The Greatest Show on Earth* (1953) cites the 1940s *Road to* series with a guest appearance by Hope and Crosby. The famous entertainers are seen in the audience, eating popcorn while watching Dorothy Lamour sing "Lovely Luawana Lady," not performing in the show themselves. This equation of showbiz and consumption is not an isolated moment in the DeMille film. The diegetic audience gets almost as much attention as the circus acts, with DeMille routinely cutting away to close-ups of spectators watching the show in rapt attention and literally consuming a seemingly endless supply of popcorn, ice cream, and peanuts. In the plot – its main conflict arising from the financially threatened circus's effort to stay on the road for a full season – when the star attraction (Cornel Wilde) cripples his arm in a fall, the aerialist ends up selling balloons to the audience as his means of remaining with the show. That audience, moreover, dominated by children, is characterized within the diegesis and by DeMille's voice-over as regressive: even adults like Hope and Crosby are shown to be juvenile in their enthusiasm for the "excitement and adventure" of the show. Repeatedly, the circus boss (Charlton Heston) tries to convince the corporate owners not to shut down the tour for the sake of all the children in small towns everywhere across America. Not surprisingly, when the fugitive clown Buttons (James Stewart) is finally apprehended by the police, before leaving the big-top in handcuffs, he hands over his faithful little dog to a child in the audience. Talk about taking home a great souvenir!

The Greatest Show on Earth is essentially a throwback to the road films of the 1940s. Its circus community, joining talented misfits together to form a home on the road, is cast from the same mold as the sideshow act in *Saboteur*. But Buttons's presence in the show, with the famous face of James Stewart hidden by clown makeup, like the clown's own strong identification with the children in the audience, helps to distinguish how this film characterizes the relation of utopian entertainment and its consumers: as Irving Howe warned of mass culture in 1948, "The identification is ultimately with our role of social anonymity" (502). *The Greatest Show on Earth* celebrates this role as the hallmark of pleasurable consumption, in contrast to the way that fame and the production of entertainment go together hand in hand in *Sullivan's Travels* and *Without Reservations*. Furthermore, after the spectacular train wreck destroys the big top, the show itself becomes stationary; it literally loses its locomotion. With the circus immobilized, the performers have to go into Cedar City in order to bring the anonymous audience to the show, dramatizing the real catastrophe threatening the circus – the postwar rupture between home and the road – which the DeMille film continually tries to negotiate by showing how the utopian ethos of popular entertainment can be achieved through its consumption.

That the circus, the greatest *traveling* show on earth, has trouble drawing enough crowds to justify its long tour on the road is perhaps much more significant than the plot of DeMille's film recognizes. In comparison to the previous decade of wartime social disruption and mobility on the one hand, and postwar demobilization and relocation on the other – a rhythm of social displacement– replacement that also characterizes a road film's typical structure – the 1950s was a rather sedentary period: few films of this decade, for example, go on the road. "Home" came to mean not the nation as unified by the road, as in wartime, but domesticity as the mainstay of the postwar middle-class family and as evidence of the nation's great prosperity in contrast with postwar Europe and Asia.[7] Automobiles, far from being seen as a means of transportation or liberation, were sold as commodities and prized as status symbols; their setting was the ranch-house garage, not the open road. In fact, the automobile industry borrowed from Hollywood in displaying its new product in an annual "motorama" that, whether in a local convention center or an industrial film, looked more like big-screen musical revues than anything else, complete with glitzy, elaborate sets, musical numbers, and chorines. The car itself became part of "a show, an exhibition" (Marling: 146).

It is therefore quite fitting that, when Lucille Ball and Desi Arnaz, the stars of television's *I Love Lucy*, take to the road in the movies as newlyweds Tacy and Nicky Collini in *The Long, Long Trailer* (1954), one of the 1950s' few outright road movies, like turtles they carry their home with them. The Collinis' shiny yellow trailer – first seen by the couple at a motorama – sports the latest modern kitchen appliances, such as a sleek refrigerator and gas range with a see-through oven door. It even has a sunken living room, and the bedroom is large enough for twin beds. Its cupboards, moreover, are so stocked with dishes and cookware of every size and shape, its closets so stuffed with matching fleece towels and Tacy's Helen Rose wardrobe, that Nicky cannot find space for his clothes, let alone the golf clubs he tries to bring aboard. All this mobile home needs for its finishing touch, Tacy says more than once, is a deep freeze. She persuades her husband-to-be to buy the trailer, "a little place we could call our own," because Nicky's work as a geological engineer will require them to move around the country, but he discovers, to his dismay, that their portable home is actually like "a train" pulling behind their new convertible: "forty feet of train," to be more exact. As well as resembling the era's large cars themselves – weighted down with surplus chrome and tail fins, filled from engine to trunk with "the usual power accessories, deep-pile upholstery, padded interiors, coil springs, and bargelike proportions" (Marling: 141) – the trailer uncannily calls to mind DeMille's voice-over description of the circus in the opening of *The Greatest Show on Earth*: "A massive machine whose very life depends on discipline, motion, and speed. A mechanized army that rolls over any army in its path." The whole point of this trailer, once it hits the road and overwhelms every car coming in its path, is to make you forget that you're on the road.

On the face of it, the road plot of *The Long, Long Trailer* has nothing to do with either the entertainment industry or Hollywood, but then this film does not need to invoke the trope of showbiz to represent the road as the nation because it literally takes home on the road. Rather than overtly representing the unifying spirit of American popular culture through showbiz, the road in this film provides a seemingly unended series of opportunities for consuming. As they travel cross-country in this home on wheels, Tacy fills up the trailer with boxes of canned fruits and vegetables that she acquires along the way, and, more ominously as it will turn out, rocks from every stop, carefully labeled. "Every one reminds me of some wonderful place that we've been," Tacy tries to explain, planning to display all these mementos from their honeymoon when they reach Colorado and set up the trailer as their home, suggesting how she intends to place home life and the road side by side. However, anticipating a climb up a narrow mountain road to 8,000 feet, Nicky orders his wife to throw everything out in an effort to reduce the trailer's considerable weight. Since she cannot bring herself to part with her souvenirs, Tacy hides the rocks throughout the trailer; when Nicky discovers her deceit, he dumps everything out, precipitating their temporary estrangement at the start of the film and his framing voice-over.

The Long, Long Trailer nonetheless projects the utopian ethos of showbiz onto the road through the well-known television personae of its two stars. In its theatrical trailer, Arnaz's voice-over repeatedly refers to the characters as "Lucy" and himself, and, even within the film, the fictional names of the couple encourage such conflation of star and television identities with their characters, since "Tacy" and "Nicky" sound too much like "Lucy" and "Ricky" to be accidental (Harvey: 166). Moreover, the year after they made *The Long, Long Trailer*, Arnaz and Ball took to the road again in their television series, with Lucy and company going to Hollywood in a famous series of episodes spanning two seasons (and airing from 1954 to 1955).[8] Of course, during her stay in Hollywood, Lucy Ricardo still wants to break into showbiz. She gets and ruins a walk-on in a motion picture, for example, and, though burnt from too much sunbathing in an effort to look like a star, awkwardly appears in a fashion show with other Hollywood wives; for that matter, the Ricardos and their friends, the Mertzes, put on an amateur show in Ethel's home town of Albuquerque before they get to LA, and Ricky has gone there to star in a movie himself. But most of the comedy in Lucy's long, long trip to Hollywood comes from her position as a starstruck fan collecting souvenirs of her trip to bring home, from Richard Widmark's signature on a grapefruit to John Wayne's footprints at Grauman's Chinese theater. When they pack for their return to New York, Ricky complains about the weight of her luggage, which turns out to be crammed full of her mementos from Hollywood (save for Wayne's cement block, which she *almost* gets away with).

This long story-arc in the television series illuminates how the road functions in the 1950s to project the utopian value of entertainment through consumption. Given the fact that it followed so closely upon the wheels of *The Long, Long Trailer*, the television road trip to Hollywood helps to clarify what the road means in this film, too. True, the Collinis' road trip reverses direction (headed out of Los Angeles on Highway 101 northeast to Colorado), and the film uses the colossal, well-appointed trailer, "an incongruously massive blot on the western landscape," to satirize "the lure of technology and mobility which possesses a newer, rootless middle class" (Harvey: 168–9). All the same, the road narrative here ends up just as the television series does: like Lucy, Tacy sees her road trip as an occasion to consume pieces of America as souvenirs of her journey, quite literally so, intending to incorporate the road into the exterior of her home once she and Nicky stop traveling. To be sure, in contrast to Lucy's trip to Hollywood, popular entertainment does not overtly contextualize the utopian sense of home on the road that Tacy experiences through her consumerism, but it is never entirely absent from *The Long, Long Trailer*: from the television personae of the two stars, to the film's many references to director Vincente Minnelli's "own movie legacy" in its casting and mise-en-scène (Harvey: 168), to the film adaptation of a bestseller that Tacy describes at length to Nicky as they make their tense climb up the mountain.

As Lucy Ricardo's television road trip confirms, Hollywood is still the capital of show business in the 1950s and, as the final destination of cross-country travel on Route 66, still the end of the road across the US. A road trip to Hollywood made by Dean Martin and Jerry Lewis in their final film together, *Hollywood or Bust* (1956), likewise acknowledges the road's reorientation of showbiz culture around the utopian pleasures of consuming entertainment. Immediately before the credits unroll in *Hollywood or Bust*, a voice announces: "This motion picture is dedicated to you . . . the American movie fan." Lewis impersonates first this fan, then similar ones from Britain, Japan, France, Russia, allowing the introduction to conclude: "There are movie fans everywhere, and you can be sure they all want to go . . . Hollywood or Bust."

Within the diegesis, Lewis plays Malcom Smith, a movie fan so avid in his consumption of Hollywood that he not only sees a film repeatedly, but can cite even the most minor details from its credits. Malcom pairs up with gambler Steve Wiley (Martin) when the two win a red convertible in a movie theater give-away and immediately head for the West Coast. For Malcolm, much as for Lucy Ricardo, the road will lead him to the "land of stardust, land of glamour," as the title song exclaims, so it simply marks a transition: from going to the movies in New York City to running riot in a Hollywood studio in his effort to meet his favorite actress, Anita Ekberg. For Steve, it is a means of escaping gambling debts, since he plans to sell the car as soon as they hit LA. More significantly, and in contrast with *Without Reservations*, the road in *Hollywood or Bust* may follow Route 66 sign for sign but the nation Malcom and Steve cross with companion Teri Roberts (Patricia Crowley) has all the regional specificity of a studio backlot, despite the insertion of second-unit location footage. No chance of meeting the Ortegas here! As the three travelers drive from state to state singing about the attractions of the west, all they have to do to signal the regional difference of each locale in this musical number is change their hats, in effect turning the road into a hunt for souvenirs much as Lucy and Tacy do. When Malcolm finally gets to Hollywood, the film capital then reinforces his status as a consumer of showbiz, the ultimate, childlike fan. While would-be-singer Teri gets a job performing

Plate 5.4 Jerry Lewis, Patricia Crowley, and Dean Martin sing about the attractions of the West, with some added canine accompaniment, in *Hollywood or Bust*.

in the movies, the one who becomes the real star in pictures is Malcolm's dog, characterized on the trip through his voracious appetite for hamburgers, who ends up co-starring with Ekberg in *The Lady and the Great Dane*.

Contrasting the glamour and the capital expenditure of show business with the banality of the country between New York City and Los Angeles, *Hollywood or Bust* considerably differs from *Without Reservations* and the other 1940s films I have examined: this film uses the road to juxtapose the nation and show business. In those 1940s films, the road is utopian because of its association with the production of entertainment; showbiz represents Americanness everywhere and effaces the nation's diversity, which the war had made much more visible. Taking a road trip is thus almost like being at home, as in *Sullivan's Travels* and *Saboteur*, even when the road ends up turning that utopian feeling inside out, as in *Detour*. Instead of using show business to characterize the nation's uniformity by reproducing the utopian feeling of USO shows, so vividly represented in the Hope and Crosby series, the 1950s films work it into the texture of their road trips in order to celebrate the consumption of entertainment, which, with the advent of television, will ultimately find a more suitable venue in the home and not on the road. As a result, the difference between showbiz and "home," rather than their equivalence, as in the 1940s road films, comes to motivate the traveler's position on the road as a consumer of entertainment in the 1950s.

At that historical juncture, when interstates and shopping malls were not yet as common or as integrated into the economy of traveling as they are today, the nation itself was ambivalent about the uniformity of the mass culture that would become much more pronounced in later decades, further changing what the road means in films from *Bonnie and Clyde* (1967) and *Easy Rider* to *Natural Born Killers* (1994) and *To Wong Foo, Thanks for Everything! Julie Newmar* (1995). Although *To Wong Foo* in particular tries very hard, by evoking the same set of showbiz tropes, to recall the utopian past of those earlier movie trips to Hollywood, this film's three drag queens get stalled on their road almost as soon as they set out for the movie capital, just as the film itself gets mired in ideological contradictions about gender, sexuality, race, class, and regionalism.[9] By contrast, when the USO took its camp shows on tour in the 1940s, showbiz had a very different function in unifying and giving coherence to the nation's homogeneous identity by projecting a utopian ethos onto the road, one which, in the 1990s, *To Wong Foo* tries to reinflect as queer style and *Natural Born Killers* to deconstruct as tabloid television. But it was already becoming clear in the 1950s that the road movie could no longer support the utopian associations of the nation with "home" and showbiz that it had so powerfully carried in the 1940s, when America's roads provided a ready setting for imagining such cultural unity – and for promoting its fiction of social coherence.

Notes

1 For an account of how the Office of War Information influenced cinematic represen-tations of American home life, the war effort, and combat during the war years, see Koppes and Black, and Doherty.

2 The series, all produced at Paramount and starring Dorothy Lamour with Hope and Crosby, consists of *Road to Singapore* (1940), *Road to Zanzibar* (1941), *Road to Morocco* (1942), *Road to Utopia* (1946), *Road to Rio* (1948), and *Road to Bali* (1953). With *Road to Hong Kong* (1962), Hope and Crosby revived the series in the early 1960s, relegating Lamour to a guest appearance as herself, and making the film for United Artists in the UK.

3 For example, before agreeing to do his guest appearance in *My Favorite Brunette* (1947), Crosby demanded and received a $25,000 payment from Hope, who had a financial interest in the film (Marx: 216). Crosby's refusal to do it for free cooled the friendship considerably.

4 See Krutnik "Spanner," and Krutnik and Neal for additional commentary on the come-dian comedy.

5 My emphasis here, though, should not detract from the *Road to* series' potential for representing the liberatory effect of the road as well, since its queer subtext is undeniable – and just as historical, embedded in the buddy relation of war culture and

the camp coding of showbiz. See my essay "Queering the Deal: On the Road with Hope and Crosby," *Out Takes: Essays on Queer Theory and Film*, ed. Ellis Hansen (Durham, NC: Duke University Press, forthcoming 1997).

6 Or writer-director Preston Sturges's next film, *The Palm Beach Story* (1942), another road movie, which refers back to the screwball comedies of the 1930s. According to Sturges, he made *Sullivan's Travels* precisely to tell his fellow film-makers that they "seemed to have abandoned the fun in favor of the message," and "to leave the preaching to the preachers." Yet he also felt that "the ending wasn't right" because he could not find a way of correlating what Sullivan learns on his travels with the resolution of the love story (295).

7 On the domestication of postwar culture, its relation to both home life and consumerism, see May.

8 The film was produced during the series' television hiatus in 1953 and it premiered in February, 1954; the road trip story arc of the series began filming in October, 1954, and commenced airing in December of that year, spanning the second half of the 1954–5 season and the first half of the 1955–6 season. See Andrews: 313–39.

9 See the essays by Pamela Robertson and Sharon Willis later in this volume for discussions of this film's cultural politics.

Works Cited

Andrews, Bart. *The "I Love Lucy" Book*. New York: Doubleday, 1976.

Bérubé, Allan. *Coming Out Under Fire: The History of Gay Men and Women in World War Two*. New York: Plume, 1991.

"Bob Hope: Memories of World War II." Videocassette and TV special. NBC. August 5, 1995.

Dean, Paul. "100 Classic Reasons to Save Route 66." *Los Angeles Times* (October 25, 1993), Home Edition: E-1. *Los Angeles Times* Archives. Online. August 7, 1996.

—— "Still Getting Kicks on Route 66." *Los Angeles Times* (September 27, 1992), Home Edition: E-1+. *Los Angeles Times* Archives. Online. August 7, 1996.

Doherty, Thomas. *Projections of War: Hollywood, American Culture, and World War II*. New York: Columbia University Press, 1993.

Dyer, Richard. "Entertainment and Utopia" (1977). Rpt. *Only Entertainment*. London: Routledge, 1992. 17–34.

Feuer, Jane. *The Hollywood Musical*. 2nd ed. Bloomington: Indiana University Press, 1993.

Gallico, Paul. "What We Talked About." *While You Were Gone: A Report on Wartime Life in the United States*, ed. Jack Goodman. New York: Simon, 1946. 28–63.

Harvey, Stephen. *Directed by Vincente Minnelli*. New York: Harper, 1989.

Hersey, John. *Into the Valley: A Skirmish of the Marines*. (1942). Rpt. New York: Pantheon, 1989.

Hope, Bob. *Have Tux, Will Travel*. New York: Simon, 1954.

Howe, Irving. "Notes on Mass Culture" (1948). Rpt. *Mass Culture: The Popular Arts in America*, ed. Bernard Rosenberg and David Manning White. New York: Free Press, 1957. 496–503.

Koppes, Clayton R. and Black, Gregory D. *Hollywood Goes to War: How Politics, Profits and Propaganda Shaped World War II Movies* (1987). Rpt. Berkeley: University of California Press, 1990.

Krutnik, Frank. "The Clown-Prints of Comedy." *Screen* 25.4–5 (1984): 50–9.

—— "A Spanner in the Works? Genre, Narrative, and the Hollywood Comedian." *Classical Hollywood Comedy*, ed. Kristine Brunovska Karnick and Henry Jenkins. New York: Routledge, 1995. 17–38.

Krutnik, Frank and Neale, Steve. *Popular Film and Television Comedy*. London: Routledge, 1990.

"Letters from GIs." Bob Hope Memories of World War II. Online. Bobhope.com. August 18, 1996.

Marling, Karal Ann. *As Seen on TV: The Visual Culture of Everyday Life in the 1950s*. Cambridge, MA: Harvard University Press, 1994.

Marx, Arthur. *The Secret Life of Bob Hope*. New York: Barricade, 1993.

Mast, Gerald. *Can't Help Singing: The American Musical on Stage and Screen*. Woodstock, NY: Overlook, 1987.

May, Elaine Tyler. *Homeward Bound: American Families in the Cold War Era*. New York: Basic, 1988.

McCormick, Thomas J. *America's Half-Century: United States Foreign Policy in the Cold War*. Baltimore: Johns Hopkins University Press, 1989.

Movie Lot to Beachhead by the Editors of Look. New York: Doubleday, 1945.

Mugge Robert, dir. *Entertaining the Troups: American Entertainers in WWII*. 1989. Image videodisc.

Oakley, J. Ronald. *God's Country: America in the Fifties*. New York: Dembner, 1990.

"Our Story Part One." 1944. USO camp shows. USO World Home Page. Online. August 18, 1996.

"A Proud History." USO World Home Page. Online. August 18, 1996.

Sturges, Preston. *Preston Sturges*, ed. Sandy Sturges. New York: Simon, 1990.

Tynes, Teresa, "Everybody's Big Break: World War II Camp Shows and the Creation of American Television Culture." Society for Cinema Studies conference, New Orleans. February 14, 1993.

6

WANDERLUST AND WIRE WHEELS

The existential search of *Route 66*

Mark Alvey

"Tod says I got unrest," muses Buz Murdock (George Maharis) in the 1960 pilot of *Route 66* ("Black November"), explaining to an old mechanic in a small Southern town the reasons he and his buddy Tod Stiles (Martin Milner) climbed into a Corvette and set out on the road a few months earlier. "So what's wrong with unrest? It's as good as anything. Besides, we're all stuck with it".[1] In 115 subsequent episodes over four seasons, that unrest pushed Tod and Buz (and, later, Tod and Linc Case [Glenn Corbett]) down untold miles of highway, through most of the continental US, into countless encounters with troubled souls. Television's seminal road series, *Route 66* was remarkable for thoughtful character drama, its blending of series and anthology forms, and a groundbreaking cross-country location agenda. Unrelentingly restless and habitually bleak, *Route 66* was the early 1960s' answer to both Kerouac and the Joads – not the usual stuff of prime-time adventure, to be sure. Shunning domesticity on a medium – and network – loaded with family comedies, echoing *On the Road* and anticipating *Easy Rider*, premiering at the dawn of the New Frontier and ending in the shadow of the Vietnam War, *Route 66* occupies a unique place in both the television terrain of the 1960s and the popular culture of the road. In the following pages I examine *Route 66* in an attempt to explain its distinctive use of the road as a story-telling device and thematic trope, and illuminate its singular search for meaning in 1960s America. *Route 66*'s peculiar approach to series drama, and its employment of the road as a dramatic principle, were the product of a specific industrial moment, the essential starting point for our discussion.

"A Peripatetic *Playhouse 90*": The Anthology Hits the Road

Route 66's narrative design emerges directly from the conditions shaping Hollywood television circa 1960. The series draws on two somewhat antithetical trends prevailing in prime-time drama during that period, action-adventure and

Plate 6.1 The *Route 66* road couple (George Maharis and Martin Milner) and their famous Corvette. Courtesy Columbia House Video Library.

the "semi-anthology." Action shows, notably a spate of imitative Westerns (à la *Cheyenne*) and detective shows (*77 Sunset Strip* et al.) from Warner Bros., became the primary symptom of a perceived "crisis" of programming mediocrity and imitativeness bemoaned by critics and industry insiders (predating Newton Minow's "vast wasteland" rhetoric by several years). The semi-anthology, so dubbed by *Variety*, was one effort by telefilm producers to upgrade their dramatic product in the wake of the criticism, a differentiation strategy that fused anthology-style stories with continuing-character conventions in an effort to increase story variety· and narrative flexibility. *Wagon Train* (1957) was widely considered the founding example, and *Naked City* imbued the form with a contemporary sensibility in 1958, using a police-procedural premise as a pretext for stories about New York. *Naked City*'s creators, producer Herbert B. Leonard and writer Stirling Silliphant, mounted *Route 66* two years later.[2]

A superficial glance at *Route 66* might place the series squarely in the action camp. It was nominally an adventure, chronicling the far-flung travels of a disparate duo: Tod, the blue-eyed, Yale-educated, thoughtful one, whose apparent affluence had vanished – save for a Corvette – with his father's death, and his buddy Buz, dark-visaged, streetwise, and impulsive, a tough-but-sensitive orphan from Hell's Kitchen. The show's commercial credentials seemed impeccable: two handsome young leads, a sleek convertible, a picaresque premise à la the wandering westerner – and a guaranteed modicum of mayhem in each installment: Silliphant's original presentation for the series concluded with the promise that each episode would be "packed with at least two or three top-staged brawls (built into the character of Buz)." These apparently escapist elements, however, were eclipsed by the program's more serious dramatic agenda, the seeds of which were outlined in the presentation as well:

> The theme – search, unrest, uncertainty, seeking answers, looking for a way of life.
>
> The people – are young enough to appeal to the youthful audience, old enough to be involved in adult situations.
>
> The stories – will be *about* something, will be honest, and will face up to life, look for and suggest meanings, things people can identify with, and yet there will be the romance and escape of young people with wanderlust.
>
> The locales – the whole width and breadth of the US, with stories shot in the actual locations, à la Naked City. What we did for one city, we now propose to do for a country and for many of its industries and businesses.
>
> The only series about contemporary America on the air. Not a cops and robbers, not a Western, not a private eye.

Even with the promise of formulaic fistfights – an obvious gesture to the persistent commercial viability of "action" – the creators clearly were trying to distance their product from the typical run of television adventure and, significantly, emphasize the series' relative independence from genre constraints. "This was a very impossible thing to sell to a studio, you can understand," Silliphant recalled in a 1987 interview. "'It's an existential search, gents, we don't know what it is;' and they're going to say, 'Well, when you know what it is, come back and tell us.'"[3] Leonard and Silliphant have both reported that Columbia-Screen Gems executives opposed the project early on, and in fact refused to underwrite the pilot, arguing that no advertiser would buy a show about "two bums on the road" ("Remembrances": 54; "Dialogue": 15).

Given the industry's ostensible quest for innovation, however, and the growing currency of serious drama and "semi-anthologies," the series' unusual premise augured well for its ultimate sale to CBS. (And in retrospect it doesn't seem so difficult to visualize Chevrolet embracing a series that featured its signature sports car as a "third character."[4]) Even with its leavening of fistfights and youth appeal, *Route 66* has a far more distinct kinship with the early 1960s trend toward social-realist drama (e.g., *The Defenders, Dr. Kildare, East Side, West Side, Slattery's People*) than with the action cycle represented by *77 Sunset Strip*. And among these other social dramas and semi-anthologies *Route 66* was unique, for, while it shared their contemporary setting and serious tone, unlike them it was not bound to a familiar generic arena (courtroom, hospital, newsroom), nor were its dramatic conflicts circumscribed by such defined institutional settings (law, medicine, politics). Its only genre forebear was road fiction, and its only dramatic backdrop America.

The road premise was perfectly suited to the semi-anthology format. *Wagon Train* had established the basic pattern for this variation, with the pioneer journey providing a framework, and a pretext, for episodic character studies built around "guest stars." Guest stars, in fact, became a staple commercial element of television drama during this period, and *Route 66* would go on to feature proven Hollywood stars like Joan Crawford and emerging talents like Robert Redford.[5] For its subject matter, *Route 66* leaned toward contemporary psychological drama, often with a dark edge; as Silliphant told *Time* in a 1963 profile, "We are terribly serious, and we feel that life contains a certain amount of pain" (61). It was the show's penchant for psychology and seriousness that led to the legendary complaint from one CBS vice-president for its failure to adhere to network president James Aubrey's programming "dictum" of "broads, bosoms, and fun."[6] Another network executive, concerned with the show's "downbeat" tone, warned its producers that the series should not be considered "a peripatetic *Playhouse 90*" ("Hearings": 13–14).

Willingly or not, the network official captured much of the show's aesthetic character. *Route 66* functions as an anthology of psychological dramas and character studies predicated on the intersection of Tod and Buz's odyssey with the lives of other people. The episodic stories are interconnected by the journey, and suffused with the restlessness that fuels it. It is instructive to note that the title first proposed for the series was *The Searchers*, suggesting a fundamental principle of its story-telling structure.[7] As with most road texts, *Route 66* is a tale of both search and flight, and as a serial narrative characteristic of American commercial television, its central meaning lies not in some finite goal at the end of the road, but in the discoveries made along the way.

The Narrative Trajectory of *Route 66*

While its wandering premise and virtual freedom from genre constraints offered a potentially limitless variety of stories, *Route 66*'s anthology structure, and its serious intent (eschewing formulaic jeopardy plots and violent heroics), fostered a tendency toward dramas of personal or psychological crisis. From Silliphant's perspective, the "search" framework of the series necessitated "anthological" stories – "they had to be about the people in these locations." Thus, *Route 66* emphasizes not the tales of the searchers themselves, but those of the various souls encountered by Tod and Buz (and Linc, Tod's new partner beginning in 1963) in their stops along the highway.[8] Typical of many semi-anthologies of the period, the guest stars generally serve as protagonists of a given episode – their motives, not those of the continuing characters, propel the narratives. In episode after episode, the guys either drive into town just as a particular individual or group is confronted with some sort of crisis, or cross paths with the protagonists at an early stage in the dramatic conflict. Although the wanderers invariably become involved emotionally in the central situation, their narrative agency is usually limited. As Todd Gitlin has remarked apropos of the cops in *Naked City*, the nomads of *Route 66* generally "faded into the background while the foreground belonged to each week's new character" (66).

A first-season episode entitled "Ten Drops of Water" is a good illustration of the structure of *Route 66*, and the kind of role the searchers generally serve in the series. After a chance encounter with a boy and his stubborn mule on a dusty road not far from Kanab, Utah, Tod and Buz soon become involved in the struggle of the Paige family to save their drought-stricken ranch. Tod and Buz learn from a neighbor that Homer and his older brother and sister, Virgil and Helen, have been running the ranch alone since their parents died four years ago; they are fiercely independent. In short order the family's well gives out; Virgil tries to get a loan at the bank to buy enough water to hold them until the well can be fixed; Virgil chases the mule away when he tries to drink from the trough, and the animal runs into the desert, and Homer follows; soon a dust storm flares up, and Tod and Buz join Helen to hunt for Homer; Virgil remains to work on the well. Finally a desperate Virgil stumbles to the neighbors' ranch and asks for help. In the last act, the mule is dead, the pump is fixed, the water is flowing again. But Helen wonders about next time; Homer doesn't want to live in a place where there's not enough water for a poor old mule. After asking Tod and Buz if Oregon is as lush as he's heard, Virgil walks over to speak to his neighbor, presumably about selling the ranch. In the final scene, Homer visits his parents' grave, and the family drives away.

Tod and Buz are strictly ancillary narrative agents here. Manifesting a common trope of the series, the boys try to help, but ultimately have no real power, and thus no effect. They contribute physical assistance in attempting to fix the well (to no avail), assist Helen in searching for Homer in the dust storm, and, most pertinent to the central conflict, they offer advice, suggesting to Virgil that perhaps he should give up. But it is the Paige family's story, and ultimately it is Virgil who makes the pivotal decision to sell the ranch. In this episode Tod and Buz literally cross paths with the protagonists, and thus provide an entry into their story, but have no significant stake or function in it.

Characteristic of *Route 66*, and the semi-anthology strategy in general, many of the key dramatic scenes take place outside the narrative purview of the series regulars: two scenes of Homer at his parents' grave; Virgil making his case to the banker; Virgil and Helen discussing their plight. Even though Tod and Buz are present through much of the narrative, they are largely irrelevant to the story, "fading into the background" of the central dramatic conflicts. The wanderers have no social authority (unlike the doctors, lawyers, and psychiatrists of other social dramas of the era); they are ultimately helpless to assist the family. Likewise, they have no real narrative authority. As if to emphasize just whose story this really is, as the credits roll, the final shots of the episode depict the Paige family heading up the road in their pickup, not Tod and Buz in the Corvette.

Silliphant has suggested, quite aptly, that the searchers' primary function was "bearing witness" to the lives and stories they encountered. On occasion the guys do serve a slightly more active function by catalyzing an episode's central dramatic conflict, but their subsequent agency still remains marginal. In "Mon Petit Chou" (1961), for example, Tod becomes smitten with a young chanteuse, arousing the jealousy of her manager, an embittered piano-player – sparking an exploration of their relationship. Tod has little else to do (until a climactic fistfight with the piano-player); he and Buz are off screen for nearly half of the episode. There are occasional exceptions to the "anthological" episodes, in which one of the regulars takes center stage. In "The Thin White Line" (1961) Tod takes a nightmarish odyssey through the streets of Philadelphia after accidentally being slipped a hallucinogenic drug; his point of view dominates the entire episode, and there are no major guest stars. In "The Mud Nest" (1961) Buz stumbles onto a family that he thinks might be his, and searches for the woman who could be his mother; here Buz's goals motivate the story, and he appears in every scene. In "Fifty Miles from Home," the 1963 episode that introduces Linc, he functions in effect as the guest star-protagonist, with the story focusing on his ambivalence about returning home to a hero's welcome after his tour of duty in Vietnam. Such episodes are interesting, indeed distinctive, insofar as they provide closer and more sustained explorations of the emotional makeup of the regular characters, but they are exceptions to the typical pattern of the series. By and large, as Gilbert Seldes observed in his *TV Guide* review of the series, "our heroes come as close to being innocent bystanders as they can." This relative marginalization of its "heroes" distances *Route 66* from the bulk of the Westerns and action dramas of the period (the character studies of *Wagon Train* excepted). Tod and Buz are rarely active protagonists; they are invested neither with social authority nor the moral authority of genre heroes, nor do they regularly face thrilling perils that they must resolve by force or cunning.

But if the involvement of Tod and Buz at the episodic level of the series is generally marginal and limited, it still serves a crucial function, and one that transcends purely narrative concerns. In "bearing witness," Tod and Buz offer a compassionate window onto the troubles of other people. As bystanders, and, crucially, outsiders in the communities and conflicts through which they pass, they serve to generate insights into the motivations and mysteries of the characters they encounter. In "Welcome to Amity" for example, a young woman returns to her hometown after a long absence in order to move her mother's grave from a pauper's field to the highest point in the town cemetery. The community opposes her project, however, and the only people she can hire to dig the new grave are two strangers – Tod and Buz. The boys continually question the attitude of the townspeople, but are met with angry resistance. The past, and the woman's motives, finally are revealed in a confrontation between her and her aunt. Except for digging the grave, haranguing some of the locals for their intolerance, and, finally, comforting the woman at the grave-site, Tod and Buz function at the margins in this story. However, in this and similar episodes, the searchers' efforts to help and support their troubled acquaintances provoke answers which would not be available without their perspective. In bearing witness, Tod and Buz function as the emotional and moral "eyes" through which we view these stories; their reactions, and their judgments, provide a kind of reference point for the viewers'. This is not to suggest that the searchers possess any moral certitude, or know any of the "answers." As Philip Booth writes in his essay on the series, "The questions they ask of themselves, and the world, rarely admit of a simple 'right' answer" (12). As "heroes," Tod and Buz are confused, helpless, and fallible, but as "witnesses" they provoke a more intimate understanding of the lives they intersect on the road.

The preceding discussion has stressed the degree to which the travels of Tod and Buz function primarily as a pretext for relatively autonomous anthology-style stories. From a broader perspective, however, the search of *Route 66* constructs a significance of its own. While Tod and Buz seldom have a concrete narrative agenda at an episodic level – motivated largely by compassion, and their "good samaritan" impulses – their restlessness constitutes a macro-level narrative foundation for the series. Buz articulates it in the first episode when he muses on his own "unrest," and in subsequent episodes they explain their wandering as a search for "a place to plant roots," or "a place where we really fit"; Linc too is explicit about seeking a purpose, finding meaning. Admittedly, the thread of continuity present in *Route 66* is more a function of this thematic realm of the "existential search" than of causally driven or historically developed narrative structure.[9] Still, as Silliphant has suggested, there are "two levels working at all times" in the show: the search, and the individual stories. My argument for the search functioning as a "pretext" for the show's anthology dimension is grounded in the fact that it is never the dominant subject of any one episode. Yet, although it is emphasized only in passing, and seldom articulated explicitly, it is always there. Even as background, it is constantly present, connoted by the Corvette, the bedrolls, the rooming houses, the road, even the very fact that Tod and Buz are seldom in the same place in the next episode. Indeed, the wide-ranging and ever-changing locations themselves – the production covered twenty-four states (and Toronto) in four years – vividly reinforce the show's restless subtext. If *Route 66* is an anthology of individual character studies, it is, simultaneously, a saga of wanderlust and unrest. One could perform a kind of figure-ground reversal on the series' intertwined trajectories and argue that the anthology dimension is, in fact, merely the pretext for the wandering, rather than the other way around.[10] From this perspective, *Route 66* can be said to have long-term, even serial, narrative stakes. These stakes – the goals of the search – are often submerged, yet they are crucial to the series. From the long view, the series is as much about the search, and the wandering itself, as it is about the various people and conflicts encountered along the way. With both narrative levels in play, *Route 66* manifests in a unique way the tension between the ongoing and the episodic, between the serial and the anthological dimensions of semi-anthologies, and indeed of all episodic series.

The notion that *Route 66* possessed a larger, over-arching narrative identity is borne out to some degree by the fact that the series does finally come to a self-conscious narrative closure, a two-part finale in which Tod gets married.[11] Unfortunately, this rather momentous narrative event is afforded scant dramatic weight in terms of "the search"; there is virtually no exploration of the impact this wedding will have on the wanderers, save for one scene in which Linc ponders his choices (declaring that he's tired of roaming around the country with no clear destination, but also opposed to staying in the same place with no purpose). The dramatic and structural significance of this pivotal moment in the series, and the lives of these two characters, is addressed only in the final seconds of the episode. In the last scene Linc tells Tod he is "going back home for a while." Tod protests that he and his bride will be driving the same direction, but Linc reminds him, "That's a two-seater you got there, old buddy." Tod responds with a sad smile. Linc simply says, "See ya," and walks out the door. Tod looks pensive for a moment, then turns to embrace his new partner, his new life. In the last shot of the series, Linc leans on the Corvette for a moment, giving it a last longing look, and walks up the driveway toward the road.

Although the narrative trajectory of the *Route 66* saga is concluded all too abruptly, the series does end on a note of uncertainty, with one of the principals still on the road. Tod, perhaps, has found what he was searching for; Linc's future is more ambiguous. He is heading home, for now, but it is clear that he has yet to find the meaning he sought when Tod (and we) first met him – he is still searching. In this sense, the long-term stakes of the program are left tantalizingly open. And even though Tod presumably is "settling down," his marriage does not with a stroke of finality erase whatever questions, disillusionment, and yearning drove the previous four years and 20,000-odd miles of searching. As Buz said in the very first episode, "we're all stuck with" unrest. This unrest, which pushes the wanderers down the road, and drives the series, takes us beyond strictly formal and narrative concerns to the larger cultural and thematic patterns manifested in the search.

The Existential Road-Map of *Route 66*

In retrospect *Route 66* seems to be a more apt title for the series than the one originally planned, since its stories tend to focus less on the searchers and more on their various encounters. The historical, cultural, and mythic implications of Route 66, "The Main Street of America," impart a highly charged metaphoric significance to the title.[12] Although the searchers traveled far beyond US Highway 66, the notion of "the road," and that road in particular, evokes both the long stretches of highway as well as the dots on the map, each containing its own instances of human drama. To understand *Route 66* we must understand both the restlessness that fuels search, and the fleeting discoveries made in each encounter. The unrest that underlies the show is inextricably linked to, and also transcends, its particular historical context. The road has been a multivalent cultural symbol for every era in the life of America, and *Route 66*, emerging in the wake of Ike and the Beats, arriving with JFK and a New Frontier, captures in a singular way the nation's passage from the disquiet of the 1950s to the turbulence of the 1960s.

Because of its highway-bound backdrop and its nomadic social dropouts, as well as its timing, *Route 66* has drawn inevitable comparisons to Jack Kerouac's *On the Road* (the program premiered three years after the publication of the novel), usually posited as a clean-cut, sanitized variation on the novel.[13] According to biographer Dennis McNally, Kerouac found the similarity so compelling he twice tried to enlist attorneys in filing suit against Silliphant for plagiarism, but both advised him that his cause was groundless (272). When asked about the resemblance in 1962, Herbert Leonard replied, "I never heard of the book until a few weeks ago" (Gehman: 17). Of course it's inconceivable that one or the other of the show's creators had not heard of the controversial bestseller. Even so, Kerouac's attorneys advised him well; the resemblances between the two texts are superficial – it is their differences that are truly provocative.

It is instructive to examine both of these road works in light of Paul Goodman's *Growing Up Absurd* (published the same year *Route 66* premiered), the classic study of various disaffected subcultures of young American males, including "juvenile delinquents" and the Beats. The factors that Goodman saw driving these youths' disillusionment and rejection of dominant society in the late 1950s are consistent with those manifested by Tod, Buz, and Linc in *Route 66*: a lack of purpose, identity, and community. Certainly the discontent, and the wanderlust, of *Route 66*'s searchers link them to the restless nomads of Kerouac's America. Yet the unrest and dissatisfaction at the root of both *On the Road* and *Route 66*, though related, are not identical. In Goodman's view the novel expresses only "the woeful emptiness of running away from even loneliness and vague discontent" (280). Both texts can be said to be motivated by a search for meaning, but *On the Road* seems to be fueled by an almost visceral need, a thirst for experience (partially as grist for the aspiring writer), visions, kicks. Out on *Route 66*, Tod and Buz and Linc are each escaping, to some degree, from the pain of the past, but also looking for an identity, a purpose.

The "search" itself plays out quite differently in each case. Remarkably little of Kerouac's novel actually takes place on the road. The highway is presented in a headlong rush of cities and states, with thousands of miles sketched in a few sentences, and little consideration of the stops along the way. Kerouac's alter-ego Sal Paradise spends most of the novel hurtling between New York, Denver, and San Francisco; his destinations are concrete, and once he arrives he stays for a while. There is a manic quality to the book's restlessness, an erratic, temporary feel to its travels. In some respects Sal is more a Beat tourist than a social drop-out. "What I wanted was to take one more magnificent trip to the West Coast and get back in time for the spring semester in school," he proposes at one point. "I said good-by to my aunt and promised to be back in two weeks and took off for California again" (107, 110). Such passages bear out Goodman's observations on the curious ambivalence of the Beats to their middle-class backgrounds (often obscured amidst the Beat mythology). Ultimately, as Goodman writes of *On the Road*, "One is stunned at how conventional and law-fearing these lonely middle-class fellows are" (280).

Indeed, as David Marc points out in his book *Comic Visions*, *On the Road* and Kerouac's other novels "betray a profound ambiguity concerning the relative merits of suburban family life and alternative modes of existence" (67). Sal Paradise, Marc writes, "wanders the continent with Whitmanian abandon, but dutifully returns to the white-picket-fence home of his aunt in New Jersey every time he feels 'the pull of my own life calling me back'" (67). Tellingly, Sal refers to his aunt's house as "home" throughout the novel, and returns there several times, in addition to visiting his brother and his "Southern relatives." In addition, Sal Paradise has not only this biological family, but also an extended family of wild men and poets in Denver and California.

From this perspective, Kerouac's bohemians are scarcely more dissident or disaffected than the ostensibly "sanitized" drifters of *Route 66*. Tod and Buz, of course, have no family, no roots, no home but the Corvette. They have no destination in mind; their route is uncertain. Their trek is not a brief fling on the road before getting back to the business of everyday life. The road, during these several years, *is* their life; their timetable is ambiguous and open-ended. Only Linc has a "back home" to go to, and he distances himself from it for a time, not so much ambivalent as alienated.

Above all, *On the Road* is the story of Sal Paradise, a tale narrated in the first person by an extraordinarily self-centered narrator. *Route 66*, as we have seen, is comprised of many stories, and concerns the lonely souls of America's backroads as much as the searchers themselves. In *On the Road*, Goodman points out, "there are hundreds of incidents, but throughout most of the book, nothing is told." It would be unfair to say that the novel ignores its transient characters, but Sal's attention to and involvement in their lives is undeniably fleeting. As Goodman suggests with great insight, "The entire action of *On the Road* is the avoidance of interpersonal conflict" (279–80).

The dominant thrust of *Route 66* is largely the opposite: the *embrace* of inter-personal *involvement*. Despite their unrest, Tod and Buz are not alienated from society. Whatever it is they are seeking, the meanings they find ultimately involve making some connection or contribution to the lives of others. Indeed, if anything, *Route 66* draws more on the chivalric tradition than the Beat generation; tellingly, a 1961 audience survey commissioned by the show's sponsors indicated that *Route 66* viewers held "the 'knight errand' [*sic*] role of the two stars" to be central to the series (Summary: 2). Their paladin function was updated, of course; television historians Castleman and Podrazik have proposed that the guys tended to function as "unofficial social workers and psychoanalysts" in the series (144) – an accurate enough assessment, although, as we've seen, their intentions seldom translated into effective agency. Even the advertisers recognized – and celebrated – the centrality of "other people" to the series, as evidenced in the promotional tag that preceded each episode: "There's no pot of gold at the end of the rainbow, nor a pan of silver at the end of *Route 66*. Just people, a far more rewarding discovery" (quoted in Booth: 12).[14]

In discovering people, Tod and Buz satisfy a part of their quest, if perhaps unknowingly. Linc is more conscious of this realization. In the final episode of the series he declares that the only way to find meaning ("get turned on") is "to find something to do for people – people who need you." If Tod and Buz do not always articulate it so explicitly, they continually effect it in practice. In "A Bridge Across Five Days," Buz befriends Lillian, a middle-aged woman trying to move back into mainstream society after eighteen years in a mental hospital. Lillian calls Buz late one night, after the workplace argument that first brings them together. Buz is puzzled by the call – does she want an apology, is there trouble? She tells him, "I'm trying to build a bridge." Buz recognizes the phone call as a cry for help, and is saddened that Lillian had no one else to call but him, a virtual stranger. At its most explicit level the bridge Lillian refers to (and the bridge of the title) is the transition she is trying to make into the "normal" world. But her words also suggest another kind of bridge: a bridge to another person, a bridge out of isolation, beyond loneliness, across alienation.

Although not all of *Route 66*'s stories articulate the idea so explicitly, many of them center on such attempts to forge the connections between human beings, the relationships that often seem so difficult to build and maintain, but are ultimately essential to social life. The stories do not argue that love conquers all, nor that every problem can be solved by the intervention of well-meaning "heroes." They acknowledge, as Buz does in "Voice at the End of the Line," that "every one of us is born into solitary confinement; and we spend the rest of our lives sending out a small SOS we hope someone will hear." Some of us are rescued from this isolation. Some aren't.

This vision of America is markedly different from that presented by most television programming during this period – the most pertinent fictional context against which *Route 66* must be read. American television has always displayed and celebrated the domestic sphere in its fiction, even as the appliance's centrality in the home helped cultivate it in social life.[15] Horace Newcomb has called the family "the central symbol of television," and this was nowhere more true than the early 1960s (261). Prime time during this period was dominated by situation comedies, most of which centered on some version of family life. The cop shows and professional dramas too exhibited the extended (or surrogate) "workplace" families, and usually portrayed or at least alluded to the familial relationships of their members. Even the Westerns took a turn for the domestic in dynastic sagas like *Bonanza* and *The Big Valley*. Only the handful of rootless frontier heroes like Cheyenne and Maverick were as restless and disconnected as Tod and Buz.

As a *contemporary* drama, however, the distance *Route 66* puts between itself and the picket-fenced American dream is singularly significant. Here again the series resonates to some degree with its Beat precursors. In her book *The Hearts of Men*, Barbara Ehrenreich argues that two strains of postwar male rebellion, the Organization Man's contempt for his 9-to-5 grind, and the Hefner-Playboy's rejection of married domesticity, reached their apotheosis (albeit briefly) in the Beats (52). *Route 66* obviously is more consistent with this flight from suburban stasis than with most of its prime-time contemporaries (although it must be said that, like the Beats, the searchers are remarkably free of Hefner's "philosophy" of materialistic concupiscence, the Corvette notwithstanding). To be sure, *Route 66* does not *reject* domesticity, but it is just as ambivalent about it as *On the Road*, if not more. The directionless journey of the searchers keeps them far removed from domestic stability. The corollary to the series' wanderlust was an assumption (sometimes explicit) that the guys eventually wanted to settle down; however, the narrative imperative of the series' premise continually staved off that option. In occasional episodes one of the wanderers would fall in love, but for one reason or another the relationship never worked out. One goal of the search, fleetingly articulated as "a place to put down roots," or "a place where we fit," is shown to be difficult to achieve, and problematic to maintain. The series did not say "no" to middle-class domesticity, just "not yet."

Route 66 never depicts the comfort and familiarity of the suburban home, or the domesticated workplace. With few exceptions, the world Tod and Buz travel in is by definition a world divorced from family and domestic ties. Theirs is an America of rented rooms, motels, trailer parks, and bunkhouses. Tod and Buz never pass through the suburban sphere of Rob and Laura Petrie, the middle-American landscape of the Cleavers or the Andersons, nor the welcoming small town of Andy Taylor and Aunt Bea. The people whose paths they cross are often just as rootless and disaffected as they are, hardly the people next door: a tormented jazz musician, a heroin addict, a washed-up prizefighter, an aging RAF pilot (turned crop-duster), a runaway heiress, Cajun shrimpers, a weary hobo, an eccentric scientist, a small-time beauty contest "promoter," hard-scrabble farmers, Cuban-Basque jai-alai players, a newly paroled con (framed by her abusive lover), a grim Nazi-hunter, a blind dance instructor, a dying blues singer – the list could go on, alienated outsiders of every conceivable type, all marginalized by fate, hurt, or choice.

The darker edge of the program's stance on domestic life is most clearly illustrated by the remarkable number of orphans, loners, and fractured families that pass through the series. Tod and Buz are alone in the world; Linc is estranged from his father; runaway orphan kids figure in at least two episodes, not to mention the Paige children; Lillian ("Bridge Across Five Days") was an orphan, and finds that her own daughter regards her as dead; "Man Out of Time" depicts an old mobster haunted by the memory of his dead son; Joan in "Welcome to Amity" reveals that she hates her mother's memory; the protagonist of "Love is a Skinny Kid" returns home to confront her mother, who had the girl "committed" as a child and told the town she was dead; the woman whom Buz thinks might be his mother in "The Mud Nest" tells him her child had in fact died in infancy; in "Like a Motherless Child" Buz befriends an aging prostitute wracked with guilt over the child she gave away; the eccentric heiress of "How Much a Pound is Albatross" lost her family in a plane crash and is running from her grief. Little wonder, perhaps, that the network that aired *Father Knows Best*, *Dennis the Menace*, *Father of the Bride*, and *Andy Griffith* on other evenings during this time might have found such fare disturbing.

Unlike so much of television fiction, then and now, *Route 66* does not affirm and celebrate family and domesticity, but rather foregrounds how fragile and problematic such social relationships can be. Its restless search, and many of its stories, constitute an admission that the lures of suburbia, home and hearth are not inevitably stable and comforting. The notion that "we're all stuck with" unrest, and that each one of us is born into loneliness, is central to the series. *Route 66* could be said to constitute both a search for community, and a testament to the difficulty of achieving it.

None of this should be taken to suggest that *Route 66* presented an urelentingly pessimistic view of domesticity, or of American society. The show's narrative variety admitted morality plays, tender love stories, and even the infrequent comedy or (very infrequent) murder mystery.[16] But the bulk of the stories bore out Silliphant's characterization of the series as "terribly serious," and the CBS executive's "downbeat" complaint. Some episodes close on a note of hope, others with a cry of anguish. The stories necessarily end, but the problems are not always solved. And every episode ends with the understanding that the searchers are still looking.

This picture is suggestive of the larger cultural patterns at work in *Route 66*. As I suggested earlier, the series occupies an interesting historical position as a cultural text, in terms of both its imagery and its position at the dawn of a new decade. The road, the restless mobility of the two wanderers, and even the Corvette evoke several familiar currents of postwar America: prosperity, consumption, leisure, mobility, even tourism. Although their search was borne of unrest, these admittedly clean-cut drop-outs and their gleaming convertible spoke to the middle-class wanderlust of postwar families on summer vacations as much as the disaffection of the Beats.

The road itself, and the search it connotes, are likewise complex. Every search has two sides, one of optimism and one of dissatisfaction, and *Route 66* is no exception. The road offers both escape and hope. The rear-view mirror reflects what's left behind – pain, perhaps joy, but not the right "fit"; the horizon offers the possibility that the lack will be satisfied. The Corvette itself is a curiously conflicted symbol in the series. At a general level it exemplifies the nation's (and the American male's) postwar "love affair" with the automobile. It is a sports car, with a powerful engine and only two seats, signifying speed, mobility, independence (not a "family car"); yet it is sometimes put to work (helping people) as a winch, towing a trailer, pulling a mule (it looks strangely out of place on a Utah ranch and a New Mexico pueblo). It is an expensive convertible, a status symbol (prosperity, consumption); but it is Tod's only real asset, and his single memento of his father; he must drive forklifts and pitch hay to put gas in it (in one episode he sells its wire wheels to stake a morally righteous crap game). Thus, the Corvette and its occupants manifest a curious mix of the bourgeois and the beat.

Route 66 takes its own place in the imagery of the road in American popular culture, and it does so in a way peculiarly resonant for 1960. Tod, Buz, and Linc, in their youth, their movement, and their unrest, echo not only the Beats but the young rebels of 1950s cinema personified by James Dean and Marlon Brando. They also anticipate the counter-cultural anti-heroes of the late 1960s,

Plate 6.2 In the third season Glenn Corbett (pictured here with guest star Susan Oliver) joined Milner on the road. Used by permission of the Wisconsin Center for Film and Theater Research.

particularly that even more disaffected duo that would follow them down the highway in a search for America at the end of the decade in *Easy Rider*. The more pessimistic side of the series not only spoke to the contradictions of bourgeois domesticity, but also presaged the malaise and division that would evolve by the end of the decade, beginning with the assassination of JFK and culminating in Vietnam.

Indeed, *Route 66* was remarkably prescient about that most divisive national issue of the late 1960s. Although the series was rarely topical in the same way as some of its contemporaries like *East Side, West Side* or *The Defenders* (episodes dealing with heroin addiction and right-wing extremism being two notable "issue-oriented" exceptions), it was certainly the first American television series to explore the nation's involvement in Vietnam on a consistent basis. Silliphant worked the issue into the series because of his "obsession" with Vietnam and its history, and his conviction that "we were getting into a load of shit," just as the French did before us. However, Linc's stance on the war, and thus the show's, is undeniably ambivalent. When he first returns stateside (in "Fifty Miles From Home"), he tells his mother he does not want the hero's welcome his hometown has planned, because "it's the killer they're honoring." Yet he also suggests that he found meaning in helping South Vietnamese farmers stand up for themselves. In this sense Linc doesn't question America's involvement in the war, in fact he affirms it to some degree. Still, he is clearly ambivalent about his own role in it; Vietnam is not a mission to which he is willing to return. The experience obviously troubles him, and the issue returns to haunt him in subsequent episodes. Vietnam becomes a recurrent topic in the series, and certainly a subtext for Linc's character, throughout the show's final season. Admittedly, *Route 66* broached Vietnam well before American involvement had escalated to tragic levels, which is undoubtedly why the subject could be addressed directly and somewhat critically. That the series manifested a distinct ambiguity on the war should hardly be surprising, not only because the war was a vague and distant conflict in 1963, but because it is still divisive thirty years later, still being re-fought, re-thought and revised in popular film and television discourse.

Again, the search of *Route 66*, like every search, entails optimism as well as discontent. The show's more hopeful dimension paralleled the optimism of a new beginning that some glimpsed in American society in 1960 with the election of John F. Kennedy.[17] It could even be argued, to engage in a bit of Kennedy-era reflectionism that is only partly facetious, that the show's nomadic duo constituted their own two-man domestic Peace Corps, symptomatic of the era's new spirit of activism. In a sense *Route 66* stands as a fitting metaphor for the New Frontier, manifesting an implicit optimism, a conviction that a horizon of hope, a renewal of meaning, lies just over the next hill. At the episodic level, the series constituted a journey to discover – rediscover – America itself, in its deserts, warehouses, bayous, cabstands, mountains, steel mills, barges, and bar-rooms, and of course, its people.

But the search continues, speaking to the unrest that "we're all stuck with," the restlessness that perhaps can never be satisfied. We last see Linc walking toward the highway to stick out his thumb, the end of his search indefinite. Although Tod's roaming is ostensibly over, the final image of the series is the Corvette, pointing away from the house (and the camera), toward the road. The empty convertible, with luggage strapped to its rack, connotes restless pause, incipient movement – and four years of wandering – far more than closure and stasis. What is that feeling, that nameless ache that drives the searchers out on the road? Kerouac could not define it, but he evokes it not half-badly in *On the Road*: "What is that feeling when you're driving away from people and they recede on the plain till you see their specks dispersing? – it's the too-huge world vaulting us, and it's good-by. But we lean forward to the next crazy venture beneath the skies" (130). The search, of course, is an end in itself, restlessness its own destination. The endless road is a goal, satisfying, only for the moment, the need to just go. In this the guys in the shiny Corvette were not so different from Kerouac's bohemians in their beat '49 Hudson, expressing an unrest that is not confined to any one decade or generation. As Buz acknowledges in the first episode, reflecting on his own unrest, "Sure – we're looking. Tod says if we keep moving we'll find a place to plant roots and stick. With me? It's fine, just . . . moving."

Road's End

Leonard and Silliphant have both referred to the Corvette as "third character" of *Route 66*. But the series featured an even bigger star: America. As Gilbert Seldes observed in his 1962 *TV Guide* review, "I am sure they bring their New York or Hollywood plots with them. They also bring an eye for the place, a curiosity about what makes one city different from another," he wrote. "And while each program differs from the others, all of them together differ from the run of TV program series – they are played in different air." The show's wide-ranging location agenda gave it a unique visual realism that no studio backlot could duplicate, from the glitter of Reno to the forests of Poland Spring, Maine, from the hill country near Austin, Texas to the skyscrapers of Chicago, the docks of Astoria, Oregon to the sails in Tampa bay. Prior to the series' cancellation in 1964, the production was slated to move to Europe for a fifth season, and switch to color. While the two restless expatriates certainly would have encountered untold dramas on the *autobahn*, the Rue de Madeleine, and Twickenham Road, it is fitting that a show first proposed as a series about contemporary America ended its journey here in the USA.

Other searchers followed Tod and Buz down the highway in the early 1960s, as the image of the wandering samaritan continued to be employed as a dramatic device in prime time. *Bus Stop* (1961) inverted the premise, using the stopover setting of William Inge's play as a pretext for stories of troubled transients; *Frontier Circus* (1961), *Straightaway* (1961), *Stoney Burke* (1962) each concocted a nomadic premise (itinerant circus troupe, stock car racers, and the rodeo circuit, respectively) for anthology-style story-telling. As the decade wore on and Camelot crumbled, the restlessness of television's nomadic anthologies gave way to a more pronounced malaise, and the narrative impetus to wander became more concrete. *The Fugitive* (1963–7) retained the nomadic knight-errant formula, adding a more concrete serial structure (and a compelling dose of paranoia) in the form of the chase subplot; *Run For Your Life* (1965–8) employed an incurable illness as its guiding narrative stimulus; *Then Came Bronson* (1969) had a more abstractly existentialist premise, with the title character drawn to the road by a friend's suicide.

In 1993 the Corvette took to the highway once more in a nominal sequel, a summer series (on NBC) that put Buz's illegitimate son (inexplicably) at the wheel with a glib Generation-X partner in the passenger seat. Although the new *Route 66* lasted only a few weeks, by revisiting the roaming-anthology premise of the original, it evidenced television's continuing quest for narrative flexibility, and the durability of the semi-anthology (as well as Hollywood's inherent penchant for recycling). From *The Fugitive* to *The Incredible Hulk*, *Run For Your Life* to *Quantum Leap*, *Then Came Bronson* to *Johnny Bago*, *Movin' On* to *Crossroads*, *Highway to Heaven* to *Touched by an Angel*, television has continued to exploit the tradition of the wandering samaritan as a means of blending the story variety of an anthology with the continuing series format. *Route 66* established the template in 1960, launching a singular effort at contemporary television drama.

In his biography of Kerouac, Dennis McNally accuses Silliphant and Leonard of lifting "the archetypal freedom image" from *On the Road* (272). If it were possible to plagiarize an archetype, of course, one could make a similar case for Kerouac pirating from Cooper, Melville, and Hemingway, not to mention *Detour*, *I Am a Fugitive From a Chain Gang*, *They Made Me a Criminal*, *The Grapes of Wrath*, and *It Happened One Night*; indeed, McNally himself acknowledges Kerouac's debt to Mark Twain, and Kerouac's alter-ego Sal Paradise invokes both *Sullivan's Travels* and Steinbeck during his journey. *Route 66* simply followed Kerouac on the historical highway of American road fiction, and made its own contribution to the literature of the road, one that is every bit as provocative and important. That the series mounted its dramatic agenda on television, in a Corvette, on the road – literally – is to its creators' everlasting credit.

Notes

1 All dialogue has been transcribed from videotaped episodes of the series. Episodes quoted or summarized at length are documented in "Works Cited." Air dates cited therein are from Gianakos.
2 For contemporary examples of the "crisis" rhetoric see "Is There a Programming Crisis?," Cunningham, Horowitz, and Hackett. The essential study of Warner Bros. television and its action cycles is found in Anderson. On the "semi-anthology" strategy see Rosen, "TV Anthologies," and Gelman. On *Naked City* see "We Can Make 'Em" and "Naked Truth." For production background on *Route 66* see Jenkins, and "Rough Road."
3 All attributions to quotations from Silliphant are from the author's 1987 telephone interview unless otherwise noted.
4 As both Silliphant and Leonard dubbed the Corvette in the author's 1987 telephone interviews. Chevrolet remained a 50 percent sponsor throughout the show's four-year run.

5 A sampling of *Route 66* guest stars would include Buster Keaton, Dorothy Malone, Douglas Fairbanks, Jr, Ethel Waters, Sylvia Sidney, Boris Karloff, Tuesday Weld, Rod Steiger, Robert Duvall, Susan Oliver, Walter Matthau, Suzanne Pleshette, Leslie Nielsen, and Lee Marvin.

6 The "Aubrey dictum" tale is recounted in Barnouw, Bergreen, Halberstam, and Watson. See also "Hearings": 15.

7 Silliphant's pilot script for *The Searchers*, "The Wolf Tree," dated October 7, 1959, is housed in the Stirling Silliphant Collection, UCLA Library Dept. of Special Collections. See also "Two 'Searchers'."

8 Maharis left the show in a contract dispute in 1963. Secondary sources like Brooks and Marsh and *Columbia Pictures Television* report that Maharis left the series owing to a bout with hepatitis, and Silliphant and Leonard made the same claims in their 1987 interviews with the author. However, what may have begun as an illness became a spate of lawsuits and accusations, with Maharis accused of "malingering," attempting to halt production in order to break his contract. The case was settled out of court in October of 1963. The Herbert Leonard papers at UCLA contain an extensive file on "Lancer Productions vs. George Maharis." See also, for example, "For the Record," "A Knock," and "Lancer Brief."

9 The series does not construct a consistent and ongoing sense of continuity. Any concrete geographical and chronological links between episodes are infrequent and fairly superficial, as when the fellows refer in passing to their next destination, or the rare instances in which they are in the same location and job in successive episodes. Some consecutive episodes do exhibit coherent geographical progression, but others diverge wildly – probably in a nod to geographic variety – as, for example, when Tod and Linc appear in Maine, Minnesota, Colorado, and Vermont in consecutive episodes in the fourth season. Likewise, like most episodic series of the era, the continuing characters of *Route 66* do not exhibit a developed sense of memory or history. Although we know Tod can quote Rimbaud, Buz digs Thelonious Monk, and Linc is estranged from his father, ultimately the guys are more types than characters – Tod the wide-eyed Yalie, Buz the streetwise orphan from the Lower East Side, Linc the veteran troubled by what he has seen and done in Vietnam – fleshed out just enough to provide the requisite amounts of empathy or passion to catalyze or complement the guest star's story.

10 My thanks to Horace Newcomb for sharing this insight with me.

11 The 1964 series finale, "Where There's a Will, There's a Way," is a silly and contrived "comedy" tale of a family of con artists vying for an inheritance (likely a pastiche of *It's a Mad, Mad, Mad, Mad World*, which was released the previous year), an episode that Silliphant himself has called "sloppy work." Double-dealing antics dominate the two-part episode, the crux of which is a provision in an old swindler's will that requires his daughter's marriage to Tod (fortunately, the couple fall in love first).

12 On the lore of the old highway itself see Wallis.

13 See, for example Newcomb; Marc, "Screen Gems": 24; McNally: 272; Jarvis: 7.

14 The series is even self-conscious about its pattern of altruistic errantry on occasion, as when Tod and Buz have this exchange in the opening moments of "Eleven the Hard Way":

> *Tod*: Just for kicks why don't we stand on the sidelines for a change, y'know, no jobs and no involvement.

Buz: In *Reno*?

Tod: Well let's just take a forty-eight hour furlough from other people's troubles; give my bruises a chance to heal.

Of course, within minutes the boys are mixing it up with some toughs who try to rob the episode's protagonists.

15 On television's construction of the domestic see Spigel; for an overview of television families see Taylor.

16 One of the best comic examples is a comedy of errors starring Buster Keaton and Joe E. Brown ("Journey to Ninevah"); one of the silliest stars Boris Karloff, Peter Lorre, and Lon Chaney, Jr, as themselves, gathered at a motel near Chicago's O'Hare airport to close a deal on a new horror film venture ("Lizard's Leg and Owlet's Wing").

17 See, for example, O'Neill; Wasserman; and Watson.

Works Cited

Anderson, Christopher. *Hollywood TV: The Studio System in the Fifties*. Austin: University of Texas Press, 1994.

Barnouw, Erik. *Tube of Plenty*. 2nd rev. ed. New York: Oxford, 1990.

Bergreen, Laurence. *Look Now, Pay Later*. New York: Mentor, 1980.

"Black November." Writ. Stirling Silliphant. *Route 66*. Dir. Philip Leacock. CBS. October 7, 1960.

Booth, Philip. "*Route 66* – On the Road Toward People." *Television Quarterly* 2 (Winter 1963): 5–12.

"A Bridge Across Five Days." Writ. Howard Rodman. *Route 66*. Dir. Richard Donner. CBS. November 17, 1961.

Brooks, Tim and Marsh, Earle. *The Complete Directory to Prime Time Network TV Shows*. 5th ed. New York: Ballantine, 1992.

Castleman, Harry and Walter Podrazik. *Watching TV*. New York: McGraw-Hill, 1982.

Columbia Pictures Television: The Studio and the Creative Process. New York: Museum of Broadcasting, 1987.

Cunningham, John P. "'Creeping Mediocrity,' Bringing Boredom to TV." *Advertising Age* (December 2, 1957): 65–7.

"Dialogue on Film: Stirling Silliphant." *American Film* (March, 1988): 13–15.

"The Fingers of God." *Time* (August 9, 1963): 60–1.

Ehrenreich, Barbara. *The Hearts of Men: American Dreams and the Flight From Commitment*. New York: Anchor Books, 1983.

"Eleven the Hard Way." Writ. George Clayton Johnson. *Route 66*. Dir. William A. Graham. CBS. April 7, 1961.

"Fifty Miles From Home." Writ. Stirling Silliphant. *Route 66*. Dir. James Sheldon. CBS. March 22, 1963.

"For the Record." *TV Guide* (December 15, 1962): A-1.

"For the Record." *TV Guide* (June 22, 1963): A-1.

Gehman, Richard. "He's Always Racing His Motor." Part 2. *TV Guide* (April 21, 1962): 17–19.

Gelman, Morris J. "The Hollywood Story." *Television* (September, 1963): 27+.

Gianakos, Larry James. *Television Drama Series Programming: A Comprehensive Chronicle, 1959–1975*. Metuchen: Scarecrow, 1978.

Gitlin, Todd. *Inside Prime-Time*. New York: Pantheon, 1983.

Goodman, Paul. *Growing Up Absurd*. New York: Vintage, 1960.

Hackett, Harold. "A Plea to Widen TV's Horizons for More Creativity." *Variety* (January 1, 1960): 80.

Halberstam, David. *The Powers That Be*. New York: Dell, 1979.

"The Hearings That Changed Television." *Telefilm* (July–August, 1962): 13+.

Horowitz, Murray. "Vidfilmeries' Soul-Searching." *Variety* (November 29, 1959): 31.

"Is There a Programming Crisis?," *Television* (February, 1957): 50–2.

Jarvis, Jeff. "The Couch Critic." Review of *Route 66* [1993 version]. *TV Guide* (June 12, 1993): 7.

Jenkins, Dan. "Talk About Putting the Show on the Road!" *TV Guide* (July 22, 1961): 12–16.

Kerouac, Jack. *On the Road*. New York: Signet, 1957.

"A Knock Develops on 'Route 66'." *TV Guide* (January 26, 1963): 22–5.

Leonard, Herbert B. Telephone interview. May 18, 1987.

"Lancer Brief Bumps Maharis Off Sullivan." *Variety* (12 June, 1963): 35.

Marc, David. *Comic Visions*. Boston: Unwin Hyman, 1989.

—— "Screen Gems: 25 Years of Prime-Time Storytelling." In *Columbia Pictures Television*: 23–9.

McNally, Dennis. *Desolate Angel: Jack Kerouac, the Beat Generation, and America*. New York: Random House, 1979.

"Naked Truth." *Newsweek* (March 4, 1963): 79.

Newcomb, Horace. *TV: The Most Popular Art*. Garden City, NY: Anchor Press, 1974.

O'Neill, William L. *Coming Apart*. New York: Quadrangle, 1971.

"Remembrances of Four Columbia Producers." In *Columbia Pictures Television*: 44–54.

Rosen, George. "TV Debut: 'No Mischief' Season." *Variety* (September 5, 1962): 1+.

"Rough Road." *Newsweek* (January 2, 1961): 60.

Seldes, Gilbert. Rev. of *Route 66*. *TV Guide* (February 10, 1962): 4.

Silliphant, Stirling. Telephone interview. 11 May, 1987.

Silliphant, Stirling. Presentation pages for *Route 66* [1959]. Herbert B. Leonard Collection, UCLA Theater Arts Library, University of California, Los Angeles.

Spigel, Lynn. *Make Room for TV*. Chicago: University of Chicago Press, 1992.

Summary of Social Research Inc. data on *Route 66* May 19, 1961. Herbert B. Leonard Collection, UCLA Theater Arts Library, University of California, Los Angeles.

Taylor, Ella. *Prime-Time Familes*. Berkeley: University of California Press, 1989.

"Ten Drops of Water." Writ. Howard Rodman. *Route 66*. Dir. Philip Leacock. CBS. November 11, 1960.

"TV Anthologies Hit Peak With 8 in 1963–64." *Variety* (June 26, 1963): 27.

"Two 'Searchers,' Leonard and Girard." *Variety* (September 23, 1959): 30.

"Voice at the End of the Line." Writ. Larry Marcus. *Route 66*. Dir. David Lowell Rich. CBS. October 19, 1962.

Wallis, Michael. *Route 66: The Mother Road*. New York: St Martin's, 1990.

Wasserman, Harvey. *America Born & Reborn*. New York: Collier, 1983.

Watson, Mary Ann. *The Expanding Vista: American Television in the Kennedy Years*. New York: Oxford, 1990.

"We Can Make 'Em Just as Cheap or Cheaper in N.Y.: Herb Leonard." *Variety* (February 26, 1958): 26.

"Welcome to Amity." Writ. Will Lorin. *Route 66*. Dir. Arthur Hiller. CBS. June 9, 1961.

"Where There's a Will, There's a Way." Writ. Stirling Silliphant. *Route 66*. Dir. Alvin Ganzer. CBS. Part I: March 6, 1964. Part II: March 13, 1964.

7

EXPOSING INTIMACY IN RUSS MEYER'S *MOTORPSYCHO!* AND *FASTER PUSSYCAT! KILL! KILL!*

Julian Stringer

I

The road movie habitually promotes two narrative situations. In the first, one or more goal-oriented protagonists take off as a means to escape, either from pursuers (*A Perfect World*, 1993; *True Romance*, 1993) or from a hitherto boring lifestyle (*Five Easy Pieces*, 1970; *Lost in America*, 1985). In the second, one or more protagonists seek to "find themselves" existentially, either through sex (*Something Wild*, 1986), violence (*Natural Born Killers*, 1994), or by messing with nature (*Easy Rider*, 1969). In utilizing these stock situations, the road movie differentiates itself from other genres by defining distinct parameters of action and by aspiring to complete a particular emotional trajectory. The progression is toward a unified and fulfilling subjectivity. Road movie logic maintains that the further you drive from civilization the more easily you can shake off its constraints, the more people you leave behind the closer you can get to yourself. Typically, such narratives either promise that social pressures will evaporate into thin air, or else they encourage indulgence in the solitary contemplation of inner space.

These generic aspirations are extremely unstable, however, as the road movie everywhere presents contradictory impulses. It could be argued that a road movie isn't a road movie if it doesn't testify to the impossibility of the existential project, because setting off onto the highway necessarily entails the transportation of significant amounts of cultural baggage. In other words, the myths of escape and self-discovery are chimerical, just two more mirages along the way – other people always end up tagging along. Road movies would be less interesting than they are if they didn't offer a variety of quirky characters to be intrigued by, which is one reason why the genre has thrown up so many buddy films, and why tales of the lone traveler seem so quaintly eccentric (especially if narrated by a cultural outsider, such as Romanian poet Andrei Codrescu in the 1993 film *Road Scholar*).

The exceptions only prove the rule. In an American genre so concerned with the geographical *vastness* of space lies a concomitant emphasis on the physical *closeness* of people. While seeming to offer liberation and introspection, the road movie closes down on that freedom by constructing social contracts among people who are intimate with each other. The open highway does not offer escape and a mystical "finding of the self" so much as the chance to redefine and recontextualize existing or emergent social relationships. Human interaction drives us. Paradoxically, then, in masquerading as one of the most anti-social of all cultural forms, road movies constitute a polar opposite. Presenting characters who travel through expansive landscapes in self-enclosed vehicles, they situate the work of ideology in the creation of new intimacies.

In his book *Seeing Films Politically*, Mas'ud Zavarzadeh discusses what he terms the "cultural politics of intimacy" in a way that can help the thinking through of this central generic paradox. For Zavarzadeh, intimacy is usually taken to lie outside of culture and history – it is viewed as interpersonal, not social, transhistorical, not historically conditioned – even though relations of intimacy are "always already limited by the historical situation in which the subject is located and thus by the subject positions available" (Zavarzadeh: 114). The desire to escape culture by going on the road is doomed to failure because characters take culture with them through forging alliances with the people they meet.

It may be possible to construct an historical typology of the road movie by tracing the various ways in which the genre manages the cultural politics of intimacy. It is not my intention to try and do this here, but I would point to a number of relevant questions that can be asked of any specific example. On what terms are intimacies between characters constructed? By what means do films from particular historical periods propose to redefine and recontextualize particular social relationships? How are those relationships read by different social audiences? My suspicion is that the genre has moved in a generally conservative direction when it comes to the question of who is likely to become intimate with whom.

Road movie protagonists may look through the window and see the whole world ahead of them, but they usually end up becoming intimate with people just like themselves. As Zavarzadeh elaborates, in our culture "one 'chooses' one's intimates not 'freely' but in an overdetermined way from within the constraints of class, sex, race, and religion, to mention only the most significant ones" (Zavarzadeh: 114). (So white people are more likely to attach themselves to other whites than to black people, and male teenagers are unlikely to hook up with female senior citizens – a tendency borne out by the common class/ethnic interpellations of otherwise revisionist texts like *Thelma and Louise*, 1991, and *The Living End*, 1992, as much as by the more traditional *You Only Live Once*, 1937, and *Sugarland Express*, 1974.) The road movie tends to disallow the dialogic coming together of different classes, sexes, races, and religions by refusing to engage critically with the socially and historically conditioned nature of human interaction. However, it does not have to be this way. If road movies have only recently begun to deploy physical and emotional attachments for radical (feminist and gay) purposes, the chance to form intimacies with anyone who happens to pass through a common environment opens up possibilities for interesting future meetings.

Many of the genre's more historically distinct titles encourage a form of mass cultural intimacy through their existence as cult films produced so as to please a knowing, collaborative audience. Motorbike and custom car films from the 1960s, for example, buy into the overdetermined constraints on intimacy so as to promote a group fantasy of subcultural cloning for the white youth market. Yet some also parody the genre's stock narrative situations to such an extent that their relations of intimacy are exposed. *Motorpsycho!* (1965) and *Faster Pussycat! Kill! Kill!* (1966 – hereafter *Pussycat*), two films made virtually back-to-back by celebrated exploitation director Russ Meyer, illustrate this process particularly well.

II

Motorpsycho! and *Pussycat* are genre afterthoughts from an *auteur* not generally thought of as a road movie practitioner. Sandwiched between examples of Meyer's more familiar soft-porn work (*Mudhoney*, 1965; *Mondo Topless*, 1966), the two titles are distinguished by some beautiful black-and-white cinematography, and by an effective use of location shooting in and around the Delta area of the Sacramento River. In addition, each can be dated fairly precisely through the references it makes to specific moments of contemporary white pop culture – the former by building on the cult of the maniac initiated in 1960 by Alfred Hitchcock's *Psycho* (not to mention "Motorpsycho Nightmare," Bob Dylan's song of a few years later), the latter through its "trash aesthetic" links to earlier female car-club movies such as *The Fast and the Furious* (1954) and *Dragstrip Girl* (1958; see Rose: 21). Generically, however, both lie off the beaten track. While achieving a synthesis of the road movie and sexploitation approaches, each also suggests the dark fatalism of a *film noir* death trip (cf. *Gun Crazy*, 1949; *Detour*, 1945; *They Live By Night*, 1949; *The Postman Always Rings Twice*, 1946).

Since both titles have their origins in stories written by Meyer himself, and because *Pussycat* is structured to resonate off against the memory of *Motorpsycho!*, the two films can be taken as brother and sister texts that are intimate with each other. *Motorpsycho!* may be the less familiar to readers. It concerns three bikers,

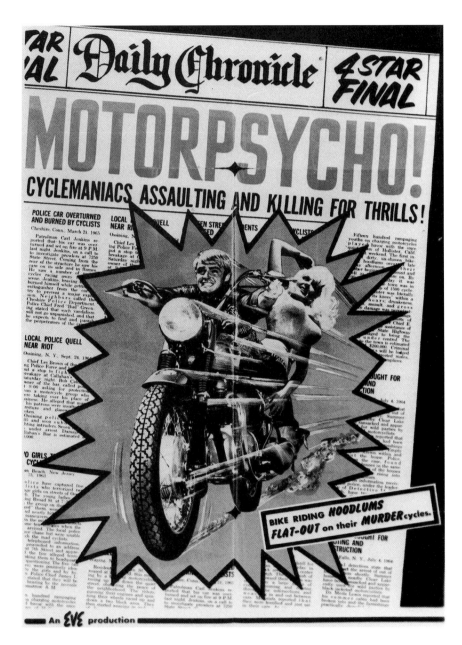

Plate 7.1 The cult of the maniac.
Stephen Oliver in *Motorpsycho!*

Brahmin (Stephen Oliver), Dante (Joseph Cellini), and Slick (Thomas Scott), who molest and rape Gail Maddox (Holle K. Winters), the wife of a small town vet, Cory Maddox (Alex Rocco). As they move on, the gang terrorize a married couple, killing the husband and leaving his young wife, Ruby Bonner (Haji), for dead in the desert. Ruby later teams up with Cory as the latter stalks the bikers in his pickup. After some violent confrontations, the three hoodlums self-destruct. Slick is murdered by his own kind, Ruby kills Dante in self-defence, and, after regressing back to his traumatic experiences of wartime Vietnam, Brahmin is blown up by the dynamite-throwing Cory. In the end, the "good" vet and Ruby are left alive and intact, free to drive away from the desert to safety.

This basic scenario is consciously invoked in *Pussycat* through a number of textual inversions. Here, the gang comprises three sports-car-riding female go-go dancers, led by the charismatic (but psychotic) Varla (Tura Satana). Just as the first scene of *Motorpsycho!* depicts three bikers victimizing a heterosexual couple, *Pussycat* opens with Varla and her two associates, Rosie (Haji) and Billie (Lori Williams), killing a man in the desert, then abducting his girlfriend, Linda (Susan Bernard). While refueling at a gas station, the women become interested in a local muscle man known as "The Vegetable" (Dennis Busch). Soon, however, they are even more taken with his eccentric father, the wheelchair-bound "Old Man" (Stuart Lancaster), when they learn that he keeps a cash fortune stashed away in his home. In the process of trying to get their hands on the money, the gang self-destructs. Varla kills Billie, "The Vegetable" kills Rosie, and, after the "Old Man" and Varla themselves meet violent deaths, Linda and Kirk (Paul Trinka – the nominally "good" son) are left alive and intact, free to drive away from the desert to safety.

As the above synopses suggest, these road movie protagonists are treated as mere archetypes who, devoid of psychological complexity, help melt the genre down to its bare essentials. Out there in the desert, nomadic wanderers bump into strange individuals and have to cohabit with them. The relationships that develop are very antagonistic; in neither film can any single character be said to progress toward a unified and fulfilling subjectivity – other people always get in their way. With his career background in heterosexual soft-porn, Meyer pits each protagonist against his or her antagonist so as to prepare the ground for an energetic clash of mutually incompatible intimacies. By highlighting the *confrontational* nature of existent and emergent interpersonal relationships, the two films allow one constituent feature of the genre to be exposed a little more clearly. Stephen Bayley may have come up with the best description of *Motorpsycho!* and *Pussycat*'s attractions as road movies when, describing a 1956 Chevy Corvette, he claims that "if young adult libido were expressed in terms of metal, plastic and plating it would look like this" (Bayley: 15): Meyer is the one to imbue such themes with the dynamism of dialectical conflict.

Plate 7.2 An energetic clash of mutually incompatible intimacies.
Tura Satana and Paul Trinka in *Faster Pussycat! Kill! Kill!*

Consider, for example, how antagonisms are suggested through the deployment of particular formal devices. Both films foreground an ironic use of written dialogue and spoken delivery. The presentational style favored by most of Meyer's star performers complements the director's understanding of human interaction as a never-ending struggle for power and control. Most conversations degenerate into shouting matches, people get close to each other so as to manipulate the upper hand, and lines are spoken ironically, as if being delivered in quotation marks. This latter effect functions to separate the actor from the role s/he plays, thus blocking any aspiration towards the completion of a coherent emotional trajectory. At those moments when characters articulate their thoughts a little too passionately, a camp effect is produced. Intimate relationships are presented as steamy and up-close, but, simultaneously, as distanced and at one remove.

A good example of this process occurs about half-way through *Pussycat*, at the time when the go-go dancers are debating the best way to infiltrate the house where the money is. All three bask in the warm California sun, stretched out on the body of Varla's sports car as if posing for the cover of a drag racing magazine. Adopting a sweet voice and mild tone, the charismatic (but psychotic) leader demonstrates how she will go about explaining their predicament to their unsuspecting prey. Falsely reporting that Linda "flipped" when her boyfriend was killed in a racing accident, Varla maintains that their hostage "Ran away from home. Her family's big socially and doesn't want any publicity. So they asked us to find the girl. We *found* her." On these words, Varla's expression softens a little more. Smiling at Rosi, a conspiratorial arch in her eyebrows, she curves her body suggestively and coos, "Just like we're gonna find some of that l-o-o-o-n-g green." Suddenly, however, Billie pokes her face in, exclaiming, "Oh, that's so phoney it's almost believable!". Switching mood faster than a fiddler changes elbow positions, Varla turns nasty. "You don't have to *believe* it," she snarls. "Just *act* it."

At this moment, Tura Satana's canonical butch performance is bewilderingly contradictory. When Varla oscillates between the projection of an "emotionally present" mode of *friendship* and a confrontational mode of *hostility*, it becomes impossible to read her actions in any naturalistic manner. Forms of intimacy which are normally separated out have been indiscreetly bridged.

Conversations like the one briefly described above often take place within the mise-en-scène of a vaguely defined social space. Meyer's decision to shoot both films in an isolated landscape, rather than on the highway, works to support the sense that characters are moving around each other in ever-decreasing circles. Protagonists occupy borderless zones, indistinct topographies. With each new move, the violence that provides Meyer with his key metaphor for the incompatibility of personal needs and desires escalates. In both *Motorpsycho!* and *Pussycat*, characters are trapped on all four sides by people they are then forced to become intimate with – a situation that can be taken as paradigmatic of the entire genre.

In addition, each film's narrative trajectory is not compatible with the road movie's ideology of escape into inner space. Russ Meyer has never been that interested in sticking to the neat cause–effect linear progressions demanded of Hollywood plot lines, and he was not about to start with *Motorpsycho!* and *Pussycat*. Both dwell on what Craig Fischer terms "*descriptive* passages of violence, sexual intercourse, and other activities considered taboo by mainstream cinema." In other words, "the mode of address of exploitation films involves a fluctuation between Hollywood narrative and the description mode characteristic of pornography" (Fischer: 18).

When placed within the context of the road trip, this narrative hybridization creates something of a problem (after all, road movies are meant to be about what happens in the movement between two destinations, two identifiable geographic markers). Because Meyer's characters exhibit little motivational drive, because they harbor few goals beyond the ambition to make money and get laid as often as possible, they fall obstinantly short of achieving that "more stable spiritual or social state" (Corrigan: 144) that Timothy Corrigan sees road movie protagonists as aspiring to develop. None of these characters are looking to "find themselves." As products of the pornographic imagination, their natural state is to be as intimate as possible with other people.

III

Given the gender dynamics of both the road movie narrative and the soft-porn spectacle, it seems fitting that *Motorpsycho!* and *Pussycat* work to expose generic intimacy by orchestrating the disintegration of a hot-blooded threesome. For if the travelling trio is not as prevalent a road movie trope as that of the outlaw couple, it is still pretty common (*Easy Rider*; *The Adventures of Priscilla, Queen of the Desert*, 1994). Three people alone on the road can experience many divergent, shifting emotional attachments. As they journey forward, incompatible relationships can be jettisoned, and more sympathetic emotional links established. This is usually achieved, however, through a power struggle, whereby two of the partners "exchange" the third as an object of desire. To be more precise, since so many road movies are same-sex buddy films, the emphasis is usually on how a single female gets to be passed between the hands of two men within the terms of an erotic triangle (*Scarecrow*, 1973; *Rain Man*, 1988).

Saying this is merely to repeat what Eve Kosofsky Sedgwick has written about in her work on homosocial desire and the exchange of erotic objects between men in English literature. Sedgwick's observations are of direct relevance for the exposure of particular sexual intimacies in the road movie. According to her, "the bond that links the two rivals is as intense and potent as the bond that links either of the rivals to the beloved . . . the bonds of 'rivalry' and 'love', differently as they are experienced, are equally powerful and in many senses equivalent" (Sedgwick: 21). Such bonds and rivalries are most acute when caught up in the experiences of a threesome who travel through expansive landscapes in self-enclosed vehicles.

As regards *Motorpsycho!* and *Pussycat*, I want to follow these insights up by briefly pursuing two lines of inquiry. First, I would like to suggest how exaggerated performance signs (delivery of dialogue, use of body language, etc.), together with the generally antagonistic nature of all close relationships, turns on a specific acknowledgment by the texts themselves of the presence of the extradiegetic cult spectator. Second, it is necessary to add that the intimacies generated out of these triangular intensities have to be distanced from the cultural taboos that cohere around their logical end-point, namely male homosexuality.

The first issue is raised when Russ Meyer makes his own cameo appearance in *Motorpsycho!*. Playing the role of the police sergeant sent to investigate the rape of Gail, he takes a look at her unconscious body by lifting up the blanket that covers her legs. "Looks like they did a *real* job, doc.," he says. "Those three hoods must have had a *ball*." This line is delivered in an ironic, jokey manner, but it elicits a responsible, professional reminder from the doctor next to him that the woman has been "*assaulted, criminally assaulted*." A few seconds later, Meyer picks up on his favorite theme once again as he rides to hospital with the grief-stricken husband. "She'll be alright in a week or so," he exclaims. "After all, nothing happened to her that a woman ain't *built* for." Cory remains silent. However, after the sheriff goes on to ask how well his wife knew her attackers (implying that "sometimes a woman will encourage . . . "), he shuts him up. "Look at her face!" Cory shouts with irrefutable conviction. "Look at those bruises! Does that look like she was having a party? She was *assaulted. Criminally assaulted*."

The point of this short exchange is that it represents a male sexual duel for control of the female body. Set within the confines of a cramped vehicle (shot, moreover, at low level, and in the tightest framing of the entire film) the two men struggle to assert their rights of intimacy. The struggle moves in two directions. Within the fictional world of the diegesis itself, Cory's concerned point of view is validated through his justifiable anger at the cop's offensive remarks. At the extradiegetic level, however, the knowledge that it is Meyer himself who talks about "balling" is enough to ensure that his lines are read as deliberately excessive. While it may be going a bit far to claim that such simultaneity forces the viewer actively to reflect on his/her own complicity in the sexual rivalries being acted out, the scene does point to the latent text–audience identifications within the heart of any celluloid erotic triangle.

Following Sedgwick, though, we might also say that any male/male intimacies established on a Russ Meyer road trip have to be disavowed. This is necessary not just because his films are usually homophobic (*Beyond the Valley of the Dolls*, 1970; *Beneath the Valley of the Ultravixens*, 1979) but because the fragility of masculine identity requires that sexual tension between men be deflected. Accordingly, *Motorpsycho!* gives its three bikers two women (Gail and Ruby) in exchange for such reassurance. As no erotic triangle can guarantee a totally even distribution of power, gender asymmetries have to be constantly smoothed over.

Pussycat's greater generic success hinges on the fact that it breaks the shackles of such a demand. Meyer's women can get away with more interesting forms of intimacy. Because, to quote Sedgwick once again, our society constructs a "relatively smooth and palpable continuum of female homosocial desire" (23), the latter film is more adapt at exploring the emotional bonds and rivalries that exist between three female protagonists. (There is no equivalent in the earlier film to the cat-fight between Rosie and Billie, or the sight of Rosie chewed up with jealousy as she spies Varla rolling around in the dirt with Kirk.) Since, within patriarchy, female/female relationships can be safely eroticized, Meyer's cinema more successfully integrates such descriptive passages within the drive and excitement of a road trip. Paradoxically, while the bikers are unified as a *group* but the go-go dancers are divided as *individuals*, the women strive harder to be passionately intimate with each other.

In *Motorpsycho!*, the town where most of the action is set resembles a place that anyone might pass through while on the road; more than that, the street where the three bikers first molest Gail Maddox is named Blythe Way; and, more than that, we know right from the start that these "no-good-bike-ridin'-punks" are heading for a specified location, Las Vegas. This is to say that even though they wind up in the middle of nowhere, dead, the three men still retain a semblance of individuality and particularity.

In *Pussycat*, by contrast, nothing is specified, everything is abstract. Here, most of the action takes place in a geometrically stark landscape that might suffice for a live-action re-make of a Roadrunner cartoon; the "Old Man's" house is five miles from the nearest telephone; moreover, as the film's last line of spoken dialogue makes clear, these three women are most emphatically "not going anywhere." Even though they wind up in the middle of nowhere, dead, their lack of particularity necessitates the affirmation of intimacies.

A brief comparison of both films' opening credit sequences is enough to illustrate what I mean. These scenes are thrillingly characteristic of Russ Meyer's idiosyncratic editing style. With *Motorpsycho!*, the director starts out with a title card superimposed over a close-up of a transistor radio blaring out rock music – the radio is dangling between the legs of a young man – before moving on to a brief insert of the front wheel of a motorbike. Next, there is a dramatic cut to a long shot of the three psychos riding their machines in neat formation (as this shot is a track-out executed from the rear of a moving car, it can be taken as representative of the kind of "framed perspective of the vehicle itself" that Timothy Corrigan proposes as an identifiable road movie composition [146]). The next couple of edits juxtapose similar shots of the three men riding together with close-ups of machine parts. While the men look cool at a distance, their bikes are fetishized in isolated detail.

This ambitious credit sequence provides the inspiration for *Pussycat*'s opening scene, but the latter works in a much more suggestive manner. After an hilarious and deservedly famous introductory monologue ("Welcome to violence: the word and the act. While violence cloaks itself in a plethora of disguises, its favorite mantle still remains – sex!"), a shock cut takes us to Varla dancing on the go-go stage. As the Bossweeds crank out their eponymous trash anthem, her body glows as a shimmering light against the grey backdrop. In the next two shots, Meyer edits together images of Rosie and Billie dancing, presumably, by her side. The montage sequence continues with the three dancers now framed in a single composition while disembodied male audience members ogle and shout their support in intercut head-shots. No wonder this sequence exudes such heat. "When I'm shooting, I get a semi-hard on," Meyer told an interviewer in 1981.

"It's not that I'm touching myself. But subliminally, it all comes right through the reflex – bang! – into my noggin and down to my gritch" (quoted in Kelly: 43).

After thirteen short edits, the camera is moved outdoors to frame a steering wheel. Immediately, Meyer cuts to the driver, Varla, tearing down the open highway. Throwing back her head to laugh, she turns in her seat and looks back at her companions on the road behind. Eyeline matches establish where the three women are in relation to each other (Varla–Rosie–Billie), thus exposing how power flows through the apex of their triangular relationship.

Motorpsycho! presents its three young bikers as a group who are comfortably close to each other, but it lets the camera's pornographic gaze safely fetishize their motorbikes, not their bodies. *Pussycat* fetishizes its women's bodies by fragmenting them into shots of individual dancers who parody forms of intimacy for a paying public. This latter sequence works more ambiguously, then, as if it were a fragment of some lost film by the great master of Soviet montage, Sergei Eisenstein. Compare the opening of *Pussycat* with the first five shots of Eisenstein's debut film, *Strike* (1925). With economy and brilliance, Eisenstein presents two close-ups of a solitary capitalist framed and abstracted against a plain grey background. He then juxtaposes these with single shots of three different factory locations – the inside, the outside, and the administration quarters. As Judith Mayne has shown, the result is that Eisenstein creates ideological tension through a discontinuous style. Eisenstein's use of dialectical form everywhere suggests contradictory relationships:

> The boss seems to be watching the workers, although there is no visible spatial unity in the shots. The three views of the factory are disconnected and could well be three different factories. The close-up of the boss is unanchored and undefined within a context: behind him there is only an indistinct grey background. This discontinuity could be seen as representative of the boss's mastery of space and time – he is, after all, symbolic of the power that controls any factory, seen from whatever angle. Yet, this discontinuity also could be read as an indication of weakness, that is, the fragmented nature of the boss's power. Ownership is undermined by fragmentation, and controlling vision is undermined by discontinuity.
>
> (Mayne: 69–70)

I feel compelled to praise Meyer's editing strategies along similar lines. *Pussycat*'s women are presented exploitatively, yet their individual charisma liberates them from the frame's constraints. Varla has to turn her head physically so as to laugh at her companions (thus suggesting the "unnaturalness" of her "unfeminine" behavior?), but this small motion sets her apart from everyone else, signaling that she is where the action is. Each cut insidiously fragments and disempowers a group of outlaw women, yet in both films intimacies between

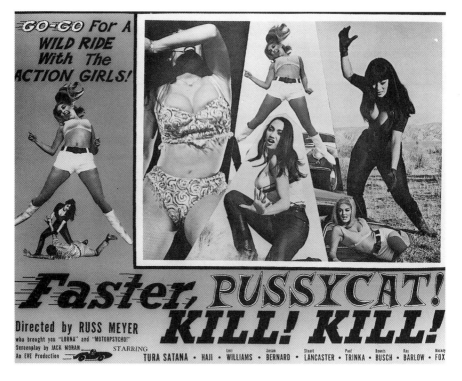

Plate 7.3 Faster Pussycat! Kill! Kill!
The oblique suggestion of physical closeness through montage.

group members are bound to shatter in the face of consistent antagonisms anyway. If *Motorpsycho!* presents physical closeness in single compositions, *Pussycat* suggests it obliquely, through montage. The later film works better because it more effectively expresses the irreconcilable conflicts that Meyer takes to define all road trip intimacies.

IV

With their exclusive focus on the thrills afforded by sex, violence, money, speed, and power, these two films confirm an observation made by critics of other popular genres, namely that low-budget genre film-making anticipates the styles and themes of bigger-budgeted titles by foreshadowing their concerns. (*Motorpsycho!* precedes the breakthrough biker film of the 1960s, *The Wild Angels*, 1966, by a year or so; the neo-feminist *Pussycat* anticipates *Thelma and Louise* by twenty-five.) "B movies" hide in the light of more "respectable" cultural objects by basking in their neglected obsessions, uncloaking their repressed fascinations. Meyer's films are sometimes claimed to be of interest for precise historical reasons

– while *Motorpsycho!* was one of the first American films to refer to the subject of returning Vietnam vets, *Pussycat* helped establish the currently-in-vogue "lethal lesbian" stereotype – but fixing them as road movies also confirms their function as irritants to more willfully accommodating examples of the genre.

Relations of intimacy, in both valued and devalued road movies, are historically specific, however, and it might be interesting to research further the contextual meanings that surround both films. *Motorpsycho!*, for example, seems to exhibit the same kind of repulsed fascination for the Hell's Angels that gripped journalist Hunter S. Thompson in a similar time and place, while *Pussycat* could raise in one's mind the memory of the desert "dune buggy attacks" of Charlie Manson's own murderous "family." But maybe it is enough simply to observe that each runs against the grain of its time.

In the mid-1960s, as other genre practitioners spread the existential vapor that infiltrated the lungs of mobile flower children, as young people dropped out and searched for roads that would lead to the solitary contemplation of inner space, Meyer was wallowing in the mire. Returning sex and violence to the central place they habitually occupy in the politics of road movie intimacy, he asserted, before the fact, the punk dictum that you should "never trust a hippie." Astonishingly, the turns that the genre has proceeded to make since 1965–6 only suggest the wisdom of this cultural position.

While *Motorpsycho!* has yet to find its place in the sun, *Pussycat* has established itself as a cult classic. Now, at a time when road movies and 1960s camp nostalgia are in, it even has its own parody in the form of an MTV video for Janet Jackson's song "You Want This." It feels these days as if increasingly large numbers of film-makers and movie-goers want to escape social pressures by seeing their surrogates on screen drive through vast landscapes. But does the increased visibility of *Pussycat* – and *Wild at Heart* (1990), *Sherman's March* (1985), *Near Dark* (1987), and all the rest – indicate that we also want to get closer to each other, to share intimacies? If that is so, what form does that desire take, and how far are we prepared to travel in the examination of what most connects us with each other?

Works Cited

Bayley, Stephen. *Sex, Drink and Fast Cars*. New York: Pantheon, 1986.

Corrigan, Timothy. *A Cinema Without Walls: Movies and Culture after Vietnam*. New Brunswick, NJ: Rutgers University Press, 1991.

Fischer, Craig. "*Beyond the Valley of the Dolls* and the Exploitation Genre." *The Velvet Light Trap* 30 (1992): 18–33.

Kelly, Matthew. "The Breast of Russ Meyer." *Swank* 28 (May, 1981): 42–5.

Mayne, Judith. *Kino and the Woman Question: Feminism and Soviet Silent Film*. Columbus: Ohio State University Press, 1989.

Rose, Cynthia. "*Faster, Pussycat! Kill! Kill!*". *Monthly Film Bulletin* (December, 1981): 243.

Sedgwick, Eve Kosofsky. *Between Men: English Literature and Male Homosocial Desire*. New York: Columbia University Press, 1985.

Zavarzadeh, Mas'ud. *Seeing Films Politically*. Albany: State University of New York, 1991.

8

THE ROAD TO
DYSTOPIA
Landscaping the nation in
Easy Rider

Barbara Klinger

A man went looking for America and couldn't find it anywhere.
(Ad copy for *Easy Rider*)

In 1988 George Bush proudly noted that the United States had made a successful recovery from the excesses of the "Easy Rider society" of the 1960s (Dowd: A11). In the Reagan–Bush era, reference to *Easy Rider* (1969) instantly conjured up demonic images of the hippie counter-culture with its long hair, experimentation with drugs and sex, and violent social protests. For this more conservative political era, such images represented a permissive degeneracy and destructive militancy that had to be eradicated for the nation to thrive.

Unlike many films from the past, however, *Easy Rider* didn't have to wait for retrospective canonization (however dubious in its motives). It was literally a legend in its own time, serving as an instant emblem of its generation. *Easy Rider*'s story featured two hippies named Wyatt/Captain America and Billy (played, respectively, by Peter Fonda and Dennis Hopper), who travel from Los Angeles to New Orleans on their motorcycles only to find dramatically increasing hostility from local citizens along their journey. Budgeted for $375,000, Hopper's directorial debut made over $50 million worldwide during its original release and won the 1969 Cannes Film Festival Award for "Best Film by a New Director."[1]

While the film generated substantial debate, critics from the alternative and mainstream presses alike generally saw it as a spectacular document of its times that effectively represented the hippie ethos as well as the serious rifts between counter- and dominant cultures. The critic for the *Washington Post* hailed the film as "lyrical and brilliant, the reflection of its generation . . . like a Bob Dylan song on celluloid," while Rex Reed wrote that "by taking up where Kerouac and Lawrence Lipton and all the Holy Barbarians left off, Fonda and Hopper

179

have produced the definitive youth odyssey of the 1960s" (233). Similarly, in the counter-culture's alternative press, reviewers called *Easy Rider* "the first 'commercial' . . . motion picture to embody the new youth consciousness" (Miller: 16), the "first . . . to deal with aspects of hip life honestly and without exploitation . . . and . . . confront the reality of America" (Glushanok: 20–1).

While it is difficult to pinpoint why certain films are instantly recognized as generational landmarks by their audiences (particularly while others with similar characteristics, such as *Alice's Restaurant*, 1969, fail to be), it is clear that, because *Easy Rider* synthesized so many mainstays of 1960s youth and popular cultures, it had more than a fair chance of being immortalized by those whose interests it seemed to represent. Most obviously, one could point to *Easy Rider*'s concentration on hippie life and its twin social themes of freedom and repression. One could also note the film's relationship to popular culture via its use of rock music, allusions to Roger Corman's successful AIP motorcycle and drug-experimentation films (such as *Wild Angels*, 1966; *The Glory Stompers*, 1967; *Hell's Angels on Wheels*, 1967; and *The Trip*, 1967), generic revisionism of the film Western, and deployment of stylistic and narrative techniques associated with the New American Cinema. All of these tied the film firmly to tropes of the counter-culture, from libidinous pleasure, spontaneity, and rebellion to aesthetic hipness.[2]

But it is abundantly evident from the reception of the film that part of what captivated *Easy Rider*'s audiences was simply its depiction of a motorcycle journey across the United States. On the one hand, the film appeared as the apotheosis of the car, motorcycle, and highway cultures that had escalated since the 1950s thanks to factors as various as the National Highway Act of 1956, which created a gigantic system of interstate highways, Beat writer Jack Kerouac's *On the Road* (1957), which deified the experience of cross-country travel by freewheeling male individuals as an antidote to bourgeois complacency, and the highly publicized presence of the Hell's Angels, the pack of "renegade" chopper riders who were a source of public fear and fascination by the 1960s.[3]

On the other hand, the film related these intersecting features of 1950s and 1960s culture to a commentary on America that brought together the powerful allure of the road with a contemporary cultural critique. The traveling quest, one of the hallmarks of the road movie (Corrigan: 144–5), structured numerous 1960s Westerns (such as *Butch Cassidy and the Sundance Kid*, 1969, and *The Wild Bunch*, 1969), but was also featured more explicitly in such road trip fare as *Two for the Road* (1967), *Alice's Restaurant*, *The Rain People* (1969), *Midnight Cowboy* (1969), and French director Jean-Luc Godard's *Weekend* (1967; shown in the United States in 1969). While films centered on excursions through the countryside were hardly the only source of cultural critique in the cinema during this period, critics were quick to see the allegorical implications afforded by the road movie. The characters' journeys in many of these films directly commented on the state of contemporary society. More specifically, *Easy Rider* and other US road movies of the 1960s carried a certain message about America during a time when the nation's identity was contested. As one reviewer acknowledged,

> The "search for America" undertaken by Captain America and his sidekick Billy is not geographical, it is literally a quest to find out where America's head is at. The people and places represented in that quest are evocative of different states of consciousness co-existing unpeacefully in this country and all over the world. Each stop on the road is an encounter with a different awareness of what is real and what is of value.
>
> (Miller: 17)[4]

Commentators further rooted both the appeal and the message of the film in the "vast discrepancy between the visual beauty of the movie . . . and the ugliness of the climate of life in the late sixties" (Brode: 282). The film juxtaposed "America the beautiful" with "Amerika the ugly": the pristine wilderness of the landscape, representing the great potential of the country's historical past, with the profane sentiments of its fascistic and bigoted inhabitants, threatening the very foundations of democracy in the present.[5]

Reactions to *Easy Rider* at the time of its release focused, then, on how its road trip embodied the counter-culture's attitudes toward the state of the nation. But when located within the context of other portraits of the United States during the late 1960s, the film's depiction of the country is in fact not so straightforward. Placed within the visual discourses on nationhood of the time, *Easy Rider* emerges as a film of conflicted historical and ideological identity.

The example of *Easy Rider*, as a quintessential road movie situated within one of the most tumultuous times in twentieth-century US history, allows us to grasp how the road film, in particular its generically obligatory journey through landscapes and territories, participates within broader creative and cultural efforts to define the nation. This contextual frame complicates what commentators have long seen as *Easy Rider*'s transparent personification of late 1960s' rebellious youth consciousness.

Landscaping the Nation

The connection between images of the landscape and the construction of national identity is not new. As Angela Miller says of nineteenth-century US landscape painting, its mission was "to give to nationalism an organic basis, to root it in the geography of the continent" (167). In the 1960s, sources such as *The Saturday Evening Post*, *National Geographic*, *Life*, and *Look* magazines produced pictorial essays about America clearly intended to glorify the nation. As we shall see, these essays, featuring a range of American topographies from the city to the wilderness, acted

AMERICA

as a linchpin for patriotic rhetoric. This rhetoric provided a continuum with traditional nationalism during a time when the very definition of 'America' was being challenged by the Civil Rights and youth movements.

But, as one might suspect, such democratic portraits of America did not monopolize representation. Mass circulation magazines as well as other sources, most notably Pop Art, were busy disarming earlier idyllic and romantic images of America. These sources portrayed apocalyptic, disaster-filled scenarios of modernity via competing depictions of the country's landscape. Through either an ideological identification with the counter-culture or a kind of hysteria born of 1960s political violence, alternative depictions of the nation emerged and flourished alongside the more conventional.

While, as Homi Bhabha points out, nationalist discourses attempt to project "the idea of the nation as a continuous narrative of national progress" via "the narcissism of self-generation," the concept of nation is always deeply ambivalent. It is inflected by numerous differences not the least of which is that between the official attempt to project an appearance of endurance and "a much more transitional social reality" (1). Because the concept of the nation is always caught between these two temporal dimensions, its chief figure is ambivalence, a "wavering between vocabularies," that creates enough of an indeterminacy to produce a "Janus-faced" discourse on the nation during any given time. This duality is bound to affect deeply representations signifying "'nationness'" (2–3). Because of the uneven development of historical forces during a period, meanings "may be partial because they are *in medias res*; and history may be half-made because it is in the process of being made; and the image of cultural authority may be ambivalent because it is caught, uncertainly, in the act of 'composing' its powerful image" (2–3). One could reasonably imagine that the ambivalent status of the concept of nation, caught between tradition and the transitional forces of the historical moment, would only be exacerbated during times when the nation is under siege, as it was during the 1960s.

At first glance, though, *Easy Rider* seems to escape this complexity. Its treatment of the road appears to generate a clear-cut counter-cultural message about the state of the nation in the late 1960s. As it rewrites the landscape according to the youth and Civil Rights movements of the time, it seems only to document and embrace a transitional nationalism that attacks the presuppositions of a formerly stable Americanism. The journey of the hippie protagonists of *Easy Rider* reveals a geographical regionalism politicized according to the radical movements of the time.

Wyatt and Billy are California hippies, incarnating, respectively, the "cool" existential and wild paranoid hippie types drawn from the state most recognized as a counter-cultural mecca. The terrain most idealized in the film – the Southwest – is at once the land of displaced peoples championed by the counter-culture (e.g., Native Americans and Hispanics) and the site of iconography for the hippie movement, since hippie clothing and lifestyles mimicked the buckskin naturalism of the early settlers. The Southwest is also the locus of the hippie commune Wyatt and Billy stay in briefly, the commune being one of the chief insignias of the new 1960s alternative youth culture. In the Southwest, the protagonists enjoy the freedom of the road, the hospitality of those they encounter, and the beauty and mystery of the region's wilderness. Conversely, the South, the small-town South in particular, is demonized in *Easy Rider* as the region most identified in the 1960s with militant ignorance, racism, and violence. The South was the land of George Wallace, white separatist governor of Alabama, and the site of bitter and deadly Civil Rights struggles since the 1950s. It was also, as Merle Haggard's hit country tune "Okie from Muskogee" (1969) communicated, not a place that welcomed long-hairs. It is in the South that Wyatt and Billy meet discrimination, violence, and their own deaths: "rednecks" jail them because of their long hair, hurl insults at them at a local café, attack them while they're sleeping (killing George, the American Civil Liberties Union lawyer played by Jack Nicholson), and, ultimately, murder both Billy and Wyatt on the highway (with a shotgun hung on a rack in a pickup truck). While there are idyllic images of cypress trees and the Old South, Southern scenery is dotted with African-American poverty and the intrusive icons of modern life and industrialization (gas stations, refineries, etc.).

On the surface of the film, then, the terms of youth and Civil Rights protest are materialized in the trajectory of the road trip through politically value-laden regions. In addition, *Easy Rider*'s regionalism acted iconoclastically in relation to several previous features of the road movie, thus enhancing its revisionist status and counter-cultural credentials. It reversed populism's faith in small-town America epitomized in Frank Capra's *It Happened One Night* (1934) and the Western's conventional east-to-west trajectory with its promises of freedom and opportunity. Even the comically self-reflexive quest for frontier fortune (e.g., Alaskan gold) in Hope and Crosby's *Road to Utopia* (1946) is reversed as *Easy Rider*'s protagonists 'score' their drug money in the beginning of the film only to lose it in the end.

But, upon closer inspection, we can see that *Easy Rider* is not simply a counter-nationalistic film. To the contrary, it vividly crystallizes the tension between nationalism as a process evolving through time and nationalism as a thing already realized, a thing to be preserved from the assaults of history. This ambivalence becomes particularly clear when the film is linked to other representations featuring the American landscape during the late 1960s. The film's "geopolitics," as well as its use of the American highway and landscape, are intertwined with representations in the mass media and art scene that took America as their subject. *Easy Rider*'s highways and landscapes are positioned between two extremes: the affirmative patriotisms of Americana in the mass media and the raucously critical demystifications of Pop Art, between the romantic, nostalgic yearnings of the former and the violent, apocalyptic mood of the latter. As a result, *Easy Rider* is a work on "nationness" which is very much in process, riven with conflicts over the meaning of the American icons of the road, the wilderness, and the city.

America the Beautiful

In 1957, *The Saturday Evening Post* published a collection of photographs entitled *The Face of America*. This collection featured the various regions of the country in their rural, suburban, and urban splendors within a seasonal framework ("The Face of America in Spring," "The Face of America in Summer," etc.). The collection yielded a sense of the changeable and cyclic, yet constant and enduring characteristics of the land. We see sections of the country and citizens' activities – from certain ritual moments such as cherry blossom time in Washington, DC and an annual Thanksgiving dinner in Vermont to landscape monuments such as the Grand Canyon to more quotidian events such as a baby parade in Ohio. These pictures, the accompanying copy tells us, demonstrate the "spirit of a free nation" based upon "new images of . . . old enduring values." While each child born "throws himself with ingenious energy into the challenge of contributing his own personality and vocation to the character of the place where he was born . . . he partakes of a larger vision than that of his local place and his daily job. It is this which makes him a transcontinental citizen of this country" (5–6). No matter how regionally or individually distinct one's lifestyle may be, one is a citizen of the United States of America, an identity which transcends the particulars of regional and individual loyalties. Thus, *The Face of America* promotes the geographical particularities and diversities of the country, its "riches," while it situates them within a unified nation – a dual rhetoric unsurprising in the midst of the Cold War.

The beginning of the Cold War had already resulted in proliferating portraits of American democracy in the US media. As Elaine Tyler May has argued about other kinds of images during the 1950s, this tactic sought to differentiate the United States from the communist Soviet Union, showing the superiority of a way of life based on democracy, equality, and freedom. Thus, as in the copy for *The Face of America*, Cold War rhetoric proclaimed the nation's diversity (as opposed to the alleged homogeneity of the Soviet Union), while demonstrating its unity (in the face of the Communist threat) as a means of defining its superior status as a nation. Idealized photographs of American landscapes were pressed into service as ideological weapons against Communism.

While the Cold War continued to provide the incentive for nationalistic sentiments stressing diversity, unity, and democracy throughout the 1960s, by the end of that decade massive civil unrest in the form of the Vietnam War protest, the radical youth movement, race riots, and the black liberation movement, as well as the assassination of political figures such as Malcolm X, John F. Kennedy, his brother Robert, and Martin Luther King, dramatically enhanced the instabilities of the Cold War era by questioning the democratic claims that had traditionally served as the basis of national identity. To the counter-culture and Civil Rights workers, democracy was compromised by imperialism, racism, and repression as the United States fought a questionable war in Southeast Asia and battled African-Americans and youth protesters on the domestic front.[6] The unrest of the 1960s and the continuing Communist threat provided a situation in which a secure national identity was both violently contested and desperately required. Thus, the discourse about America the beautiful had a double duty to perform in relation to the officially perceived threats of the Cold War and protest culture. Magazines endorsed images of America the beautiful to address the instabilities of the period, containing them by contextualizing them within familiar historical and ideological references.

Perhaps the enlistment of color photography to serve the purposes of patriotic rhetoric is nowhere more evident that it is in the pages of *National Geographic* magazine in the late 1960s.[7] To concentrate for a moment on a particularly representative case, the magazine's report on the state of Oregon ("Oregon's Many Faces" by Stuart Jones) demonstrates this rhetoric's major motifs. The article characterizes Oregon through its landscape, people, and related industry and resources. Oregon's landscape is varied, "full of scenic marvels" (74) and "elbow room" (77). Further, it exists in vivid connection to America's past, particularly the pioneer and pilgrim eras. Mount Hood, for example, "signalled journey's end for pioneers trekking west on the Oregon Trail" (77), while the names of Oregon cities (e.g., Portland, Salem, Newport) echo the names of pilgrim settlements in New England. Contemporary celebrations further invoke the past, such as the "September jamboree" with its "rodeo, chuck wagon dinners, and Indian pageants" (91). Oregon's people are "an extremely mixed bag with a unifying love for independence of thought, people who would reject the very idea of wearing a label" (77). Moreover, it is a state which has resolved various racial conflicts. Oregon has a policy of "integrating Indian children into the state school system" (90). The Native American population runs the flourishing "Kah-Nee-Ta Vacation Resort" (90). As for the Japanese who had been interred in camps during the Second World War, they state that "wartime scars healed long ago. Oregon has been good to us. We harbor no bitterness" (95). A local commentator on this issue remarks further that the Japanese themselves "deserve great credit, of course, but I like to think that the special spirit of Oregon also played a part. Here a man is judged by what he is, not by his race, religion, or pigmentation" (95). As for industry, Oregon is booming because of businesses such as metallurgy

Plate 8.1 National Geographic presents one of Oregon's scenic marvels:
its mountainous coastline.

and lumber. As the author states, "with 26 million acres of commercial timber
– enough to rebuild every house in the United States – Oregon leads the nation
in forest products" (92–3).[8]

Throughout this rhetoric the past is reciprocally related to the present in a
manner that certifies the heritage of democracy and progressive capitalism based
on a sense of the never-ending frontier. The vast space signals the diversity and
grandeur of America's physical geography, harkening back to the vistas of the
pioneer days, while the state's cities demonstrate affiliations with the first
European settlements in New England. Town and country signify historical
continuity and the importance of the American past. True to the ideal principles
of the frontier, Oregon also embraces egalitarianism in the form of racial
tolerance, particularly when its race-citizens contribute productively to advancing
the capital profile of the state, as the Native Americans and Japanese have done.

Oregon appears to embrace some Civil Rights platforms (i.e., tolerance and school integration) for non-blacks, but only insofar as these progressive features can be linked to the ideals of frontierism, rather than to an explicit social or political agenda.

That the issue of racial conflict has somehow been magically resolved is particularly clear in *National Geographic*'s coverage of Southern cities. In an essay on Atlanta the main references to the Old South are to its restoration from the ravages of the Civil War or to the continuation of its traditions (in the form of the debutante ball, for example). The New South is exemplified through the tropes of progress (e.g., Atlanta as the home of Coca-Cola, an important epidemiological center, and a new municipal showcase). Appreciation of the dramas and charms of the past coupled with a contemporary faith in technology, progress, and the essential fairness of the American character resolve all social inequities and lead to a bright future (Ellis: 246–81). That such discourse could take place amidst proliferating public tragedies of racial violence is a testament to the durability of traditional patriotic rhetoric rooted in idealized frontier ideology.[9]

Pictorial verification of the continued existence of the frontier is key to *National Geographic*'s patriotic messages. Essay after essay attempts to demonstrate that the United States is still a frontier – full of new resources and new territories, a vision which Oregon as a state with enough lumber to rebuild every house in the country aptly incarnates. Thus, *National Geographic* features pieces on Alaska's outback, the US Virgin Islands, the ocean (called the "deep frontier"), the moon, and the growing interstate highway system.[10] The magazine relentlessly discovers new frontiers which in turn secure the manifest destiny of the United States.

In 1969, of course, Apollo 11 was launched and Neil Armstrong walked on the moon. Like other magazines, *National Geographic* featured prolific photos of the moon, often in the fold-out page format (which suggested that a typical page could not capture the immensity of the moonscape). The moonscape is forbidding and barren, but a space which represents dreams of new frontiers that are not unlike the old. The moon crater Copernicus "just about matches in size our largest national park, Yellowstone [about 400 miles across]" (Cook: 245). Writers show us what a settlement on the moon would look like (complete with swimming pool) by virtue of the "frontiersmen of the space age" – engineers and technicians who will help colonize the moon (Weaver: 229). The moonscape, compared to Western icons and situated within the rhetoric of discovery, adventure, and expansion, represents the extraterrestrial reach of America's frontier know-how as well as the promise that the frontier is not dead.[11]

But another, perhaps less expected terrain for the enactment of a neo-frontier expansionist ethos, is the interstate highway system the government had begun funding in 1956 with the passage of the National Highway Act. A 1957 cover article in *Time* magazine calls road building "the American Art," remarking that the "panorama of road builders stringing highways across the land reflects a peculiarly American genius, one that lies deep in the traditional pioneering instincts of the nation" ("Construction": 92). Later accounts continue to extol American ingenuity and progress, while ensuring continuities with the glorious past. As the writer for "Our Growing Interstate Highway System" exclaims, "A giant nationwide engineering project – the Interstate Highway system – is altering and circumventing geography on an unprecedented scale." Highways extend "to the wild green yonder" where we can see "young trailblazers" stopping at a rest stop to get a drink (Jordan: 199). Further, a drive along the Interstate system "provides a vivid lesson in the geography of the U.S. The new highways cut through the brooding forests and silent deserts, they course the endless prairies, skirt rivers that helped shape the destiny of a continent, and knife through high, lonely mountains" (201). To develop the ramifications of this conjunction of geography and the legendary past, the writer adds, "Everywhere you find history too – battlefields, monuments, yesterday's frontiers" (204). But unlike excursions in the past, the interstates provide all of the amenities – "wide shoulders, easy vision at night, emergency telephones, scenic overlooks and rest areas . . . even underpasses for hikers and wildlife" (197). The photographs of the highways make them appear as spectacular as the naturescapes and cityscapes they transect; roads stretch endlessly through the equally endless American terrain.

Thus, frontierism is tirelessly presented in the pages of *National Geographic* and other sources. The landscape continues to affirm frontierism and the promise of space. It is a space by definition democratic since in theory no class systems or unfair hierarchies exist there; a space then where individual renewal, property relations, and industry can be achieved within a democratic framework.

Easy Rider's cinematography of the US landscape shares this embrace of The Land. As Rex Reed succinctly puts it, the film "looks like a nature study filmed on an opium trip" (233). The film indulges in picturesque road montages, referred to as "travelogue" sections by its original reviewers, which allowed spectators to "experience the vastness of America's physical beauty" (Brode: 20). *Easy Rider*'s rapturous portrait of the landscape is further magnified by cinematic strategies emphasizing the protagonists' *experience* of the landscape via the use of traveling point-of-view shots. Through the use of such dynamic point-of-view shots and exhilarating rock music, that experience is effectively cathected into the viewer.

There are several sequences in *Easy Rider* that rhapsodize the American landscape via the picturesque road montage. The first, supported on the sound-track by Steppenwolf's *Born to Be Wild*, depicts the joy of riding through shots of Wyatt and Billy on their motorcycles, followed by panoramic point-of-view shots of the desert Southwest. After having dinner with an Anglo farmer and his Mexican family, *Easy Rider* features extended passages of Southwestern scenery with the Rocky Mountains, forests, deserts, and buttes, including our heroes'

Plate 8.2 Part of a picturesque road montage from *Easy Rider* with Wyatt, Billy, and the Rocky Mountains.

sunset arrival in Monument Valley. These scenes again alternate between objective shots of the riders on their bikes and subjective shots of their experience of the landscapes they pass. The Byrds' "Ballad of Easy Rider" and The Band's "The Weight" play over this second road montage. The combinations of road montage and musical passage act as interludes between narrative actions. These devices cue the audience that it is time to watch and take pleasure in the spectacle – in this case, men, motorcycles, the open road, and the beauties of nature.

That the American wilderness is to be admired as a vision is made clear through this assembly of cinematic elements. Moreover, in the second montage sequence, there is nearly a 360-degree pan of the horizon at Monument Valley, a device necessary, the film-maker seems to be saying, to capture the spot's grandeur reverently and completely. Throughout these montages, the cinematographer, Haskell Wexler, allows sunlight to hit the lens of the camera, flaring the shots with dazzling reflections off the lens and occasional rainbow-effects (an innovation of the New American Cinema). This technique gives the landscape a literal radiance (while also alluding to the enhanced perceptions of the land through the marijuana-influenced view of Wyatt, Billy, and their hitch-hiking companions).

This vision of the wilderness is carefully tied to a sense of US history, at least as it has been immortalized in images from the classic Western. The campfire scenes in *Easy Rider* self-consciously recall similar scenes from the Western. Instead of staying in motels (where they are not welcome), Wyatt, Billy, their commune-bound hitch-hiker, and George bed down at night like the pioneer adventurers before them. On their first night out, Billy makes the parallel clear when he pretends that they are "fighting Indians and cowboys on every side . . . out here in the wilderness." True to some of the principles of New American Cinema revisionism, the film-maker updates these past conventions by establishing numerous parallels between the Old and New West. For example, Hopper juxtaposes Billy's buckskin garb with Wyatt's motorcycle leathers and horses with motorcycles (particularly when the repair of Wyatt's motorcycle is compositionally matched to shoeing a horse at the Anglos' farm). But curiously few signs of modernization affect the depiction of the Southwestern landscape itself.

As Robert Ray and others have noted, revisionist Westerns of the 1960s were remarkable for reversing conventions associated with the frontier ethos, particularly in signaling the closing of the frontier and thereby suggesting that the frontier image was no longer valid (296–325). *Easy Rider*'s west-to-east trajectory would be an example of how this particular film demonstrates the end of the frontier and the hopes it held for individual freedom and national progress. However, the film's concentration on such celebratory images of the West – beyond indulging in the atavistic romanticism which Ray suggests many revisionist films of the period do – further belies its strategies of reversal. This becomes particularly clear when we place *Easy Rider* within the context of other road movies of the time, as well as the "America the Beautiful" pictorial context surrounding it.

The frontier is alive and well in *Easy Rider*, situated, as it has traditionally been, in the West. Not all road movies of the time embraced the Western landscape in such ecstatic terms. *Alice's Restaurant* fails to exploit pictorially the physical resources of either the West or the Northeast that serve as a backdrop to its main hippie character's meanderings. Like *Easy Rider*, *The Rain People* sets out to demystify the sense of purpose and optimism that pervades the conventional road picture. But, unlike *Easy Rider*, it refuses to idealize the American landscape. The road Natalie (Shirley Knight) travels from the East to the Northwest is alienating – it's a world of plastic motels, roadside phone booths, gas stations, flat farmlands, fast food, obligatory scenic outlooks, claustrophobic small towns, and trailer parks. *Midnight Cowboy* more surrealistically depicts the banality and lurking violence in the heart of the West (Texas), as well as the impersonality and sexual chaos of the city (New York). Its dusty Texas roads, small-time cafés, and traumatic sexual experiences vie with the horrific images of a city occupied with sad "perverts" to yield a sense of a country without any sustaining relationship to a mythic past. Jean-Luc Godard's *Weekend*, a French film screened in the United States in 1969, offers the most profane vision of individual initiative, the road, and modern French landscape imaginable with its bickering, murderous bourgeoisie couple, endless traffic jams complete with burning wreckage, and unspectacular locales that bespeak the modern condition. Thus, the road movie was in no way obliged to offer the viewer extravagant scenery as a part of its allegorical take on the contemporary state of the nation.

In insisting on the continued presence of the frontier and its promises of freedom, *Easy Rider* allies itself rather unexpectedly with the discourses on "America the Beautiful" offered by *National Geographic* and other mass-circulation magazines. While the film inserts the counter-culture into the wilderness, the presence of hippies does not automatically derail the nationalistic symbolism so intimately associated with the grand scenery. Indeed, when hippies were represented positively in the media, it was often through their relation to the early pioneers, rustic living habits, and love of the earth.[12] Thus, the pairing of hippies and national scenery in *Easy Rider* does little to disturb the traditional meanings of the latter, since the media had already co-opted the hippie movement in Old Western terms.

More important, like *National Geographic*, *Easy Rider*'s pictorial strategies function as a travelogue through picturesque America. Through its ultra-photogenic aesthetic, the film advertises the physical grandeur and continued availability of America's frontier territories, just as it suggests through its protagonists, the Anglo/Mexican family they encounter, the youth commune, and other aspects of their journey through the West, that this territory still promises freedom, diversity and tolerance, and a continuing influx of new pioneers. Since its Southwestern scenes never attempt to demystify the West nor the exhiliration the road can still offer the American male, the film both preserves mythic memories of the historical past and demonstrates their continuing relevance to measuring the health of the American nation.

While *Easy Rider* demonstrates the death of those ideals once the characters leave the frontier and enter civilization, its preoccupation with Western landscape as a marker of our past and present glory perpetuates the fiction of the frontier ideology. When George remarks about the sad state of intolerance in the contemporary United States – "This used to be one helluva good country" – we might very well ask, "when?" The frontier eras represented escape and opportunity for many, but they also involved deprivation, untrammeled violence, and the virtual extermination of Native Americans, among other things. In nation-alistic discourses, however, the US landscape becomes a series of landmarks commemorating not only past adventures which have marked the nation's historical progress, but the daring openness and initiative of the American character itself.

Thus, by creating its counter-cultural message through regionalism, *Easy Rider* participates in a patriotic mythology which obscures the failings of the frontier myth. Through its vast, unpopulated, unmodernized, romantic vistas of natural Western glories, the film unquestioningly supports one of the foundations of American ideology – frontierism – a myth that had become a virtual lingua franca in traditional nationalistic discourses in the late 1960s. *Easy Rider*'s main difference from *National Geographic* discourse is that it utterly refuses to show the modern West. Modernity is a stigma associated with civilization – in this case, the South. In this sense, the film's atavistic romanticism sustains an even more traditional view of the frontier than its more overtly conservative discursive companions.

If "grand national scenery . . . is the nursery of patriotism" (A. Miller: 8), then *Easy Rider* is a strange bedfellow to the counter-revolutionary strategies of 1960s mainstream magazines and other sources. The images of the West assure the viewing audience of the enduring presence of the historical past and the ideals of patriotism through what amounts to a transcendental view of America as an "idyllic wonderland" which is "untouched by human hands" (Stich: 46).

But while mainstream magazines devoted to traditional nationalism extended their paean to efface regional differences (e.g., connecting the West with the Northeast and the South with the North through images of urban and industrial growth), *Easy Rider*, as we have seen, indulges in a regionalism according to 1960s politics. Not only is the West idealized, but the South is demonized. *Easy Rider*'s South bears the burden for all of civilization's maladies, including small-town racial prejudice, xenophobia, and the negative effects of modernization, urbanization, and industrial growth. We can partially understand this negativity about the South as more generally about civilization, given the film's revisionist Western credentials. That is, in the Western, there is often an ambivalence about the physical and spiritual effects of civilization on the frontier. This ambivalence is updated and additionally emphasized by such 1960s phenomena as the hippies' retreat from the city and the identification of the South with bigotry. But, as in its depictions of the Western landscape, *Easy Rider*'s generic revisionism and counter-cultural position only partially explain its situation within 1960s politics and culture.

The dystopian aspects of the film joined it to negative press accounts about the state of America, as well as to a decade-long interrogation of American icons and myths by Pop artists. These broader connections suggest that *Easy Rider*'s message was a patchwork of traditional and transitional views on the meaning of America within the social melee of the youth revolution.

Amerika: Death, Disaster, and the Apocalypse

After Wyatt and Billy are arrested and jailed for parading without a permit in their first encounter with Southern hospitality, they return to the road, along with George, who has decided to accompany the pair to New Orleans. Following their release, the road depicts the beauties of the Southern landscape and its open spaces. To the Holy Modal Rounders' "If You Wanna Be a Bird," George and Billy cavort on their cycles, communicating once again the alliance of cycle, landscape, and male freedom.

Soon, though, the mood of the film clearly changes, abruptly signaled by Jimi Hendrix's nihilistic "If Six Was Nine," a stark counterpoint to the more carefree celebrations of the road earlier on the soundtrack. Instead of wilderness, we see cemeteries, Southern mansions, mangrove trees, and small towns decorated with American flags. The road montage also fleetingly depicts the African-American experience in the South by showing shacks and poverty on the outskirts of the towns through which the protagonists pass.

After this montage, Billy, Wyatt, and George suffer more prejudicial treatment at the hands of the locals when they stop for lunch at a café. The locals loudly refer to them as "refugees from a gorilla love-in," among other things. Shortly there-after George is murdered by "rednecks" as he sleeps. When Billy and Wyatt go on to New Orleans to the House of Blue Lights, where they meet two prostitutes and go on an acid trip during Mardi Gras, the iconography of the city enhances the sense of disconnection from the wilderness. The road montage is replaced by an hallucinogenic fragmentation of the city and its graveyard (with the Electric Prunes' "Kyrie Eleison" on the soundtrack). The religious and funereal imagery of this sequence paves the way for the last scenes on the way to Florida. As mentioned earlier, the Southeastern landscape displays the marks of industry – power lines, gas stations, and refineries. On a road in proximity to the Southern urban landscape, Wyatt and Billy are blown off their motorcycles by shotgun-toting Southern "rednecks." As Wyatt's motorcycle explodes into flames, an aerial shot places the wreckage within the context of a landscape vista to clinch the tragic proportions of the assassination. Roger McGuinn's version of Bob Dylan's "It's Alright Ma (I'm Only Bleeding)" literalizes the apocalyptic dimensions of the final act.

Along with its more affirmative cultural commentary on the state of the nation, *Easy Rider* also partakes of apocalyptic, disaster-filled predictions on the future of the country. While *Easy Rider*'s politicized regionalism centers this apocalypse in the South, it uses the region to depict the closing of the frontier, the death of freedom in a modern landscape contaminated by fascistic intolerance and violence.

In the mass media, images of the closed frontier broadly involve the impact of technology on the environment, the decline of the American city, and the dangers of US highways, among other things. In an essay for *Look* ironically entitled "America the Beautiful," for example, David Perlman outlines the grim future for the globe if technological developments continue to progress unimpeded. Giving us a less than optimistic view of the meaning of space travel, Perlman notes the "cancer-like" spread of pollution across the world as seen by the astronauts (25). In the United States "four million cars vomit unburned hydrocarbons . . . lead and cancer-causing nickel additives . . . 16 million rubber tires vaporize on the abrading freeways, and invisible but deadly asbestos particles shed from brake linings" (25).

Another essay in the same issue proclaims that our future is in danger because of pollution and careless use of natural resources: "Hardly a century ago, the American landscape seemed equal to our relatively unlimited power to destroy . . . before 50 million buffalo were slaughtered, Indian nations humbled or exterminated, mountains and forests denuded. . . . We have created ugliness where there once was beauty" (Wolf: 32). Picturing a mother and son in gas masks because "urban air stinks" (31), the writer comments that while we "escaped from an Old World into a New Eden . . . there are no New Edens" (32). Similarly, *Life* featured essays on "The Highway as a Killer," which reported that "each week 1000 Americans die in auto crashes" ("Highway": 25) and "The Case of Fear in the Cities Beset by Crime" (Rosenthal: 17–23), which detailed the escalation of crime statistics and residents' changing perceptions of urban life.

Such essays help depict the "Janus-faced" aspect of nationalism – its polarized, unstable, multiple articulations. In this case, alarmism competed with optimism, redefining the United States through a sense of a heritage willfully and violently lost and progress grown out of control. These forces have made the frontier a distant memory in danger of never being resuscitated. Cars destroy the landscape, environment, and public health, while highways contribute to a mounting death toll. The thrill of the ride and the road no longer symbolize a frontier legacy and democratic freedom, nor even the affluence of leisured suburbanites and their teenagers. Instead, they symbolize the irresponsibility of modernity, portending disaster.

Of all of the media forms of the 1960s, Pop Art provides the definitive critique of the romanticism of vehicle, the road, and the US landscape. Within a substantial reworking of American iconography in general, Andy Warhol, Allan D'Arcangelo, Duane Hanson, Larry Rivers, and others treated the underside of the promises of the highway, including speed, mobility, and the experience of the vastness of the American landscape tinged with history. As Sidra Stich writes, Pop Art featuring the highway often attested to the "dominance of the road as an American image and mobility as a characteristic aspect of American life." But Pop Artists did not see the highway, as had Kerouac and others, "as a metaphor for freedom or an escape route away from the doldrums of the workaday world; the road is little more than a conveyor belt that runs through a repetitive, vacuous, monotonous environment. And travel is no longer an adventure yielding novel perceptions as much as it is an excursion to replicas of the already known and familiar" (Stich: 69). The canvases of D'Arcangelo (*U.S. Highway 1*, 1963; *Full Moon*, 1962) and Edward Ruscha (*Standard Station, Amarillo, Texas*, 1963), for example, show how the ubiquitous emblems of highway asphalt and the gas station completely dominate the landscape, ultimately effacing it. Via Celmin's work (*Freeway*, 1966) shows freeways depicted through the windshield of a car from the point of view of the passenger to emphasize the homogeneity and monotony of the landscape and the detached, alienated quality of the motorist's experience (71–2). In Llyn Foulkes's painting of Death Valley (*Death Valley U.S.A.*, 1963), inscribed "This painting is dedicated to the American," the landscape is desolate; any utopian promises of expansionism it may have once held are transformed by an eviscerated, forbidding, completely deromanticized topography (170–1).

Such art arose in reaction to the 1950s growth of motel and fast-food chains, prefabricated housing, suburbanization, and the incursion of small industry, businesses, and billboards on the highway. But Pop Art also reacted to a myriad of incidents in the 1960s, from the escalating war in Vietnam, domestic civil strife, and the dramatic decline of the city to statistics about highway casualties and the media exploitation of traffic accidents. By 1959 at least 1.25 million Americans had died in traffic accidents, exceeding the number of war dead in the United States (Corrigan: 147). In 1969 alone, 56,000 Americans died in such accidents (Stich: 172). In Hollywood during the 1950s and 1960s, Montgomery Clift's devastating car accident and the deaths of James Dean and Jayne Mansfield in car crashes lent an aura of romantic tragedy to the speed and glamor of being on the road. Marlon Brando's turn as a motorcycle rebel in *The Wild One* (1954), the spate of 1960s AIP motorcycle films, the notorious quintessence of 1960s outlawry, the Hell's Angels, and teenage boys' fantasies about motorcycles and rebellious masculinity, only enhanced the danger and excitement associated with fast wheels, youth, and the freedom of the road. Death in this context could make one a legend, as it did James Dean.

Pop Art responded to the exploitative necrophilia of the press and the overly romanticized Hollywood depiction of road catastrophes through a series of shocking, but removed images of death and disaster on the highway. Duane Hanson's *Motorcycle Accident* (1969) portrays a lifelike sculpture of dead youth, sprawled on the ground still attached to his motorcycle. Perhaps more than any other Pop Artist, Andy Warhol devoted himself to death and disaster imagery. Warhol silk-screened and painted a series of car crashes from newspaper photographs between 1963 and 1964, vividly exemplifying and critiquing the media's ghoulish concentration on highway disasters. These include: *5 Deaths, White Burning Car III, Orange Car Crash 14 Times, Green Disaster #2, Ambulance Disaster, Saturday Disaster*, and *Foot and Tire*. Serial repetition of many of these photo-images renders them mundane, de-spectacularized. They deglamorize the mythos of the car crash as a romantic end to youthful rebellion by depicting the banal gruesomeness and grotesquery of highway accidents. Each victim is

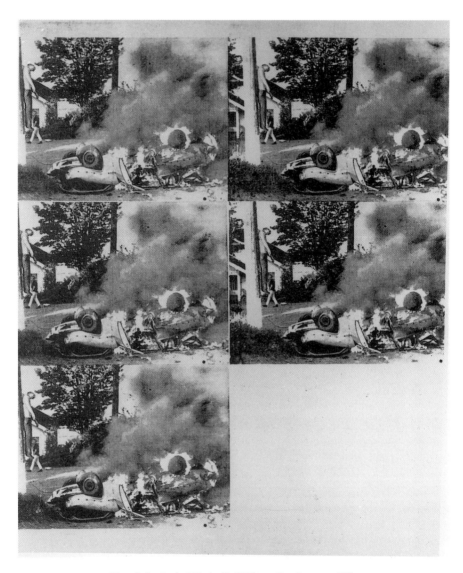

Plate 8.3 Andy Warhol's "White Car Burning III".
The American dream of mobility turned into a nightmare. © 1997 Andy Warhol
Foundation for the Visual Arts/ARS, New York.

transformed into a death-and-disaster still life, variably impaled on telephone pole spikes, hanging out of car windows, trapped beneath cars, and uniformly converted into blood-spattered, human wreckage which blends into the automotive wreckage. The victims are "everyman/woman" in a scenario that turns the "American dream (of social mobility and leisure) into a nightmare" (Printz: 16).

The preoccupation of some Pop Artists with death sought to reflect the omnipresence of violence, particularly against the backdrop of the 1960s, through an unsentimental, deromanticized lens which was clearly at odds with American aesthetic traditions showing the valor in death. As Stich writes, "for the first time in American art . . . death is treated forthrightly as a fearful, alienating counterpoint to idealistic conceptions of the American dream . . . in postwar art death is not related to either spiritual or heroic themes. . . . Rather, death is shown to be a brutal end, a purposeless finality, a haphazard disaster caused not by divine or natural means but by human madness or political strife" (163).

Easy Rider's second half, with its banal small towns, industrialized highways, and fiery vertiginous motorcycle death finale invokes this spirit of revisionist reassessment of the state of the nation, rather than the "red, white, and blue" pronouncements of the affirmative media. In addition, though, while its finale suggests the martyrdom of its heroes, thus invoking a tragic romanticism (again, especially in contrast to *The Rain People* or *Midnight Cowboy*), the abruptness of Billy and Wyatt's roadside assassinations avoids the "freeze frame" and slow-motion hail-of-bullets endings of *Butch Cassidy and the Sundance Kid* (1969) and *The Wild Bunch* (1969), respectively, thus minimizing the legend-making connotations of these devices. However, *Easy Rider* shares little of Pop Art's radical techniques of distanciation with respect to its subjects. While there are affiliations between the alarmism of the mass media and the critical iconoclasms of Pop Art, it is in a more general sense that *Easy Rider* dovetails with the transitional forces redefining America at the time.

Films during the late 1960s helped create what Todd Gitlin has referred to as an "edgy, apocalyptic popular culture" bred by catastrophic political violence (202). As Gitlin has pointed out, the paranoid and apocalyptic culture of the late 1960s was often materialized through extreme filmic violence, as in the endings of *Bonnie and Clyde* (1967) and *The Wild Bunch*, where the protagonists were shot literally to pieces in slow motion. Gitlin calls *Easy Rider* "a lyric on behalf of paranoia, saying to the counter-culture: yes, you'd better fear those ignorant Southern fascist hard-hats." The counter-culture was "transfixed by the image of their demons as they watched this cautionary tale" (202). Films on the left and the right and the music of Bob Dylan, the Rolling Stones, and the Doors "thrived in *and reproduced* an apocalyptic, polarized political mood." Gitlin's ultimate point here is that the aestheticization of violence in films of the 1960s and the dark

Plate 8.4 *Easy Rider*'s version of the apocalypse: the assassinations of Billy and Wyatt on the road by "rednecks," Wyatt's motorcycle in flames.

pulsations of rock music helped create "*in ensemble* . . . a symbolic environment that was conducive to revolutionism out of context, to the inflation of rhetoric and militancy out of proportion to the possible" (202). In one sense, the left movement got sidetracked from dealing directly with political issues by media images that displaced activism through spectacles of violence offering a negative vision of the potential of the counter-culture and its aims to survive within a repressive society. From Gitlin's point of view, apocalyptic imagery in the media polarized the political struggle so monumentally that effective, radical political action seemed hopeless.

While the fatalism of this imagery may have helped ultimately to compromise the political struggles of the late 1960s, its production of the reverse image of American dreams of freedom, mobility, and individual initiative nonetheless created a public profile of a nation at odds with competing traditions based on America the Beautiful rhetoric. *Easy Rider*'s excursions into the dystopian regions of American national identity coupled with its abrupt demolition of its hippie heroes places it firmly within the transitional discourses of the time that were dramatically rewriting the optimism of the frontier ethic.

The Janus-faced Nation

Easy Rider's relationship to the two major national discourses of its time – the traditional and the transitional – reveals that what has appeared to be its clear generational message, its advocacy of the hippie and its denunciation of society, is fraught with inconsistencies and ambiguities. The film's canonization obscures its contradictions, contradictions rooted in the social discourses about nationness in this revolutionary historical moment. The film is at once a travel poster proclaiming the continued presence of the grand Old West and its historical and mythic associations, and a nightmarish portrait of small towns, cities, and the end of the frontier (and the world). It is a celebration of the freedom of the road and the beauty of the landscape and a dissertation on the end of the road and the repulsive banalities and industrial blight that disfigure the scenery. In examining *Easy Rider*'s treatment of the road and the landscape, we can see that there is no single "smooth" message offered by the film about its times. *Easy Rider* is a quintessential example of a film caught between two languages. Even as it attempts to fashion itself as a timepiece about the hippie generation and its conflicts, the film moves between the language of traditional patriotism founded in the visions provided by "grand national scenery" and a language of revisionism seeking to dismantle traditional notions of Americanism by detailing the nightmarishness of its roads, inhabitants, and modernized landscapes. *Easy Rider* thus invokes both affirmative and critical visions of 1960s America, making it more of a measure of its times than either its original or later audiences could imagine.

Notes

1   *Easy Rider* was also nominated for several Academy Awards, including best supporting actor (Jack Nicholson) and best original story and screenplay (by Peter Fonda, Dennis Hopper, and Terry Southern).

2   Each of these areas deserves more discussion, particularly *Easy Rider*'s intertextual references to texts that had been embraced by youth culture. The film had multiple ties, for example, to the exploitation film. The stars of the film – Hopper, Fonda, and Jack Nicholson – had all worked for Corman at AIP, as had their cinematographer, Laszlo Kovacs. Fonda had starred in *Wild Angels* and *The Trip*, while Hopper had starred in *The Glory Stompers*. In addition, because of Fonda's previous exploitation film appearances, his best-selling poster (featuring him astride a Harley-Davidson motorcycle), his highly publicized drug bust for marijuana possession, and his status as actor Henry Fonda's son, he was already an icon of youth culture hipness and rebellion.

   Easy Rider also belonged to a trend in film production that seemed to promise a revitalized US cinema. Hopper's film was part of the New American Cinema (as was *Bonnie and Clyde*, 1967, another cult film of youth audiences). New American Cinema featured a "spontaneous" style influenced by the French New Wave and a generic revisionism that sought to critique and reverse conventions that had dominated classic Hollywood films for decades. *Easy Rider* invoked the Western through its vistas of

Monument Valley and the Southwestern wilderness, its substitution of motorcycles for horses, and its characters, whose names – Billy and Wyatt – were meant to invoke Billy the Kid and Wyatt Earp, the latter a role previously played by Peter's father Henry in John Ford's *My Darling Clementine* (1946). The film also reversed one of the most sacred tenets of the genre – the movement from east to west which had traditionally promised liberty and plenty for all – by having its protagonists travel from California to the Southeast, wherein they encounter increasingly hostile challenges to their freedom leading up to their joint assassinations by Southern "rednecks."

3 *Easy Rider* openly quotes from *On the Road* in several scenes, most notably when a character from the commune asks Peter Fonda why he won't stay. He replies, "I don't know, I just gotta go." This echoes Dean Moriarty's less existentially cool conversation with Sal in *On the Road*: "Whee, Sal, we gotta go and never stop going till we get there." Sal: "Where we going, man?" "I don't know but we gotta go" (237). Moriarty later says, "It's the world – my god! It's the world! We can go right to South America if the road goes. Think of it! Son-of-a-*bitch*! Gawd-*damn*! . . . Damn! I gotta go!" (277). *Easy Rider* also uses a whorehouse scene as a point of culmination for its traveling heroes, but substitutes the alcohol-driven delirium of *On the Road*'s scene (286) with its own delirium-inducing substance – LSD. While paying tribute to the West, the mystique of the individual, and the awe-inspiring value of the US landscape, *Easy Rider* revises *On the Road*'s tone of exhilaration to produce a cautionary tale about the road, questioning its ability to lead to adventure, potential, and freedom. That Kerouac died in October of 1969, during the film's initial run, adds a note of poignancy to this end-of-the-road tale. Last, for a sense of the impact of Hell's Angels during the 1960s, see Thompson.

4 For example, one reviewer of Godard's *Weekend* points out that "traffic jams represent the embodiment of the world state at present" (Arkadin: 12), while another writes that in Godard's world the Schuylkill Expressway would represent not a road at all, but a "symbol and a glorious one. The Schuylkill expressway symbolizes the END OF THE WORLD according to Jean-Luc Godard" (Eisenberg: 19). In a review of *Rain People*, the reporter for *Helix* writes that

> America seems to have special claims on the journey story about people who are on the run. . . . it's a very familiar story but still one that's full of energy and fascination because . . . the very American-ness of the whole song-of-the-road obsession dovetails . . . with the feeling that . . . the public and private sense of national and personal identity have just got to end up running dab smack into each other. . . . *The Rain People*'s journey has an abundance of interesting stops along the way and presents some of the most keenly felt observations to appear in a year of many keenly felt American movies.
> (P.H.: 14).

For other examples of this kind of allegorical reading, see Schickel and Milne. Schickel writes, "The road does lead through modern America, and inevitably the [characters] must collide with the casual unthinking brutality of a nation that talks much of freedom but will not tolerate radical personal experience" (241). Milne comments that "the last image of the film is as desolate a condemnation of the errors of civilization as the series of funeral pyres which dot the roadside in Godard's *Weekend*" (211).

5　"Amerika," as the alternative press liked to call the United States during the late 1960s, signified both a literal and figurative perversion of "America" to address what many saw as the fascist, repressive operations of the country's government and bureaucracies, evidenced in such phenomena as the nation's imperialistic engagement in Vietnam, coercive and violent treatment of protesters, racial discrimination, and puritannical attitudes toward sexuality.

6　There are numerous books that detail the youth and Civil Rights movements of the 1960s. See for example: Gitlin; Peck; Branch; Blum; Farber; and Anderson.

7　For an in-depth analysis of *National Geographic*'s rhetoric in relation to Third World countries, see Lutz and Collins. Other magazines of the 1960s, such as *Life* and *Look*, also eulogized and romanticized the United States through landscape imagery in an attempt to perpetuate the enduring legacy of democracy. For example, *Life* magazine ran a series entitled "To See This Land America," which featured New England and "the beauty and movement of New York as viewed from a Manhattan apartment." In an amusing attempt at grandeur that also sought to tame the barbarity of the urban industrial environment through natural references, the writer comments that he can see from his window "a concrete plant more serene than an Alp" (69). In an issue with a flag cover, *Look* magazine ran a piece entitled "American Images." Like *The Face of America*, this piece displayed a series of images that gave a panoramic view of American cities, prairies, hills, airports, dime stores, and lunch spots to depict the diversity that had arisen from the nation's original expansionist impulses. As the writer comments, "We came from somewhere else to find a lyric haunting land whose boundless newness offered constant hope for ever better things beyond. Most Americans remain obsessed with our innocence in all its gawky grace and sunburst spontaneity" (Hedgepeth: 22).

8　For more of this kind of coverage of the West (and Midwest) in *National Geographic* during the late 1960s, see also Matthews: 668–79; Ellis: 347–71; Fisher: 114–47; Linchen: 157–201; and Graves, "San Francisco Bay, the Westward Gate": 593–637.

9　See also here Graves, "Mobile, Alabama's City in Motion": 368–97.

10　See, for example, in *National Geographic*: Abercrombie: 540–63. We are told that in Alaska's outback a "pioneer woman of the 20th century . . . cooks pancakes for her husband . . . who is out checking his traplines" (561). The igloo "boasts an all-electric kitchen" (549). See also Mitchell: 67–103 and Macleish: 139–50. Other feature stories that underscore this mission of the magazine include "New Map Charts an Expanding Nation", 220–1.

11　It should be pointed out that mass-circulation magazines were not univocal, presenting only a flag-waving US frontierism. At times they displayed the same ambivalent feelings about the nation marking the more extreme contrasts between *National Geographic* and Pop Art. Particularly, alarm about urban decay/violence and the effects of progress/technology on the environment temper more positive accounts. See Perlman: 25–7; Wolf: 28–32; and Rosenthal: 17–23.

12　See, for example, "The Commune Comes to America," *Life*'s magazine's cover story about youth communes. The writer remarks,"Youthful pioneers leave society to seek from the land and one another a new life" (16b); "Their hair and their dress, their pioneer spirit, even their Indian teepees evoke the nation's frontier beginnings" (20b). The writer also finds that the youth in the communes are "surprisingly pristine" as they practice religion, ban drugs, and uphold "traditional American monogamy" (20b).

Works Cited

Abercrombie, Thomas J. "Nomad in Alaska's Outback." *National Geographic* (April 1969): 540–63.

Anderson, Terry H. *The Movement and the Sixties*. New York: Oxford University Press, 1995.

Arkadin. Rev. of *Weekend*. *Dallas Notes* (November 19–December 2, 1969): 12.

Bhabha, Homi K. "Introduction: Narrating the Nation." *Nation and Narration*, ed. Homi K. Bhabha. New York: Routledge, 1990. 1–7.

Blum, John Morton. *Years of Discord: American Politics and Society, 1961–1974*. New York: Norton, 1991.

Branch, Taylor. *Parting the Waters: America in the King Years, 1954–63*. New York: Simon & Schuster, 1988.

Brode, Douglas. *Films of the 1960s*. Secaucus, NJ: Citadel, 1980.

"The Commune Comes to America." *Life* (July 18, 1969): 16b–23.

"Construction: March of the Monsters." *Time* (June 24, 1957): 92.

Cook, David W. "How We Mapped the Moon." *National Geographic* (February, 1969): 240–5.

Corrigan, Timothy. *A Cinema Without Walls: Movies and Culture after Vietnam*. New Brunswick, NJ: Rutgers University Press, 1991.

Dowd, Maureen. "Bush Boasts of Turnaround from 'Easy Rider' Society." *New York Times* (October 7, 1988): A11.

Eisenberg, Lee. Rev. of *Weekend*. *Distant Drummer* (April 3–10, 1969): 19.

Ellis, William S. "Atlanta, Pacesetter City of the South." *National Geographic* (February, 1969): 246–81.

—— "Wisconsin's Door Peninsula." *National Geographic* (March, 1969): 347–71.

Farber, David. *The Age of Great Dreams: America in the 1960s*. New York: Hill & Wang, 1994.

Fisher, Allan C. "San Diego, California's Plymouth Rock." *National Geographic* (July, 1969): 114–47.

Gitlin, Todd. *The Whole World is Watching: Mass Media in the Making and Unmaking of the New Left*. Berkeley: University of California Press, 1980.

Glushanok, Paul. Rev. of *Easy Rider*." *Rat* (July, 1969): 20–1.

Graves, William. "Mobile, Alabama's City in Motion." *National Geographic* (March, 1968): 368–97.

—— "San Francisco Bay, the Westward Gate." *National Geographic* (November, 1969): 593–637.

Hedgepeth, William. "American Images." *Look* (July 15, 1969): 22–9.

"The Highway as a Killer." *Life* (May 30, 1969): 24–35.

Jones, Stuart E. "Oregon's Many Faces." *National Geographic* (January, 1969): 74–115.

Jordan, Robert Paul. "Our Growing Interstate Highway System." *National Geographic* (February, 1968): 195–219.

Kerouac, Jack. *On the Road*. [1957.] New York: Penguin, 1991.

Linchen, Edward J. "Colorado, the Rockyies' Pot of Gold." *National Geographic* (August, 1969): 157–201.

Lutz, Catherine A. and Jane L. Collins. *Reading National Geographic*. University of Chicago Press, 1993.

Macleish, Kenneth. "A Taxi for the Deep Frontier." *National Geographic* (January, 1968): 139–50.

Matthews, Samuel W. "Nevada's Mountain of Invisible Gold." *National Geographic* (May, 1968): 668–79.

May, Elaine Tyler. *Homeward Bound: American Families in the Cold War Era*. New York: Basic, 1988.

Miller, Angela. *The Empire of the Eye: Landscape Representation and American Cultural Politics, 1825–1875*. Ithaca: Cornell University Press, 1993.

Miller, Francis Jr. Rev. of *Easy Rider*. *The Great Speckled Bird* (September, 1969): 16.

Milne, Tom. Rev. of *Easy Rider*. *Sight and Sound* (Autumn 1969): 211.

Mitchell, Carleton. "Our Virgin Islands, 50 Years Under the Flag." *National Geographic* (January, 1968): 67–103.

"New Map Charts an Expanding Nation." *National Geographic* (February, 1968): 220–1.

Peck, Abe. *Uncovering the Sixties: The Life and Times of the Underground Press*. New York: Pantheon, 1985.

Perlman, David. "America the Beautiful." *Look* (November 4, 1969): 25–7.

P.H. Rev. of *Rain People*. *Helix* (November 20, 1969): 14.

Printz, Neil. "Painting Death in America." *Andy Warhol: Death and Disasters*. Houston: Houston Fine Art Press, 1988. 11–23.

Ray, Robert. *A Certain Tendency of the Hollywood Cinema, 1930–1980*. Princeton: Princeton University Press, 1985.

Reed, Rex. Rev. of *Easy Rider*. *Big Screen, Little Screen*. New York: Macmillan, 1971. 233.

Rosenthal, Jack. "The Case of Fear in Cities Beset by Crime." *Life* (July 11, 1969): 17–23.

Saturday Evening Post. *The Face of America*. Garden City, NJ: Doubleday, 1957.

Schickel, Richard. Rev. of *Easy Rider*. *Life* (July 11, 1969): 10.

Stich, Sidra. *Made in the U.S.A.: An Americanization in Modern Art, the '50s and '60s*. Berkeley: University of California Press, 1987.

Thompson, Hunter. *Hell's Angels*. New York: Random House, 1967.

"To See This Land America I & II," *Life* (March 3, 1967): 50–7; (March 10, 1967): 58–69.

Weaver, Kenneth F. "That Orbed Maiden . . . The Moon." *National Geographic* (February, 1969): 207–32.

Wolf, Anthony. "Our Future Is in More Danger." *Look* (November 4, 1969): 28–32.

9

FEAR OF FLYING

Yuppie critique and the buddy-road movie in the 1980s

Ina Rae Hark

Dean drove from Mexico City and saw Victor again in Gregoria and pushed that old car all the way to Lake Charles, Louisiana, before the rear end finally dropped on the road as he had always known it would. So he wired Inez for airplane fare and flew the rest of the way.

Jack Kerouac, *On the Road*

Linda: The movie you're basing your whole life on, *Easy Rider*, they had nothing, they had no nest egg.
David: Bullshit! They had a giant nest egg. They had all this cocaine.
Linda: That's not true.
David: It *is* true. Linda, they sold cocaine.

Albert Brooks, *Lost in America*

In the space of a little more than a year, from November 1987, to December 1988, three buddy-road movies appeared in theatres: *Planes, Trains and Automobiles* (1987), *Midnight Run* (1988), and *Rain Man* (1988). They shared a number of elements, beginning with the same master narrative: One buddy is a self-involved man with a distaste for intimacy who is battling a deadline to achieve some highly desired personal goal. For reasons that will become clear shortly, I will call him the "high flyer." The other man, whom I will label "the neurotic," is as apparently deficient in capitalist/masculinist qualities as the high flyer is in excess of them. Either truly mentally handicapped or simply fussy, nagging, and feminized, the neurotic and his personal idiosyncrasies initially drive his companion to distraction; they also interfere with the expeditious completion of a cross-country trip necessary to accomplish the first man's goal before the deadline expires, putting them both on a road filled with many detours and also eventually cutting off any access to financial reserves. Gradually, however, commitment to the previously scorned road companion becomes more important to the high flyer than making the deadline or closing the deal.

Given that buddy-road movies had been in disfavor in Hollywood for nearly ten years, it is rather astonishing that three such similar "odd couple" or "anti-buddy"[1] narratives should suddenly appear. This essay will argue that this apparent coincidence was part of a larger project of popular culture after the beginning of Reagan's second term to articulate its discomfort with the excesses of 1980s economic practices and the yuppie lifestyle they spawned. Other shared elements of the films, like the sacrifice of a valuable watch (read Rolex) to keep the couple going, and a climactic stop-over in Las Vegas, which is used to symbolize the true nature of the booming, speculative, deficit-driven economy, clearly point to such an aim. Some of these similarities doubtless derive from the fact that *Midnight Run* director Martin Brest was set to direct *Rain Man* at a point in development when its script looked a lot more like that of *Midnight Run* than that of the film Barry Levinson finally made (see Ansen: 53). But the elements cited appear in enough of the other anti-yuppie films of the era, as well as frequently serving as metaphors in analyses of the 1987 stock market crash that symbolized the end of Reaganomics, to qualify as a part of the *zeitgeist* rather than as simple borrowing. That each pair takes to the road only after an unsuccessful attempt to fly directly to the city where the deal-maker's goal can be realized emphasizes a binarism that became especially pronounced in the 1980s: flying embodies capitalistic success; the road is for economic losers.

To critique yuppie culture would seem to dictate a deconstruction of this binarism, so that the failure implicit in being grounded and broke is shown to constitute success of a different but more authentic kind. The three films make various moves in this direction, but they ultimately wish to recuperate patriarchal capitalism and hegemonic masculinity. These road movies show none of the ferocious anticapitalism of Jean-Luc Godard's *épater le bourgeois* road satire *Weekend* (1967); indeed they shift the ground of the critique so that business success or failure is finally not even at issue. They focus on transforming the character who embodies 1980s values into a "better person," not detaching him permanently from capitalistic practice. Micheline K. Frank, in her study of these films, reads them in ahistorical humanistic terms as a celebration of the underlying brotherhood of all men despite their superficial differences; she praises their plots, which repeatedly put the characters through "a psychic or spiritual journey" that results in "the formation of a bond or affiliation between the men and the individual overcoming of prejudice that involves reclaiming parts of the self" (123). The reform is thus not economic, but psychological, and the shift from culture critique to redemptive psychodrama is sufficient to blind Frank to the former aspect of the films altogether. This recuperative strategy almost exactly prefigures that of George Bush when he inherited the Reagan mantle, to call for "a kinder, gentler" America while fully embracing the "voodoo economics" he had at one time appeared to denounce.

While implementing this ideological project, however, the films themselves get detoured by their own recuperative strategy. At this historical juncture, the attempt to recuperate consumer capitalism by putting two white, heterosexual men on the road together has the unintended consequence of radically interrogating the premises of hegemonic masculinity. Conceiving yuppiedom as a problem of personal avarice and self-absorption, rather than as a result of economic practices, the films effect a cure that does often make the high flyer a better person. Unfortunately, the two chief recuperative moves, depriving him temporarily of capital resources and having him bond with a feminized neurotic buddy, also make him vulnerable to the emasculating potential of poverty and homosocial intimacy.

The film-makers evoke the potently masculine myth of Road Man, hoping to erase these implications. Instead they create an ideological gridlock, for emasculation is deeply imbedded (if unacknowledged) in the myth.[2] Maintaining the road man's masculinity depends on simultaneously justifying his avoidance of capitalist success (symbolized by the fear of flying) and dispelling the threat of bisexuality that has inhered in male road narratives from their inception, e.g. *Huckleberry Finn* as well as *On the Road*. Buddy-road movies of the 1980s, therefore, almost reflexively explain both why the buddies didn't travel by plane and that they aren't gay.

On the other hand, these films also reveal the road man as linked to the successful businessman in a number of implicit ways that the culture usually represses. If road men simply embody high-flying capitalism and masculinism in a different register, the threat of emasculation is eased, but the culturally constructed significance of the road as oppositional space then needs closer examination. This raises in turn the question of just how radically opposed to patriarchal capitalism even the most self-congratulatory examples of the "wild"[3] and "alienated" American road mythos actually are. As this essay will argue, the failure of the re-emergent buddy-road movie of the late 1980s to resolve these contradictions provides an insight into why the genre essentially had to reinvent itself once more in the 1990s before it could regain a preeminence it hadn't enjoyed since the end of the 1970s. To do so it is necessary first to examine the various ways the 1980s responded to that golden age of road movies of the previous decade.

Bypassing the Road

There's no highway in the sky, as the title of the 1951 James Stewart–Marlene Dietrich film puts it, and road movies therefore don't take place on airplanes. A close relative, the travel-disaster movie, can be set there, but without the ever-changing landscape, the possibilities of switching vehicles in mid-journey, and the potential for escape and isolation, vital semantic[4] elements of the road genre simply cannot transfer from the highway into the skyway. So, as the era of frequent-flyer[5] miles dawned, the road movie, which had been revived, and revised, with *Bonnie and Clyde* (1967) and *Easy Rider* (1969) and had flourished throughout the early 1970s, approached a vanishing point. With the end of the Vietnam War, and the resignation of Richard Nixon, the oppositional fervor that had fueled so many road movies had cooled; the *zeitgeist* no longer underwrote the rebellious, alienated, dropout or outlaw position road movie protagonists regularly adopted. Gas lines, energy crises, rising prices at the pump, and a more ominous view of hitch-hiking from the perspective of both driver and passenger alike had done much to take the sense of liberatory adventure out of the road. The return of the blockbuster with the success of *Star Wars* (1977) dampened Hollywood interest in the offbeat and downbeat narratives that road classics of the 1970s contained. Road movies of the late 1970s and early 1980s, populated mostly by rural Southerners and Southwesterners, were played for broad farcical laughs or car-crash pyrotechnics. The *Smokey and the Bandit* series (1977, 1980, 1985) was sadly exemplary: no longer the figure of an existential quest, the road had become a mere slapstick spectacle.

The election of Ronald Reagan in 1980, and the institution of his economic policies, quickly replaced the marginalized road man with a very different cultural icon: the yuppie business hotshot. "The Yuppies," Jean Baudrillard avers, "are not defectors from revolt, they are a new race, assured, amnestied, exculpated, moving with ease in the world of performance, mentally indifferent to any objective other than that of change and advertising (advertising everything: products, people, research, careers, lifestyle)" (110). Baudrillard also notes that although the Reagan generation grew up during the troubled 1960s and 1970s, they managed to root out "even any subconscious memory of those wild years" (110), including those years' fascination with the road man. While an avid car fetishist, with his BMW or Mercedes, the young *urban* professional sticks to the interstates and city beltways and is unlikely to be grounded in the vast rural spaces and isolated secondary roads favored in road movie iconography, with its "still resonant topography of vanishing points, billboards and motels, the extra-societal wilderness where the snug compression of urban culture peters out into a long empty stretch of entropic disorder" (Atkinson: 14). The hustling deal-maker of the "go-go eighties" is more likely to view these sorts of roads only from an altitude of 35,000 feet: "*Newsweek* saw yuppies as 'the vanguard of the baby-boom generation,' which had 'marched through the '60s' and was now 'speed[ing] toward the airport, and advancing on the 1980s in the back seat of a limousine" (Ehrenreich: 198).

Airplane travel, both as an actual material practice and as a metaphor, functioned throughout the 1980s as a marker for the particular functions of capitalism under Reagan. Like capital in the era of supply-side economics and unbridled speculative investment, the airline industry had also been deregulated. These respective deregulations allowed persons not previously so empowered to gain access to capitalist success and to plane travel. In an arena where the two systems merged, that of booking corporate business trips, the multiple fares and competing travel packages available through deregulation prompted many businesses to institute corporate travel management departments. In his book on this subject, James Poynter observes that the bewildering profusion of deals provided savvy travel managers an opportunity to turn the previous "cost center" of business travel into a "profit center" (85).

This simultaneous deregulation of capital and air travel more or less assured that in the 1980s the person for whom travel is a means to an end, who is goal-oriented with an eye on final destinations and ultimate victories – in other words, the person successfully inscribed into capitalist patriarchy – will be found on the runway not the highway. Having produced a culture of deals and deadlines that frowned upon detours, the decade felt little kinship with the road movie's languorous and frequently interrupted journeys. Conversely, the typical road movie protagonist, who by definition has chosen not to fly and tends to be either economically marginal, on the run, working at a low-prestige "road" job like truck driver or traveling salesman, or taking time away from business to go on holiday, thus cannot serve as an identificatory figure for workaholic yuppies. No wonder the decade that journalists frequently tagged as "high-flying" had little use for the road genre.

The metaphorical designation of the 1980s as a high-flying decade well represented this marked expansion of profit-making horizons, the insistence of Reaganites that the sky was the limit for the booming economy. Equally, however, the metaphor pointed up the repressed side of Reaganomics, that the high-flying economy was built on air – corporate and consumer debt and government deficits. *Time* described this "Reagan Illusion" as "the idea that there could be a defense buildup and tax cuts without a price, that the country could live beyond its means indefinitely" (Church: 20); *The New Republic* similarly characterized the 1980s boom as based upon "the willing suspension of disbelief that you can live beyond your means indefinitely and never have to pay up" ("Dreamer": 4). When the forces that fueled the boom ran out, there would be neither a slowdown nor a pause, but a crash. The *New Republic* observed: "The market was like Wile E. Coyote in the Roadrunner cartoons, who runs off the edge of a cliff and keeps right on going, until he looks down and then plummets" ("Dreamer": 4). On "Black Monday" the market looked down.

Grounding the High-flying 1980s

October 19, 1987, the stock market fell 508 points. *Time* began its cover story "After the Fall" as follows:

> Decades have a way of crashing to a close during the blink of an hour. . . . The '80s, as befits their high-flying adrenaline rush, have dissipated a few years early, sputtering to an end during the stock market's terrifying final hour of free fall on Monday. Even though Wall Street may eventually stabilize, the tenor of the times will never be the same.
>
> (Church: 20)

The representation of the market crash in the metaphoric terms of a plane crash resonates through other aeronautical tropes within the magazine's coverage. Wall Street's pre-crash style is dubbed "high-to-higher flying"; a plot summary of the eerily prescient Oliver Stone film *Wall Street*, slated for December 1987 release, says of protagonist Bud Fox: "Enticed, Fox takes off into the stratosphere of high finance, only to crash land a year later" ("Rise": 53). *Business Week* similarly cited global equity market "turbulence" as an after-effect of the crash (Bartlett: 31), and headlined an article about "Bloody Monday II" on October 26, "Better Keep Those Seat Belts Fastened" (Bartlett: 38), blaming this second market drop on "a lot of white-knuckled investors."

To *Newsweek*, those investors reflected "a gambler mentality that has always been a part of playing the markets" ("Market": 33) and that would make Las Vegas such a natural milepost for a number of the anti-yuppie road movies. All those relinquished watches that would circulate through the films also had their real-life post-crash correlative: "At First State Pawners, an upscale pawnshop in Chicago's financial district, the lines of customers Monday afternoon were so long that clerks worked 45 minutes overtime taking in Rolex and Piaget watches, diamond necklaces, and even engagement rings" (Martz: 18).

The crash provided a convenient landmark around which nagging doubts about Reagonomics and the yuppie lifestyle could definitively crystallize. "The 5-year-old bull market [that] turned obscure corporate takeover artists into celebrities while making some investment bankers crooks and greenhorn MBAs millionaires" (Laderman, "Bull": 48) had produced pop-cultural unease from at least mid-decade.[6] The insider trader scandals that culminated in the Ivan Boesky indictment in 1986 only accelerated public skepticism, so that both *Wall Street* and Tom Wolfe's *Bonfire of the Vanities*, which had been written before the crash and reached bookstores just weeks after it, confirmed in people's minds that the market meltdown represented on a broad scale the kind of personal chastisement that the popular culture had been inflicting on arrogant yuppies for several years.

While these two texts scripted nothing short of a complete nosedive for the highest of high flyers, those modeled on the Milkens, Boeskys, and Trumps, most anti-yuppie movies targeted those who, often through careers in advertising or marketing, had aided and abetted the rampant consumerism and commodity fetishism that encouraged the piling-up of personal debt in the same way that Reagonomics fueled the nation's burgeoning deficits. A number of genres were serviceable for this purpose. Grant argues for a cycle, the "yuppie horror film," that reconfigures "the classic horror film's otherworldy supernatural" as "the material and economic pressures of this world that is too much with us" (4). More benign fantasies, which utilize the trope of having a yuppie body occupied by a kinder or more innocent spirit, are seen in films from *All of Me* (1984) to *Heart and Souls* (1993); four such films, *Like Father, Like Son* (1987), *Big* (1988), *18 Again!* (1988), and *Vice Versa* (1988), appeared in the same period as the yuppie buddy-road movies.

Yet it was most appropriate that, as suspicions grew about whether yuppie high-flyers should be grounded, the road movie would re-emerge as a vehicle of critique. Baudrillard, writing his meditation on America under Reagan, observed: "Drive ten thousand miles across America and you will know more about the country than all the institutes of sociology and political science put together" (55–6). This sense that to understand the authentic nature of America in the 1980s, to observe what the Reagan illusion masked, one must take to the road would be shared by a growing number of film-makers by the end of the decade. Not being French culture critics, they did not arrive at Baudrillard's paradoxical conclusion that the authentic America resided in its very inauthenticity. In varying degrees the road stands in all of them as a site of nostalgia, authorizing a counter-illusion rather than an authentic portrait of the "real" 1980s America.

One of the first of these road movies, *Paris, Texas* (1984), was a product not of mainstream Hollywood but of the independent art cinema. Directed in English by Wim Wenders, the German film-maker who is to road movies what John Ford (or maybe Anthony Mann) is to Westerns, and co-written by noted off-Broadway playwright Sam Shepard, *Paris, Texas* shares with a more commercial and recuperative successor like *Rain Man* the pairing of a high flyer with his neurotic brother and a critique of yuppie values worked out through a series of symbolic associations of each man with airplanes and vintage automobiles. Walter Henderson's (Dean Stockwell) life is disrupted by the call that informs him his brother Travis (Harry Dean Stanton), missing and presumed dead four years earlier, has just walked out of the desert dazed and confused in rural Texas. Walter flies out from LA to the nearest Texas airport and then drives around in search of his missing brother. Travis, when found, is nearly catatonic and keeps trying to set off again on foot without his brother. He gradually becomes more lucid and communicative, just in time to assure Walter that he has no intention of leaving the ground. Despite Walter's incredulity that his brother could be afraid to fly, Travis has a panic attack, and they have to leave the plane and drive to LA.

Various images and events in the film link Walter to the high flyer trope. He has a thriving business as a billboard manufacturer that nevertheless keeps him under constant time pressure; he complains bitterly that the two extra days Travis's refusal to fly will add to the trip will imperil his company's prospects. The towering billboards themselves inscribe Walt into the consumer-driven yuppie economy and, because they all seem to feature the fetishized bodies of beautiful women, are "images of social commodification and degradation, representing critical problems of gender relations" (Kolker: 130). Moreover, in further associations of Walt and high places, he and his family have just bought a hilltop suburban house near the airport, over which planes fly regularly. (Travis goes through a phase of watching them land and take off through binoculars.)

By the time Travis has been back in Los Angeles for a few days, his neuroses and amnesia have abated to the point that he is ready to reconstruct his identity primarily for the purpose of repairing the broken paternal bond with his son, Hunter, whom Walter and his wife Anne have informally adopted. Since Travis has disappeared from America at precisely the point the 1980s began, he needs advice on how to mimic the archetypal 1980s man whom his brother clearly embodies. He is coached by the family's Latino housekeeper, who counsels him: "To be a rich father . . . you must look at the sky, never the ground." This line could sum up the high flyer trope: it links financial success ("rich") and patriarchy ("father") and associates both with the skyway, not the highway.

As the rest of the film makes clear, however, Travis's struggle to overcome his own neuroses cannot include exchanging them for his brother's. Walter's 1980s obsessions exist primarily to show the type of man Travis will *not* become in his efforts to reconstruct his *tabula rasa* of a life. For one thing, catatonic or coherent, Travis throughout the film remains stubbornly grounded. The spectacle of Harry Dean Stanton striding purposefully across the desert, down the highway, across a bridge, or on the sidewalks leading to his son's school, is one of the key images in *Paris, Texas*. He recuperates his masculinity and his fatherhood not by becoming a high flyer like Walter but by reconfiguring his relationship to the ground into one that carries a powerful charge of phallic masculinity. He buys a vintage, tail-finned Ford Ranchero truck and sets out with Hunter to find his estranged wife, Jane (Nastassja Kinski). Neither pedestrian or passenger, he re-creates himself as a king of the road.

This second road trip in the film involves a deadline; Travis must get to a Houston bank in four days in order to spot Jane as she makes her monthly wire transfer of funds for Hunter to LA. Were this one of the recuperative yuppie films, and were Walter still driving, many complications would arise on the road, and the automated bank would comment ironically on the brothers' financial desperation. Since the film is content to critique the 1980s through Walter but then to leave him and his values behind, nothing of the sort occurs. Walter lends Travis cash and credit cards, which, like Hunter, Travis seems unlikely to return, and then literally disappears from the diegesis. The trip is marred by no catastrophes, and father and son reach the bank in plenty of time. During the remainder of the film, the signifiers of yuppie critique no longer function because the figure under scrutiny has shifted to that ghost of the 1960s and 1970s, Road Man.

Roger Ebert in his review of *Paris, Texas* asserts, "It has more links with films like *Five Easy Pieces* [1970] and *Easy Rider* and *Midnight Cowboy* [1969], than with the slick arcade games that are the box-office winners of the 1980s" ("Paris, Texas"). Clearly the film shares some of Travis's considerable nostalgia for the world of these genre precursors, a nostalgia reflected in his choice of a decidedly non-contemporary vehicle for his travels. But nostalgia cannot erase the decade-long absence from movie screens of such films, a period during which attitudes toward some of the less appealing sides of their protagonists' personalities had hardened. For if the lure of the road is the lure of independence from laws, time clocks, and responsibilities, the transcendence of getting and spending, of what Aitken and Lukinbeal call "place-based sedentarism," that independence also entails an inability to stay in one place, accept responsibility, or maintain a committed relationship to a wife and family.

The prototypical road man in this regard, of course, is Dean Moriarity in Kerouac's *On the Road*. A prodigious car thief in his youth, Dean is a master of the automobile, whether in zooming cars in and out of their spaces as a parking lot attendant or speeding along empty prairies at 110 miles per hour. He is also a faithless lover and terrible provider. Dean departs the novel with three wives, past and present, four children "and not a cent . . . all troubles and ecstasy and speed as ever" (247). It is this model of the road man that Travis evokes in his long monologue to Jane, when he tells of the alternately possessive and neglectful husband, prone to drunken rages and abusive behavior to his wife and child, who finally just abandons them. Whether this is an accurate retelling of their past relationship, or a recasting of Travis in the image of his own father (the teller of the bad joke about Paris . . . Texas, who died in a car accident) or a pure fantasy, a "narcissistic play with the images of family and home" by a man merely "in love with his own symptoms" (Corrigan: 156), is not clear. Nor is it clear whether Travis's reuniting son and mother but abandoning them once more to drive the Ranchero off into the night and the end credits vindicates or condemns the road man's independent, irresponsible ways. Robert Kolker may view the act as Travis's redemption, expressing the "enduring sadness of the now enlightened man who purposefully, perhaps even heroically, removes himself from the temptations of violence in the domestic scene" (136), but Corrigan claims it instead demonstrates how, in the 1980s, a crisis of male subjectivity reaches such a pitch that "that predominantly male road movie invariably turns into, for its producers and its audiences, a sci-fi film that is historically incomprehensible" (159).

A year after *Paris, Texas* was made, actor-writer-director Albert Brooks's *Lost in America* (1985) diagnosed, as does Corrigan, a profound narcissism in the 1980s nostalgia for the road. Brooks astutely unmasks the romance of the road as a mere fantasy alternative to high flying, assumed by temporarily disenchanted yuppies still firmly entrenched in their own self-centered materialism. *Lost in America* spoofs such a man in David Howard, a perpetually dissatisfied, though very successful, advertising account executive. When David, instead of receiving the executive promotion he had been counting on, is transferred to New York to work on the Ford Motor Company[7] account that his agency has just obtained, he resigns in a fit of pique, liquidates his assets, buys a state-of-the-art Winnebago motor home, and vows to live with his wife Linda on the road like the heroes of *Easy Rider*, a sacred text of his baby-boomer youth. Making this daring life reversal possible is the $145,000 "nest egg" the couple retains. When Linda feels almost mystically compelled to spend the night in a Las Vegas hotel, "the worst money-grubbing place in the world," and then to gamble away nearly all of their nest egg, David refutes her claim that "our dream's still the same, only we don't have any money" with the fact that, on the road without money, they are merely "in the middle of nowhere with nothing." As the dialogue that appears in my epigraph reveals, the nostalgic memory of *Easy Rider* as a utopian text celebrating the liberatory pleasures of turning one's back on the capitalistic rat race comes up short with the realization that Wyatt and Billy were deeply enmeshed in capitalistic practices, albeit excitingly outlaw ones.

Paris, Texas never shows us the day-to-day reality of Travis's life on the road once the money borrowed from Walt runs out. *Lost in America*, on the other hand, goes into great detail to depict the realities of living on the road without a nest egg. With their finances able to carry the gas-guzzling Winnebago only as far as small-town Arizona, the Howards find themselves living the lives of the working class they have never been: trailer parks, minimum-wage jobs, moronic teenagers as their supervisors. Does this experience make them better people? No, it simply convinces them to travel cross-country to New York City as soon as they have the means so that David can "eat shit" to get his job back. The end title cards inform us that after the west-to-east road trip the couple has once again success-fully replicated, and even enhanced, their LA life in Manhattan.

The mythic Road Man evoked by *Paris, Texas* reflects an oppositional fantasy of liberation from the constraints placed on man the breadwinner, whose relation-ship to money grew out of a nexus of responsibilities to home and family. As Barbara Ehrenreich points out, however, such liberatory fantasies did not always have to entail declaring an independence from money; they might simply require a new way of relating to it. The consumer culture "was increasingly reaching out to men as consumers in their own right . . . Men earned the money, why shouldn't they spend it on themselves?" (218). As a consumerist yuppie, David Howard can therefore not tolerate a freedom of the road that comes at the price of his nest egg.

Masculinity and Money

The differences between Travis Henderson and David Howard point up two competing views about the effects of a steady income on masculinity. One has its *locus classicus* in Kerouac's *On the Road*, of which Manohla Dargis writes, "Fast cars, whisky, women, a few last, soiled dollars – the hipster's journey was the pleasure principle on wheels" (16). Potently sexual, Road Man embodies that modern form of masculinity that Jeff Hearn identifies as "founded on speed and fragmentary, fleeting images" (198). A man on a passenger plane can conquer time and space much faster, but it's the fact that the man behind the wheel or on the bike is generating that speed, steering those curves, and deciding which exit ramp to take that gives his journey its phallic frisson. Dargis's phrase "few, last soiled dollars" sums up the discontinuity between this masculine potency and gainful employment. In *On the Road* those "soiled" dollars are usually begged, borrowed, or stolen (often from women). Jobs, when held, are in marginal occupations (security guard, parking lot attendant), temporary in duration, and performed slackly.

The road men who conform to the Kerouac pattern typify the "existential hero," one of several categories of twentieth-century masculinity described by Anthony Rotundo: "The hero who lives by this belief is suspicious of authority, wary of women, and disgusted with corrupt civilization. If he would be true to the purity of his male passions and principles, he must – and can only – live at the margins of society" (286). From another perspective, however, such a marginal existence is not masculine at all, despite the sleek, speedy vehicles at the road man's command. From the point of view of a sedentarist breadwinner, *On the Road*'s Dean and Sal are bums; from the point of view of the young urban professional, they are downscale losers. On the other hand what could be a more masculine territory than the cut-throat world of mergers, leveraged buyouts, bond trading, arbitrage and entrepreneurship that the "greed is good" ethos articulated by *Wall Street*'s Gordon Gekko promoted? At the very least, as Andrew Tolson observes, success in one's job is hardly an unmasculine behavior:

> In Western, industrialized, capitalist societies, definitions of masculinity are bound up with definitions of work. Whether it is in terms of physical strength or mechanical expertise, or in terms of ambition and

competitiveness, the qualities needed by the successful worker are closely related to those of the successful man.

(quoted in Brittan: 84)

Rotundo notes that, from the nineteenth century onward, there arose the sentiment that "If a man was without 'business' he was less than a man" (168). Even some existential heroes heed the call of capitalism. They may, to be sure, feel less constrained by responsibilities, more courageously independent than the dull organization man – Rotundo's "team player" – but the "passionate masculinity" that they embody has a long history of compatibility with business success, particularly the kind of high-risk buccaneering that dominated the 1980s. As Rotundo concludes his description of the existential hero: "[he] has an economic counterpart in the cult of the entrepreneur who pursues his vision outside the contaminating influence of corporate institutions" (286).

Moreover, in the world of patriarchal late capitalism, the romantic notion that freedom from a regular paycheck carries a macho charge constantly runs up against the emasculating implications for a man who never has enough money and has to demean himself for what little he can scrape together. If the road is to be a way of life rather than a delimited transformative phase within a generally stable patriarchal capitalist existence, these implications become harder and harder to dismiss. Road television series like *The Fugitive* (1963–6) and *The Incredible Hulk* (1979–81) implicitly played on the suffering of their physician protagonists, whose life on the run caused them to "toil at many jobs"[8] of the blue-collar, non-professional variety. No wonder those "social outcasts, voluntary dropouts" that Robin Wood observes the protagonists of 1970s buddy-road movies to be invariably wind up dead (230). The demise that Wood argues is necessary to protect their heterosexuality from the intimate bonds of the road is equally necessary to preserve their masculinity from the stigma of monetary lack and low-wage ignominy.

Even the perception of Kerouac's own self-congratulatory self-representation of a masculinity more authentic because independent of a paycheck is probably overstated. Many pages of *On the Road* are devoted to recounting how much money Sal has spent, how much he has left, and where he can get some more (usually from his long-suffering aunt). Warren French, in a revisionist reading of the novel, quotes Kerouac's fear that "I was beginning to cross and recross towns in America as though I was a traveling salesman – raggedy travelings, bad stock, rotten beans in the bottom of my bag of tricks, nobody buying." French notes that "Driving fast and dangerously is an exhilarating experience for a while, but people, like cars, finally run out of gas" (40, 44). Albert Brooks simply adds that they run out of gas money as well.

Deadlines, Deals, and Detours

Planes, Trains and Automobiles, *Midnight Run*, and *Rain Man*, despite using the sudden loss of money on the road as a principal move to critique yuppie values, eventually recuperate any repudiation of the value of capital. The hegemonic masculinity already undermined by the homoerotic pressures of road intimacy and the buddy plot requires the remasculinizing effect of financial solvency. The films' recuperative strategies pivot on collapsing the apparent distinctions between the road man, the high flyer, and the neurotic. The initial impression that the three figures represent discrete relations to capital and very different types of masculinity is dispelled by the film's conclusion.

Each of the films employs its subgenre's semantic elements somewhat differently to achieve these ends. *Planes, Trains and Automobiles* stresses the collapse of class distinction as a marker of high flyer status and also reveals the mythologized road man as homologous with a social type whom yuppie ideology scorned: "Upscale spending patterns created the cultural space in which the financially well matched could find each other – far from the burger-eaters and Bud-drinkers and those unfortunate enough to wear unnatural fibers" (Ehrenreich: 229). The film opens with a close-up of an expensive watch. It reveals to marketing executive Neil Page (Steve Martin) that his New York boss's indecision over whether to implement Neil's new campaign threatens to make him miss the 6 p.m. flight for which he has reservations. The flight will not help Neil score a business coup but enable him to spend as much time as possible with his family in Chicago during the Thanksgiving holidays. Since Neil is shown to appreciate his wife and children (and to express skepticism over the value of the products he pushes), a serious interrogation of capitalist practice is essentially taken off the table prior to the beginning of the road trip. We may wonder why he then must subsequently endure a nightmare of delays and detours that allow him to arrive home only just before Thanksgiving dinner is put on the table. The locus of the critique is here not yuppie workaholism or acquisitiveness but yuppie self-enclosure in a sense of entitlement, refinement, and obsession with style, connoisseurship, and fitness. This ideology will be challenged through Neil's travels with the obese, garrulous, insecure, and definitely déclassé Del Griffith (John Candy), who, with his penchant for junk food and unfashionable clothing containing far too much synthetic material, serves as a lifestyle Other for Neil, whom Roger Ebert accurately describes as a "fastidious, anal-compulsive snob" ("Planes").

Because of his late arrival at the airport, even though the plane's departure has been delayed, the indignant Neil is forced to fly coach instead of first class, and, worse, to be "taken up" by Del. After a blizzard diverts their plane to Wichita, Del sometimes generates obstacles to Neil's goal: in the sleazy motel he books them into, a thief steals their cash; his carelessness causes their rental car to catch fire, incinerating Neil's credit cards. Just as often, however, he comes through to help him get back on the road and meet his deadline. For, although Del is hardly the cool hipster of *On the Road*, he is a skilled road man, with a network of friends all over the country and innate survival skills when resources are slim. He is also the truth of the road man, rather than the myth, that nightmare that haunted Sal Paradise: a traveling salesman of shower curtain rings (which he is nevertheless able to sell as exotic jewelry when he and Neil are strapped for money). As the film's denouement reveals, Del has, since the death of his beloved wife Marie, actually lived on the road. He has no permanent address and carries all his worldly goods in the gigantic trunk that so exasperates Neil on several occasions.

Unlike Travis Henderson, Raymond Babbitt, and *Midnight Run*'s Jonathan Mardukas, Del's neuroses don't make him avoid airplanes. This film instead, as its title suggests, demonstrates the growing illusoriness of a hierarchical distinction between high flyers and road men. By the late 1980s, deregulated air travel was inspiring the same sorts of second thoughts as was the deregulated economy. For the previous elite cadre of air travelers, deregulation had curtailed much of their former convenience and comfort, while at the same time expanding access to those of the Del Griffith class. Poynter describes nostalgically the pre-deregulation experience of the frequent business flyer:

> If a passenger flew frequently between cities, he knew the schedules, the carriers, and the fares because none of them changed with any degree of frequency. He knew his ticket would be accepted by every air carrier on which he flew . . . and he knew his baggage would probably arrive at the final destination with him. Service was excellent and so were the meals.
>
> (2)

As corporations formed their own travel management bureaus to cope with the chaos of a deregulated industry, the lure of turning corporate travel from a "cost center" to a "profit center" could severely curtail the pleasures of travel. Poynter cautions: "The concentration on savings can sometimes be so substantial that corporate travel departments lose sight of the fact that if the business traveler must suffer through substantial inconvenience and hardships, the purpose of the business trip may be jeopardized and the company can lose more money than it saves" (85). A decade later, indeed, information technology has made it unnecessary for true high flyers to leave corporate headquarters at all. A 1996 television commercial for Haworth office furniture systems, showing a graphic of an airplane bouncing through a thunderstorm as it traverses a map of the US, superimposes the caption "Travel like this is Out," then cuts to a view of a video teleconference, a type of travel that is now "In."

Relentlessly stripped of all his accustomed travel comfort as the film progresses, Neil finally bonds with Del after he manages to check into a cheap motel in exchange for their last seventeen dollars plus his prized watch, and the two of them get drunk on mini-bottles from the in-room bar. Realizing that Del has no family, Neil invites him home for Thanksgiving dinner; they walk up the street of Neil's tony Chicago suburb carrying the trunk together and looking for all the world like Laurel and Hardy in *The Music Box*. Yet, while Neil gradually comes to feel gratitude and compassion for Del, he never quite seems to overcome his sense of revulsion with Del's company. Moreover, the other working-class characters that form Del's network of road acquaintances are presented as distasteful caricatures. This undercuts the seeming point of the film, Neil's learning to appreciate the value of folks outside his hermetic yuppie circle. Indeed, Del's pathetic neediness, his rejoining Neil time and again after Neil has indicated, often in ways that are extremely hurtful to Del, that he would prefer to travel solo, essentially turns the film into a fantasy wish-fulfillment for all those poor working-class slobs who wish to be accepted by the suburban elite, rather than a lesson on the evils of yuppie snobbery.

Such double-think also operates in *Rain Man*, where the revelation that the high flyer is really a road man is offset by the inscription of the *déclassé* neurotic into the world of consumption and high style. The film opens with a shot of a flying

Plate 9.1 Charlie Babbitt proves a natural road man.
Dustin Hoffman and Tom Cruise in *Rain Man*.

car. At least that's the trick the camera plays; the car is one of the imported Lamborghinis at the heart of Charlie Babbitt's (Tom Cruise) big $75,000 deal being lowered by a crane onto the LA docks. The image, however, sums up a central fact about Charlie: he's a natural road man who pretends to be a high flyer. Not only is he a car dealer, but he was alienated from his wealthy father Sanford Babbitt because he "stole" a joyride in Babbitt senior's prized 1949 Buick Roadmaster, which Sanford had made off-limits to Charlie. In a gesture of wounded irony, the father, in his will, leaves Charlie the Buick, but no money. If his autistic brother Raymond's (Dustin Hoffman) fears of flying on any airline that has ever had an accident provide the ostensible rationale for putting the pair on the road for their trip back to Los Angeles, the road proves Charlie's natural element. Although he has to do all the driving, he never seems to tire. He manages to obtain satisfaction for Raymond's rigid demands wherever they go, including a farm house showing Wapner at three, a neat trick since The *People's Court* is a syndicated program shown by each local station that purchases it at a time of the station's own choosing; thus it is an almost magical coincidence that the farm community would receive it at the same hour Raymond got used to its being broadcast in Cincinnati. Although his credit card maxes out and he has to pawn his Rolex, the brothers never lack funds for food, shelter, and gas. The material desperation that inflects the buddy-road adventures in *Planes, Trains and Automobiles* and *Midnight Run* doesn't surface here.

By the end of the film Charlie has bonded to Raymond and finally made an emotional commitment to his girlfriend Susanna (Valeria Golino), yet *Rain Man's* last scene shows Charlie alone at the train station, his business in ruins, and Raymond headed back to the Walbrook home, already too distracted to give Charlie a goodbye wave as the train departs. One thinks of the end of *On the Road* as Sal last glimpses Dean Moriarty, cold and ragged, from the receding Cadillac limousine into which Sal's more upscale friends deny Dean access. This is in fact the irony of *Rain Man*. Charlie's involvement with Raymond causes him to miss the deadline on his deal, lose all his money, and yet be so ennobled by the love for his brother that grows throughout the trip that he refuses a bribe of $250,000 to relinquish his demand for custody of Raymond. In the end Charlie gives up Raymond for Raymond's own good, rather than money, and seems to be rewarded with . . . *nothing*. He effectively reenacts with Raymond the unsatisfactory relationship with his father, whose resemblance to Raymond the film stresses in many ways. Lest the film actually demonstrate that there are things more valuable than money and style, while Charlie is shedding the yuppie trappings of his high flyer charade, he is, moreover, re-creating the sympathetic, but wealthy, Raymond in just such a 1980s image.

Sanford Babbitt,[9] a businessman who leaves an estate "in excess of three million dollars," is "a man who had difficulty showing love." The son to whom he leaves this money, Raymond, "cannot understand his own emotions" and also "doesn't understand the concept of money." Raymond is old enough to be Charlie's father, he resembles Sanford physically, and he saves, as did Sanford, an old photograph of himself and young Charlie during the many years they have been separated. Charlie, too, has problems expressing affection, and his obsessive phone calls to check on the faltering deal at every stop on their much delayed travels establishes a theme of all three of these buddy-road movies, that the high flyer is more neurotic than the neurotic.[10] It is almost a foregone conclusion, given the film's linking of capital and emotional dysfunction, that, when Charlie does learn to love, he will wind up broke.

Raymond also turns out to have his father's touch for making money, as his autistic savant skills enable the brothers to earn enough cash at the blackjack tables in Las Vegas at least to pay off Charlie's debts, redeem the Rolex, and fund the rest of the journey to Los Angeles. All that separates Raymond from completely reincarnating the patriarchal image is the Del Griffith style promulgated by the consumer habits of his institutional environment. Although Charlie can't wean him from fish sticks, cheese puffs, and Jell-O, he does provide him with stylish designer suits, consumer items that facilitate the late capitalist investment in the commodified image (a camera, an Abbott and Costello video, and a Sony Watchman television to provide complete mobile access to Wapner), and a new motto: "K-Mart sucks." Charlie, revealed as Road Man and liberated from capitalist machinations by traveling the back roads with his brother, sends back to Cincinnati on the train[11] a Rain Man now firmly, if unwittingly, enmeshed in capital and yuppie lifestyle prejudices.

Midnight Run more seriously challenges capitalism by firmly linking money both to criminality and to a literal trafficking in human lives. Its protagonist, Jack Walsh (Robert De Niro), attempts to navigate the shoals of patriarchal capitalism by distinguishing "clean" money from dirty, rather like Clyde, in *Bonnie and Clyde*, does when he lets a farmer waiting to make a deposit at a bank the Barrow gang is robbing keep the money because it is his and not the bank's – as if all a bank's money didn't at one time belong to someone other than the bankers. For most of its length the film exposes the speciousness of such logic, before suddenly adopting it at the eleventh hour to insure a happy ending and a recuperation, if not of all capital, at least of the small business ethic. Meanwhile it trots out all the semantic elements of the recuperative yuppie film, only to have them break loose from their usual narrative functions and then resettle in very strange places.

Jack, on a Monday, is given a Friday midnight deadline in order to close a $100,000 deal that will enable him to open up his own business. Although Jack here assumes the yuppie high flyer's initial diegetic position, no phrase could be further from the truth in describing him. Exiled from Chicago and the police force because he wouldn't play ball with heroin kingpin Jimmy Serrano (Dennis Farina), he is a rumpled ex-cop with a profane vocabulary, who has "two forms of expression: silence and rage." Jack works for a sleazy Los Angeles bondsman, Eddie Moscone (Joe Pantoliano), recapturing criminals who have jumped bail; his $100,000 windfall will come from the apprehension of embezzler Jonathan Mardukas (Charles Grodin), coincidentally an accountant for one of Serrano's front companies, whose failure to appear will cost Eddie $450,000 and put him out of business. One of Rotundo's classic existential heroes, Jack has been estranged from his ex-wife and daughter for nine years, and believes himself the only honest man in a corrupt criminal justice system. In short, Jack fits the profile of Road Man to a tee, except that he has a terrible time holding onto motor vehicles. Apparently not the owner of a vehicle himself, he rents, borrows, or steals a series of cars and trucks, only to be forced to abandon each during his and his prisoner's hectic cross-country escape from three groups of men who want Jonathan for their own purposes. Even when he finds himself back at the Los Angeles airport with over three hundred thousand-dollar bills, he can't get a cab driver to accept one, and the movie concludes with his exasperated "Looks like I'm walkin'."

If the high flyer isn't quite a high flyer, and the road man not quite a road man, the neurotic isn't just a neurotic, either. Jonathan is on the surface a typical yuppie, constantly voicing 1980s health concerns over Jack's cholesterol and incessant smoking. Jack tells him that the other passengers in first class are "a better class of people, your class, probably all embezzlers too." When a child remarks that "you don't look much like a criminal," Jonathan replies, "I'm a white-collar criminal." If Jonathan's class markers align him with Neil Page and Charlie Babbitt, however, he also displays a whole range of "Felix Ungerisms" and phobias (primarily the fear of flying which gets the pair ejected from their plane before takeoff) that align him with Del Griffith and Raymond Babbitt.

But even these contradictions do not sum up the slipperiness of placing Jonathan within the 1980s buddy-road paradigm. For Jonathan's personality is completely performative. He isn't really afraid to fly; in fact, he's a pilot. Intent on manipulating his captor in any way that might save him from being sent to jail – and certain death at the hands of Serrano, now a Vegas mobster from whom he has diverted $15 million, giving most of it to charity – Jonathan puts on the neurotic, fearful, fussy manner that he knows a man like Jack will expect from an accountant, traits that will both delay the trip from New York to Los Angeles and cause Jack to lower his guard. The sequence in which Jonathan pretends to be a federal officer looking for counterfeit twenty-dollar bills so that the buddies can obtain money for food showcases his skills at self-creation. As nearly as one can ascertain, Jonathan is not so much a yuppie as a 1960s activist turned bean counter, who still believes in liberal causes and sharing the wealth (he chides Jack for under-tipping). When the media reported his Robin-Hood-style crime, they

Plate 9.2 Broke and stranded on the road.
Robert DeNiro and Charles Grodin in *Midnight Run*.

dubbed him "the Duke," a sobriquet based on his surname but in its suggestion of masculine icon John Wayne an ironic contrast to the nerd Jonathan only appears to be. Both criminal and incarnation of morality, daring opponent of mafiosi and wimpy health nut, Jonathan embodies the porous demarcations between Road Man, neurotic, and high flyer that permeate *Midnight Run*.

Although none of its characters works anywhere near Wall Street, the film's narrative structure can be instructively allegorized by seeing Jonathan as a tempting hostile takeover target pursued by three unwelcome merger partners. Eddie Moscone needs him back in order to salvage an unwise investment; Federal agent Alonzo Moseley (Yaphet Kotto) needs his testimony in order finally to convict Serrano; Serrano, to protect himself both from the Feds and others in his criminal organization, needs him dead. Each of these three "CEOs" has two chief flunkeys: Jerry the office manager and bounty hunter Marvin Dorfler work for Moscone; two nervous assistants keep Moseley posted on the pursuit of Walsh and Mardukas; henchmen Tony and Joey coordinate Serrano's efforts to "hit" the pair. Each of these entities has its own corporate style. The bail bondsmen and skip-tracers wear scruffy leather and denim and chain-smoke. The FBI men sport conservative suits, white shirts, and identical sunglasses. Jimmy and his men are the flashy dressers and high-livers. Indeed, it is Jimmy the vicious mobster who actually represents yuppie values, sarcastically telling Jack during one of their confrontations: "I see you're still spending all your money on clothes."

Yet discrete signifiers of one group keep sliding into the others. Moseley has tried to quit smoking but is always borrowing Marvin's cigarettes and failing to return them. Moseley ("Agent Foster Grant") and Jack circulate Jack's shades between them, and Jack steals both Moseley's badge and his car. Moseley is also somewhat neurotic, asking his aides if their reports are "going to upset me" and threatening to have a heart attack when things get tense. Jerry and Marvin both betray Eddie's interests to the mob, which pays more generously than the employer who is always trying to lowball them out of a fair wage for their efforts. There are also a series of impersonations. Jack and Jonathan both use the stolen credentials to pose as Moseley; Marvin poses as Jack to trace him through, and then cancel, his credit card; Jack later impersonates Marvin in order to find out if the mob has captured Jonathan. All of these self-proclaimed "businessmen" converge on Las Vegas's airport, a dual symbol of 1980s speculation, in the film's chaotic finale.

Despite their opposing temperaments Jack and Jonathan stand outside this corrupting business nexus. Jack left behind his profession, home, and family rather than go on Serrano's payroll, as all the other cops in his precinct had done. Jonathan, upon discovering that he was on Serrano's payroll, gave up any chance of continuing a normal life in order to divest Serrano of his illicit earnings. In the business analogy Jack serves as the "White Knight" who preserves Jonathan from being taken over and who for good measure sends Serrano into bankruptcy, i.e. Federal custody for kidnaping and conspiracy.

Like Charlie Babbitt, Jack eventually comes to care more for Jonathan than for money, and, although they make it back to LA before the deadline, lets him go. Unlike Charlie, he gets his money anyway. Jonathan, who happens to have over $300,000 secreted in a money belt, gives the sum to Jack so that Jack can give up bounty hunting and open his coffee shop. This gesture completely contradicts the film's ongoing critique of capitalism. First of all, considerable doubt has been cast on the feasibility of the coffee shop idea. Although it is easy to see the attraction of the coffee shop setting to a former cop and road man – many such shops appear in the diegesis – Jack's abrasive personality hardly seems suited to a career in a service industry; and, as Jonathan the accountant warns, "a restaurant is a very tricky investment; over half of them go under in six months."

Second, both Jonathan and Jimmy ridicule Jack's notion that one can separate "clean" money from dirty. Jack on the one hand despises anyone who accepts bribes; it goes against his code of honor either to accept $1 million to hand over Jonathan directly to the mob or to take a payoff from Jonathan in exchange for letting him go. But he is willing essentially to accept blood money for turning in "the Duke" to legitimate authorities, even though he admits to admiring Jonathan's actions against Jack's long-time foe. "Why don't you go for the big money, you're doing his work for him anyhow," Jonathan queries. "The reason I do this shit in the first place is because I wouldn't work for that lowlife asshole," Jack retorts. The fallacy of this reasoning is in fact apparent to Jimmy Serrano, who insists that he will have to kill Walsh rather than buy him off: "I know Walsh; he won't take any money from me. He's a very self-righteous type of guy. . . . In his mind this [turning the Duke in] is clean. He gets what he wants, I get what I want. The guy's a fucking burnout." Jack draws similar fine distinctions when he goes to his ex-wife to borrow money (he eventually accepts the use of her car as well) but will not accept the babysitting earnings his teenage daughter offers. So, when Jonathan decides to reward Jack for freeing him, he is careful to explain, "It's not a payoff, it's a gift. You already let me go." Of course, ironically, this money, and the shop it will finance, originate in Serrano's criminal activities.

If all these films easily recuperate the financial solvency whose lack threatens their protagonists' masculinity, their efforts to deflect potential queer readings are much more awkward. Partially they are compromised by their nostalgic[12] melding of several different past road movie traditions. Their plots belong to a reintegrative tradition popular in the 1930s and 1940s in which the road trip has a definite end, and the protagonists, having learned important lessons along the way, reenter mainstream society. These films generally featured heterosexual couples, and marriage was their true final destination. The male protagonists as "odd couple" derive clearly from male comedy teams that feature a straight man/comedian pairing, notably Crosby and Hope and Martin and Lewis. When such couples take to the road, endings are again happy, with the homosocial relationship between the two men triangulated through a woman in the pattern famously explicated by Eve Kosofsky Sedgwick. Finally, the films reference those oppositional buddy movies of the previous decade where marginalized figures cannot be reintegrated into society, and frequently one or both buddies end up dead, jailed,[13] or catatonic. And it is the links to these latter figures, who "have placed themselves outside the pressures of patriarchy, which are all that stand in the way of the acceptance of constitutional bisexuality" (Wood: 230), that causes all three films difficulty in bringing closure to their buddies' relationships, given that neither marriage or death is a desired option.

The increased discussion of gay issues throughout the 1980s and the surfacing of queer readings of ostensibly straight texts were clearly on the mind of the makers of the yuppie buddy-road films. Even if nothing in the diegesis suggests a homoerotic attraction between the buddies, the films repeatedly imply and then disavow it. In the motel where Del and Neil are forced to share a bed early on in their journey, they awake to find that each is embracing the other as if he were his wife. (This scene follows Neil's cruel diatribe of the night before when he exclaims that after spending an evening with Del Griffith "I can take anything . . . it's like going out on a date with a chatty Cathy doll.") A scene of comically homophobic macho posturing follows. Although Raymond Babbitt is incapable of any emotional intimacy, and is Charlie's brother, one sequence of *Rain Man* goes overboard to intimate that the audience might think there is something queer about their relationship. After his success at the tables, Raymond attracts the attention of a hooker, who is suspicious of Raymond's claim that the much younger Charlie is his brother; she clearly intuits a gay couple who won't be needing her services. Raymond, however, responds with interest to the woman's proffered "date" and insists that Charlie teach him to dance. After the brothers slow dance against the glittering Vegas skyline, Charlie feels the urge to give Raymond a hug. This intimate gesture sends Raymond off into one of his panic attacks, however. At this moment Susanna arrives unexpectedly from LA, subsequently dances with and kisses the jilted Raymond in an elevator, and safely triangulates the buddies' relationship for the rest of the drive. In *Planes, Trains and Automobiles*, Del's love for his dead wife translates into his desire to reunite Neil with his spouse, providing a similar triangulation.

Midnight Run is the only one of these films actually to convey, primarily through the affect of the performances of De Niro and Grodin, any kind of deep emotional bond between the buddies. Roger Ebert comments: "It's rare for a thriller to end with a scene of genuinely moving intimacy, but this one does, and it earns it" ("Midnight Run"). And, while the film is careful to show us that Jonathan loves his wife, and that Jack hasn't gotten over the wife who left him, the women's role in stabilizing the homosocial triangle is somewhat equivocal. Jack, who has for years held onto an erratically time-keeping watch, because it was his ex-wife's first gift to him, finally heeds Jonathan's advice, "Sometimes you just have to let go, get yourself a new watch"; but instead of discarding the old watch, he gives it to Jonathan to replace the Duke's expensive timepiece, traded to some Native Americans in exchange for their truck. The passing of this love token to Jonathan, even if it signifies a love now irrevocably past, raises the symbolic stakes of the relationship between the two men. The gesture does not inspire an immediate disavowal, but it is followed by a separation of the buddies at the film's conclusion that has the most finality of any of the three. Whereas *Planes, Trains and Automobiles* leaves us with a freeze-frame of a beaming Del looking on as Neil and his wife embrace out of the frame, and *Rain Man* shows a solitary Charlie who has promised to come to Cincinnati to visit Raymond in a week, *Midnight Run* precludes any possibility of a future reunion. Jack turns to say a last goodbye to Jonathan only to have a cut to Jonathan's former position reveal that he has vanished, back to his fugitive, hidden life. It is as if nothing but Jonathan's complete dematerialization will neutralize the otherwise not disavowed intimacy of their relationship. None of the films, however, is able to tolerate a final image of the buddies united in the frame.

Dead End

Reviewing *Rain Man*, John Simon writes: "There ensues a typical comic road movie *cum* mismatched buddy movie (are those still two genres or have they become irrevocably fused?)" ("Rain All Over": 52). With the three films just discussed having appeared in so short a period of time, it's no wonder that Simon thought a new genre hybrid had blossomed. But the hybrid would fail to propagate its next generation. Partially this involved the demise of the yuppie as a target of critique even as corporate profits and the stock market recovered (Ehrenreich: 241–3) but recession and downsizing insured no return to yuppie arrogance. More so it related to a growing incompatibility between the reintegrative goals of road comedy and the dismantling of hegemonic masculinity inherent in the post-Kerouac road. As this perception seeped into the general cultural consciousness, the reluctance in both 1970s and 1980s Hollywood buddy-road movies featuring a white, heterosexual male duo to keep the buddies together at the end of the film would translate in the 1990s into a reluctance to start such a pair down the road in the first place.[14]

Certainly few figures resembling the high flyers scrutinized in this essay have headed down the road together with a buddy during the current decade. In the 1990s the road movie revival would take off either from the postmodern landscape and heterosexual outlaw couple of 1990's *Wild at Heart* or from the displacement of the straight male buddies as road protagonists inaugurated by 1991's *Thelma and Louise* and subsequently coming to encompass a whole range of gender, sexual, and racial Others. Many of the decade's reintegrative buddy-road comedies, like *The Adventures of Priscilla, Queen of the Desert* (1994), *Boys on the Side* (1995), or *To Wong Foo, Thanks for Everything! Julie Newmar* (1995), featured same-sex buddy trios, one or all of whose members were openly gay. If on the one hand the historical interest of *Planes, Trains, and Automobiles*, *Midnight Run*, and *Rain Man* resides in their recuperation of capitalist patriarchy while critiquing yuppie lifestyle excesses, on the other they mark the historical endpoint for the straight man, in all his connotations (law-abiding, not comically neurotic, heterosexual), on the road; for the road has come to represent, to the culture at large, the space where hegemonic masculinity is undone.

Notes

1 These are the terms used respectively by Frank and Simon. The former suggests the link with Neil Simon's Felix Unger and Oscar Madison. Haskell refers to the protagonists of 1970s buddy movies as odd couples also.

2 As Stuart Aitken and Chris Lukinbeal note elsewhere in this volume, "with many road movies . . . [there is a sense of] a psychic freedom that offers emancipation but, in actuality, practices emasculation" (353).

3 "Wild" is the privileged adjective Hollywood employs to describe the liberatory yet dangerous road ethos. Examples range from *Wild Boys of the Road* (1933) to the many biker movies inspired by *The Wild One* (1954) and *The Wild Angels* (1966), to *Something Wild* (1986) and *Wild at Heart* (1990).

4 I am using this term according to the method for genre analysis theorized by Altman.

5 Tom Snyder, in a study of Route 66, links a disconnection from the authentic nature of the US to the advent of inexpensive air travel: "A lot hasn't changed in the country in the last 30 to 50 years. People who travel the route get a feeling of what this country was – and still is. It's easy to forget that now with our frequent flier programs" (quoted in Schenden: E-8).

6 Grant (13) cites a 1985 *New York* magazine article, "Second Thoughts on Having it All," as a marker of this concern and notes that it coincides with the first appearance of what he defines as a "yuppie horror cycle." Significant road movies, whether or not they critique yuppies directly, begin their return during 1984 to 1986, with *Paris, Texas*, Jim Jarmusch's *Stranger than Paradise* (1984), *Lost in America*, *The Sure Thing* (1985), and *Something Wild* the most notable titles.

7 One would think that a road man would love to promote a car company, but the implicit joke here is that the Mercedes-obsessed David is deeply insulted at being asked to hawk a plebeian American automotive product.

8 This was part of the heavily ironic prologue intoned by the narrator over *The Fugitive*'s credits, one of the dubious opportunities that the train wreck "freed" Richard Kimble to pursue.

9 The Babbitts, of course, bear the surname of Sinclair Lewis's archetypal business fraud.

10 Suzanne Moore remarks of the film: "But then I guess that the logical conclusion to the sort of rampant individualism that Charlie displays at the beginning of the film is actually an *autistic culture* where such pathetic and routine-traits pass for communication and where intimacy means a kind of dying" (38).

11 Obviously the skittish Raymond has not kept up to date on Amtrak's safety record.

12 As in *Paris, Texas*, each film features vintage vehicles, the rented, olive-green sedan in *Planes, Trains and Automobiles*, the Native Americans' banged-up truck in *Midnight Run*, and, most prominently, the 1949 Buick Roadmaster convertible so central to *Rain Man*.

13 A clear predecessor to the 1980s buddy-road movies also is the escaped-prisoners-on-the-run *The Defiant Ones* (1958), which combines the plot trajectory and dead-end

male bonding of the 1970s buddy movie with the psychologically redemptive themes of earlier screwball comedy. Both Frank and Simon cite this influence.

14 The language from some reviews of *Bulletproof*, a *Midnight-Run*-influenced buddy-road movie of 1996, reveals the likely reason why. John Anderson says that the film takes "the homoerotic subtext of the buddy movie" and accessorizes it with "chains, hand-cuffs, some manner of bondage equipment" to produce "the romance of the year" (16). Richard Corliss observes: "After a while the standard gross-out talk of action movies – the gay-baiting gags and threats of fellatio – makes for an odd subtext. All these swaggering men who say they hate each other are really in love" (91). It is notable that the figure of normative masculinity here, and in the similar *Fled*, released during the same summer 1996 season, is portrayed by an African-American (Damon Wayans, Laurence Fishburne), as if any identificatory figure for straight, white men can no longer tolerate such a discursive context.

Works Cited

Altman, Rick. *The American Film Musical*. Bloomington: Indiana University Press, 1987.

Anderson, John. "Bad 'Bulletproof' Misses its Mark." *The State* [Columbia, SC] (September 13, 1996): Weekend section 16.

Ansen, David. "Who's on First?" *Newsweek* (January 16, 1989): 52–6.

Atkinson, Michael. "Crossing the Frontiers." *Sight and Sound* 1 (1994): 14–18.

Bartlett, Sarah. "Starting Over." *Business Week* (November 9, 1987): 31.

Baudrillard, Jean. *America*, trans. Chris Turner. London: Verso, 1988.

Brittan, Arthur. *Masculinity and Power*. London: Basil Blackwell, 1989.

Church, George J. "After the Fall." *Time* (November 2, 1987): 20–33.

Corliss, Richard. "The Next Worst Thing." *Time* (September 16, 1996): 91.

Corrigan, Timothy. *A Cinema Without Walls: Movies and Culture After Vietnam*. New Brunswick, NJ: Rutgers University Press, 1991.

Dargis, Manohla. "Roads to Freedom." *Sight and Sound* 3 (1991): 14–18.

"The Dreamer Awakes." *The New Republic* (November 9, 1987): 4.

Ebert, Roger. "Midnight Run." *Chicago Sun-Times* (July 20, 1988): n. pag. *Internet Movie Database*. Online. May 8, 1996.

—— "Paris, Texas." *Cinemania*. 1994 ed. CD-ROM. Redmond: Microsoft, 1994.

—— "Planes, Trains, and Automobiles." *Chicago Sun-Times* (November 25, 1987): n. pag. *Internet Movie Database*. Online. May 8, 1996.

Ehrenreich, Barbara. *Fear of Falling: The Inner Life of the Middle Class*. New York: Pantheon, 1989.

Frank, Micheline Klagsbrun. "Unchained: Perspectives on Change." *Journal of Popular Film and Television* 18 (1990): 122–9.

French, Warren. *Jack Kerouac*. Boston: Twayne, 1986.

Grant, Barry Keith. "Rich and Strange: the Yuppie Horror Film." *Journal of Film and Video* 48.1–2 (1996): 4–16.

Haskell, Molly. *From Reverence to Rape: The Treatment of Women in the Movies*. Harmondsworth: Penguin, 1974.

Hearn, Jeff. *Men in the Public Eye: The Construction and Deconstruction of Public Men and Public Patriarchies*. London: Routledge, 1992.

Kerouac, Jack. *On the Road* (1957). Rpt. New York: Penguin, 1976.

Kolker, Robert. *The Films of Wim Wenders: Cinema as Vision and Desire*. Cambridge: Cambridge University Press, 1993.

Laderman, Jeffrey. "Better Keep those Seat Belts Fastened." *Business Week* (November 9, 1987): 38–9.

—— "How the Bull Crashed into Reality." *Business Week* (November 2, 1987): 48–50.

"The Market on the Couch." *Newsweek* (November 2, 1987): 33.

Martz, Larry. "After the Meltdown." *Newsweek* (November 2, 1987): 14–20.

Moore, Suzanne. "The Death of Intimacy." *New Statesman* (March, 10 1989): 38.

Poynter, James M. *Corporate Travel Management*. Englewood Cliffs, NJ: Prentice Hall, 1990.

"The Rise and Fall of Bud Fox." *Time* (November 2, 1987): 53.

Rotundo, E. Anthony. *American Manhood: Transformations in Masculinity from the Revolution to the Modern Era*. New York: Basic Books, 1993.

Schenden, Laurie K. "Get Your Kicks on Route 66." *Los Angeles Times* (September 15, 1994): E-8. *Los Angeles Times Archive*. Online. April 26, 1996.

Sedgwick, Eve Kosofsky. *Between Men: English Literature and Male Homosocial Desire*. New York: Columbia University Press, 1985.

Simon, John. "Good Citizenship, Dubious Packaging." *National Review* (September 30, 1988): 57–8.

—— "Rain All Over." *National Review* (February 24, 1989): 52–3.

Wood, Robin. *Hollywood from Vietnam to Reagan*. New York: Columbia University Press, 1986.

Part III

ALTERNATIVE ROUTES

10

THE NATION, THE BODY, AND THE *AUTOSTRADA*

Angelo Restivo

In 1965, Pasolini coined the term *neo-italiano* to refer to the emergence of a new national language, one that threatened to displace once and for all the regional dialects that had, throughout Italian history, defined the parameters of reality for "national subjects" who had remained essentially regional in their primary affiliations (Brunetta: ch. 27). At the time, few Italians were more aware than Pasolini of the ways in which language itself constructs subjectivity; and thus, we can easily argue that Pasolini's neologism can be applied not only to the emergence of a new, hegemonic national language, but also to an essentially new *subject* – precisely, the "Italian" – constructed out of the rapid modernization of the nation brought about by the economic boom of the late 1950s and early 1960s.

One of the most dramatically visible signs of this economic miracle was the *autostrada*, the Italian version of the American interstate highway. But more than that, the *autostrada* became a trope for the ways in which economic modernization inscribed itself within the practice of everyday life. The *autostrada del sole*, for example, was charged with symbolic significance: as the backbone of the highway system, this *autostrada* didn't just connect the north to the south; it sped the driver from the prosperous, bourgeois northern provinces to the impoverished, semi-feudal provinces of the south, so that the journey was the traversing not simply of space, but of consciousness as well.

This new proximity between radically different Symbolic orders, combined with a new, "mobile" subjectivity constructed by the automobile, put into play within the nation a number of contestatory discourses. Different regions and different economic interests (including those of transnational capital) attempted to fix meaning at the sites where more traditional ideas of the nation were in flux. This essay will look at the way a popular Italian road movie reveals (symptomatically) the problem of defining the new Italian. Then, we'll look at the strategies deployed by advertising to construct the Italian as "mobile consumer." Finally, Pasolini's documentary *Comizi d'amore* (*Love Meetings*, 1964) not only provides a document of the way in which the discourses of modernization "cut into" the local and the traditional; but the film itself – as the work of a radical film-maker – attempts to produce a discourse that hopes to resist the hegemonizing forces at work in the nation.

An Italian Road Movie

Dino Risi's comedy of 1964, *Il sorpasso* (*The Easy Life*), doesn't present us with the kinds of aesthetic problematics that arose in the more "serious" films of the period, probably because of the traditional "populism" of the form of the *commedia all'italiana* of the 1950s. However, it does exemplify that turn toward complexity that Brunetta sees as marking the Italian comedy of the boom years (Brunetta: 588–9). "*Il sorpasso*" is the act of passing another automobile on the road, and the film organizes itself around the frenetic but aimless driving of the main character Bruno (Vittorio Gassman) and his more serious-minded "buddy" Roberto (Jean-Louis Trintignant). The film is a veritable catalogue of the emerging "lifestyle" of the new Italy; and, while it situates itself almost exclusively in the terrain of the new, it is always against the backdrop of an old way of life that only occasionally surfaces with a shock.

The film begins with Bruno speeding in his car through Rome, trying to find a telephone just as everything is closing for the *ferragosto* vacation. This opening – which culminates in a storefront grate closing just as Bruno tries to reach for a phone – aptly condenses both the old and the new. For, in a society still tied to the old tradition of long mid-day breaks, the problem of finding something open at a particular time is quite common; but the fact that for Bruno it is a *problem* already marks the film with a double sense of time, and marks Bruno as "out of sync" with the rhythms of the city. Yet the irony here is that it is *ferragosto*, and the entire city (and later, the nation) is closing all at once so that everyone can be part of the enforced conformity of the new leisure society.

Bruno and Roberto meet by chance, as Roberto is looking out his window when Bruno stops for the telephone. Roberto is a student of law, living alone in a rather dreary, modern apartment in the periphery of Rome, an urban space thrown up quickly in the 1950s to accommodate the tremendous influx of population from the country. Bruno comes up to make the phone call, and significantly, the woman he is trying to reach isn't home, which not only reinforces the series of missed encounters that opens the film, but also marks Bruno's frenetic activity as essentially futile. Then, when Bruno goes to the bathroom to wash up, he ends up breaking (off-screen) the vase that Roberto was about to warn him to be careful of. This break, of course, becomes the first in a series of ruptures to the hitherto smoothly functioning – if "repressed" – world of Roberto.

Roberto, studying for his upcoming exams, seems immune to the vacation mania that has taken hold of the nation; as such, he stands for the older *homo economicus* of renunciation, savings, and investment. This represents a significant inversion of terms in the duo Roberto/Bruno, for Bruno is the elder, and what he teaches his young *compagno* is the obsolescence of the old ways that still govern Roberto's life. Significant too is the fact that Roberto is played by a foreigner, while in the role of Bruno we have an actor central to Italian cinema as an institution. Bruno in many ways exhibits the traits of a certain Italian (and more specifically Roman) "type," who lives by the art of *arrangiarsi*, a kind of improvisational way of getting by through a combination of bravado, seductiveness, and "smarts." By making this typical southern Italian figure into the prototype of the new Italian, the film (perhaps unconsciously) suggests that it is the very adaptability of the Italian, the "chameleon-like" quality that is so often to foreign travelers a central trait of the Italian stereotype, that allows the discourses of consumption to remold the Italian character so easily. For in many ways, adaptability and improvisation are the very traits that are required to be activated in such postmodern spaces as, say, the shopping mall. In any case, this inversion of semic combinations – the youth with the foreign and the sublimated, the older with both traditional Italy and obsessive mobility – is something we will return to shortly.

After the scene in Roberto's apartment, Bruno convinces Roberto to abandon his studies for a while and join him in a *giro* – a "spin," we could say – in the car. Needless to say, they can't find an open bar or *trattoria*, and so the *giro* widens as they drive into the countryside. In fact, as the film progresses, the movement encompasses ever more kilometers, until by the end of the film we are in Viareggio, on the Riviera, where finally we are presented with the social totality that is "Italy" – a society clad in bathing suits and diverting itself with dancing the twist. And throughout the ride, the film has presented us with the images and sounds of a mobile, consumerist Italy. One of the film's principal visual motifs is the broken machine: first, a broken cigarette vending machine; then, the door handle of the toilet at the cheaply constructed rest stop; and ultimately, the wreckage of the automobile itself. This is an Italy not of permanence but of disposability, and the film's soundtrack is dominated by the incessant beat of equally disposable pop tunes, the most prominent of which is Domenico Modugno's "Dimmi quando," the lyrics of which – with its obsessive repetition of the "when, when, when" in the indirect question "Tell me when you'll want me" – is the perfect anthem to the perpetual present of the consumer.

In terms of what we might call, after Jameson, the film's allegorizing function, most crucial are the two set-pieces that involve family visits, first to Roberto's aunt and uncle, then to Bruno's ex-wife and daughter. The aunt and uncle, solidly bourgeois, live in an old villa in the countryside, a villa where Roberto often spent time as a child. Here, the portrait painted is strictly "Italian gothic," complete with "eccentric" (that is, homosexual) butler, the unmarried daughter who will linger at home until she turns into an old maid, and the local peasant who resembles the "Maciste" of the Italian cinema of the 1910s and 1920s. While Bruno later indicates to Roberto his contempt for the whole group, as a guest he deploys all his formidable charm to insinuate himself into the family, to the point where Roberto not only becomes jealous, but begins to doubt his understanding of his own past. For Bruno – in asides to Roberto – continually reads the "gothic subtext" to the family narrative: the butler, he explains, is called "Occhio fino" because he is a *finocchio*, a "fag"; the uncanny resemblance between Roberto's fatuous cousin and the somber peasant, he notes, is sure proof that Roberto's aunt needed "wilder" sex than her bourgeois husband could provide. In these scenes, Bruno is anticipating the role that later Terence Stamp would play in Pasolini's much more deadly-ironic *Teorema* (1968): in one scene, he wins the heart of the spinster by undoing her hair and showing her what she'd look like as a "Roman girl." Bruno's ultimate triumph is the acquisition of the uncle's grandfather clock: he cons the uncle out of the patrimony that rightly belongs to Roberto, so that he can wrest it from family ties and put it into circulation. In fact, Bruno makes at least part of his living by recycling the antiques of a dying social class.

In contrast to Roberto's family, Bruno's is thoroughly modern: atomized, alienated, mobile and pleasure-seeking. Bruno's decision to make a surprise late-night visit to his ex-wife is at least partly motivated by a series of failed erotic encounters; it is as if these relatively unimportant failures remind him of the one failure that is important, that of his marriage. Now, at this point in Italian history, divorce has not yet become legal; it is, however, a major focal point of public discourse (as we shall see) and as such is a kind of barometer of just how successfully modernization has been accomplished. In any case, Bruno and Roberto are thoroughly drunk when they look up Gianna at one in the morning; nevertheless, Gianna, who hasn't seen Bruno in well over a year, takes the two men in as if this were an expected occurance. Gianna is so completely contemptuous of Bruno's "masculinism" that she puts up with him as if with a wayward child. Thus, in a film that is otherwise thoroughly masculinist in its enunciation, there emerges in the subtext of this scene that crisis in the sexual relation that is concomitant to modernization, and that in the American cinema had found earlier expression in the *noir* and melodrama of the 1950s.

Thus it is no surprise that Bruno, almost as a defense mechanism, suddenly adopts a patriarch's concern over the whereabouts of his 15-year-old daughter at one in the morning; nor does it come as a surprise when she walks in with a "boyfriend" – Bibi – who is years older than Bruno. For in popular culture generally, one of the ways in which the "crisis in masculinity" that accompanies modernization finds expression is through a pathological Oedipalization of the daughter's sexual choices: in the American cinema of the 1950s once again, we can cite *Written on the Wind* (1956), *Imitation of Life* (1959), and *Rebel Without a Cause* (1955) as particularly prominent examples of this. In the American scenario, the generalized collapse of the Law renders all the men in the films incapable of living up to the phallic mandate; but within the melodramatic economy, this failure is turned back upon the woman, whose "voracious" qualities then work to gender the entire economy of consumption as "feminine." In *Il sorpasso*, we can see a similar dynamic with Bruno's wife and daughter, where their pursuit of material security renders them – in the context of the men unable to provide it – unfathomable.

In *The Political Unconscious*, Fredric Jameson demonstrates how the semiotic rectangle can be used to uncover the ways in which a given text attempts to "solve" the textual antinomies that reflect real, historical contradictions (166–8). In the case of *Il sorpasso*, we could say that the principal contrary that the text produces is that between work (and the work ethic embodied in Roberto) and mobility (or the road), which would produce the following:

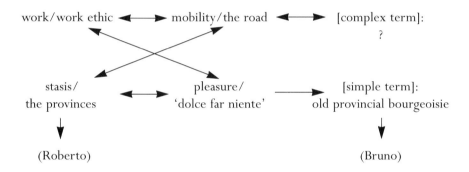

What the semiotic square makes apparent is that the social tension around which the film constructs itself (or which, in Jameson's terms, the film allegorizes) is the movement of hegemony from the old provincial bourgeoisie to a new class; and that it is precisely in the attempt to visualize this new hegemonic class that the film "stumbles." What is unimagineable in *Il sorpasso* – what indeed is the principal stumbling block for the cultural imagination as a whole – is the subject who embodies both mobility and the (northern European or "Protestant") work ethic; in short, the new class of technocrats who were transforming both economy and culture throughout the 1950s. As soon as Roberto is uprooted from his sheltered world, the film can imagine his trajectory ending only in his sudden and arbitrary death in a car accident.

"*Point de Capiton*"

Il sorpasso, then, makes visible for us a kind of "void in the Symbolic" which confronted Italy in 1964. It was around this opening that all types of discourses – in advertising, journalism, and politics as well as popular culture – competed in an attempt to pin down the meaning of this new Italian, and thus to be able to deploy it for ideological ends.[1] It is for this reason that the study of a national magazine like *L'Espresso* becomes so important: within the pages of *L'Espresso* in the years 1960 to 1965, we can see played out in a variety of discourses the always-unfinished process of constructing the national subjectivity.

Italy, then, achieves the unification only promised in the Risorgimento of the nineteenth century at precisely the moment in which it becomes a society of consumption. This is why national advertising – by the multinational oil companies, for example – provides us with an especially rich discursive field to read against the high art of the period: for advertising, better than any other discourse, shows us exactly how the signifier "Italy" is a signifier under which slides an entire array of signifieds. A particular advertisement can be seen as the attempt to halt the sliding of signification (see Zizek: 96) in such a way that the nation and the product seem inextricable; this is especially true for the advertising of products such as

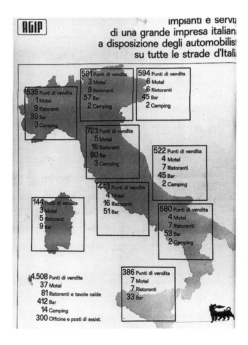

Plate 10.1 Ad from *L'Espresso* (June 5, 1966) shows the national map constructed around mobility and consumption.

gasoline, where the use of the product is intimately connected to a radical change in social practice (in this case, the expansion of the use of the automobile within both the urban space of Italy and the entire national space itself). Ultimately, these ads work to construct new "cognitive maps" of Italy, reinscribing the various regions of the nation into new narratives of consumption and mobility.

The sense of a new age at hand that advertising is playing upon is directly connected to the suddenness of Italy's economic miracle. Italy has changed radically in little more than a decade, while the Italian subject has remained locked in discourses and political configurations that emerged out of the Second World War. A page of advertising in *L'Espresso* of January 19, 1964 is remarkable in the ways that – by a totally contingent juxtaposition of two advertisements – it uncovers this historical rupture. On the top half of the page is an ad from the chemical group SNIA, touting a new synthetic fabric "with all the advantages." The headline of the ad is "E' arrivato" (loosely, "It's here!"); and the ad depicts a stylishly dressed woman confidently striding toward the reader, as if she is about to walk right off the page. On the bottom half of the page, *L'Espresso* is seeking new subscribers by offering a three-record set of songs from the European resistance. Spread across the ad is a ragged band of partisans, rifles slung across their shoulders, and the Italian flag waving off in the corner. On the one hand, history is seen as a march toward the future, where the most logical attitude for the Italian to take is a turning back on the past. On the other hand, we see the ways in which that past – still a potent force in a country where the Communist Party has between one-fourth and one-third of the electorate – is becoming commodified and turned into nostalgia. And while we must be careful not to draw the wrong conclusions from a (perhaps) totally fortuitous juxtaposition, we can nevertheless note the irony in the "sexuation" the ads present: there is one "Woman," walking toward us with no baggage and no regrets, while below her, a rag-tag group of men are scattered in the distant Italian landscape, almost as if they were ridiculous "worker bees" setting the stage for the triumphant emergence of the queen.

It is significant, too, that the chemical company ad is *drawn*; it is not a photograph. One of Fredric Jameson's most interesting observations about the materiality of video (as a quintessentially postmodern medium) is that its formal precursor is best seen, not as the narrative forms of fiction, but rather the material forms of animation. As he puts it, "animation constituted the first great school to teach the reading of material signifiers (rather than the narrative apprenticeship of objects of representation . . .)" (*Postmodernism*: 77). Now, this observation is highly useful when looking at the historical conjuncture we are dealing with: for, in terms of the construction of the postwar nation, it was precisely the neo-realist cinema which staked everything on the question of representation, and on the concomitant "apprenticeship" of the national audience. And indeed, in the 1960s it is precisely these two questions – that of representation, and that of pedagogy – which are facing serious film-makers, and this precisely in their attempt to create a discourse of *resistance* to the growing cultural homogenization wrought by the hegemonizing forces of the economic miracle.

Ultimately, then, the logic of the *point de capiton* is the logic of social antagonism and contestation within the ideological field, as the various camps try to "pin down," or conversely to subvert, what it means to be a citizen of this new nation. And here is thus where de Certeau's distinction between strategy and tactics becomes useful. For insofar as the discourses of advertising and of the new national language are so palpably material in their effects – because the changes in the object-world of Italy are so seemingly unstoppable – these discourses can be seen as strategic moves by the hegemonizing classes. And thus the only appropriate response from the film-maker is to adopt a set of tactics which will draw the lines of battle at the level of the particular, the local, and the everyday (see de Certeau: 34–9). And it is *this* aspect of the earlier neo-realist tradition that the new film-makers of the 1960s find useable, even as they realize the extent to which the first wave of neo-realism was recuperated by the national project of the Christian Democrats.

Advertising, then, brings us to the junction of hegemony and everyday life. The British cultural historians Bommes and Wright put it particularly well when they note that hegemonizing discourse functions by "deploying/restaging everyday life in particular coded sites, images, events" (Bommes and Wright: 290). Advertising, cinema, and television all are engaged in articulating spatial relations through which the nation, and the national narrative, are experienced. In a sense, then, we can say that the nation, Italy, is being "re-mapped" in this period, particularly through advertising in magazines like *L'Espresso*.

Gulf Oil Company employed a technique of "touring" famous national spaces, with all the sophistication and pizzazz of art photography. The series employed the headline "Corre sfrecciante . . . Gulf carburante" ("Run without breaking . . . by burning Gulf"), and an almost full-page picture of a time-lapsed car speeding through one or another landmark public space, such as the Piazza della Signoria in Florence. Here again, the advertising is attempting to reinscribe the space of Italy with new signifiers; in particular, it attempts to resolve the contradiction between the speed of the automobile and the cramped and labyrinthine urban spaces of Italy. What comes to mind here is the futurist ideal of *Velo-città*, their attempt, in the action painting, to inscribe within the Italian city the idea of modernity and "speed." The ads, with their time-lapse photography, seem consciously to allude to the futurist action paintings, and we can recall that futurism was the aesthetic most aligned with the construction of the nation during the Fascist period. As James Hay perceptively notes, futurism was determined to create "hyper-technological tropes" in order to produce "new ways of perceiving temporal and spatial relations in Italian cities" (41), where, of course, the dominant organizational principles come from the high Middle Ages and Renaissance.

The series done by Shell Oil is the most interesting and complex of the automobile-related ads. Each ad in the series features a child constructing a narrative of travel with the family. Often, there is a large picture of a happy or pensive child, with a little story underneath. The case of "Luisa" is different, however; her advertisement is constructed of six photographs which, together with her commentary underneath each one, constructs a narrative. Luisa tells the story of how she and Daddy (who are "great friends") take little trips every Sunday. The six pictures creating the narrative are, first, a stop at a restaurant along the *autostrada* ("all of glass"); then Piazza delle Erbe in Verona ("a really beautiful city"); then two photos detailing the pit-stop at a Shell station, where a helpful attendant notices the fan belt is loose; then Montecchio and the castle of Romeo and Juliet ("there are still castles!"); and, finally, the *autostrada* by night, as the father–daughter couple return home.

On the most obvious level, we see how the ad naturalizes leisure travel by inscribing the unfamiliar or novel scenes within the age-old landscape of Italy. At another level, the ad mobilizes the Oedipal scenario, as the young girl runs off with Dad every Sunday (where's Mamma?), dreaming of castles and Romeo and Juliet, and snuggling up to Dad on the road home. Thus, we see the process whereby the ad attempts to "colonize the unconscious," by allowing leisure travel and Shell Oil to negotiate the sexual desire that runs through the family.

Insofar as all these ads are working upon the urban spaces of Italy, they bring to mind Benjamin's notion of the "porosity" of Naples, the idea that the urban space of Naples is doubly inscribed, and that the sudden juxtaposition of an earlier, pre-industrial society with that of the present jolts the pedestrian with an awareness of historical rupture (Benjamin: 163–73; Buck-Morss: 26–7). Certainly, these ads do present us with the shock of historical disjuncture, of the juxtaposition of two modes of economic organization within the same space. The ads, however, work within a completely discursive economy, purged of the historical "Real" which underpins the Benjaminian experience of Naples. This is the reason we can describe the nation-space created by these ads as postmodern: each potential referent is turned into a pure sign, in the manner described by Baudrillard (21–5), and each relates to the other as pure difference, whose meaning becomes fixed through the mediation of the commodity. This is the "hidden logic" underlying Pasolini's key notion of "homogenization" (Pasolini: 71–6), the dark side of the economic miracle.

Pasolini and the Limits of Resistance

The cultural ramifications of Italy's modernization were in fact the central preoccupation of Pasolini's cinema of the 1960s, from the explorations of the new Roman underclass in *Accattone* (1961) and *Mamma Roma* (1962) to his allegory of the derealization of bourgeois life in *Teorema* (finished in the explosive political climate of 1968). The *autostrada* – though under construction and thus deserted – makes an appearance in the 1966 *Uccellacci uccellini* (*Hawks and Sparrows*). But from the point of view of the inscription of modernization into the local and the everyday, more useful is Pasolini's 1964 documentary *Comizi d'amore*. In a sense, this documentary is the "trace" of a road trip: it was made "on the fly" as Pasolini scouted locations for *The Gospel According to St. Matthew* (1964). The trajectory is thus governed not by the road, but by rhetoric. And this allows Pasolini to interrogate the very map of Italy, exposing cross-sections that remain hidden from the dominant discourse.

It is important when looking at this film to consider both its enunciated "content" and its enunciation: the enunciated providing an important historical document of the Italian subject's encounter with modernization; the enunciation attempting to "shape" the material in such a way as to perform an act of resistance itself. In calling the film "a national inquest on sex," Pasolini (most likely consciously) alludes to Zavattini's neo-realist ideal of the "film inquest." Nevertheless, for the viewer today, the question that comes up is the same one that haunted the neo-realist project generally: to what extent does an act of resistance unconsciously partake in the very logic of the thing being resisted? Or, to put it in de Certeau's terms, to what extent is the film a tactical resistance to the hegemonizing discourses, and to what extent does it actually reflect the very strategy of those discourses? Certainly, the very act of putting on the table the issue of sex, the very act of "speaking sex," is – Michel Foucault teaches us – precisely the social project of modernity. In this sense, the film is certainly complicit in this project; and this repeated double-bind that Pasolini found himself in is certainly a major explanation for his later artistic movement to the premodern and the Third World.

But there is a sense in which *Comizi d'amore* is profoundly subversive; the spectator is forced to realize the *constructedness* of the Symbolic Order, is forced to see how the Symbolic Order is an arbitrary covering-over of some traumatic Real – of the body, of sexuation, of history. This is evident from Pasolini's very clever opening strategy for the film, where Sicilian children are being asked how babies are born. Of course, this is the question that represents in general the child's first attempt at a self-conscious examination of sexuality, and so children's narratives here are inevitably filled with gaps and contradictions which need somehow to be resolved. In the documentary, we see how the signifiers of the birth narrative

– Mama's stomach, the stork, God – begin to slide under the pressure of Pasolini's "logic."

Pasolini's privileging of the narratives of the Sicilian children reveals a larger strategy in the documentary: that is, as we move through the interviews with adults, we begin to see the same kind of sliding of signification when the received discourses on sexuality meet their stumbling blocks.[2] Generally, the film employs two distinct enunciative strategies: first, a series of interviews by Pasolini with various ordinary Italians in everyday situations, in which these Italians speak surprisingly frankly about whatever is on their minds; and second, a series of interruptions to these interviews, where Pasolini sits with a group of rather prominent intellectuals (including journalist Oriana Fallaci and psychoanalyst Cesare Musatti) to discuss broader issues of sexuality and social change. On the surface, this strategy of interruption seems to reflect a "retrograde," televisual procedure of contextualization, where no "body" is allowed to speak for him/herself, without mediation from both media-annointed "experts" and the studio hosts who deliver everything up to the viewer. However, here the discourse of the intellectuals is not the contextual frame through which all the rest is viewed, but rather illustrates in living form the ways in which the various voices of the film "rub against one another." It illustrates, that is, *the very problem of the constitution of the object of study*.

In this sense, the presence throughout the film of Pasolini's *body* becomes the critical self-reflexive move of the documentary.[3] For in documentary practice generally, the key ideological move is toward the disembodied voice, which becomes the vehicle for knowledge, for the universal. It is the presence of the body – as Joan Copjec rightly notes – that introduces the disruption of the particular into the attempted totalization ("The Phenomenal Non-phenomenal": 184). Bill Nichols has noted how crucial is the body to documentary, in that the invocation of the body becomes a kind of "guarantee" of the *referent* (as opposed to the signified). He goes on to argue that the body becomes a kind of "stand-in" for "experience as yet uncategorized within the economy of a logic or system" (249–55). Or, to put it in psychoanalytic terms, the body stands as guarantor of the Real, even as it itself is traversed by the discourses of the Symbolic. This is a particularly fruitful way to look at Pasolini's documentary: it is *all* bodies. But they are narrating bodies, incessantly called upon to find ways of making sense of the new forces shaping their lives.

One of those forces – the one which was understandably of central interest to Pasolini – was the emergence of that "modern phenomenon," the homosexual. It is precisely in the discussion of homosexuality where Pasolini is able to bring into focus most clearly the ways that modern discourses were received at the local level, where tradition and resistance asserted themselves in fascinating and improbable ways. In fact, homosexuality in this film can be seen as the strand that interconnects all the other modernizing discourses about the body – from hygiene to prostitution to women's rights. Here, we can note with Foucault that there are three areas which needed to be defined/regulated in the movement from pre-bourgeois to bourgeois culture: childhood, women, and the family (and by extension, non-procreative sexualities; Foucault: 104–5).

The *Legge Merlin*, for example, was the national law that closed all the (state-run) brothels in Italy, including the famous *case chiuse* of Naples. Clearly, this law was a product of the "enlightened" and modernizing discourses that were disseminated, for example, by *L'Espresso*. In the documentary, a Neapolitan man links the new law with an increase in homosexuality among the young; in fact, what we are seeing is the *emergence* or the "invention" of homosexuality within a Symbolic Order which had hitherto held to more "antique" notions of desire. Thus, homosexuality becomes in the film the most interesting site of contestation.

L'Espresso in the early 1960s ran several articles attempting to "understand" homosexuality. The national magazine calls homosexuality "certainly one of the arguments of the day," and constructs homosexuality in several ways. First, there is speculation that it is a product of leisure society, and the post-economic miracle of Italy. This argument is given relatively little weight. Second, there are discussions of the biological/psychodynamic issue, which understandably is not resolved. Third, much focus is placed on the issue of therapy, and here (remarkably) the discussion is quite "advanced." The magazine privileges an existential therapist whose therapy is centered on "being in the world," where the idea is to find a way for the patient to live his sexuality in a "non-destructive" way (i.e., by following the heterosexist models of bourgeois marriage). Finally, the article concludes with a doctor's quote that, in the end, Proust understood everything.

So far, there is little to surprise us: for, as Foucault notes, the bourgeois project is to construct homosexuality as "a personage, a past, a case history, and a childhood" (43). But when we move to the documentary evidence of attitudes in the south of Italy, we begin to see that homosexuality – insofar as it "exists" at all – exists in a radically different way from that constructed by *L'Espresso*. Pasolini interviews a group of young men in a piazza in Catanzaro. Among the group of six or seven men, attitudes toward "inverts" range from pity to disgust. Finally, one of the boys says, "Even though I go with them, it disgusts me." And then his friend says, "I go with them too."

This is quite a remarkable moment in the documentary. Obviously, among these boys there is a concept of "other" being employed, but how this other is defined is completely unclear. The boys are openly frank, among their friends, about their own participation in homosexual acts; what, then, is an "invert"? Perhaps – and this is speculation, for it is not brought out in the documentary – they are operating on a model of active/passive in defining the other: that is to say, the important thing in defining masculinity is the act of insertion, and not the gender of the person receiving. But in any case, the symbolic system they operate in allows for the practice of homosexuality without a concomitant need for definition or medicalization; and the interesting thing about an active/passive binary opposition is the way in which – in the privacy of a sex act – who is to know if one decides to "cross the line" (i.e., occupy the passive position)?

In the south, there is a performative view of "sex," as opposed to the essentializing view of the emergent bourgeoisie (and of "modernity" in general). In a scene in a piazza in Naples, a Neapolitan argues against the *Legge Merlin* because he sees the law as encouraging sexual relations between young men; he says that before, the young men could find sexual outlet for 300 lire, whereas now, with prostitution moved to the streets, the cost has risen to 3000 lire. He then turns to a young man next to him and says, "Tell him about the urinals." The boy then explains that young men spend all day at the urinals, whereupon the older man interrupts and explains that they later spend their "earnings" on the prostitute. Finally, the man pins the problem on the widespread unemployment in Naples.

As the new discourse on sexuality becomes concrete in the form of a law that impinges upon daily life, we can discern specific class and regional effects (see Foucault: 127). The Neapolitan, engaging as he is, leaves us with more questions than answers. Is he implying that those sexual encounters did not go on before the *Legge Merlin*? Considering the way that young women were traditionally jealously guarded in southern families, sex among young men was rather inevitable and tolerated. Is it possible that the boys could have spent their "earnings" on other than the prostitutes, having already been sexually satisfied? In any case, homosexuality is here not even mentioned, and a performative model of sexuality is put forth. The economic problem – which indeed is real for the young Neapolitan – is, in the discourse of sexuality, the smokescreen behind which the issue of pleasure can be left undecided.

To summarize the various discourses constructed around Italy's economic transformation, we can construct once again a semiotic square, this time around the notion of space:

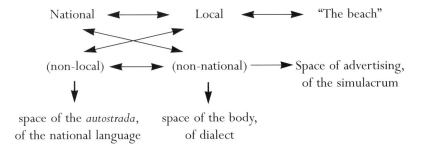

The lower terms represent the social contradiction as it presented itself in its most tangible form: Italy, traditionally a "nation" of strongly insulated regions speaking their own dialects, is confronted with a new sense of space brought about by the superhighway ("limited access," of course) engineered by a new technocratic elite speaking a standardized national language (evident in written form in the weekly *L'Espresso*).

The simple and the complex terms, on the right, present us with the ways in which popular discourses attempted to mediate the contradiction through spatial strategies; but what is highly interesting is the ways in which both these terms contaminate each other. That is to say, the space constructed by advertising was

Plate 10.2 This news story from *L'Espresso* (May 29, 1966: "Assault on the beaches of Italy") reminds us of how Risi and Pasolini deploy the beach as the site of the new social totality of Italy.

largely non-local and non-national, governed, as we have seen, principally by the forces of transnational capital in the process of consolidating its "third stage." Yet in order to do that, it needed to deploy local places in such a way as to reassure the mobile, consuming subject that s/he was still "Italian." To do this, it deployed the simulacrum, creating out of national places a system of pure signs.

The beach appears in both *Il sorpasso* and *Comizi d'amore*, and in both films it is the place in which the new social totality is imagined: as a mobile, undifferentiated mass diverting itself in a national ritual of vacation.[4] As a cinematic trope, however, the beach brings with it the image of an "edge," of the place where the nation ends: thus it functions as a kind of limit-point, the paradoxical, unsignifying space which allows all the other spaces to form the signifying system. This is why, in both films, there is a sense when we go to the beach on holiday that we are confronting a literally meaningless spectacle; and both films derive their ironic humor from this very idea.

Finally, when Pasolini goes to the beach, it is – as he says in an intertitle – in search of the "real Italy." And what he privileges when he gets there is the narrative of the Tuscan father with his young son in tow, delivering to Pasolini's camera the traditionalist notion that the state is simply an extension of the family. This discourse is, of course, the fundamental tenet of the Fascist, "corporatist" idea of the nation, which Italy had embraced only a few decades before. What Pasolini uncovers, then, is the ghost that haunts any attempted mediation between the national and the local, and which the advertising of the period subtly reinvokes: the ghost of Fascism.

Notes

1 The groundwork for this conception of advertising is laid out in Zizek: 87–100.
2 For the Lacanian view of sex as "stumbling block," see Copjec, "Sex": 16–24.
3 The centrality of the body in Pasolini's work as a whole has been discussed in Viano: 14–15 and Greene: 45.
4 Here my argument is methodologically indebted to Fredric Jameson's semiotic mapping of space in *North by Northwest*. See "Spatial Systems": 47–72.

Works Cited

Baudrillard, Jean. "The System of Objects." *Selected Writings*, ed. M. Poster. Stanford: Stanford University Press, 1988.

Benjamin, Walter. "Naples." *Reflections: Essays, Aphorisms, Autobiographical Writings*, trans. E. Jephcott, ed. P. Demetz. New York: Harcourt, Brace, Jovanovich, 1978.

Bommes, Michael and Patrick Wright. "'Charms of Residence': The Public and the Past." *Making Histories: Studies in History, Writing, and Politics*, ed. R. Johnson et al. London: Hutchinson, 1982.

Brunetta, Gian Piero. *Cent'anni di cinema italiano*. Roma: Editori Laterza, 1991.

Buck-Morss, Susan. *The Dialectics of Seeing: Walter Benjamin and the Arcades Project*. Cambridge: MIT Press, 1991.

Copjec, Joan. "The Phenomenal Non-phenomenal: Private Space in Film Noir." *Shades of Noir*, ed. J. Copjec. New York: Verso, 1993.

—— "Sex and the Euthanasia of Reason." *Supposing the Subject*, ed. J. Copjec. New York: Verso, 1994.

de Certeau, Michel. *The Practice of Everyday Life*, trans. S. Rendall. Berkeley: University of California Press, 1984.

L'Espresso, May 23, 1965; May 30, 1965; ("Omosessuali si nasce?", "La Paura della donna").

Foucault, Michel. *The History of Sexuality*, vol. 1, trans. R. Hurley. New York: Pantheon, 1978.

Greene, Naomi. *Pier Paolo Pasolini: Cinema as Heresy*. Princeton: Princeton University Press, 1990.

Hay, James. "Invisible Cities/Visible Geographies: Toward a Cultural Geography of Italian Television in the 90s." *Quarterly Review of Film and Video* 14:3 (Spring 1993).

Jameson, Fredric. *The Political Unconscious: Narrative as a Socially Symbolic Act*. Ithaca: Cornell University Press, 1981.

—— *Postmodernism, or, the Cultural Logic of Late Capitalism*. Durham, NC: Duke University Press, 1991.

—— "Spatial Systems in *North by Northwest*." *Everything You Always Wanted to Know About Lacan . . .* , ed. S. Zizek. New York: Verso, 1992.

Nichols, Bill. *Representing Reality: Issues and Concepts in Documentary*. Bloomington: Indiana University Press, 1991.

Pasolini, Pier Paolo. *Lettere luterane*. Torino: Einaudi, 1976.

Viano, Maurizio. *A Certain Realism: Making Use of Pasolini's Film Theory and Practice*. Berkeley: University of California Press, 1993.

Zizek, Slavoj. *The Sublime Object of Ideology*. New York: Verso, 1989.

11

"WE DON'T NEED TO KNOW THE WAY HOME"
The disappearance of the road in the *Mad Max* trilogy

Delia Falconer

"'Whither goest thou, Australia, in your bumpy car in the middle of the night?' – that's 'Jack Outback.'"

"Rebel" (Max Cullen), *Running on Empty*

The roads that rifled through *Mad Max 1* do not exist in the third film [*Beyond Thunderdome*]. There are only trails blazed at the moment of wandering.

(Gibson: 173)

In *Mad Max* (1979), set a "few years in the future" on the outskirts of a decaying city, the policeman Max (Mel Gibson) battles biker gangs on Anarchie Road. In *Mad Max 2* (1982), which takes place after a devastating oil war, these asphalt roads have been replaced by dirt tracks as Max, now an embittered wanderer, comes unwillingly to the aid of a commune of desert dwellers. In the third film of the trilogy, *Mad Max Beyond Thunderdome* (1985), in which Max helps a group of feral children find their way home, even these dirt roads have disappeared into a trackless landscape of desert dunes, fertile gorges, and post-nuclear dust.

In this essay, I will examine this progression away from the road as a particular and complex (re)negotiation of Australia's spatial history. In the first film, the road appears as a specific and violently contested site. By the last film it has disappeared into a landscape of mythic "sights." This disappearance, I will argue, represents both the road's liberation from colonial narratives of empire and its absorption into a *deregulated* postcolonial spatiality. *Beyond Thunderdome* suggests that this latter landscape, which is market-driven, corporatized, and globally orientated, holds utopian possibilities, but only, perhaps, for "indigenized" Australians, who are willing to regard land and stories as "resources," and to ignore historical inequalities and conflicts in the consensual spirit of "postness" and progress. In doing so, it both reflects and refines a corresponding shift in discourses of Australian nationalism during the 1970s and 1980s.

The following discussion intervenes in two modes of analysis which have been used in critical readings of the spatiality of the *Mad Max* films. The first is eager to read these films as postmodern cultural productions, symptomatic of the spread of that "corporate space" of multinational capital, described by Fredric Jameson, which makes "an older kind of existential positioning of ourselves in Being – the human body in the natural landscape, the individual in the older village or organic community, even the citizen in the nation-state – exceedingly problematical" (127). Christopher Sharrett, for example, claims that the first two *Mad Max* films shrewdly expose, by means of obvious quotations from the American movie canon, "the spiritual and intellectual bankruptcy of '*the*' modern landscape" (82, italics and inverted commas mine), which is characterized by simulacra, schizophrenia, and the "collapse of totalizing theories of history" (90). Ariane Rummey sees in *Mad Max 2* a simulacral landscape without secrets, colonized by American military technologies such as Pine Gap, reflecting "the deterritorialized condition" (49) of postmodern space, and bearing out Paul Virilio's claim that "technology is our new nature" (46). The hero who undertakes a quest through this landscape, she writes, has simply evolved in Australian films from an "intrepid bushman" to a "fast driver" (46).

This mode of analysis suggests that the road, as a representative technology of postmodernity, always imposes a certain inevitable cultural logic upon its users. Such a metonymic[1] tendency appears often in recent analyses of the road. Both Margaret Morse and Jean Baudrillard, for example, read "the" highway as a quintessentially postmodern site (and "driving" as a symptomatic activity) while avoiding its different modes of use and access.[2] It concerns me, however, that such symptomatic readings cannot account for change within postmodernity, as Meaghan Morris notes (*Great Moments*), but can only identify perpetual transformation as its characteristic state. As she argues, the fact that they cannot read local tactics of negotiation often results in "the universality of a global-yet-American cultural logic [being] accepted, and affirmed, in the moment of critique" ("Tooth and Claw": 264). Such readings also assume that a transnational "postmodern subject" emerges from the consumption of the "latest" technology. As Evan Watkins points out, this assumption replicates the logic of "obsolescence" by which late capitalism operates,[3] and disqualifies those who do not have access to new forms of technology as "relics and throwaways . . . who haven't moved on with the times" (3). These are issues of particular relevance to the trilogy, since the films are preoccupied with issues of consumption, obsolescence, and survival.

Therefore, while many of the observations made by Sharrett and Rummey are useful, they do not offer a "thick" reading of the use of landscape in the *Mad Max* films. Nor do they offer the possibility of intervention. While they recognize the space of each film as "postmodern," these readings seem able to account only for the stylistic similarity of the films, rather than being able to account for their move "off-road." The notion of intertextuality which they depend upon (the American film canon) ignores the specificity of the Australian road movie's own history, as well as other practices and discourses, such as advertising and tourism, which the *Mad Max* films also draw upon. Nor do they seem capable of reading in whose interests the cultural logic of "postmodern space" is framed and negotiated by the films. Rummey's statement that "the colonizers [of the Australian landscape] have switched from the British to the Americans does not hold much significance" (52) is particularly troubling, for it ignores the public reception of these films in Australia, which recognized them as very "Australian" in an historically original way. This reception involved the redefinition of Australian nationalism away from a British imperial model towards "middle class, suburban, populist, consumerist, entrepreneurial and developmental dimensions" (James, "Australia": 72). The economic success of these Australian products in an international marketplace was presented as being synonymous with the success of the Australian people, at a time when the landscape, in turn, was valued for its "productivity."

The second sort of analysis with which I am uncomfortable claims the films for a "resistant" postcolonialism. In his reading of *Beyond Thunderdome*, Ross Gibson suggests that by "leaving the road" in the third film Max abandons an adversarial relationship to the land, and begins instead to "trace the contours of the continent, reading it a little more cannily, moving according to its dictates, and growing from it" (175). I would certainly agree that the last film of the trilogy enunciates a celebratory attitude of "postness." It does this, as Gibson claims, through its insistence on producing myths of origin for, and ways of consuming, the land-scape, incorporating the "foreign" and privileging new beginnings over a nostalgic belief that one might "go home again . . . [to] an English Australia" (172). Yet, in determining how *successfully* the film deconstructs the imperial drive to conquer space by establishing a *post*colonial environment, Gibson's analysis fails to inter-rogate the possibility that such a move might embrace other forms of imperialism. His reading of the film as "mythic" tends to present Australia's postcolonial landscape as a a perpetual present of "postness," characterized by the law of trans-formation, which is positioned against a more "real" past. In such an analysis, then, in which the present can only be read in terms of empty "styles," Gibson runs the risk of "effacing . . . the indecisiveness of actual conflicts" (Morris, "Tooth and Claw": 265) by which Australia's landscape is produced as "postcolonial." There is also a possibility that his reading naturalizes the infusion of corporate tourist-driven representations of Australianness into the landscape, which the films, as "events," depended upon for a positive reception.

This essay, then, treats the *Mad Max* films as such events, in which international success and increasing budgets are as much part of the trilogy as the films themselves. Rather than reading them as "proofs" of the ideology of postwar capitalism or a postcolonial sensibility, I will offer a "thick" analysis which examines the specificity of their negotiation and framing of these conditions within and beyond the films. In the next section I will examine how these global changes were articulated by the growing climate of economic rationalism in Australia in the 1970s and 1980s; its specific material effects on the Australian film industry; the consequent strategies of appropriation used by its road movies; and changing discourses of nationalism during this period which, in turn, envisaged and produced a new sort of landscape. I will examine how, in each of these microhistories, the issue of globalization attracts ambivalence, since on the one hand it threatens older ideals of nationalism, but on the other it also offers new roads out and in. In particular, I will unpack the historically original association of entrepreneurship and citizenship. In the third section of this paper I will offer a close analysis of the films in order to understand how they negotiate and figure this terrain. I will trace the development from a violent fluctuation of affect associated with the road's hybridity in *Mad Max* to a more positive rapprochement with a touristed landscape in *Beyond Thunderdome* as the film moves off the road.

During the 1970s and 1980s, a climate of economic rationalism slowly began to replace the imperial model of a discrete "Fortress Australia" with the ideal of an aggressive dialogue with the world economy. The deregulation of the Australian financial system in the early 1980s was perhaps the most concrete signifier of the breakdown of a colonial model of nationhood, insofar as the floating of the dollar harnessed the Australian economy to the international marketplace by surrendering official control of the exchange rate. Interest rates were deregulated, and foreign banks encouraged to enter Australia. The resulting reconceptualization of Australian space, as permeable and open instead of protected and discrete, was clearly articulated by Bob Johnson of the Reserve Bank, when he described deregulation as "the overt breaking of our isolationism. Without it, there is the mentality of living behind the moat. The float linked the Australian economy, for better or worse, with the rest of the world" (Kelly: 87).

Sam Rohdie, Elizabeth Jacka and Susan Dermody have sketched excellent histories of the corresponding "float" of the Australian film industry into the global marketplace. Although the Australian Film Commission continued to provide financial assistance to this industry, its supportive role began to change around 1980. Instead of funding "Australian" content and seeking to produce quality art films primarily for domestic consumption, it encouraged Australian films, through the 10BA Tax Act, to shift "from production values to market values, [and] from a domestic to an international orientation" (Rohdie: 30). The effect of this Act was that during the 1980s Australian films tended to be funded by overseas investors, and their marketing depended upon "presales" to overseas markets and foreign-dominated film distribution networks. This, in turn, effected a standardization of the industry's products.[4] Established genres from the Hollywood canon were renovated in a new locale. "Australianness" consequently emerged as a set of tropes aimed, tactically, at gaining global audiences. The success of Australian films often depended upon attracting recognizable American actors to attract overseas audiences and funding. Thus, as Rohdie argues, "the State produced ideology of a national film culture and national film art simply masks an economic reality (general for the Australian economy) for which terms like 'national' make little sense" (28–9).

Kennedy Miller, the producer of the *Mad Max* films, is an interesting player in this reorientation of the marketplace. As exploitation/road movies, its films represent market-driven genre pieces with an emphasis on "entertainment" over local content. Over this period, Kennedy Miller made a virtue of the cultural hybridity of its films, presenting itself as a very "Australian" success story. In a "survivalist" discourse crossing the borders of film and media texts, its ability to weather the exigencies of international film-funding capital through appropriation was presented as a triumph of postcolonial initiative. It was praised for its ability to turn international film genres (or, in the case of *Beyond Thunderdome*, the star system of the international rock scene) into "resources." As I shall demonstrate, a survivalist discourse and an emphasis on the transformative use of myth are foregrounded with increasing flamboyance and self-consciousness in each successive film. The story of Max is, increasingly, the story of Kennedy Miller, "fast drivers" in the new economic landscape.

This shift is figured in a number of other Australian road movies of the 1970s and 1980s. The Australian car industry has a history of vulnerability to the international market, particularly in the 1970s and 1980s.[5] Consequently, in Australian road movies from this period, the road and car seem to stand in suggestively for the film industry itself.[6] As Paul Carter has noted in *The Road to Botany Bay*, the road stands as an enabling trope and trace of British imperialism in Australia. Yet, ironically, in these films "escape" from its colonial history is often enabled by appropriating the American car and borrowing from the American road genre. These are valued for their associations with freedom, consumption, and national progress, but are also tainted with feelings of nostalgia and displacement. In these road movies the road is thus at once here and elsewhere, leading away from colonial models, perhaps into danger. The road and car, as hybrid sites, attract intense ambivalence. The road movies of this period are characterized by a sense of celebration and a corresponding fatalistic fascination with vulnerability in this search for new landscapes.

The Cars that Ate Paris (1973), for example, is almost allegorical of this change. Paris is a conservative outback township which is protected from "outsiders" by a British Loyalist mayor. Yet, ironically, it depends for its living upon those "outsiders," whose cars are hijacked and gutted by the inhabitants for parts, and turned into hot rods, sinister but comical symbols of hybridity. Indeed, the name "Paris" suggests an "otherness" at the very heart of the Australian countryside.[7] In *Backroads* (1977), the road is a site of complicated economic, racial, and sexual exploitation; its corporate overdetermination is underscored by visual metaphors of the destructive capacity of imported technology and culture on its original human and nonhuman inhabitants. Yet a stolen American car (introduced as a character in its own right in the title sequence – "DJS.530 '62 Pontiac Parisienne") is also a fetishized means of self-expression and escape for both Aboriginal and white drivers. *Running on Empty* (1982) is the most celebratory representation of the infusion of American products and culture with the Australian road. Mike (Terry Serio), the hero, strikes up a friendship with Rebel, the blind owner of a small outback petrol station, who drives a '57 Chevy and uses a recognizably "beat" lexicon. Rebel is linked fantasmatically with the glory days of the American road in the 1950s, when cars were large and you could have "all the gas you could burn for a dollar." It is interesting that in the last two films the reality of contemporary economic imperialism (Mike and his mechanic mate Tony have to push their car along the outback roads because petrol rationing has limited their mobility) is partly displaced by a nostalgia for a mythic American past. Yet, ironically, in both films the cars do not deliver what they promise. This ambivalent canon forms part of a refiguring of Australian space which the *Mad Max* films articulate for a local audience, at the same time as they envisage an international one.

Although the Oil Crisis demonstrated our vulnerability to the world market, national pride was subsequently focused upon technology, centered on our resources boom in the early 1980s, and the rearticulation of Australian identity around corporate, entrepreneurial ideals. The historical antagonism between big business and the "average" Australian was renegotiated into an ideal of shared interests, when, in 1983, the new Prime Minister Bob Hawke introduced the Accord (enterprise bargaining between companies and unions). Paul James observes that nationalistic discourses shifted so far toward an internationally entrepreneurial ethic during this period that "it would no longer seem incongruous that large corporations, including, eventually, transnationals like Esso, would advertise themselves through reference to their Australianness" ("Australia": 73).[8] He argues that the emphasis in many advertisements which tried to construct an affective nationalism was no longer on assimilating transnational corporations into Australian national culture, but rather on creating the Australian citizen as a proud "world customer."

The affective strength of this reorientation could be observed in the media spectacle of the 1983 America's Cup, in which corporate interests and Australian individualism were assimilated into a narrative of pragmatic survivalism for an international audience. The victory of the yacht *Australia II* (owned by a Western Australian business syndicate headed by British-born businessman Alan Bond) facilitated an historically original vision of a new Australian capitalism which represented "the 'man in the street'" (James, "Australia": 10). James claims that the winged keel, which facilitated the victory (invented in 1962 but "discovered" by clever postcolonial appropriation), was presented as embodying "the linkage of the new Australian capitalism and quiet technological confidence" ("Australia": 11). It seemed that we no longer needed to define our identity against Britain[9] – what mattered was that the America's Cup victory was achieved in the fraught waters of multinational capitalism, and that "we" had negotiated them more cunningly than the Americans.[10] The near future was envisaged, then, as a coming of age for Australia, a postcolonial "Change," after which older internal conflicts, dogged by history, were to be replaced by international competitiveness, consensus, and the strategic appropriation and manipulation of international technology and capital. It is clear, then, that a positive attitude toward this reconciliation is in part responsible for a waning of anxiety in the last *Mad Max* film.

Thus the concurrent refiguring of Australian space as "landscape without *shadows*" (Morris, "Panorama": 162), was not simply an inevitable effect of globalization. Instead, as Morris argues, this construction of the landscape in tourist discourses and media spectacles actively promoted Australia as a space for "visiting, investing, cruising, developing" (162). Instead of invoking the "old frontier code of discriminatory closure" (184), which was commemorative and nostalgic and valued the historical associations of place, these media events instead valued the openness of the landscape to mobile bodies and capital. Australia was presented as panoramic, universalized, "a vast reservoir of exotic yet familiar (cross-culturally accessible) resorts and photographic locations" (161). Its infusion with technology was welcomed, for it suggested that "nothing secret, mysterious, troubling or malcontent could find a place to lurk or hide" (162). According to such touristic logic, the "nation" thus came into being as it attracted and facilitated the smooth flow of tourists and money from sight to sight, and the interests of citizens and big business were one and the same. In such a roadless landscape of absolute mobility, Morris notes, conflictual and hostile elements, such as "drought, grasshopper plagues, restless natives" (162), are absorbed into a varied locale as consumable elements. It is difficult, then, in such a climate of perpetual, simulacral change, to grasp the local, historical contingency of these changes to the landscape: a logic which, ironically, the readings of Sharrett and Rummey reproduce.

Yet these new "myths" of landscape had very real material effects on it in the 1970s and 1980s. It is interesting, once again, to turn to Paul James's analysis of advertisements for mining companies. He notes that during the 1980s they minimized the importance of place, infusing the outback of Australia with images of aerospace technology and dinosaurs ("Australia": 103). Space and time were thus universalized so that "[c]ultural symbols such as the 'land', the 'desert', [and] the 'suburban backyard'" (104) were detached from their specific histories and appeared as simulacral and mobile "flavors" of Australianness. In this way the new fusion of corporate interests and nationalism was naturalized and incorporated into the landscape. It was associated with the empowerment of Australians. This consequently facilitated the actual exploitation of the land. At the same time, the affective resonance of earlier, possessive constructions of the landscape was defused. I would argue that this affect was turned into a "resource" which could be "reinvested" in a number of locales. While the acknowledgment that value is not intrinsic to the landscape is a basic tenet of postmodern theories of space, it is worth noting that it was in the interest of big business to grasp this point and encourage the investment of affect into the prolific *narration* of myths of belonging.[11] Dissent was thereby characterized as damaging to Australian progress and, ironically, trivialized by association with earlier forms of imperialism.

These are significant shifts and, as I will now demonstrate, they contribute to the financial, narrative, and spatial organization of the *Mad Max* trilogy as it leaves the road. As Morris notes, such shifts in "mood" do not mean that contemporary audiences necessarily left the cinema having acceded to the films' enabling "messages" about nationalism and landscape ("Tooth and Claw": 261). Yet it is important to acknowledge the historical specificity and industrial strategy behind the framing of the landscape in order to understand how films can take part in "an active part in a politics of opinion" (261) which does have powerful and lasting material effects.

Mad Max tells the story of Max (Mel Gibson), a member of the "Bronze," a ragtag, macho police force which operates from the decaying Halls of Justice in a fading industrial city. Max pursues the Night Rider, a "terminal psychotic," in a high-speed car chase, and forces his car to crash into a derelict truck. This leads the "scoot jockeys," a biker gang led by the Toecutter, to target Max and his family for revenge. The gang members trace Max, who has quit the force, to an idyllic beach getaway, where they run over Jess, his wife, and Sprog, their child. Rejoining the force, Max kills Johnny the Boy in a cold and premeditated act which imitates the gang's incineration of Max's mate, Goose, in his car. Max chains Johnny to an abandoned car and ignites the grass near the petrol tank, giving the boy a saw, and the option to hack off his own leg or burn. We last see Max driving away from the explosion down the highway, staring into the white line at its centre.

When *Mad Max* appeared in 1979, not only the road but the film itself was a site of affective intensity. Its "violence" became the focal point of much critical discussion. One critic, Kevin Childs, remarked that "[v]iolence . . . [had] become as Australian as icy beer" (9). This last comment is interesting, since it suggests the film did seem, at least for Australian audiences, to articulate something disturbing and new at the "heart" of Australia. In part, this feeling of rupture was due to the unresolved tension between the film's ambiguous apocalypticism and its indulgence in the pleasures offered by taking to new roads. It was compounded by the feeling that there was a lack of fit between the notions of Australianness valued in official discourses and the recognizable "change" this film articulated.

"Civilization," in the form of the very recognizable 1970s Australian suburban coastal lifestyle enjoyed by Max, Jess, and Sprog, is directly under siege in *Mad Max*.[12] The government bureaucracy, which theoretically should protect it, is almost helpless, relying upon scavenged parts and fuel to keep Max's police car, the "last of the V-8s," going. The souped-up V-8 is an historically specific object of nostalgia in this futuristic scenario since it is the archetypal vehicle of choice of the suburban "hoon." Its more staid suburban counterpart, the "family" station wagon owned by Max and Jess, is also attacked by the vengeful scoot jockeys. Even the archetypal iconography of the Australian outback, of tinder-dry grass and barbed wire, is contaminated by a sense of threat (it is by lighting the grass that Max ultimately exacts his revenge). Clearly, then, the spatial organization of the film displays a high level of anxiety, at a moment of inflation and vulnerability to the global oil market, about the political effectivity of that older Australian nationalism characterized by a protective government and defensible borders.[13] This new sense of space, represented by the road, represents a threat to the settlement values of a dominant white car-centered "lifestyle." In one of the more horrifying scenes in the film, a young couple's car is "raped" by bikie hordes before they are dragged through its shattered orifices and also raped. To be on the road in *Mad Max*, then, is to experience the vulnerability of bodies and cars to outside, often apparently random, forces. The road is particularly frightening because, once familiar, it has become foreign.

Morris suggests, in addition, that the widespread reaction horror on the part of Australian audiences derived in part from the film's refusal to offer a moral solution to the violence it presented ("Fate": 129).[14] In the context of the Australian film industry in the 1970s, she argues, *Mad Max*'s "affective unpredictability" (129) presented violence in an historically original way by depicting it as something which arises as a result of chance, coincidence, and random forces. She claims that this marked its difference from social realist road films of the same period, like *Backroads* and *F J Holden*, which explained violence away in a highly moralized and politically motivated landscape, and depicted failure as the inevitable result of the heroes' quests. Max is a disturbing hero, in this context, for ultimately he does not seem to represent any positive values. Indeed, the film is preoccupied with a sense that its characters' motives are "contaminated." Fifi, Max's boss, wants to give people their heroes back because they have stopped believing in them. However Max questions his own motives, telling Jess, "I'm beginning to enjoy it. Any longer out there and I'm one of them, you know? A terminal crazy. I need a bronze badge to say I'm one of the good guys." The Bronze seem to be as interested in the pleasures of fast driving, car maintenance, mateship, and leather as in the pursuit of justice. They seem to embody a reactive masculinity, rather than any clear notion of the law. For example, a criminal who has been released legally by the bureaucracy is told, "We'll see you on the roads, scag, we'll see you on the roads." The film betrays an anxiety that a landscape without a definable "centre" may offer no "moral center" or set of values on which heroism may be based.

Yet, as Morris notes, although *Mad Max* was "shocking on first appearance" ("Fate": 129), it also had "utopian force" (130), because it did not present its narrative or the road as the result of a set of fixed, overdetermining circumstances. Mel Gibson's portrayal of the defiance and negative reactivity of the hoon struck an appreciative chord with audiences as a new, unapologetic hero. I remember, too, that when this film came out the marriage of the Australian landscape to American movie codes made it feel particularly exciting and epic. According to the logic of the "cultural cringe," our urban lifestyle and feelings of anxiety had been mythologized and made "serious" by the film's bold rejection of social realism and use of the American movie canon. Significantly, in the figure of the bikies the film exploits American B-grade road movies in order to make our landscape "matter" in relation to America as a cultural "centre."[15] The film's presentation of the road as a volatile and unpredictable space – in which each collision was "an orchestrated spectacle, not an emblematic moment" (Morris, "Fate": 129) – also had the effect of opening it up to competing affective investments. Similarly, although cars are represented as a dying technology (which, as Sharrett notes, "has found little use but to be placed on a circular unproductive course, simply to be used up and destroyed" [83]), the film's ability to use and destroy fourteen vehicles in the course of filming suggests the potential delights of a landscape colonized by a film technology which "travers[ed] the surfaces of space, bodies and equipment" (O'Regan: 127).

In these ways, the success story of *Mad Max* preempted the reorientation of the Australian film industry and nationalist discourses around international success. It set itself up as the "near future" in reaction to the limitations of a social realism which had prevailed in government-supported film culture. *Mad Max* was made entirely with private funds ($380,000) at a time when it was the industry norm to receive up to 50 percent government funding for a film. It was public knowledge that funding had not been applied for because the government was thought unlikely to invest in such a film. Tom O'Regan notes that *Mad Max* was produced "before the tax incentives, before talk of film as 'industry', before meeting the audience, before working within Hollywood and international norms of what constituted cinema had come in" (119). Significantly, *Mad Max* was actually used in the 1980s as an exemplary success story for re-gearing government film policy in terms of exports to global markets. It is important to note that it was instrumental in the development of new industrial strategies which would legitimate the "violence" at its center, and provide new critical discourses through which it could be appreciated. This success, celebrated by the media, government, and film industry, is part of the narrative of *Mad Max*, and it would be read into the subsequent *Mad Max* films. Max's maverick temperament and behavior stood in for the film-makers'.

At this point in time, however, few critics were able to describe the "Australianness" of *Mad Max* in positive terms. The film seemed to be an assault on an industry (and a critical audience) trained to value "serious" and "original" work, and on audiences who seemed dubious and guilty about the pleasures being offered them. Significantly, the key to "understanding" the film for some critics – and thus to distancing themselves from its violence – seems to have been to describe it in purely "mythic" or "simulacral" terms. According to one (American) critic, Michael Sragow, "[t]his movie [would] baffle anyone who doesn't realize that the entire production is an amoral, anarchistic joke." Critics who disliked the film were also forced to analyze it in stylistic terms, claiming that its violence was lacking in social value because it simply imitated models from overseas. Sandra Hall concluded that "there is no originality in [Miller's] work" (66), while according to Martha DuBose, it was "so consistently superficial that one cannot excuse its appeal by ascribing to it higher motives or themes" (21). Thus, by creating what O'Regan terms "a hyperrealised Australia: a cinematised Australia" (126), the makers of *Mad Max* contributed, in an ambivalent fashion, to the reorientation of Australian nationalism away from imperial models dependent on notions of integrity and security, while, at the same time, trivializing the real effectivity of this change as "myth."

Mad Max 2 is situated entirely in the desert outback. Since the conclusion of the first film, an apocalyptic oil war has occurred. Max, who has become an embittered wanderer, living on scavenged petrol and tins of dog food, comes across a commune of white survivors,[16] led by Pappagallo (Mike Preston), who are besieged by a pack of scoot jockeys.[17] In contrast to the crazed, nomadic forays of the pillaging scoot jockeys, the commune embraces a settler ethic, seeking to extend the dirt paths around their commune out to the coast. Inside their circle of modern-day covered wagons (a yellow bus and car bodies), the settlers are refining fuel in order to get to the Gold Coast – represented by a postcard of a bikini-clad woman – where there is nothing to do, as one character puts it, but

Plate 11.1 Mad Max 2.
Casualties of the petrol wars.

"breeeeeed." Max gains entry to the compound by trading for gasoline the life of a commune member he has rescued. Partially won over by the affection of a feral boy (Emil Minty) who has attached himself to the compound, Max agrees to drive the petrol rig during the group's escape. His maneuvers allow the others to escape and Max, almost amused, discovers that the petrol truck actually contains sand. He is alone, and on the road again.

The film's move away from asphalt roads, those traces of colonization, is made possible by the way in which it treats history. To dwell on the history of the landscape, or to argue over claims to it, the film suggests, is to stand in the way of a better future. In this way, the progressivist discourse of nationalism as internationalism which had developed since the making of the first film is used to close down much of the ambiguity of the landscape. Instead, in line with advertisements which incorporated big business and technology into the land-scape, the movement off-road into the desert, with its associations of "emptiness," produces a more universalized, "useful" landscape, which does not yearn for a lost way of life. Yet, because the film still values location over narration, the tracks north still have to be defended.

The narrative of *Mad Max 2* is framed by a prologue and an epilogue, which describe its action from the standpoint of a peaceful future after the conflict. In the opening monologue, an old man recalls "a time of chaos" and a "wasted land." He remembers the oil war which "two mighty warrior tribes" started "for reasons long forgotten." These, however, have occurred long before the important narrative the film will tell, of how Max, "a shell of a man," "learn[ed] to live again" and to find some meaning "in this blighted place." Immediately, the volatility of the road is subsumed within the framework of "imperial history" which, as Paul Carter has argued, narrates historical events as if they were inevitable, rather than the results of local negotiations. The oil crisis is relegated to a past much dimmer and more mythic than the recognizable world of *Mad Max*. It is presented as the result of redundant nationalisms, no longer important in this new world, with no mention of the corporate origins of oil crises. Max, too, is positioned as the survivor of a redundant lifestyle; his car, in the words of a commune dweller, is the "[l]ast of the V-8 Interceptors, a piece of history." This narrative frame also reinscribes the landscape, in line with earlier colonizing discourses, as a *tabula rasa* or empty stage, waiting to be written on by "civilization." Max is faced with the choice of accepting the "future" offered him by Pappagallo of a communal life, or of continuing to roam without purpose the dying world of roads.

In contrast to its predecessor, *Mad Max 2* offers a strong distinction between "good" and "evil" characters. A productive use of resources distinguishes the commune members from the scoot jockeys. According to Pappagallo, the rig is "more than just a tanker of gas." It is the commune's "lifeline to a place beyond that *vermin* on machines, to a place where we can start again." He is presented as a man of few words, who is manufacturing petrol responsibly in order to offer his people a future. By contrast, the environmental devastation of the central "waste-land" of Australia is positioned in the past and attributed to the desire for warfare on the part of "irrational" nation-states. Civilization is thus equated with the *naturalized* exploitation of resources for a better future, a move which recalls the Esso advertisements described above. This "clean" use of technology replaces the older forms of heavy industry, characterized as "men and machines" by the framing monologue. The long chase sequence at the end of *Mad Max 2* – a spectacular choreography of trucks, cars, and stunt people – testifies to the film's corresponding ability to muster resources productively. The glossiness of its mise-en-scène replaces the rough-hewn quality of the exploitation genre, and begins to replicate the smooth negotiation of landscape which characterizes tourist spectacles.[18]

"Foreignness," "unnaturalness," and contamination, by contrast, are not shared by the opposing parties, as they were in *Mad Max*, but associated only with the scoot jockeys, who are in turn associated with the "political," "historical," "conflictual," and "obsolete." Max must clearly choose sides in order to regain his humanity. The Lord Humungus (Kjell Nilsson), the leader of the siege, may have been an army officer, as Sharrett notes, since he carries a wooden case containing his revolver, military decorations, and old photos. His speeches, which use a profusion of political rhetoric ("I am gravely disappointed that again you have made me unleash my dogs of war"), are made through an old-fashioned micro- phone, and are suggestive of the Nuremberg rallies. Presented as "merely a member of an order already extinct before the holocaust began" (Sharrett: 87), he is thus marked as "unnatural." The use of gay S&M elements in his costume seems also aimed to establish the non-productivity of the scoot jockeys in contrast to the "breeeeeeding" commune members. In these ways, the film presents the exploitation of Australia's natural resources as a progressive, environmentally sensitive action – at the same time as the "historical" and the conflicts over territory it involves are expelled from the landscape as greedy hangovers of an imperialism "living off the corpse of the old world," as Pappagallo puts it. Foreshadowing the construction of landscape in the next film, the Gold Coast of Queensland, a tourist site whose importance as a place is determined by market values, marks the desired locus of civilisation within *Mad Max 2*.[19]

In a final narrative of incorporation, we discover, at the end of the film, that the opening monologue was delivered by the Feral Kid, who has grown to adult- hood and become the leader of the "Great Northern Tribe." This white child wears a fur tunic and carries a silver boomerang and is thus coded by this pastiche of "native elements" as having become, in a sense, "aboriginal." I would like to read him as a symbol of reconciliation, of hopeful hybridity, but his function in disavowing the colonial history of the land is highly suspect. This promotion of a consensual and technologized image of space appeared, problematically, at a time when the Australian government was beginning to consider indigenous claims upon the land. The Kid's "indigenized" voice ironically attaches to the narrative a racist construction of Aboriginal "authenticity" while at the same time dismissing as "long forgotten" the actual power struggles of a pre-apocalyptic history. History is thus severed from the film's present, which is figured as a matter of "survival" – of "postness" – rather than of politics. The Feral Kid's metal boomerang, then, unites aboriginality with a productive exploitation of resources. The film consequently offers a mythic trajectory for Australia, in line with our emergent "new nationalism," in which historical relations must be ignored in order to facilitate a productive future, and settlement can be rewritten and authenticated as "indigenousness." Those in possession of superior assets and technology, it appears, become "aboriginal" in a world where older claims have been obliterated by necessity.

The child's "taming" and incorporation into the Great Northern Tribe thus replays early celebrations of the colonial inscription of "civilization" onto the *tabula rasa* of Australia, but in this refiguring of the story from a new beginning, contemporary discourses of postcolonial nationalism are read back into a universal, timeless landscape of "postness" where all parties are vulnerable and all claims are equal. Tony Bennett notes that a discourse of development was often annexed into the public imagery of Australia's leading business corporations during the 1980s which positioned Aborigines as the first questers in a long wave of development toward the future prosperity represented by big business. The Bond[20] Corporation's Bicentennial beer advertisement, for example, represented national history as the triumph over adversity of successive waves of settlers, "whose differences are finally annulled as they make their way through to their ultimate historical reward and destiny: a glass of Swan lager" (78). Thus, the past is presented as a "cumulative process which has delivered the nation into the present as its accomplishment. Yet that present, while marking an accomplishment, does not mark a completion; rather, it stands poised as a moment between a past and a future cast in the same mould" (79).

It is significant that *Mad Max 2* made its location (near Broken Hill, one of Australia's principal mining towns) a tourist attraction. Other film companies also followed Kennedy Miller in exploiting this "empty space." This provides a nice example of how Kennedy Miller's manipulation of film technology and capital in *Mad Max 2* were closely articulated with corporate discourses designed to shape the identity of Australia around entrepreneurial and touristic endeavours. This is encapsulated by Peter Blazey's description of another film producer, Hal McElroy, who, like Miller, presented himself as an internationalist in opposition to that "nationalist majority of the industry which he regard[ed] as yet another manifestation of cultural cringe" (11). McElroy is depicted walking around Broken Hill in Miller's wake, wearing cowboy boots, and scouting its potential as a location. Blazey describes him as "a bounty hunter looking for an international pot of gold. It is a quest which Broken Hill, attuned to the fluctuations of the London base metals market, understands" (11).

The conclusion of *Mad Max 2*, in which the commune's mining interests incorporate indigeneity, allows its sequel, *Mad Max Beyond Thunderdome*, to move beyond obvious mobilizations of the frontier code. In this film, Max, still a wanderer, is ambushed in the desert by an airplane pilot who steals his rig from him. He tracks it to Bartertown, which he is not allowed to enter unless he has something to trade. He offers his skills to Aunty Entity (Tina Turner), the town's leader, in exchange for his rig. Aunty Entity sends him into the underworld of Bartertown, where methane is extracted from pig droppings by slave labor, in order to pick a fight with its rebellious leader, Masterblaster (who is actually two people: an intellectual Master who compensates for his dwarf stature by sitting on the shoulders of the retarded giant, Blaster). Max does as he is told, and Aunty Entity stops the argument, transferring it to Thunderdome, according to law; for, in order to avoid warfare, all disputes are to be solved in this arena by hand-to-hand combat. However, when Max cannot bring himself to kill the childlike Blaster at the end of the gladiatorial contest, he is sentenced (by wheel of fortune) to the gulag. The feral children from the Crack in the Earth rescue him from the desert, mistaking him for "Captain Walker" who, according to prophecy, will lead them to Tomorrowmorrowland. After it becomes clear that Max is not their messiah, Savannah Nix (Helen Buday) leads the children to Bartertown. Max follows them, and together they free the slaves. In a long desert car chase, Max acts as a decoy to divert Aunty and her centurions (led by the lead singer of Rose Tattoo, Angry Anderson), while the children and Master escape in the airplane which appeared at the beginning of the film, founding a new society in the nuked remains of Sydney.

Beyond Thunderdome was produced in a climate receptive to its themes and methods. The strategies of quotation and incorporation with which *Mad Max* flirted anxiously had been absorbed by 1985 into our national success story. Consequently, *Beyond Thunderdome* is far less affectively fraught. Indeed, it has a strangely jokey, tongue-in-cheek quality: even life-and-death conflicts are rendered comic. The disappearance of the road as a site of contestation indicates that place is not felt to "matter" in the same ways it did in the first two films. Instead of concentrating on battles to establish and defend sites against intruders, the film's narrative centers on story-telling, and the feral children's oral narratives constitute a large part of the action. *Beyond Thunderdome* thus reflects contemporary tourist and corporate discourses about space by focusing on the *representation* of place, rather than on place itself.

Certainly, Ross Gibson is correct to claim that the imperial ethic of discriminating closure no longer seems to be at issue in this film. What *Beyond Thunderdome* substitutes for this, however, is a deregulated space, in which to be "home" is simply to choose from a range of easily exchanged locales, all of which must be acknowledged collectively *as* home. The cinematic space is strangely abstracted: it ranges from the Edenic gully, the Crack in the Earth, to Saharan desert sands (the "gulag"), and an "archetypal" post-nuclear town more reminiscent of *Blade Runner* than of any real place on earth. In a *post*-apocalyptic world, the value of these sites is determined less by disputing claims, or reevaluating history, than by projecting a consensual story of the future (for both Aunty Entity and the children are powerful story-tellers). Consequently, all quests are presented as the inevitable results of a postwar necessity which has destroyed all older claims to the land: as the song over the opening credits goes, "You're one of the living, you've gotta stick together." The film closes with Tina Turner singing, "We don't need another hero, we don't need to know the way home." There is an ironic logic in this move, since *all* the settler inhabitants of Australia are constructed as dispossessed but "indigenized" innocents in search of their authentic homeland.

Beyond Thunderdome thus extends the articulation of indigenousness with the

Plate 11.2   Mad Max Beyond Thunderdome.
Max (Mel Gibson) helps the feral children find their way home.

successful management of natural and human resources in *Mad Max 2*. The Crack in the Earth is inhabited by a band of white feral children, who are marked as "indigenous" by a pastiche of "native" dress styles and rituals.[21] Although the name of the gorge marks it significantly as the heart of the land, it is represented as only a temporary residence within a settlement frame, and the children's harmony with nature is equally ersatz. The history which ties them to this place – inscribed on the earth itself with cave murals, and performed in oral narratives which obviously allude to Aboriginal culture[22] – turns out to be false. Max is not Captain Walker, the children's expected rescuer. Significantly, the children yearn to be "salvaged" from their symbiotic relationship with the earth, so that they can return "home" to the city, Sydney (called Tomorrowmorrowland and represented by tourist images on slides), and recover what they have "lost." There they will find the technology to build a better future. The fact that they take Master with them suggests that the future will be orientated around "innocence" and intellect rather than brute force. The new "history" that they articulate when they arrive in the nuked remains of Sydney is the story of their own travels.

Bartertown, on the other hand, is a bordered protectionist economy, run by Aunty Entity (Tina Turner) who, as the ultimate protectionist, tries to lay down social and economic laws which bound her space. She tells Max: "All this I built.

Up to my armpits in blood and shit. Where there was desert now there's a town. Where there was robbery there's trade. Where there was despair now there's hope. Civilization – and I'll do anything to protect it." Bartertown is built from a mishmash of old technology, and uses slave labor in Underworld to refine fuel from pig shit. It is associated not only with the British empire and exploitative industrialism (through visual references to Australia's penal past) but also to the Roman Empire in the costuming of the guards and the gladiatorial combat of Thunderdome. At the moment of Australia's economic deregulation, the film thus associates protectionist economics and the British empire (the "mother country") so explicitly that we are left to conclude that Aunty's town will face a better future because of its disruption by outside forces. Yet at the same time it dehistoricizes Australia's British past by positioning it as part of a transhistorical imperialism which encapsulates both England and ancient Rome.

The casting of the African-American rock star Tina Turner in the role of Aunty Entity is especially interesting, since her Americanness is not coded (like the Roman Empire and convict Australia) as a signifier of imperialism. Instead, her "difference" seems to represent the film-makers' ability to negotiate the international world of film-making and rock promotion. When asked about casting by an interviewer (Heathwood: 125), George Miller remarked with exaggerated naivety: "as we were going to Los Angeles, we said well, why don't we see Tina Turner!" Miller's use of the American rock industry is consequently part of a narrative of Australian boldness and ingenuity. Miller also constructs the space of his own production as a kind of tourist site visited by the world's rock 'n' roll peerage:

> When we started, for some reason all the rock 'n' roll people around the world wanted even bit parts. We got some message from Angry's people and I said I liked Angry and Rose Tattoo, but he couldn't act! Then we saw some of a film he'd done and realised he had real flair. His part evolved too as a result of his ability.
>
> (Heathwood: 143)

Tina Turner thus stars in the narrative of the film's celebration of its own powers of story-telling, and its consequent ability to move capital through space. The film's ability to "salvage" and direct so many purveyors of international expertise – the special effects co-ordinator from *Raiders of the Lost Ark*, the story-board artists from *Return of the Jedi*, and Jarre, the composer for *Lawrence of Arabia* – has been reworked by the film's self-narrativization as the ultimate proof of colonial survivalism. Miller could therefore boast to Heathwood: "We have never said very much about budgets, they're whatever people want to say they are. But yes, I can tell you it was a very big budget; and yes, I think you'd have no problems saying it's the biggest budget for an Australian movie so far" (143).

Max's role shifts in *Beyond Thunderdome* from scavenger to negotiator. His function is to integrate Bartertown and the Crack in the Earth, and he moves with reasonable ease through these different locales. Even the "evil" characters are ultimately cuter than they are dangerous. The contest in Thunderdome marks this critical change in his character. Max is outmanned by the huge Blaster in a gladiatorial spectacle. Suddenly, he uses his superior technical knowledge, blowing a whistle he has picked up in the wilderness to deafen the giant. It is very tempting to read this scene allegorically as the staging of a primal scene of new Australian nationalism similar to the spectacle of the America's Cup. The media circus of Thunderdome even has its own ringmaster, and is treated to the sight of the law's performance, which transforms a game of strength into the triumph of skill. Max salvages and uses a found object in much the same way as *Australia II* used the already existent winged keel, and his positive unoriginality wins the day.

As a coda to the trilogy, Australia's colonial journey of "discovery" into the interior of the land is reversed, but not continued as far as England. "Home" turns out exist in the "tell," which Savannah Nix performs for the feral children in Sydney, holding a baby (the sign of the future) in her arms. She claims that the story she performs, the story of those who "got the luck and started the haul for home" "ain't one body's tell, it's the tell of us all." Savannah adds that the children do the tell every night, "to 'member who we was and where we came from,'" and that they light up the city to guide others in the wilderness "home." Through these means, "home" is produced by the manipulation of narrative, and appears attractive because *others* want to visit it. This corresponds to the reorientation of Australia, at this time, as a tourist site. As Morris notes, a tourist discourse encourages invasion. A touristic space "must be liberal, and open: the foreign and the primitive are commodified and promoted, ghosts are special-effects: the only 'barrier' officially admitted is the strictly economic" ("Panorama": 182). The film's theme song, then, becomes the anthem of a new Australian consciousness asserting that it "doesn't need to know the way home" because home is where it is performed. Significantly, the "knowledge" sought and acquired is not represented as a matter for political debate. Instead, it is conceived of as a practice of learning how to "use" salvaged lives and objects. In the *Mad Max* trilogy, then, the Australian landscape has been gradually rewritten as a *tabula rasa* upon which the philosophies of success in the 1980s can be joyfully written, and where international marketability and opportunistic pragmatism determine our ability to call Australia "home."

Notes

1 I have borrowed this term from Meaghan Morris (*Great Moments*: 5). Later, I use the term "event" as she defines it in the same article. I am indebted on a broader level to

her writings on Australian culture, film, and postmodernity, which I have drawn on in writing this article.

2 Baudrillard writes of the "empty, absolute freedom of the freeways" as "transpolitical" and "affectless" technologies of simulation (5). Morse describes the freeway as a representative space of postmodernity, in which one experiences the "derealisation," feminization, and fragmentation induced by a "homogeneous material culture" (200).

3 It seems doubly strange for Jean Baudrillard to align driving with "speed" and postmodern subjectivity, when in many ways the car is itself an "obsolete" casualty of those other technologies, like satellite communications, supersonic flight, and the "information superhighway," which have supposedly "derealized" the landscape.

4 Dermody and Jacka claim (*Imaginary Industry*: 12) that three main categories of films emerged from this material change: "recognisable and internationally consumable 'Australiana,'" "family fare," and "genre pictures."

5 Since the Second World War, the tariffs which protected Australian industries from the international market have gradually been removed. The Oil Crisis of 1973 increased oil prices fourfold, producing high deficits, a wages explosion, inflation and unemployment.

6 See Hey for an examination of how the film and automotive industries have influenced and supported one another since their inception.

7 A fascination with the demolition and interchangeability of car bodies and human bodies may also reflect an anxiety about the vulnerability of the Australian car industry's manufacture of bodies and parts for a global market.

8 See also McKay and Huber.

9 "It's even better than beating the Poms at cricket," remarked an unnamed spectator at the America's Cup final race (Department of Sport, Recreation and Tourism, Australian Sports Commission: 17).

10 The New York Yacht Club was "defined as embodying decadent capitalism, taking its tactics and arcane rules from its founders, the robber barons of 19th century American big business" (James, "Politics": 10).

11 For this reason I am intrigued by an Esso advertisement (1971) cited by James ("Australia": 91). Beneath a picture of seals sunning themselves on an oil rig there is the caption, "Esso calls it Halibut but the seals call it home." Here, the land is incorporated with multinational economic interests into a new sort of "place." The incorporation of the landscape is presented as natural, while the narration of belonging is presented as mobile and secondary, an "investment" which can be made, by choice, in different locales. It is an interesting and early foreshadowing of the presentation of home and narration in *Beyond Thunderdome*.

12 I would agree, therefore, with Gibson's reading of *Mad Max* as a "spectacular valediction to 1970s Australia" (174).

13 Paul Kelly claims that this older nationalism was based on the ideals embedded in Alfred Deakin's Australian Settlement, which promoted a white Australia policy, industry protection, wage arbitration, state paternalism, and imperial benevolence.

14 Phillip Adams, for example, called for the film to be banned, while Tom O'Regan "remember[s] saying aloud to no one in particular in the theatre, 'This film is evil'" (O'Regan: 126).

15 With its use of extreme close-ups, Brian May's driving score, and jerky pans and zooms, the film deliberately bears stylistic similarities to a number of American film genres, such as Westerns, B-grade beach movies, and bikie exploitation films of the

1950s and 1960s. The scene in which the Toecutter and his gang invade a small country town clearly pays homage to *The Wild One*.

16 The commune dwellers are dressed in neutral and cream tones, which connote both the preference for natural fibers of the environmental movement and the costume of "good" settlers in American Western iconography.

17 They are dressed more flamboyantly than the scoot jockeys in the first film, in a more consciously "pastiched" mishmash of "subcultural" costumes, suggestive of the influence of punk, gay S&M, B-grade Nazi movies, and heavy metal.

18 It reaches its apotheosis in *Beyond Thunderdome*, which privileges crane shots and aerial views, emphasizing a swift and nearly affectless ability to pass between locales.

19 It is interesting that in 1991 this logic found its material form. The Gold Coast was refigured by Warner Roadshow Studios as the "film and television capital" of Australia. Southeast Queensland was particularly attractive to film producers because of the "variety of scenery available" (*Gold Coast Bulletin*: 17). I am grateful to Dr Ruth Barcan for making available to me her Ph.D. research on the Gold Coast.

20 Swan breweries were owned by the same Alan Bond who owned *Australia II*.

21 Strangely, by acceding to the film's demands to be read as mythic, Gibson notes that these feral children look like John White's sixteenth-century portraits of American Indians, but ignores the film's overt references to Aboriginal culture.

22 Bob Hodge compares *Beyond Thunderdome* with the story "Jilminti," told by Dave Lamey in the Kuniyanti language and transcribed by Dr Bill McGregor. He is positive about this appropriation, claiming that each text constructs a place for the other's culture, although each affirms "its primary allegiance to its own cultural group" (287).

Works Cited

Adams, Phillip. "The Dangerous Pornography of Death." *The Bulletin* (May 1, 1979): 38–41.

Anonymous. "Coast 'to Be Capital of Aussie Films, TV'." *Gold Coast Bulletin* (June 24, 1991): 17.

Baudrillard, Jean. *America*, trans. Chris Turner (1986). London: Verso, 1988.

Bennett, Tony. "The Shape of the Past." *Nation, Culture, Text: Australian Cultural and Media Studies*, ed. Graeme Turner. London: Routledge, 1993. 72–90.

Blazey, Peter. "Film Glitter Dispels Broken Hill Gloom." *The Weekend Australian Weekend Magazine* (July 23–4, 1983): 2.

Carter, Paul. *The Road to Botany Bay*. London: Faber & Faber, 1987.

Childs, Kevin. "Doctor George Ladles out Horror," *The Age* (April 6, 1979): 9.

Department of Sport, Recreation and Tourism, Australian Sports Commission. *Australian Sport: A Profile*. Canberra: Australian Government Publishing Service, 1985.

Dermody, Susan and Jacka, Elizabeth. *The Screening of Australia: Anatomy of a Film Industry*, vols. 1 and 2. Sydney: Currency, 1987–8.

—— eds. *The Imaginary Industry: Australian Film in the Late '80s*. North Ryde: AFTRS Publications, 1988.

DuBose, Martha. "Violent, Lacking in Social Value." *The Sydney Morning Herald* (July 7, 1979): 21

Gibson, Ross. *South of the West: Postcolonialism and the Narrative Construction of Australia*. Bloomington: Indiana University Press, 1992.

Hall, Sandra. "Cashing in on Cheap Thrills." *The Bulletin* (April 24, 1979): 66.

Heathwood, Gail. "Hello Tina, Max is Back." *Vogue* (May, 1985): 124–5, 143.

Hey, Kenneth. "Cars and Films in American Culture, 1929–1959." *The Automobile and American Culture*, eds. David L. Lewis and Laurence Goldstein. Ann Arbor: Michigan University Press, 1980. 193–205.

Hodge, Bob. "Aboriginal Myths and Australian Culture." *Southern Review* 19.3 (1986): 277–90.

James, Paul. "Australia in the Corporate Image: A New Nationalism." *Arena* 63 (1983): 69–106.

—— "The Politics of the Winged Keel." *Arena* 65 (1983): 6–14.

Jameson, Fredric. *Postmodernism, or, the Cultural Logic of Late Capitalism*. London: Verso, 1991.

Kelly, Paul. *The End of Certainty*. St Leonards, NSW: Allen & Unwin, 1992.

McKay, Jim and Huber, Debbie. "Swan Sport and Ideology: 'They Said You'd Never Make It . . . '" *Arena* 83 (1988): 117–29.

Morris, Meaghan. "Panorama: The Live, the Dead and the Living." *Island in the Stream: Myths of Place in Australian Culture*, ed. Paul Foss. Leichhardt, NSW: Pluto, 1988. 160–87.

—— "Tooth and Claw: Tales of Survival, and *Crocodile Dundee*." *The Pirate's Fiancée: Feminism, Reading, Postmodernism*. London: Verso, 1988. 241–69.

—— "Fate and the Family Sedan." *East–West Film Journal* 4.1 (1989): 113–34.

—— *Great Moments in Social Climbing: King Kong and the Human Fly*. Double Bay: Local Consumption Publications, 1992.

Morse, Margaret. "An Ontology of Everday Distraction: The Freeway, the Mall, and Television." *Logics of Television: Essays in Cultural Criticism*, ed. Patricia Mellencamp. Bloomington: Indiana University Press, 1990. 193–221.

O'Regan, Tom. "The Enchantment with Cinema: Film in the 1980s." *The Australian Screen*, eds. Albert Moran and Tom O'Regan. Ringwood: Penguin, 1989. 118–45.

Rohdie, Sam. "The Australian State: A National Cinema," *Framework* 22/3 (1983): 28–30.

Rummey, Ariane. "Oltre Nature – Landscape Technology and Australian Films." *On the Beach* 13 (1988): 46–53.

Sharrett, Christopher. "Myth, Male Fantasy, and Simulacra in *Mad Max* and *The Road Warrior*." *Journal of Popular Film and Television* 13.2 (1985): 80–91.

Sragow, Michael. Rev. of *Mad Max*. *Los Angeles Herald Examiner* (May 9, 1980).

Stratton, Jon. "What Made *Mad Max* Popular? The Mythology of a Conservative Fantasy." *Art and Text* 9 (Autumn 1983): 37–56.

Watkins, Evan. *Throwaways: Work Culture and Consumer Education*. Stanford: Stanford University Press, 1993.

12

HOME AND AWAY
Friends of Dorothy on the road in Oz

Pamela Robertson

In the cinema it is not uncommon to experience involuntary memory. It can happen that we are suddenly and unexpectedly seized, in the midst of the most seemingly mundane film, by an overwhelming sensation of sensuous reminiscence.

(Stern: 39)

The truth is that once we have left our childhood places and started to make up our lives, armed only with what we have and are, we understand that the real secret of the ruby slippers is not that "there's no place like home," but rather there is no longer any such place as home: except, of course, for the home we make, or the homes that are made for us, in Oz: which is anywhere, and everywhere, except for the place from which we began.

(Rushdie: 57)

If the road movie is in some deep sense about the road itself, and the journey taken, more than about any particular destination, it is still a genre obsessed with home. Typically, the road takes the traveler away from home. Sometimes, the road leads to a new home, as in frontier narratives or tales of emigration. As often, in various kinds of escape or travel narratives, the road just leads away – away from boredom, or danger, or family, or whatever it is that produces the desire or need for something called "away" as opposed to the place called "home." While it provides an escape from and alternative to home, and home can be "anywhere, and everywhere" on the road (or, in another formulation, "anyplace I hang my hat"), the trope of the road still requires the concept of home as a structuring absence: Very often, as Corey Creekmur suggests elsewhere in this volume, from the perspective of the road, either "you can't go home again" or "there's no place like home."

The Wizard of Oz (1939), of course, paradigmatically enacts the road movie's contradiction between the desire for home and away. In *The Wizard of Oz* the

271

discovery that "there's no place like home" takes place only through leaving that home and journeying to a parallel but much more spectacular universe. It enacts Freud's *fort/da* game of home and away as a contrast between Kansas and Oz, black-and-white and colour, reality and fantasy. As Salman Rushdie says, the song "Over the Rainbow"

> embodies with the purity of an archetype . . . the human dream of *leaving*, a dream at least as powerful as its countervailing dream of roots. . . . In its most potent emotional moment, this is unarguably a film about the joys of going away, of leaving the greyness and entering the colour, of making a new life in the 'place where there isn't any trouble'. . . . It is a celebration of Escape, a grand paean to the Uprooted Self, a hymn – *the* hymn – to Elsewhere.
>
> (Rushdie: 23)

As Rushdie and Gore Vidal both point out, given the glorious magic of Oz and the extreme hard bleakness of Kansas, why Dorothy wants to go home is never entirely clear: the dream of leaving seems so strong, especially in Garland's magnificent performance. But while Dorothy dreams an escapist Technicolor dream of a no place "over the rainbow," upon her arrival in that place, that Oz, like a homesick tourist abroad, immediately and irrationally she begins to yearn for home.

If Oz, in Rushdie's gloss on it, is the "anywhere, and everywhere" or imaginary home where we all end up when we have left our original home, it is also a name given to a real place (and imagined community) on this planet. Australia is a self-proclaimed Oz. And it is perhaps no accident that in the third Oz book, *Ozma of Oz* (1907), when the obligatory disaster strikes that takes her back to Oz, Dorothy and her uncle are on board a ship to Australia – a land that for centuries appeared on maps as *terra incognita*, unknown land, and that white colonialists proclaimed *terra nullius*, land of no one (a concept officially discredited only in 1993 with the Native Title Act). The nickname Oz has been used collo-quially by Australians since as early as 1908 and increasingly since the 1970s to refer to their nation and themselves. Australia's self-creation as an Oz is tied to an ongoing nationalist project of self-definition. The nickname has emerged in intellectual circles as part of a search for national identity, in, for instance, the radical *Oz Magazine* (1963–73) and the cultural studies volume, *Myths of Oz*, on constructions and representations of Australianness. In recent years, the state has given the nickname official currency in such acts as dubbing the lottery *Oz Lotto* and calling a CD-Rom for schoolchildren about Australia's national identity *Oz ID*. Etymologically, the Australian nickname originates not with Baum's Oz but as a slang pronunciation of the abbreviations Aus. and Aussie. Yet the parallel to Dorothy's Oz lurks in Australia's other nickname, the initially ironic "Lucky

Country," and, more explicitly, in David Williamson's play, *Emerald City*, about life in Sydney.

In the last few years, living in Australia, having lived most recently in the American Midwest before that, I've thought a lot about Dorothy and her desire to return home. In that other Oz, I am fascinated by another musical road movie, a film structured around a trip west and a return home, a film that reminds me of *The Wizard of Oz*: the Australian film *The Adventures of Priscilla, Queen of the Desert* (1994).

The Adventures of Priscilla, Queen of the Desert tells the story of two drag queens and one transsexual travelling from Sydney into the Australian outback on a bus dubbed Priscilla for a high camp lipsynching drag gig in Alice Springs. As in *The Wizard of Oz*, each character has his/her own motivation for taking the trip. Tick/Mitzie (Hugo Weaving) goes to help his wife by taking over parental duty toward his son Benjamin (Mark Holmes). The transsexual, Bernadette (Terence Stamp), joins him as a means to escape her grief over the death of her husband Trumpet (named not for his musical abilities but for an extended foreskin). Adam/Felicia (Guy Pearce) is motivated by the dream of climbing King's Canyon, in the center of Australia, as a Queen. In the course of their journey, in line with the conventions of the road movie, these three main characters, all white, come into contact with a variety of people who provide a range of responses to their queerness and cross-dressing. Once fulfilled, however, Adam's dream feels anti-climactic for the three drag queens who in the incongruity of their surroundings become like Dorothy in her Oz: they want to go home.

The Adventures of Priscilla, Queen of the Desert was viewed by Australians as part of an ongoing effort to produce a truly Australian cinema and culture, a culture defined against both British heritage and American cultural imperialism. Before being screened in Australia, *Priscilla* went on the road. It premiered at the Castro Theatre in San Francisco as part of the San Francisco International Film Festival in May 1994, then screened in the "Un Certain Regard" section of Cannes a week later. It officially opened in America in August 1994, before finally opening in Australia in September, 1994. Most reviews and commentaries in the Australian press ignored the specific content of the film – in terms either of the film's genre, its queer content, or its politics – in favor of its characterization as an *Australian* film. *Priscilla* stood (along with *The Sum of Us*, 1994) as a milestone of Australia's entry into the international gay film market – its gayness and Australianness, and the presumed surprise of its being gay *and* Australian, were equally important. In selling the film to Australian audiences, critics focused primarily on its critical success at Cannes and its box-office success in America (cf. Brunette; Connelly; Holgate; McCarthy; Maslin; Urban; Williams). On the one hand, the necessity for the film to have the stamp of approval from outside Australia before being tested in Australia was evidence of a continued "cultural cringe" or national inferiority complex in Australia. But, on the other hand, Australian critics and viewers valued *Priscilla* as evidence that the film industry could compete in a global market, not only gaining international recognition by showing at festivals and winning Academy recognition for its costume designers, Lizzie Gardiner and Tim Chappel, but also drawing large box-office receipts. *Priscilla* was taken as a sign of a shift in Australian film-making, away from "the nationalist, the populist, the touristy" (Jacka: 125) – the costume dramas of the 1970s and mythified Dundeeism of the 1980s – toward a cinema that works "more with a notion of difference, adopting a position which acknowledges all the diversity within Australia but also maintains that, in spite of this diversity, there are still significant differences between what is Australian and what is not" (Jacka: 123).

This essay examines *Priscilla* as a road movie which is self-consciously about difference and diversity in Australia. I suggest that we must understand the degree to which the categories "gay" and "Australian" are defined in the film through their opposition to other categories, especially "woman," "immigrant," and "native." Rather than assert a direct path, or road, of influence from *The Wizard of Oz* to *The Adventures of Priscilla, Queen of the Desert*, this essay uses *The Wizard of Oz* as a point of departure and reference for my analysis of *Priscilla*. I explore how concepts of home and away intersect with concepts of difference in *Priscilla* and suggest ways in which identity politics intertwine with how we conceive and remember home.

"We're Not in Kansas Anymore"

Aspects of *The Wizard of Oz* and its star Judy Garland have, of course, been taken up as part of a camp counter-canon, and the film can be read as being about queer difference. Corey Creekmur and Alexander Doty elaborate on the film's links to camp and queer culture and its appeal to "friends of Dorothy" as follows: "*The Wizard of Oz* is a story in which everyone lives in two different worlds, and in which most of its characters live two very different lives while its emotionally confused and oppressed teenage heroine longs for a world in which her inner desires can be expressed freely and fully" (Creekmur and Doty: 3). They identify possible queer-encoded characters in the "sissy lion, an artificial man who cannot stop crying, and a butch femme couple of witches." Against its own domestic motto, *The Wizard of Oz* offers a narrative about leaving conventional models of domesticity and creating alternate families and alternate homes. Even back in Kansas, Dorothy's family consists of Aunts and Uncles, stereotypically privileged figures in queer iconography. Equally important to a camp reading, I think, is the way *The Wizard of Oz* captures the feeling of being different, out of place, incongruous, not at home. This feeling of incongruity is suggested by Dorothy's oft-quoted and parodied line, "Toto, I have a feeling we're not in Kansas anymore."

Plate 12.1 Dorothy as immigrant to a culture that already consists of many varied inhabitants. Ray Bolger and Judy Garland in *The Wizard of Oz*.

The Wizard of Oz can also be read as a film about travel and emigration in a multicultural world. In this light, Dorothy is the out-of-towner or the newest immigrant to a culture that already consists of many varied inhabitants. Her trip can be seen in terms of her negotiation of difference both as she encounters new customs and "persons" (Witches and Munchkins and Tin Men and so on) and as she is rendered different and strange by her new surroundings.

As Richard Dyer suggests in his elegant piece on Garland, Garland's embodiment of difference within ordinariness is a key aspect of her camp appeal. In both a camp and a multicultural analysis, her difference is precisely her ordinariness. Removed from Kansas to Oz, Dorothy is a spectacle of ordinariness in a spectacular world. In the panopticon of Oz, Dorothy is constantly under surveillance – both the Wicked Witch of the West and Glinda watch her every move. Though she is subject to the Wicked Witch's power, and requires Glinda's occasional protection, Dorothy's difference from the extraordinary inhabitants of Oz also gives her quite surprising power over them. Recall the Wicked Witch of the West's shock at this power: "What a world, what a world! Who would have thought a good little girl like you could destroy my beautiful wickedness?" From the perspective of an outsider, Dorothy exercises moral judgments about behaviors in Oz, as when she criticizes the Lion for attacking tiny Toto, or the all-powerful Wizard of Oz for making false promises. Like the stranger with no name in a Western, Dorothy conquers Oz before returning home: she kills both Wicked Witches and demystifies and displaces the Wizard – replacing him with her friends, Tin Man, Lion, and Scarecrow – so that "All Hail Dorothy." As an unwitting émigré, however, she opts to return to familiar terrain – terrain that is familiar to her and in which she is familiar.

Like *The Wizard of Oz*, *Priscilla* enacts the experience of the road as one of displacement and incongruity. In interviews, director/writer Stephan Elliott tells again and again how he came up with the idea for the film. Seeing "a plume of feathers break from a drag queen's head-dress during a [Sydney Gay and Lesbian] Mardi Gras parade and go tumbling down a deserted street like a tumbleweed from a Sergio Leone Western," Elliott came up with the idea of "drag queens in the outback" (vii). Thus the displaced imagery of the American West in Leone's Italian landscape (or the similarly displaced Western landscape of Oz) undergoes a further displacement as a drag queen's feathers are substituted for tumbleweed and are placed in an Australian setting. The film relies on the spectacular and sometimes hilarious contrast between the gorgeous artifice of drag and the stark and alien landscape. Echoed by Adam's dream of climbing King's Canyon in full drag ("a cock in a frock on a rock"), Elliott dreams a movie based on the incongruous spectacle of drag culture and, by implication, gay culture, in the outback.

Plate 12.2 The drag queen as spectacle: Adam/Felicia (Guy Pearce) atop the eponymous bus in *Priscilla, Queen of the Desert*. Courtesy of Pictoral Pics.

In a reversal of *The Wizard of Oz*, the drag queens in *Priscilla* are spectacles of difference in a drab world, inhabitants of Emerald City who somehow end up in territories that appear to be much like Baum and MGM's conceptions of Kansas. Sometimes in *Priscilla*, the three drag queens make spectacles of themselves, as when Tick, on a bet, joined by Adam, parades down the main street of Broken Hill in drag, or when the drag act performs musical numbers (to largely unenthusiastic audiences). Being a spectacle, however, also entails being victim to homophobia, as when anti-gay graffiti are spray-painted on their bus in Broken Hill, or when Adam is nearly gay-bashed in Coober Pedy.

The film takes on the signs of gay identity politics in its focus on drag queens, who have become increasingly the chief ambassadors of queer representational politics, generally, and – via the Gay and Lesbian Mardi Gras – of Sydney's gay community in particular. It attends to the constructedness of gender (drag performance, transsexuality) and it characterizes gay identity and sexuality as potentially fluid and mobile, particularly in relation to Tick (married with a son, but not clearly bisexual) and Bob (straight, in love with a transsexual). The film engages gay politics directly not only in its ideal portrait of Tick's son, Benjamin – who *wants* his father to have a boyfriend and *wants* him to lipsynch ABBA – but also in its scenes of gay-bashing and homophobia.

However, the encounter with others on the road needs to be understood as not only an encounter between queer and straight culture but also between men and women and within the context of Australia's problematic multiculturalism. Rather than view all identities as performative, constructed, and fluid, the film insists on the authenticity and fixity of others in the film, who become part of the fixed and alien landscape. In relation to queer identity politics, the film offers an idealistic and utopian vision of tolerance, for which Benjamin is the film's objective correlative. However, the ideal of tolerance is unevenly distributed in the film, and three scenes, in particular, seem to be out of (lip)synch with the tone and politics of the movie. These scenes involve the trio's encounters with, first, a lower-class white butch woman, second, a Filipino stripper, and, third, a group of Aboriginal people. I discuss these scenes below.

"Only the Bad Witches are Ugly"

In Broken Hill, a butch white woman, Shirley (June Marie Bennett) tries to prevent *Priscilla*'s three drag queens from getting a drink in a hotel pub. Bernadette, the transsexual, decisively cuts her down: "Now listen here, you mullet. Why don't you just light your tampon and blow your box apart, because it's the only bang you're ever going to get, sweetheart." This cutting remark provokes straight male laughter in the diegesis (and presumably for the film's audience) at the biological woman's expense and enables the three drag queens to bond homosocially with the male redneck population. But what is being laughed at here? Certainly, the woman represents a threat, a cruel homophobia that must be diffused for the drag queens to be accepted. She asks: "Where did you come from, Uranus?" Her crude joke about gay male sexuality, in a sense, merits one about female sexuality. But, despite its emphasis on her biological femininity (bleeding, reproductive), the joke on her presumes a failure on her part to achieve normal female sexuality (she's unattractive, unable to get a "bang"). Also, her association with the rednecks, her apparent status as a laborer, her dirty tank top, and her lack of makeup all mark her as a lower-class woman, whom Bernadette outclasses in a drinking match as well as verbally. In opposition to butch lower-class femininity, then, this scene privileges drag queen femininity, associated with the artifice and self-commodification of costume and makeup (Tick sells Wo-Man cosmetics "for the heavy-duty woman in all of us") over "natural" "heavy-duty" femininity. The joke thus fulfills the stereotype of gay male misogyny by asserting that drag queens and transsexuals are more appealing than biological women.

"I'll Show you how to get Apples"

The trio's act in a small township pub is upstaged by a Filipino woman, Cynthia (Julia Cortez). Cynthia makes a grotesque spectacle of herself doing a striptease and shooting ping-pong balls out of her G-string, to the horror of the drag artists and the delight of all the straight men in the bar, except her white husband, Bob (Bill Hunter). Cynthia's act succeeds with the diegetic audience whereas the drag act bombs. The film spectator's point of view is already aligned with the drag queens and against the unappreciative rednecks. We must, therefore, find her act – and the redneck straight male response to it – grotesque and embarrassing.

If Shirley represents failed femininity as sexual lack, Cynthia represents an excess that also marks her as a failure. Whereas the drag act parodies female stereotypes, Cynthia seemingly inhabits them. Her act appears to represent her true self which the film paints as genuinely perverse. The film primarily restricts its narration to the actions of the three drag queens. But the narration breaks away from the trio once, to show Cynthia at home, enraged and screaming, then discovering the locked-away ping-pong balls for her act. The shots of her ecstatic discovery of the ping-pong balls serve to confirm that Cynthia's act is not an act but an acting out of her rage and her desire: Earlier, we've seen Cynthia continually shut up, shoved indoors, and dismissed.

Cynthia's difference, like Shirley's, stands out particularly at the pub, a space defined in Australian mythology as a "home away from home" especially for men (Fiske et al.: 5). Bob says that Cynthia isn't allowed in the pub because "She's got a problem with alcohol . . . she makes a complete fool of herself." Tick responds,

"Oh I know how she feels." Despite this apparent sympathy, neither Tick nor any of the other characters in the film knows or cares how Cynthia feels. Because Bob is characterized as a "gentleman" who recalls fondly his youthful visits to see Les Girls, we aren't allowed to sympathize with her rage at being left home alone while her husband goes to the pub to watch the drag act. Our sympathy for Bob, rather than Cynthia, is confirmed when she puts down the size of his "ding-a-ling" in front of the drag queens and, later, when we discover that she tricked a drunken Bob into marriage on the mistaken assumption that he was her ticket to Sydney.

As a foreign immigrant, Cynthia, whom Bernadette dubs a "mail-order bride," simply cannot or will not fit into Australian life. Cynthia – castrating, foreign, manipulative, and perversely sexualized – is thus characterized as a sort of madwoman in the attic, a figure like *Jane Eyre*'s Bertha – the foreigner who traps the good white man in a deceitful marriage, and then drags him "through all the hideous and degrading agonies which must attend a man bound to a wife at once intemperate and unchaste" (Brontë: 334). As with Bertha, her removal from the scene makes possible the formation of the ironically more "natural" couple, Bob and Bernadette. But whereas Rochester's marriage to Bertha takes place within the twisted logic of colonial expansion, and on her home turf, Cynthia's presence in Bob's life reverses the structure – blame for this marriage can be placed on the foreign immigrant whose presence in Australia, and especially in the sacred pub, is an embarrassing intrusion.

"The Horse of a Different Color"

When their bus breaks down, the men are found by an Aboriginal man who brings them back to his fringe camp. The men share a kind of cross-cultural exchange with the Aboriginal people, each group performing separately, the Aborigines singing African-American blues ("I Feel Alright"), the drag queens miming Gloria Gaynor's "I Will Survive," with one Aboriginal man, Alan (Alan Dargin), eventually joining the white men in drag.

The exchange between the Aboriginal people and the drag queens could be taken as a scene of bonding between two minority cultures. Anthropologist John von Sturmer's description of Aboriginal culture and white perceptions of it could apply equally to gay culture:

> Aboriginal societies . . . can only be treated as spectacle, as tableau. Is it because they lie beyond the possibility of a truly lived engagement? It is still the case, as it has been from the beginning, that they do not live according to "civilised" notions of society, refinement, propriety, group welfare or personal well-being. They fight too much, they drink too much, fuck too

much, they are too demanding, they waste their money and destroy property. But a lack of restraint, caution, or calculation is not necessarily an absence or a failing. It can be a superfluity. A refusal: a refusal to accept the repressive principle.

(von Sturmer: 139)

The association between Aboriginality and excess could provide a point of identification for the gay men, who are also stereotyped as excessive and turned into spectacle; and their joint performance could be a celebration and recognition of their mutual refusal of dominant conventions. However, the film does not extend this comparison because it provides no insight into Aboriginal culture. First, there is very little dialogue exchanged at all. The Aboriginal characters react but, aside from Alan, do not interact. And the film doesn't develop the relationship between Alan and the drag queens. Alan may or may not be gay – there's some suggestion of an attraction between him and Tick – but, unlike Bob, his potential role as a lover is never developed. Rather than complex characters like the drag queens, the Aboriginal people, like the butch woman and the castrating Filipino, play stock stereotypical roles *as Aborigines*. In the credits, Alan appears merely as "Aboriginal Man," a racial type or anthropological specimen, rather than a character. This, despite the fact that he is named within the diegesis.

Moreover, if the logic of this exchange with the Aboriginal characters is meant to represent the mutual recognition of two oppressed groups, we need to ask why the film fails to extend this recognition to the equally embattled figures of Shirley or Cynthia. The latter, in particular, is also stereotyped as excessive (and performative!). Less obviously hostile than the portrayal of either Shirley or Cynthia, the scene with the Aborigines seems no less stereotypical. In a sense, by privileging the Aboriginal people, and portraying them as happy singing and dancing natives, naturally and automatically tolerant, the film ultimately represents a stereotype as egregious as the grotesque Filipino. The Aboriginal characters are not so much united with the white drag queens but existing *for* them.

The scene with the Aborigines represents the hauntingly familiar use of blackness as an authenticating discourse in camp. Blackness and authenticity are inextricably intertwined in the racial imaginary through associations with folk peoples, folk culture, primitivism, sexuality, spirituality, and a host of other racial stereotypes. Because whiteness, as Richard Dyer says, "secures its dominance by seeming not to be anything in particular" (Dyer, "White": 141), representations of normative whiteness foreground race and ethnicity as categories of difference. Queer and camp representations, though non-normative in terms of sex and gender, are still consistently defined through categories of racial difference and especially blackness.

To be precise, what I am calling "blackness" in camp is almost always represented by Black Atlantic cultures and peoples. Most often, the trope of authenticity circulates around African-American culture and especially African-American music. So Mae West and Madonna, for example, both foreground their affinity with African-American culture as much as gay male culture by performing African-American music and borrowing aspects of African-American "style." What happens, then, to notions of Aboriginality as they become part of a transnational camp discourse reliant on Black Atlantic imagery and stereotypes? As Paul Gilroy asks in another context:

> What contradictions appear in the transmission and adaptation of cultural expression by other diaspora populations, and how will they be resolved? . . . Where music is thought to be emblematic and constitutive of racial difference rather than just associated with it, how is music used to specify general issues pertaining to the problem of racial authenticity and the consequent self-identity of the ethnic group?
>
> (Gilroy: 75–6)

In *Priscilla*, the Aborigines take on signs of an oppressed African-American culture through a generic and musical affiliation. They also represent a generic "blackness" as appreciative and naive audience for the drag act. But the scene also depends on unique and specific signs of Aboriginality that mark this as an Australian encounter. First, the scene with the Aboriginal people functions like an African-American specialty number in a Hollywood musical, numbers which showcase African-American talent, but are separable from the diegesis. Given the film's links to the musical, this seems hardly accidental. Second, the Aborigines perform African-American blues for the appreciative white audience and they form the most enthusiastically appreciative audience for the drag act. They thus authenticate the group's act and their gayness which, in turn, lends the aura of cool to the Aborigines, an aura denied to the rednecks earlier. Third, the Aborigines also insert the sound of the didgeridoo into the drag act, thus adding a live folk and specifically Aboriginal element to the prerecorded disco song.

Moreover, the scene at the Aboriginal fringe camp partakes of what Athol Chase describes as a stereotypical romantic nostalgia toward Aborigines "by those who see a museum or zoological value in having a 'genuine' Aboriginality available for inspection when the occasion suits." This nostalgia, according to Chase, places some Aborigines, at least, "at the nature end of the people–nature spectrum" (Chase: 23). In the scene at the camp, Adam refers to the gathering as a corroboree, or ritual gathering. By calling the party a corroboree, the film simultaneously attributes folk or religious significance to the gathering and transforms it into a spectacle for white people, much like the "Traditional Central Australian Corroborees" which have been performed as tourist attractions at the

Diamond Springs Casino Amphitheatre in Alice Springs (Fiske et al.: 128) – and similar to the drag show which is presented as a straight tourist spectacle at the casino in Alice.

As *Myths of Oz* points out, "The Aborigine is a personification of the central Australian landscape: each is equally and similarly opposed to the urban lifestyle of the typical white Australian" (Fishe et al.: 128) The sequence at the Aboriginal camp follows a segment which shows Tick choreographing numbers. During this segment, which parodies the famous Australian film *Picnic at Hanging Rock*, we get shots from Tick's point of view of various native lizards in the outback – lizards that get incorporated, along with emus, into the big number ("Finally") at the Alice Springs hotel and casino. Despite the fact that Tick has a vantage point from atop a high cliff, neither he nor Bernadette, who treks from the broken-down bus to the road looking for help, see the Aboriginal camp, which is close enough to the bus for the men to walk back to it to put on their costumes when they decide to perform. The camp seems to rise out of the landscape, or to merge with it. The association between Aboriginality and the landscape is furthered by the film's use of nondiegetic didgeridoo music when the trio first sees the outback. Like the lizards, the Aborigines provide a concrete image of the bush available for the plot when the occasion suits but disappearing from view otherwise – as Alan disappears once he has brought Tick to Bob. Not surprisingly or coincidentally, the concrete image of feathers caught on brush in the bush, emblematic of Elliott's dream of "drag queens in the outback," appears at the desertion of the Aboriginal camp.

"There's No Place Like Home"

"A myth does not analyse or solve problems. It represents them as already analysed and solved; that is, it presents them as already assembled images, in the way a scarecrow is assembled from bric-a-brac and then made to stand for a man" (Said: 312). At the end of the film, Bernadette decides to stay with Bob in Alice Springs while Tick and Adam return to Sydney with Benjamin. The home that Tick and Adam return to is defined in the film as providing a barrier between the gay community and a hostile world. Bernadette says: "It's funny. We all sit around mindlessly slagging off that vile stick-hole of a city. But in its strange way it looks after us. I don't know if that ugly wall of suburbia has been put up to stop them getting in, or us getting out." The trip out of the city and into the heart of Australia serves to confirm this appreciation for Sydney's insular and protective containment. The encounters with "them" on the outside prove the superiority of the "vile" city and reinforce the desire to keep the barriers between. Benjamin takes his place within this insular world, but the film stops all other "others" from getting in.

In *Priscilla*, as in *The Wizard of Oz*, the trip away from home serves both to increase appreciation for home and to reformulate family bonds, as Tick is able to incorporate Benjamin and fatherhood into his life. Their absence, like Dorothy's, also makes people at home appreciate Tick and Adam more. Before leaving, when Tick and Adam perform "I've Never Been to Me," the audience largely ignores their show, then one customer throws a can of beer at Tick's head. By contrast, their return performance of ABBA's "Mamma Mia" receives a wildly enthusiastic response from the audience so that, as the number ends and Tick removes his wig, he says "It's great to be home."

Whereas *The Wizard of Oz* maintains the division between the spectacular and different Oz and the colorless and ordinary Kansas, *Priscilla* allows queer difference and family values to coexist in a self-created and spectacular home. But the return home in *Priscilla*, as in *The Wizard of Oz*, can also be read as a rejection of difference and a return to familiarity. Both films emphasize the road movie's potential conservatism in the way they use the road and the encounter with others on the road to reaffirm the benefits of staying home. As camp, these road movies seemingly allow for models of difference and diversity but, ultimately, by opting for the familiarity of their own backyard, they reinscribe difference rather than acknowledge diversity.

In *Priscilla*, as in that other Oz, the discovery that "there's no place like home" takes place only through leaving that home and journeying to a parallel universe. In *Priscilla*'s Oz, as in Dorothy's, that universe is peopled with persons who superficially resemble those at home, but who are in reality the hollow projections of the travellers' nightmares. The film relies on various racist, sexist, and essentializing tropes of authenticity to position a *more authentic*, because less fixed, gay identity. In its portrayal of a porous and mobile gay identity, *Priscilla* relies on contrasting and essentialized stereotypes of "woman," "immigrant," and "native" – straw men, as it were, set up to frighten away those who venture away from home and into the Australian landscape.

"A Real, Truly Live Place"

Dorothy's Oz exists only as myth or as a fantasy substitute for any number of real places – "anywhere, and everywhere" except for home. But, when Dorothy finds herself back in Kansas, she resists the efforts of her family and friends to dismiss her Oz experience: "It wasn't a dream, it was a place. A real, truly live place!" By taking *The Wizard of Oz* as a parallel road or alternate route to *Priscilla*, I have not meant to suggest that Dorothy's Oz is *really* Australia. Rather, I would suggest that *Priscilla* creates a vision of Oz that is simultaneously mythified and characteristically Australian.

Consider, for instance, the difference between *Priscilla* and the eerily similar yet profoundly American road film, *To Wong Foo, Thanks for Everything! Julie Newmar*, which was released shortly after *Priscilla*. In *To Wong Foo*, three drag queens (one white, one African-American, and one Latino) head from the city into rural territory, but like *The Wizard of Oz* and unlike *Priscilla*, a Capra-esque fantasy ensues in which these quirky queer and multicultural outsiders transform and improve the town. They decorate their drab surroundings, bring an elderly women out of catatonia, free another woman from an abusive marriage, and unite two heterosexual couples – one young white couple and another middle-aged mixed-race couple – and so on. At the same time, the drag queens themselves are transformed by their encounter with the straight community. In the film's final scenes, the townspeople band together to protect Patrick Swayze's drag queen from a homophobic police officer, obscuring his difference by proclaiming their own: one by one, the townspeople declare, "*I* am a drag queen."

In Australia, *To Wong Foo* is generally regarded as a poor imitation of *Priscilla*, a softened and saccharine Americanization (and rip-off) of *Priscilla*'s hard-edged Australian (Ocker) cynicism. And, indeed, it is tempting to read the two films as simply representing their respective national characteristics and national cinemas. Without either denying or essentializing national differences, however, I would suggest that the different values and attitudes in the two films get played out in each film's attention to local and regional difference. In other words, the model of identity politics in each film corresponds to the film's conception of place. Once the characters in *To Wong Foo* have left New York, they are first displaced (lost, without a map) in an amorphous landscape and then moved to the fictional unsituated town "Snidersville," until they arrive in Los Angeles. Thus *To Wong Foo* takes place in a generic "anywhere, and everywhere" of the road, a no-place where differences are superficial and easily overcome. In the opposite vein, *Priscilla* places its characters very precisely in Sydney, Broken Hill, Coober Pedy, and so on. *Priscilla* maps out a very specifically Australian geography of difference, and, in doing so, it suggests that there are real differences among people and in places, and that some of these differences matter deeply. As opposed to *To Wong Foo*'s Disney-style universalizing, *Priscilla* takes on the generic form of the road movie and a transnational camp aesthetic but "speaks from a particular cultural location and with a recognisable accent" (Turner: 107).

As a film that aims to represent diversity within Australia, *Priscilla* is, perhaps, caught between Ayer's Rock and a hard place – in a kind of Hobson's choice between what Lauren Berlant and Elizabeth Freeman describe in another context as, on the one hand, "a utopian politics of identity, difference, dispersion, and specificity" and, on the other, "a pluralist agenda, in the liberal sense, that imagines a 'gorgeous mosaic' of difference without a model of conflict" (Berlant and Freeman: 152). *Priscilla* reminds us that diversity is not a single thing but consists of multiple and potentially conflicting groups and identities. We need, however, to find ways to bring these differences into constellation, without erasing them, and without privileging one difference over others. In this Australian Oz, no longer a *terra nullius* or *terra incognita*, but a "real, truly live place," if Dorothy goes seeking her heart's desire, she will have to look beyond her own backyard. She is not in Kansas any more.

Acknowledgments

Portions of this essay previously appeared in "The Adventures of Priscilla in Oz," in *Media International Australia* 78 (November 1995): 33–8. Thanks to David Boyd, Therese Davis, Arthur Knight, and Rick Wojcik for comments and suggestions on this expanded version.

Works Cited

Berlant, Lauren and Elizabeth Freeman. "Queer Nationality." *boundary 2* 19.1 (1992): 149–80.

Brontë, Charlotte. *Jane Eyre* (1847). Rpt London: Penguin Classics, 1985.

Brunette, Peter. "Queen of the Silver Screen," *The Sydney Morning Herald* (August 11, 1994): 22–3.

Chase, Athol. "Empty Vessels and Loud Noises: Views About Aboriginality Today." *Social Alternatives* 2.2 (1981): 23–7.

Connelly, Keith. "Four of the Best Push Boundaries," *The Sunday Age* (August 21, 1994): Agenda, 7.

—— "Hollywood Sings Its Desert Song," *The Sunday Age* (September 4, 1994): Agenda, 9.

Creekmur, Corey and Doty, Alexander. "Introduction." *Out in Culture: Gay, Lesbian, and Queer Essays on Popular Culture*. Durham and London: Duke University Press, 1995. 1–11.

Dyer, Richard. "Judy Garland and Gay Men." *Heavenly Bodies: Film Stars and Society*. New York: St Martins Press, 1986. 141–94.

—— "White." *The Matter of Images: Essays on Representation*. New York: Routledge, 1993. 141–63.

Elliott, Stephan. *The Adventures of Priscilla, Queen of the Desert: Original Screenplay*. Sydney: Currency Press, 1994.

Fiske, John, Robert Hodge, and Graeme Turner. *Myths of Oz: Readings in Australian Popular Culture*. Sydney: Allen & Unwin, 1987.

Gilroy, Paul. *The Black Atlantic: Modernity and Double Consciousness*. Cambridge, MA: Harvard University Press, 1993.

Holgate, Ben. "Australia's Film Formula: Cannes-Do," *The Sunday Age* (May 29, 1994): 19.

Jacka, Elizabeth. "Australian Cinema: An Anachronism in the '80s?" *The Imaginary Industry: Australian Film in the Late '80s*, eds. Susan Dermody and Elizabeth Jacka. Sydney: Australian Film, Television and Radio School, 1988. 117–30.

Maslin, Janet. "Bitchy and Buoyant on a Bus," *Sydney Morning Herald* (August 11, 1994): 21 (an edited version of her *New York Times* review).

McCarthy, Phillip. "Over-the-Top Priscilla Puts New Slant on Down Under," *Sydney Morning Herald* (August 10, 1994): 1, 4.

—— "Priscilla: A Top Little Performer," *Sydney Morning Herald* (August 17, 1994): 3.

—— "Well-Heeled Opening for Drag Queen Movie," *The Age* (August 17, 1994): 23.

Rushdie, Salman. *The Wizard of Oz*. London: BFI Publishing, 1992.

Said, Edward. *Orientalism*. London: Routledge & Kegan Paul, 1978.

Stern, Lesley. *The Scorsese Connection*. London: BFI and Indiana University Press, 1995.

Turner, Graeme. "'The Genres Are American': Australian Narrative, Australian Film, and the Problem of Genre," *Literature/Film Quarterly* 21.2 (1993): 102–11.

Urban, Andrew L. "Our Cannes-do Film-Makers," *The Australian* (May 13, 1994): 10.

Vidal, Gore. "The Oz Books." *Pink Triangle and Yellow Star and Other Essays (1976–1982)*. London: Heinemann, 1982. 55–82.

von Sturmer, John. "Aborigines, Representation, Necrophilia." *Art & Text* 32 (Autumn 1989): 127–39.

Williams, Evan. "A Wedding to Celebrate in Cannes," *The Australian* (May 20, 1994).

Williamson, David. *Emerald City*. Sydney: Currency Press, 1987.

13

RACE ON THE ROAD
Crossover dreams

Sharon Willis

Road movie protagonists, even if they travel in small groups, are usually isolated and solitary. Their silhouettes in the expanse of a landscape often graphically convey this isolation. But their journeys are inevitably social. While the standard American protagonist – the white male frontiersman-adventurer – frequently entertains a temporary relationship to community, it is usually marked by anticipation or nostalgia, and remains steadfastly remote. Whatever his relationship to a community, it is structured in and through a reciprocal gaze. If the most conventional road movies follow a protagonist whose journey inscribes a deviation or a series of deviations from an imagined proper path, when socially "marginal" protagonists – any women at all, gays, and people of color – hit the road, they themselves come to embody the deviation that their travels also represent (*Thelma and Louise*, 1991, might be the most striking case in point here).[1] That is, the central point and problem that define the journey reside in embodiment and visibility, as all meanings tend to be organized by race, gender, and sexuality. Shaped by the readings of the community that witnesses it, the meaning of the trip is inevitably understood through the meanings the witnesses assign to the bodies of the travelers.

Two recent examples of the genre that feature black and Latin characters, *To Wong Foo, Thanks for Everything! Julie Newmar* (1995) and *Boys on the Side* (1995), have in common certain formal structures. Both are shaped somewhat comedically, and both resemble fairy tales. Even more striking, the racially mixed trios that operate as these films' protagonists are distinguished by their sexuality – three drag queens and one or more lesbians, respectively. *To Wong Foo*'s travelers configure a "balanced" triangle as two older drag queens, the white Vida Boheme (Patrick Swayze) and the African-American Noxeema Jackson (Wesley Snipes) meet and take under their wings another contestant from a drag show, the Latino Chi Chi Rodriguez (John Leguizamo). *Boys on the Side* pairs Jane (Whoopi Goldberg) with "the whitest woman in the world," Robin (Mary Louise Parker), in a road trip to California, during which they pick up Jane's friend and object of

Plate 13.1 John Leguizamo, Wesley Snipes, and Patrick Swayze: a Latino, an African-American, and a European-American man in drag in *To Wong Foo*.

an unrequited crush, Holly (Drew Barrymore), who accidentally kills her drug dealer boyfriend and turns the trip into a flight.

Because these films present themselves as fairy tales, even as fables, we cannot hold them to the grounds of plausibility or verisimilitude that often anchor dramatic fictions. Instead, we have to read the collective wishes that they deploy and reinvest in order to understand the stories of community they offer in relation to our contemporary social context. As the protagonists' necessary detour becomes the whole journey, their internalized quest turns outward to benefit a whole community, raising several questions for the spectator-witness. If we examine the identificatory relays through which a spectator is invited to share the dream of community on offer in these films, we find that a series of trade-offs helps to establish the possibility of cross-gender and cross-racial identifications. By proposing a deliberately "queer" spectator position democratically open to all viewers, both films construct particular versions of a "queer" spectator position that is meant to mediate racial and ethnic differences.

To Wong Foo and *Boys on the Side* have enough in common to support a schematic, if not thoroughgoing, comparison. They share a utopian fantasy articulated through both geography and the gaze, where the cinematic technology offers a groundless, soaring spectator position that is coherent with a dream of transcending the messiness of social realities marked by conflicts around difference by appropriating difference itself. Steadfastly committed to imagining "home" as a full site that at least temporarily incorporates the stray or wandering other, these films offer a certain reassurance to a straight and white spectator that one can accomplish this transcendence without "leaving home."

At the same time, these films articulate related fantasies that imagine social conflict as pathology or dysfunction. These fantasies are linked in their figures of the law as in their associated metaphors for community – either body or family. Following their respective therapeutic agenda, the films "cure" by restoring both the community and the travelers to themselves. In *To Wong Foo*, the restoration involves expelling the farcical figure of the law, the sheriff. On the other hand, in *Boys on the Side*, the comically innocent and upright figure of the law becomes a friend and a love object to be embraced as "family." Likewise, *To Wong Foo* represents differences as reciprocally canceling in magical "figures" of difference, the queens, while *Boys on the Side* ends up eliding differences in the fluid medium of a reestablished lesbian continuum where any woman may just as well be a lesbian as not.

Such fantasies of "multicultural" community entail certain contradictions. *To Wong Foo*'s notion of the community as body is contradictory in its reliance on the radical visibility of specific bodies to consolidate community. A community imagined as body is a general body, and one which very much risks coming back to the nonspecific, that is, to the dominant. On the other hand, *Boys on the Side*'s organization around the metaphor of "family" allows it to reinstate a desexualized "lesbian continuum," and thus to render the term "lesbian" itself unspecified, if not meaningless.

In these worlds, heterosexual and white privilege appear as accidents that can be undone, first, by mere proximity to, and, second, by befriending, difference. But this is a difference detached from bodies, and consequently removed from social situation, which is exactly why both films exhibit a geographical and temporal confusion or obscurity. These happy fantasies of harmony must exist in no specific place. Magical displacement turns into a non-situatedness in which the margin cheerfully discovers itself to be embedded in the dominant.

Style and Identification

To Wong Foo, like *The Adventures of Priscilla, Queen of the Desert* (1994) before it, seems to understand the road movie genre as a vehicle for mainstreaming, as it places its gay transvestites in an isolated town, whose location remains obscure.[2] However, this film combines racial difference with sexual identity, as inscribed in its team of transvestite buddies – one black, one white, and one Latino. Examining the film's self-conscious focus on image production and on gender as masquerade, this essay will explore their importance within the film's equally self-conscious reliance on a simple formula: to introduce the "deviant" into the "normal" is to reveal the perversity, the deviance, the volatility, and flexibility at the heart of the norm. But, in the course of establishing a certain harmony between the three "queens" and the women of the town, the film manages to "forget," or to jettison like so much excess baggage, the race, ethnicity, and sexuality both of its travelers and of the startlingly hospitable townspeople.

The mainstreaming devices that accrue within the film are interestingly played out in its distribution effects: these gay characters are somehow sexually sanitized by their embodiment in action hero Wesley Snipes, heart-throb Patrick Swayze, and comic John Leguizamo, all three of whom have been highly visible in the promotional circuits, cleverly playing their own avowed heterosexualities against their appearances in women's dress.

These later effects, we find, are already embedded within the film's diegetic frame and they contribute to the mutually canceling interactions that racial and sexual specificity entertain. In this neutralization, *To Wong Foo*, like *Boys on the Side*, articulates a powerful wishfulness about community within a fantasmatic framework. Whose wish is it that a gay or lesbian of color should be an ambassador who helps to consolidate a still mostly straight, white community? How does this wishfulness fit with contemporary popular constructions of "multiculturalism," of sexuality, and of the "body politic" that supports them? My aim here is not to judge the political directions these films take as progressive or retrograde. Rather, I am inclined to sift through the ideological dust clouds they stir up in their contradictory, wishful fantasies about multiculturalism. My concern is to interrogate the ideological trade-offs necessary to produce such fantasies of community, both for the films and for their audiences.

Blockbuster Video attaches the following blurb to copies of *To Wong Foo*. "Three drag queens on their way to a Hollywood 'beauty' pageant become sidetracked in a small Midwest town and teach the locals some lessons in style and tolerance." Blockbuster's reading coheres with the film's premise, since it builds its central transitions on an equation between tolerance and style. For its discourse, and for the discourse its characters produce, tolerance *is* style. And as tolerance becomes equated with style, the narrative diffuses social conflict and levels identities in a relay of identifications expressed *as* style. In the process racial specificity is contained as embodied *only* in the trio of queens, whose discursive exchanges are consistently organized by reference to race and ethnicity. The queens shape moments of affection and intimacy through enumerations of racial or ethnic characteristics, and they stage their moments of tension through racial and ethnic difference as ritualized insult, a mimesis of the "dozens." In an exemplary moment early in the film, Noxie resists Vida over the question of bringing the "little Latin boy in drag" to Hollywood with them, asserting "I ain't driving you no more, Miss Daisy . . . Not on your queer life, I don't wanna be getting mixed up with all that

Latin mess." For her part, Vida recalls the mentoring she once offered to Noxie, "an ebony enchantress in the rough," whom she helped to "look a little bit less like Moms Mabley."

A cameo figure who emerges in the early drag show sequence that introduces the film's protagonists may effectively emblematize its project. Blonde African-American drag queen RuPaul appears as the previous year's contest winner. Phillip Brian Harper characterizes the cultural significance of RuPaul's recent career as follows:

> If RuPaul's crossover success – entailing, among other things, appearances on MTV, a duet recording with Elton John, and a role in the much-touted *Brady Bunch Movie* – has fed African Americans' old suspicions regarding white audiences' appetite for black caricature, it has also provoked a crucially important reassessment of what constitutes 'proper' racial and gender identities in the contemporary context.
>
> (190)

Equally important, however, it seems that RuPaul is becoming a figure who embodies "difference" in the abstract. When a Toronto makeup company selected RuPaul as its "spokesmodel," the company's spokesperson accounted for the choice by claiming that his company, MAC, is "about all races, all sexes, all ages," a "universalism," Harper writes, that is "embodied by no one better that RuPaul" (191). What kind of a figure is this who "embodies" difference precisely as *abstraction*?

In *To Wong Foo*, RuPaul's character is called Rachel Tensions, a name that both marks and contains such tensions within this particular body. Much the same might be said for gendered and sexualized tensions. As a figure of social tensions evoked and resolved, RuPaul belongs to a series of US popular cultural icons, including Michael Jackson, Prince, and more recently Jaye Davidson of *The Crying Game* (1992), and perhaps Whoopi Goldberg as well, who play out sexual ambiguity on the ground of a racialized body. Significantly, however, in such figures the "tension" among, race, gender, and sexuality seems to neutralize their specificities under the abstract rubric of "difference." Is it possible that race and sexuality may reciprocally render each other "metaphorical," or figurative, and thus endlessly substitutable? The term "metaphorical" comes to mind because of Toni Morrison's analysis of the culture's dependence on racialized display. "Race has become metaphorical," Morrison writes, "a way of referring to and disguising forces, events, classes, and expressions of social decay and economic division far more threatening to the body politic than biological 'race' ever was" (63). Morrison suggests that "race" "has a utility far beyond economy, beyond the sequestering of classes from one another, and has assumed a metaphorical life so completely embedded in daily discourse that is perhaps more necessary and more on display than ever before" (63). *To Wong Foo* seems to be attempting to work through the social meaning of sexualities upon the ground of a racial display that currently seems crucial to dominant popular conceptions not only of the "body politic," but of embodiment itself in relation to identity.

Such an exploration of embodiment, identity, and identification is inscribed from the earliest frames of *To Wong Foo*. Its opening sequence offers dazzling extreme close-ups of the queens applying their makeup – putting on their faces. Coded for intimacy and sensuality, the extreme close-ups function through parallel editing to match Noxie and Vida in profile, gazing left at their own images. While the editing creates a tight symmetry, the camera movement works to confuse the space through the circularity of its panning movement. While we think we are seeing Noxie directly as she looks into the mirror, the camera reveals that we, like her, have been looking at her mirror image. Figuratively, we are mirrored in her image, and she in ours. This is significant for a film that seems to suggest that the gaze is the source of the image, in a new "twist" on the question of beauty's residing in the eye of the beholder, where the beholder position is split into at least three – the narcissistic gaze of the queens, the gaze of townspeople upon them, and our gaze, alternately aligned with the first two.

Mirrors are key players in this film. Not only do they recall and produce identifications like the one cited above, where we find ourselves sharing the queen's gaze and image, but they play on fairy tale references: "mirror, mirror, on the wall, who's the fairest one of all?" And they remind us that identification works through both images and ideals. It is a mirror that brings the mysterious Julie Newmar of the film's title into the story. She comes into the picture, literally, when Vida's compact catches the reflection of a signed fan photograph of the star. So, in a sense, she has emerged as an intervention in Vida's narcissistic circuit, as an ideal image overlaid on the subjective one. From that point on, Newmar takes on a talismanic function for the three travelers, who transport the picture with them like a relic. Finally, of course, we will discover that this fairy god-mother/guardian angel figure also represents their destination, as Newmar, in a cameo role, confirms Chi Chi's success as a drag queen.

Fairies and Angels

Late in *To Wong Foo*, Vida expresses her pleasure and satisfaction at the newly ordered state of the town by punningly invoking magic: "Sometimes, it just takes a fairy." This is perfectly in keeping with the film's consistent evocations of fairies, and fairy tales. One high-heeled shoe is the only piece of evidence Sheriff Dollard (Chris Penn) holds to help him identify the suspect he is pursuing (Vida), and certainly the Cinderella reference extends to the glamorous transformation of the town's women by the three "fairy godmothers," who may also remind us of the good witch in that earlier fantasy road movie, *The Wizard of Oz* (1939). In a direct reference to magic, Chi Chi twitches her nose at a newly draped table in their hotel room, imitating Samantha from *Bewitched*. These queens transform the landscape of this colorless town and its people as quickly as they redecorate their bleak hotel room, and as instantaneously as Samantha's nose twitching accomplished its effects.

But the sequence that precedes Vida's conclusive and defining remark inscribes magical effects at the level of sound and image as well. This sequence begins with the romantic encounter between Bobby Ray (Jason London) and Bobbie Lee (Jennifer Milmore), whose names offer a light-hearted hint of gender confusion that the queens play on, but who also clearly stand as a fairy-tale couple whose destiny is written in their shared name.

Markedly shaped by its soundtrack and by the effects of steadicam technology, this sequence opens with the couple isolated in the frame against the night sky, and beginning to dance. While Bobby Ray's request seemed a bit stiff in the absence of music, as if by magic, once the couple starts dancing, apparently extradiegetic sound floods the image. As Johnny Mathis's "Hold Me, Thrill Me, Kiss Me" plays, the camera pans 360 degrees around the couple who serve as its axis of rotation. It continues circling, in ever widening arcs, as if spiralling to encompass the whole space of the town square. In the process, the camera is able to pick up several couples, newly constituted under the moonlight, as if drawn together both by the sound, and by the camera's very spiral.

These couples include Jimmy Joe (Mike Hodge), the town's one black citizen, who approaches Beatrice (Blythe Danner). As the camera focuses on the interracial pair, holding them in long shot, from a slightly high angle, we hear Jimmy Joe's words, but so amplified as to disturb our sense of space, since his voice sounds much nearer to us than he is. "Miss Beatrice," he says," I've been waiting twenty-three years to ask this. May I have this dance?" This moment is really laughable: what has been the constraint on this pair, and what has changed to allow them to bond? Through them, however, the film evokes the possibility of a constraint on interracial intimacy, but then evaporates this possible history, magically. Extradiegetic music instantly resolves itself into the diegesis, where its source is never pinpointed, and the steadicam, which floats in sweeping circular motion allows a view that is no longer bound to the ground. Freed from the constraints of more conventional axes, music and camera produce our sense of a magical, fantastical, or otherworldy perspective. But they also saturate this moment of interracial bonding. What kind of wishfulness and ideological bet-hedging emerge in an image of interracial bonding as just plain "magic"? Equally fantasmatic here is the film's construction of a town full of people who couldn't see what was right before their eyes, or cross any boundaries without the intervention of "fairies" and magic.

For the fairy tale to work, the film has to entertain the fantasy of a world without fantasy as the dystopia these queens have to transform. If there was no fantasy in the town, the film seems to connect this lack to missing concepts of "race," and to a general indifference to sexuality. But this is paradoxical, since this optimistic universe is circular: recognition of difference stimulates fantasy, but fantasy is also largely responsible for the social shape of differences.

Meanwhile, the steadicam offers us a gaze floating and gliding in a spiral that reassures us of the coherence and plenitude of the public space and, by extension, of the town itself. If that gaze reminds us of the circling aerial motion of the camera in Wim Wenders's *Wings of Desire* (1987), where angels benignly survey human activity, their intimacy and proximity to us indicated by the constant murmur of whispering voice, I think that is no accident. As the steadicam's orbit slowly widens to disclose the whole population dancing, it stops wandering around and more purposefully begins a steady diagonal ascent to the balcony where the queens, the "fairies," survey the scene and take credit for the fortunate effects of their intervention. In one sweeping camera movement, *To Wong Foo* cures the townspeople of their deficiencies at the level of desire and fantasy. Everyone is restored through the specular identification the camera produces between the town and the queens. Reciprocity is perfect in this imaginary, since this same move restores the queens' narcissism through the townspeople's admiring gazes.

We might say that the drag queens introduce desire into this deadened town. Either they introduce desire, or they catalyze desires in those who watch them. But the question is: what about their own desires? Only Chi Chi exhibits any desire and she quickly sacrifices her longing for Bobby Ray on the altar of an altruism that really translates into a sense of ethical duty to the order of the norm; she's a fairy who brings the heterosexual couple together. That the camera's wandering circles finally loop together, as if all threads in this net could be pulled tight and anchored to the satisfied surveying gazes of the three queens only helps to substantiate our sense of their angelic agency.

But later, Carol Ann (Stockard Channing) will make things even clearer. Saying goodbye to her "first real lady friend," having acknowledged that she recognized his gender all along, Carol Ann concludes, "Vida, I don't think of you as a man. I don't think of you as a woman. I think of you as an angel." At this remark, the camera again soars up above the town as the yellow Cadillac starts down the road. Carol Ann's point seems important. Angels have no sex. And this film has proceeded as if its heroes didn't either, a move that rather systematically undermines the very questions of identity the film wishes to explore.[3]

That may be the price of transforming the heterosexual universe of the town. It may be the price of a PG 13 rating as well. Finally, it's the price of Hollywood, and the film's sharpest theorist, Noxie, nearly comes out and says this for us:

"From now on, I'm not gonna worry about whether people accept me or not. I gonna make Hollywood wherever I am at." The point is, these characters have not for one minute left Hollywood. No doubt, this is why the queens can travel mapless in this world. Their apparent destination was the origin all along. Hollywood is everywhere and nowhere in the film. This should be clear from the town's resemblance to nothing so much as a conventional studio set for a Western – all façade, one unified location, the main street.

Bodies and Community

It is indeed striking that *To Wong Foo*, ostensibly fascinated by the successful drag queens, relies so heavily on the recognizable body and face of the star. Drag, in this instance, works through the consistent capacity of the star to burst through the masquerade. Playing on our awareness that Noxie Jackson is really action star Wesley Snipes, while Miss Vida is romantic lead Patrick Swayze, the film constructs these roles as "cameo" roles for the actors, a construction that is only somehow reinforced by John Leguizamo's presence. Because Leguizamo is known as a standup comedian whose career is based on his impersonations of Latino characters – men and women alike – he signifies the profession of impersonation itself in a framework where both gender and ethnicity become part of the masquerade. Marjorie Garber emphasizes the significance of readability to the masquerade: "the emphasis on *reading* and *being read*, and on the deconstructive nature of the transvestite performance, always undoing itself as part of its process of self-enactment, is what makes transvestism theoretically as well as politically and erotically interesting" (149).[4] But here, what is denaturalized at the level of the film's story and its visual effects is thereby renaturalized at the level of the actor as image.

While it relies less explicitly on fantasy as a theme, and not at all on cross-dressing, *Boys on the Side* exhibits, and exploits, an effect similar to *To Wong Foo*'s in the gender-bending that Whoopi Goldberg embodies conceptually here. In this film, as in most of her recent work, she continues to signify mostly "herself." Goldberg has acquired a curious status; she is charged in the popular imagination with representing a unique position. One of the best-paid women actors in Hollywood – for a moment, the best-paid – and certainly the highest-paid black woman in the movies, Goldberg stands apart for other reasons too. Her early career as a standup comic may have prepared her to operate as a kind of free-standing icon as well. Equally importantly, however, Goldberg is a figure who refuses to stay put, to stabilize her image, for instance, as her professional role and personal life intersect in the relationship with co-star Ted Danson established on the set of *Made in America* (1994). That film's premise has her searching for the sperm donor who may be her daughter's father. A comedy of mistaken identity and misrecognitions, the plot turns on the possibliity that she has accidentally received a white man's sperm. Upon meeting the donor (Ted Danson), she eventually falls in love with him. In her private life, Goldberg later goes on to defend then-boyfriend Danson when he is roundly criticized for a public appearance in blackface. At the time of writing, Goldberg is appearing in *The Associate* (1996), a film in which she apparently plays a woman who cross-dresses in whiteface in order to make it in the corporate world as a white man.

Tania Modleski argues convincingly that Goldberg is frequently in drag of one form or another, from Oda Mae's dressing up to go to the bank in *Ghost* (1990) to her appearance in *Jumpin' Jack Flash* (1986), where a taxi driver mistakes her for a transvestite. Reminding us of Goldberg's role as a governess in *Clara's Heart* (1988), Modleski suggests that if we consider "both extremes of the Whoopi Goldberg persona . . . those in which she represents the maternal/female (as in *Clara's Heart*) and those in which she is coded as more or less male," we find a fairly standard use of black femininity as a dominant popular culture figure: "she is "either . . . too literally a woman . . . or in crucial ways not really a woman at all" (132–3). A remarkably protean figure, Goldberg occupies the curious and volatile position of playing across gender and across race in various ways. But, curiously, this figure is thoroughly contradictory: able to play just about anyone, any identity, Goldberg still stands out as herself. Well on her way to becoming the voice and face of the Oscars, as well as of MCI, Goldberg seems to be accompanied by her small-screen personae. Her previous roles trail her like "ghosts" into the frame of each movie. It is hard to watch *Boys on the Side*, for example, without thinking of *Ghost*, and specifically of the scene in which she allows Patrick Swayze's character to "borrow" her body in order to make love to Demi Moore one last time. *Boys on the Side* once again implies and evaporates the lesbian love-making which had escaped our view in *Ghost*, as the screen image overlaid Swayze's body on Goldberg's and faded hers out – turning her into a ghost of sorts. Likewise, in *Boys on the Side*, Goldberg serves again as a kind cement to hold community bonds together, a mentor for the white people around her, and a political and emotional mediator. As a somewhat magically endowed character, Jane stands forth as insufficiently detached from the actress who plays her; while Goldberg is insufficiently submerged in her character.[5]

In a late sequence *Boys on the Side* reestablishes its "family" of women. It restores to the community Holly and Abe (Matthew McConaughey), her policeman husband, who has stuck with her through pregnancy and a jail term, and "their" daughter, Mary Todd. Then the film immediately and poignantly traces Robin's disappearance. This sequence relies on a protracted and wandering panning shot that circles Jane's and Robin's living room. This shot echoes an earlier one that establishes the multicultural quality of the community that surrounds Holly, Jane, and Robin within months of their arrival in Tucson. At that moment, the camera pans, broadly circling around the lesbian bar where Jane's birthday party is about to occur. As it circles, and circulates, this camera establishes a series of same-sex couples, along with heterosexual ones, representing a variety of visible differences in skin tone. It is this same elaborated multicultural utopian community – one that contains gay and straight couples, interracial and inter-ethnic couples, all happily socializing with uniformed police – that the film returns us to in the end. This time, however, the camera's slow, luxurious trajectory around the room coincides with the temporality of the duet that Robin and Jane sing. Robin's whispery rendition of "You've Got It" ("Anything you want, I've got. Anything you need, I've got it. Anything at all, you got it, baby") passes to Jane's stronger, healthy voice. Hers is the voice that becomes atmospheric as the length of the song coincides with the length of the shot that finally aligns the camera's gaze with Jane's, leaving her in the definitive viewing position. And, after the screen fades to black, it is through Jane's eyes again that the camera makes us search the periphery of the now sunlit room, until we discover the feared absence – Robin's empty wheelchair.

What is interesting is the film's insistence on assigning to Jane the controlling or defining gaze with which we identify. It is as if the tone and consistency of this space of utopian plenitude emanated directly from her look and her ambient voice. In a way, this moment merely confirms the position Jane has been holding all along, as the image track lines up with the soundtrack she has produced throughout. From the beginning, Jane has provided the journey's direction and its destination. But oddly, in the film's fantasmatic atmosphere, the journey from New York City to Pittsburgh implausibly takes more than one day, while time evaporates as soon as the women leave Pittsburgh. Along with time, geography disappears.

With the dissipation of any regional texture or specificity, this becomes a magical transport, an effect that coincides comfortably with the spectacle of a community springing up fully formed around these women, a community without origins. Jane/Whoopi Goldberg, then, has become the reservoir of the film's wishfulness. Part of this wishfulness involves reciprocal therapeutic effects. If Jane restores Robin's capacity for love, desire, and intimacy, when Robin reciprocates her affections, she rescues Jane from her pathology – repeated obsession with the "wrong woman," a straight woman, even though Robin's sexuality remains ambiguous. As in *To Wong Foo*, part of the wish is an equalization between subculture and dominant culture through a fantasy of an entirely equal exchange that is reciprocally transforming. In this exchange circuit, the social playing field is – fantasmatically – already leveled.

Mothers, Women, and Police

In one of *Boys on the Side*'s more stunning turns, Holly and Abe Lincoln reproduce, impossibly, fantasmatically, in "Mary Todd Lincoln," Holly's biracial baby, the child that might have resulted from a sexual union between Jane and Robin. Mary Todd Lincoln's nearly unbearable, and unbearably ironic, name stands as a testimony to the historical amnesia that seems to found this community. Part of the charming naivete that characterizes Abe Lincoln, the sensitive cop who is willing to marry a pregnant criminal, is his innocence. From his blissful indifference to Holly's past right down to his claim that his own inability "to tell a lie" is inscribed in his name, his innocence is an innocence of history. As such, this character represents the fantasy of legislating tolerance in the absence of the history that makes equal rights legislation necessary, where a benign law would automatically instantiate an equality that it could reproduce at will.

As the film zeroes in on the restoration of Robin's mother, Elaine (Anita Gillette), to her, its symmetry promotes a merging between Jane and Elaine. But even as it transforms this conventional and easily shocked mother into an idealized figure of tolerance toward racial and sexual differences, the film also substantiates its construction of Jane's and Robin's bond as a reciprocally maternalized one. Through the fantasmatic product of their unconsummated relationship, the biracial child of a lesbian union, the film naturalizes racial and sexual differences as its culminating fantasy of maternal bliss in utopian unions. This community of mothers is a world where everyone fits on a restored lesbian continuum designed to secure heterosexual stability in the face of its own fantasized tolerance. As Adrienne Rich originally described this continuum, its terms already allowed for the erasure of sex, and even desire, between women:

> If we consider the possibility that all women – from the infant suckling at her mother's breast, to the grown woman experiencing orgasmic sensations while suckling her own child, perhaps recalling her mother's milk-smell in her own; to two women, like Virginia Woolf's Chloe and Olivia, who share a laboratory; to the women dying at ninety, touched and handled by other women – exist on a lesbian continuum, we can see ourselves moving in and out of this continuum, whether we identify ourselves as lesbian or not.
>
> (158–9)

Whether this film is staunchly intent on reinstating the de-eroticized lesbian continuum, or whether it is simply haunted by its terms as a kind of return of the repressed, *Boys on the Side* produces only one moment of reference to lesbianism as sexual. In the explosively funny scene where Jane gets Robin to confess the euphemistic vocabulary through which she speaks about "down there," Robin finally succeeds, more and more gleefully, in uttering the forbidden word: "Cunt,

cunt, cunt." We may feel rewarded as repression lifts in a momentary restoration of sexuality through a word. And perhaps all the more so when the word has passed from the daughter's lips to the mother's, since Elaine applies the term as an epithet to an invasive nurse who disturbs her and Robin and Jane. But what of the lesbian here? Jane is consistently figured as choosing "the wrong woman," and this ambiguity remains unresolved in the discourse of love. Just as, through their lesbian friendship, Jane's blackness somehow erases Robin's "whiteness," even though Jane began by describing her as "the whitest woman in the world," so the entry of the mother into this circuit of love and desire obscures its lesbian character. What wish does the film fulfill in finding a little "lesbian" in everyone, in finding lesbian discourse available to all?

Diane Hamer and Belinda Budge speculate on current popular culture's use of "homosexuality as a lens for heterosexuality" (6), especially as expressed through a "present absence" (5). They argue that homosexuality has become a borrowed source of dramatic tension, since it "serves as a new and (still) shocking arena for the reworking of stories of sex and love, romance and desire" (7). Concomitantly, they suggest, popular interest in figures of homosexuality may be related to circulating cultural anxieties about gender. So, they argue, "as the artifice of conventional gender categories has been increasingly exposed . . . the difference between the two genders . . . no longer occupies such an unassailable position" (7). For these writers, "this gender anxiety is clearly finding expression in a popular fascination with homosexuality, recognized as a lifestyle in which gender roles are skewed" (7). And, therein, I would argue, lies the reassurance. If homosexuality can be reduced to a lifestyle, and if that life*style* choice involves skewing or rewriting gender roles, then these too may be a matter of style, and style is something we can all adopt. We need only take up our places on the style continuum. And style brings us back to *To Wong Foo*.

If three queens can blow into this town, become marooned there, and in the course of their sojourn effect complete transformations in both women's self-images and heterosexual relations in general, this must be a form of magic. But it is precisely the motivations of this magic that I want to explore and question. At what price does the film offer a utopian model of communication and harmony among primarily white lower-middle-class small-town heterosexuals, and this multicultural crew of urban transvestites?

Deploying the familiar Western movie theme of oppressed or frightened townspeople overcoming their differences to protect themselves and a renegade outsider who galvanizes them, when Sheriff Dollard arrives to arrest Vida, the town rallies in a particular way. A sea of women in red dresses, and eventually a throng of men and women, all in reds, surge forward to claim the identity of drag queen. As the queens melt into the mass of the crowd that valorizes their identity, the film strikes a paradox. *To Wong Foo* is diffusing some of the very identity questions on which it seems to depend in spite of itself, as gender and sexuality forcefully displace questions of race, ethnicity, or class. Oddly, though this film borrows liberally from the themes exhibited in Jennie Livingston's 1993 *Paris Is Burning*, which documents the drag ball scene among black and Latino gay men in New York City, it radically reshapes its themes. The racial and ethnic issues, the class struggle, and the contradictory desires that structure the ball, and the men's identities, the ones they claim, as well as those they assume temporarily, are expelled from the picture in *To Wong Foo*. This strange rewriting of *Paris Is Burning* converts the wrenching wishfulness of the house ball costume categories into a mass – and completely homogenizing – phenomenon, preserving only the thematics of the drag ball. The ball's dream is embodied in the metaphor of family, of matriarchy, mothers and daughters, queens and princesses, "children" straining to model ideals of femininity in order to attain legendary status. But, in this film, class issues and the racial and ethnic inflections of performance disappear altogether in the familializing and metaphorizing impulse that offers these fantasies to Everywoman.

In this gesture, despite the steps taken to explore gender itself as drag, the film reveals the anxieties that it will finally overcome strategically. According to Judith Butler, "to claim that all gender is like drag, or is drag, is to suggest that 'imitation' is at the heart of the heterosexual project and its gender binarisms, that drag is not a secondary imitation that presupposes a prior and original gender, but that hegemonic heterosexuality is itself a constant and repeated effort to imitate its own idealizations" (125). Butler continues by asserting that the need to repeat imitation

> suggests that heterosexual performativity is beset by an anxiety that it can never fully overcome, that its effort to become its own idealizations can never be finally or fully achieved, and that it is consistently haunted by that domain of sexual possibility that must be excluded for heterosexualized gender to produce itself.
>
> (125)

Perhaps despite itself, the film exhibits a moment when it appears that the queens' real role is to jump-start the mechanism of repetitive imitation so that it can send them packing right after the collective performance.

But what happens to Vida, Noxie, and Chi Chi in this mix? It is significant to remember the role of Vida's mother here. We remember that their journey into unmapped territory is precipitated by Vida's mother's condemning stare, the look that acknowledges Vida only to deny her. Somehow, everything seems to go back to the mother. Just as the origin of the journey's deviation is the disavowing maternal gaze which provokes Vida to shred the map, its end point is the approving gaze of Julie Newmar, the surrogate, good mother, whose approbation comes about through the same process that also restores Carol Ann's feminine and maternal power.

The mother's condemning disavowal, borne somehow collectively by the trio, can be lifted, it seems, only through the recognition the townspeople bestow upon them. It is as if the drag queen identity had circulated among the townspeople who alone are able to restore identity to the queens. At the point where the narcissism that has operated as compensatory for the protagonists becomes positive sheerly through the "community's" willingness to borrow it, the drag queens themselves are apparently transformed, rather like Dorothy's three companions in *The Wizard of Oz*. Carol Ann, of course, would function as Dorothy in this schema: for her there is finally "no place like home." Noxie will make Hollywood wherever she is, Vida will demand acceptance, rather than approval, from her family, as from the world at large, and Chi Chi resolves to remember that "everything I touch doesn't turn to caca. And, I'm gonna find a foundation that's a little closer to my actual skin tone." Her reappropriation of ethnic features as mask, like Noxie's vow to make Hollywood everywhere, contributes to a sense that "race" and "ethnicity" may be mere roles, fancy, or fantasy, and therefore manipulable at will. In the end, then, social identity is not only as freely assumed and as easily taken off as makeup and costume, but it is subject to our will.

In the same sweeping move that validates the queens' identity, power is restored to heterosexual women in the town. Through recourse to a feminine "policing function," the film allows the queens to discipline or expel uncooperative white heterosexual men. It is as if the white women of the town need to ventriloquize Noxie and Vida to manage their men, and, likewise, the queens must teach these women to claim their "feminine" identities as masquerade. Until femininity is stabilized – restored to its rightful "owners" – the town remains vacuous and ghostly. Vitality is restored through the auspices of newly reclaimed heterosexual feminine identity which dominates those men who refuse to change. If the best women are men in dresses, the better men stick with the women, or join them, as do Bobby Ray, Jimmy Joe, and the young toughs – all white *boys* and one black man. This is the context in which Carol Ann confers upon Vida both love and a name. Vida asserts that she has been waiting all her life to hear those words spoken to that name: "I love you Vida." When Carol Ann speaks them, it as if the heterosexual woman were the only one who could undo the reciprocal repudiation that seems to structure Vida's identity as a detour.

How may the townspeople "borrow" the drag queen identity so seamlessly?, we may ask. The film's answer is that that identity is both already known and already there for the taking. Its emblem is the attic full of funky 1960s clothes that provide the perfect costumes for the day before the social, and that miraculously render the stuttering young man who owns the store articulate, as if he had been reading the Diana Vreeland book Vida gives him all along. Everything they needed was all right there – in storage. In the grandmother's attic closet! Here we might find an echo in the fantastic moment when all of the business-attired commuters in a train begin to vogue in response to the queens' music as they drive down the highway. The fantasy seems to be that "it just takes a fairy" to activate what was there all along: heterosexual solidarity with gays, enthusiastic heterosexual imitation of gay codes and styles. *To Wong Foo* seems to wish to say that there is drag queen in all of us.[6] But, as the heterosexuals find their own wildest longings, wishes, and desires reflected in the eyes of the queens, the contradiction emerges that all issues are transformed into costuming.[7] In this context, sexuality, race, and ethnic accent become part of the pose and the costume. Underlying this transformation, I think, is a theory of the body politic as structured by relations of the general to the particular, where the queens become examples of one particularity that stands in a kind of symmetry with the townpeople's particularities. What is missing is a concept of the specific, the specificity of the social meanings assigned to bodies, rather than the abstraction of a "particularity," which finally reduces to an individuality.

Strikingly, as positive racial, sexual, and ethnic attributes become costume and pose, all negativity regarding race and ethnicity gets contained in two locations. The first is the one battle among the trio of queens; they themselves are hurling racialized and gendered insults in a closed circuit. Only Sheriff Dullard/Dollard entertains a similar discourse, or even seems to notice racial and ethnic coding at all. His excessive array of prejudices, humorously undercut by his waxing eloquent about the male-to-male sexual activity he so actively claims to find repellent, only further embellishes his pile of clichés.

By depositing all the clichés of bigotry in this character's account, and then allowing the community to expel him, and comically to scapegoat the voice of the law, the film leaves everyone else free to frolic in this fantasy of seamless, cozy, "multiculturalism."[8] Conflict, then, disappears, or is contained, almost magically. As magically as Latin and Anglo and gay and straight communities interpenetrate and incorporate jovial cops and interracial couples in *Boys on the Side*, in *To Wong Foo* racism and homophobia are made to retreat as effortlessly and as rapidly as does Carol Ann's abusive, battering husband, Virgil (Arliss Howard), who walks out of her life with a smile. If *To Wong Foo* shapes a multicultural fantasy of restored bodily plenitude with the simple expulsion of localized racist and homophobic elements, *Boys on the Side* offers the dream of an expansive multicultural family woven around permeable boundaries open to permanent exchange of the sort we see at the Latin fiesta.

Bodies Politic

Road movies often arrive at a moment when we have forgotten if the protagonists are running from something or to something, or if the story's generative site is the departure point or the destination. Similarly, when the protagonists stop temporarily in a given location or community, one is often unable to separate the ways in which this foreign element catalyzes changes in that space from the ways the space activates or encourages changes in the journey and its agents. In the case of *To Wong Foo*, however, like *Boys on the Side*, this reciprocal impact, inscribed in the reversible gaze, promotes a wish for the abolition of the social consequences of difference through identification. What kinds of body politic do these films posit through this dream of communities of identification?

What are we to make of a film like *To Wong Foo*, which is structured by the performance of racial and ethnic modalities of gender, and of gendered racial and ethnic identity, but in a context that continually reasserts the primacy of sexual difference, both through and around the queens? Who is consuming the multiculturalist fantasy here? We know this is a film for white people, because only Vida has a family, a past, an origin. All we have seen is the derisive, threatening gaze of Latino boys on Chi Chi as she flees her neighborhood to the drag show – never, apparently, to return. Noxie and Chi Chi seem to spring fully formed from communities that are nowhere to be seen. But how is whiteness constructed in its fantasy?

This must be a heterosexual whiteness, a dominant mainstream position that is adapting to a version of "multiculturalism" by culturalizing itself through the identifications it tries on. And, of course, this approach feels suspiciously like a version of multiculturalism as a "smorgasbord," where politics reduces to slogans, like "Different strokes for different folks," as Wahneema Lubiano has put it.[9] Nonetheless, the new costuming of these fantasies bears interrogation, if only to determine which forms of blindness they encourage in the dazzling visibility of the differences they display.

As Avery Gordon and Christopher Newfield have argued, the current critical attention to "whiteness" in cultural studies, as in "multiculturalist" institutional initiatives, is highly vexed

> While the attention to whiteness as a cultural system has been a very important move in the reconceptualization of race problems, it downplays the ongoing existence of white supremacy as a system of privilege. . . . Indeed, given existing racial inequalities, the reduction of all racial groups to a nonexistent level playing field poses serious problems.

> (79)

This kind of attention to whiteness has a strong impact on formulations of the meaning of "multiculturalism," particularly in relation to its embeddedness in gender and sexuality. As Gordon and Newfield put it, "Multiculturalism has also been very uncertain about where gender and sexuality fit into its notion of cultures. When the culturization of race meets up with a de-gendered and de-sexualized notion of race, the cultural move takes us two steps backward in our efforts to develop complex understandings of intersecting identities and social power" (79).

But the particular fantasies of "multicultural" community provided by these films also invoke a notion of the community as body, even while they rely on the radical visibility of certain specific bodies to consolidate community. And the body of the community, as general body, very much risks coming back to the nonspecific, that is, the dominant. As George Cunningham has argued, "The metaphor of the body politic becomes the means of figuring the common will in its most progressive sense as an assembled and orderly society that expresses itself by democratic consent" (142). But that body continues to remain unmarked. "In the same way that an unspecified image of the universal body is always sub-textually male," Cunningham continues, "it is also always, at least in our culture, subtextually white. Imagining the body politic, actually giving it an image, is the process of attaching the metaphor to a specific body" (142).

In their effort to dream a different community, both *To Wong Foo* and *Boys on the Side* offer us the image of a gaze that can give it shape. By inscribing a magically transcendent and unifying gaze in the spirals of panning shots, both these films invite everyone to imagine they are sharing an intersection of identities in that point of view. That intersection fantasmatically constitutes a community founded in identifications forged through the look. By extension, then, these films give shape to the wish that we could write our identities in a stably legible form on our own bodies, and that we could write the body politic with our own gaze – in our "own" image.

Notes

1 Few examples of black characters on the road have emerged since *The Defiant Ones* (1958) charted the journey of two fellow prisoners, one black (Sidney Poitier) and one white (Tony Curtis), who escape from a prison bus but remain linked by handcuffs, as if the only means of producing this interracial pair were to yoke them together literally. It is altogether striking that black characters seem to go on the road, voluntarily or not, in the company of white ones. A recent exception is Spike Lee's *Get on the Bus* (1996); here we might examine the function of the bus driver's whiteness in contrast to his passengers.

2 While the film's credits identify it as a town in Nebraska, the film leaves the location deliberately nonspecific. The little landscape we see suggests the Midwestern plains. Noxie, we remember, thinks they are in West Virginia. Temporality will provide no clue, either, because the length of the trip the characters have made in a car that appears incapable of traversing Manhattan is utterly implausible.

3 As Kendall Thomas has put the issue, concerning the androgyny one associates with angels: "For better or worse, we live in a world in which individual identities are forged in and through constructs of gendered sexual difference. . . . To say in such a world that someone is androgynous in this second, neutered sense is in effect to deny

that s/he exists: the androgyne has no sexual identity, which means that s/he has no identity at all. Nobody can know the androgyne's name, because there is no name by which s/he might be called" (58).

4 Garber also suggests, citing Oscar Montero, that the female impersonator calls forth a "double reading": "drag can also be an important destabilizing element that, in performance, 'questions the limits of representation.' The imperfection of her imitation is what makes her appealing, what makes her eminently readable" (149).

5 Structurally, this effect of play against the actual body/history of the actress seems to be at work in the very configuration of the friendships the film explores. Robin, the figure of AIDS in the mainstream, since she has acquired the disease through heterosexual intercourse, is wedged between and balanced by Jane as a figure for homosexuality and Drew Barrymore as a figure for addiction. Thus, the film represents the popular spectres that have emerged in moral panics surrounding AIDS, and that it clearly means to undermine through this triangular friendship.

6 Here the film's logic runs counter to Noxie's rigorous theory of drag, which goes something like this. A straight man in women's clothes is a transvestite; a woman in a man's body is a transsexual. "But a gay man with way too much style for one gender. That's a drag queen."

7 Indeed, this moment matches some of the moments in *Paris Is Burning* that Judith Butler characterizes as reinstating the norm. "The citing of the dominant norm does not," she writes, in this instance, "displace that norm; rather, it becomes the means by which that dominant norm is most painfully reiterated as the very desire and the performance of those it subjects" (135).

8 In connection with this figure and his function as alibi for the rest of the town, we might consider Judith Butler's analysis of the function of white moralism as a form of racial guilt. "This consideration of guilt as a way of locking up or safeguarding desire may well have implications for the theme of white guilt. For the question there is whether white guilt is itself the satisfaction of racist passion, whether the reliving of racism that white guilt constantly performs is not itself the very satisfaction of racism that white guilt ostensibly abhors. For white guilt – when it is not lost to self-pity – produces a paralytic moralizing that *requires* racism to sustain its own sanctimonious posturing; precisely because white moralizing is itself nourished by racist passions, it can never be the basis on which to build and affirm a community across difference; rooted in the desire to be exempted from white racism, to produce oneself as the exemption, this strategy virtually requires that the white community remain mired in racism; hatred is merely transferred outward, and thereby preserved, but it is not overcome" (277 n.14).

9 "Can multiculturalism be reduced to cultural relativism, to an empty noncritical pluralism, or to an intellectual and social smorgasbord offered to particular clients by elite institutions, or corporations? Of course it can. But part of the work of those who have been and are engaged in radical multiculturalism is to keep it from being reduced to slogans, to meaning things like 'Different strokes for different folks,' or 'To understand all is to forgive all,' or 'All we need is peace, love, and understanding'" (67).

Works Cited

Butler, Judith. *Bodies That Matter: On the Discursive Limits of "Sex."* New York and London: Routledge, 1993.

Cunningham, George P. "Body Politics." *Representing Black Men*, eds. Marcellus Blount and George P. Cunningham. New York and London: Routledge, 1996. 131–54.

Garber, Marjorie. *Vested Interests: Cross-Dressing and Cultural Anxiety*. New York and London: Routledge, 1992.

Gordon, Avery and Newfield, Christopher. "Multiculturalism's Unfinished Business." *Mapping Multiculturalism*, eds. Avery Gordon and Christopher Newfield. Minneapolis: University of Minnesota Press, 1996. 76–115.

Hamer, Diane and Belinda Budge. "Introduction." *The Good, The Bad and The Gorgeous: Popular Culture's Romance With Lesbianism*, eds. Diane Hamer and Belinda Budge. London and San Francisco: Pandora, 1994. 1–14.

Harper, Phillip Brian. *Are We Not Men?* Oxford and New York: Oxford University Press, 1996.

Lubiano, Wahneema. "Like Being Mugged by a Metaphor." *Mapping Multiculturalism*, eds. Avery Gordon and Christopher Newfield. Minneapolis: University of Minnesota Press, 1996. 64–75.

Modleski, Tania. *Feminism Without Women: Culture and Criticism in a "Postfeminist" Age*. New York and London: Routledge, 1991.

Morrison, Toni. *Playing in the Dark: Whiteness and the Literary Imagination*. New York: Random House/Vintage, 1993.

Rich, Adrienne. "Compulsory Heterosexuality and Lesbian Existence." *The Signs Reader*, eds. Elizabeth Abel and Emily Abel. Chicago: University of Chicago Press, 1983. 139–68.

Thomas, Kendall. "Ain't Nothin' Like the Real Thing: Black Masculinity, Gay Sexuality, and the Jargon of Authenticity." *Representing Black Men*, eds. Marcellus Blount and George P. Cunningham. New York and London: Routledge, 1996. 55–69.

14

REVITALIZING THE ROAD GENRE

The Living End as an AIDS road film

Katie Mills

If we find nothing else unanimous about adventure road films, we might agree that they appeal to that darker side of people's psyches where rebellion thrives, wild and free. Hence, the outlaw outlook of the road film *The Living End* (1992) engages fans of this genre, but it also deviates from our expectations in significant ways. Most viewers who sympathize with the outcast in road films are also pretty good at respecting, even if unconsciously, the rules about outlaw narratives. We come to count on the tried and true pleasures of genre, and take satisfaction in pegging the bad guys early on, noticing subtle variations on the motives that put people on the run, or second-guessing the next move in a chase scene. The question that interests me in *The Living End* is not how the rogues break the law, since they inevitably will do so, but how the film breaks the laws of *stories* about outlaws. *The Living End*, Gregg Araki's independent film about two HIV-positive gay lovers on the lam, rebels against the road genre itself in its aim to revitalize the power of cinematic story-telling in an AIDS era.

My study of *The Living End* is part of a larger project of theorizing how the road story offers marginalized communities a ready narratological structure to represent rebellion and collective transformation. Such groups then challenge the genre with their own embodied differences of gender, sexual orientation, or race. An earlier generation of alternative film-makers – the French New Wave and American avant-garde – developed an aesthetic which was intent on destroying traditional film techniques in order to disrupt the semiotics of capitalist society. Today, the return to genre and popular narrative forms by non-dominant film-makers reveals a new strategy for constructing a rebel viewing position. By analyzing the road genre in this larger sense, as a repository of images of margin-ality and autonomy, we can better understand how popular narrative provides a performative space for imaginative revisions of identity and society.

The Living End focuses, as do most road films, on the steps taken by individuals to recuperate personal power when rejected by society. The difference between the typical road film anarchist, however, and Araki's fugitives is the fact that they aren't simply loners, but gay loners involved with each other. Araki never connects his anti-heroes Jon and Luke to any larger counter-cultural community (as did *Easy Rider*, 1969, when its lone heterosexual buddies went to the hippie commune, for instance), but he throws the presumptions of the road genre – especially its focus on the heterosexual male – into high relief. By deploying the road genre as the source of collective identifications and desires in which the two elopers run amok, Araki bridges the distance between private anarchy and political affiliation. These are rebels with a cause, simply by virtue of being gay in a road film.

"End of Cinema": Araki's Debt to the Avant-garde

The end of an adventure road film is one of the most fixed aspects of the genre. Death stalks the closing of each tense outlaw film; by the time the curtains fall, at least one of the major characters has usually been killed. Similarly, death is over-determined in another contemporary genre: the AIDS film. From *Philadelphia* (1993) to *Boys on the Side* (1995), the "HIV canon" invariably winds up its plots when a leading character dies. *The Living End* combines these two genres, mixing the road film with an HIV story, to create "discontinuities" that unexpectedly twist the signature death sentence of both genres into a living end.[1] For, in this film, both HIV-positive runaways stay alive. Araki's revisionism creates a utopic space that is both a paradox and a parable: just as Jon and Luke miraculously outlive the inexorable threat of AIDS and their pariah status as gays within heterosexist society, so might the larger gay community dare to envision undying strength and desire.

Merged with the film's questions about mortality is an equally fervent inquiry into the future of cinema. Despite its diegetic flirtation with death, *The Living End* offers a metacinematic meditation on the possibilities of vital film-making and cinematic desire. With the same black humor it uses to portray the psychic cost of AIDS, *The Living End* also explores cinema's ability to retain its vigor in these plague years. Unexpectedly, Araki combines avant-garde techniques *with* their antithesis, classic filmic conventions such as narrative and genre, transforming rather than eroding dominant textual constructions altogether.[2] He pays respectful homage to film-making pioneers like Andy Warhol and Derek Jarman, and less deferentially acknowledges his contemporaries Gus Van Sant and Stephen Soderbergh. Araki insistently alludes to the work of his mentor, Jean-Luc Godard (namesake to *The Living End*'s Jon and Luke), whose car-crash road film *Weekend*

(1967) fretted about the "End of Cinema" and the revolutionary potential of alternative film-making. Through witty, informed citations of genre and auteurship, Araki transforms the earlier avant-garde's conviction that narrative is ideology into an ideological narrative about life and freedom. Rather than destroy, he constructs a different frame of reference in order to recharge the libidinal battery of film and to help build the postmodern corpus of what is increasingly called "queer cinema." *The Living End* aims its morbid irony at both the generic and metatextual levels to detour this AIDS film's *telos* away from tragedy, with its typical catharsis achieved by purging pity and fear.[3] Instead, the film rejects ethical censure and culminates in a hopeful prognosis and call to action, at least for gay men. (Unfortunately, as I shall discuss, *The Living End* at the same time perpetuates a cinematic tradition of hostility toward women.) The future of film may well require a searching inventory like that undertaken by Araki with his genre-focused deconstructions; but the revitalization of society requires it as well, since the stories we create and exchange about misfits and medical doom affect the diversity we are willing to tolerate in our fellow beings.

The Living End opens with Luke's story. To the pounding sound of industrial/ punk music, a completely black screen repeatedly alternates with claustrophobic, disorienting close-ups of a graffiti-covered wall. When the camera finally pulls back, Luke (Mike Dytri) spins in slow motion on a hill high above Los Angeles. Dressed in a muscle T-shirt and tight jeans, the young rebel drinks from a pint bottle. A mysterious noise heard over the music is finally identified as the sound of Luke painting with a spray can. In one strange location after another, surrounded by farcical sadomasochist nut-cases, he scrawls "I Blame Society" on abundantly "tagged" urban walls. Next, bare-chested, Luke hitch-hikes on sunny boulevards jammed with cars. Two crazy lesbians give him a ride, only to fail in their attempt to domineer him with a gun. Later, a wife's surreal murder of her bisexual husband, who had taken Luke home to "party," also fails to upend him.

In contrast to a very cool Luke, *The Living End* offers the story of Jon (Craig Gilmore). Streetwise and nihilistic, Luke attracts violence like a magnet, whereas Jon remains cocooned within the world of his car, apartment, and a neighborhood café. We first see Jon, dressed in floppy, baggy clothes, and driving through downtown Los Angeles on the Harbor Freeway. If Luke seems like a giant in front of this skyline, the high-rises dwarf Jon. Through flashbacks, a technique never used in Luke's segments, we learn that Jon has tested positive for HIV earlier that same day. He blames himself for the emotional and physical damage wreaked by his former lover. He forsakes company, except for Darcy, his straight female friend who worries about him obsessively. Jon's desire to isolate contrasts with Luke's constant hustling: even when back safe at home, Jon refuses the repeated invitations of an anonymous caller wanting to have phone sex. Most of the time, Jon just drives around, dictating into his tape recorder. His work as a film critic

Plate 14.1 Luke's (Mike Dytri) new-found freedom elicits a more pensive response from Jon (Craig Gilmore) in *The Living End*. Courtesy of October Films.

who is writing an article on "The Death of Cinema" is only addressed obliquely by the film, but we slowly come to understand that Jon represents the distanced voyeurism of cinema scholarship, as counterpoint to Luke's embodied and emotional engagement with life.

Jon's torpor seems to border on lifelessness, but soon enough the passive Jon and passionate Luke meet. What began as separate stories unites as a romance with two narrative positions that challenge and temper one another. Initially, when Jon encounters Luke hitch-hiking on sunny Hollywood Boulevard, he drives right by him. Then Jon runs across Luke again that night in a tunnel. Driving haphazardly, talking into his tape recorder, Jon stops for Luke only because Luke has blocked the road in the tunnel. Jon's persistent voice-over halts when Luke jumps uninvited into the car. "Drive, drive," Luke screams and although mystified, Jon reluctantly obeys. Jon never learns that Luke had just been attacked by three gay-bashers, and killed all of them with the pistol he stole earlier from the lesbians. (In one of *The Living End*'s many obvious nods to other films, the camera zooms in on the homophobes' bloody T-shirts, which are emblazoned with the names of the films directed by Araki's contemporaries: *Drugstore Cowboy*, 1989, and *sex, lies, and videotape*, 1989). The paths of the two men now run together for the remainder of the film.

The dynamics of the relationship have been established from its onset: Luke's imperative recklessness meets Jon's willingness to comply. When they spend the first night together, Luke predictably initiates the seduction. Characteristically, he remains unconcerned when Jon pushes him away to warn him that there is "something" he should know. Intuiting Jon's impending announcement about his HIV status, Luke interrupts with a flippant revelation: "Welcome to the Club." They spend the next day together, enough time for Luke's animalism to affect Jon. During a brief separation, Jon longs for Luke so much that he is ready to join his fate to Luke's when he finally reappears – in trouble with the law. Jon abandons his incomplete essay on the death of cinema, and leaves his movie-postered home to go on the run with Luke. What's at stake, as the film makes clear, is that Jon learns to leave his responsible rut and shed his self-incriminating response to being HIV-positive. We can imagine that Jon gets swept up in a fantasy of fugitive life common to road films, as if leaping quixotically from his lonely cinematic voyeurism into a film star's role with its action and adventure – reluctant all the while with playing the rebel he admires.

In the first of many reversals of the road genre, the film detours from the typical driven, adventure plot once Luke and Jon are on the run. Even though they are fugitives, and the major portion of the film takes place in a car, they just don't have the relationship to the road, to the joy of mobility, or to the landscape which characterizes many road films. They are not really fleeing any immediate threat, as are the outlaws in most road films, but are running primarily to regain a sense of meaning in a world made absurd by AIDS. Their escape thus becomes more like a vacation. On the road, they never encounter another person; all the shots show the couple alone in the car, in their hotel rooms, or standing outside their parked car. Their trip never takes them through the stock Western topography that symbolizes awesome eternity, like Monument Valley, but reveals only a post-modern wasteland of fast-food joints and ominous highway overpasses. The road segments are more like disjointed episodes of aimless cruising reminiscent of the literary picaresque genre, a tradition in American culture featuring rogues on the run and epitomized by *Huckleberry Finn*, but twisted here into nihilistic revelry. Meaning builds slowly as the viewer juxtaposes the fragmented encounters described by the film. Myriad details raise the issue of death and heighten the road genre's stereotypical courtship of death: for example, Luke draws a heart which reads, "Jon + Luke, 'till death do us part"; Jon talks about the band *Dead Can Dance*; his apartment is decorated with a toy skull in the bedroom and a skeleton in the closet; a "Choose Death" bumper sticker adorns his car; he needs to extend his deadline. These details combine with more obvious signals (e.g., Jon's essay on "The Death of Cinema" and Luke's wish to die at the height of orgasm) to amplify the narrative's macabre preoccupations. As is typical of *The Living End*'s persistent defiance of expectations, however, the film transcends these overdetermined references. Araki sets us up by using genre and these red-herring details in order to question the fate of contemporary film-making alongside that of his HIV-positive characters.

Jon's cinephilia offers a perfect pretext for the film's fluency in cinematic history and critical theory, which is revealed through the visual quotation of other films. For instance, a film festival poster on Jon's door features a sequence of stills from Warhol's *Blow Job* (1963–4), in which a man's head is thrown back in sexual abandon. This poster functions as a prominent background in repeated shots of Jon and Luke entering Jon's apartment. In several scenes, their gestures obviously mimic these poses from *Blow Job*, stressing the ties between this film in the history of gay/avant-garde cinema and the positions now occupied by Jon and Luke.[4] A poster for Godard's films also decorates Jon's wall: it emphasizes Araki's link to the French director, especially to Godard's overt interrogation of the future of cinema. Godard's influence on Araki is so great that the younger film-maker has been nicknamed the "guerrilla Godard" (Powers: 1). Although Araki cites Godard's *Pierrot le Fou* (1965) as an inspiration for his film, *The Living End* is also clearly connected to *Weekend* in its use of flamboyance as death to signal a new era of cinema. *Weekend* proclaims that "A film is life," and the fact that Araki enthusiastically embraces this position without cannibalizing it the way Godard did demonstrates that contemporary alternative cinema has moved away from the pessimism and "aesthetics of destruction" which imbued the 1960s avant-garde. Unlike *Weekend* (or Warhol's "Death and Disaster" series on auto accidents), Araki wants the road trip in his film to end well.[5] Araki clearly admires Godard, but won't settle for a re-citation of his techniques, or a weakened/*Weekend* re-run of the previous age's aesthetic gauntlet. Luke's trenchant observation in the film that the sexual freedoms of the pre-AIDS era are no longer available ("We're victims of the sexual revolution. The generation before us got to have all the fun") not only symbolizes the lost libidinal inheritance of Araki's generation, but also mirrors the need to evolve beyond the legacy of the counter-cultural film *auteurs*. Just as we now have techniques for having safe sex in an AIDS crisis, today's alternative film-makers seem to trust that they can safely partner up with genre without necessarily risking contamination by hegemony's heterosexism or racism. They manipulate the ideological forms to signify social change and challenge moral power. Araki's homage to Godard and Warhol, and to the avant-garde's meditations on the death of cinema, is no cynical *bricolage* or a schoolboy's crush; it is a zealous acknowledgment of a continuum of the past, present, and future of cinema.

The Living End takes pleasure in all its quotations, from its Godardian inspirations to the cheap thrills of traditional genre and linear narrative. Indeed, the film wallows in passion, using soft pornography as yet another filmic citation to underscore this point. As Roy Grundmann notes, "*The Living End* is largely a gay porn pastiche" (27). Similar to how Jon needs Luke to loosen him up, Araki adds sex to spice up his avant-garde intellectualisms. The numerous erotic scenes between Jon and Luke simultaneously signal porn as cinematic pleasure and a site of political self-recognition for this sexually identified community. Hot sex is a crucial, and political, aspect of an "AIDS narrative," especially to contrast gay cinema from the Hollywood AIDS film's habit of portraying a celibate and sick protagonist. Furthermore, these contradictory methods – quoting both alternative cinema *and* genres like the road film and the pornographic film – mark *The Living End* as postmodern cinema, preeminently concerned with the metamorphoses of genre and meaning.

Object A(IDS) and the Road as Chronotope of Recovery

The Living End explores how people might live through the AIDS crisis without becoming self-destructive like Luke, who blames society for his predicament, or passive like Jon, who blames himself. The fact of being infected with HIV must somehow be integrated into the world of meaning and self-knowledge that Luke and Jon had previously taken for granted. Their test results mobilize a confusing reaction of power, fear, and desire; to survive, they must embrace as part of themselves a fearful disease which our society prefers to ignore. *The Living End* takes the two extreme, opposing responses of Luke and Jon to being HIV-positive and resolves them dialectically into something more healthy.

For AIDS is the ontological wound at the base of this film, revealing the topography where, in Stallybrass and White's phrase, "ideology and fantasy conjoin" as Jon and Luke use narrative agency to survive that wound (the Latin *plāga*, wound or infection, is the root of our word "plague").[6] The rupture caused by AIDS in this film could be described by what Freudian revisionist Jacques Lacan calls the *objet a*: the surplus, the invisible, intangible, incredible mark of the world's inconsistency.[7] The *objet a* – here *objet a(ids)* – sets the two lovers off on their destructive pilgrimage, with the road offering the chronotope for ego recovery.[8] In the logic of this film, the audacity of asserting a narrative presence, the insistent creation of an "I," is the first step to reclaiming one's life. Sitting at a motel pool after they've hit the road, and dictating into his tape recorder until the batteries die, Jon notes that he feels as though he has fallen through to the other side of the looking glass. His simile suggests more than Alice's downward journey into Wonderland; it symbolizes his break from the normal developmental phase of ego formation which Lacan calls the "mirror stage." Jon's comment marks his metaphoric move away from the infant's earliest perception of itself in the mirror, when it imagines its own future body mastery, toward a second, symbolic mirror phase which signals a rebirth or resurrection of his sense of self. On the other side of this symbolic mirror (phase), we might fantasize, Jon even transcends the "imaginary signifier" of *individual* ego wholeness by means of his quest on the road but also metacinematically, by virtue of

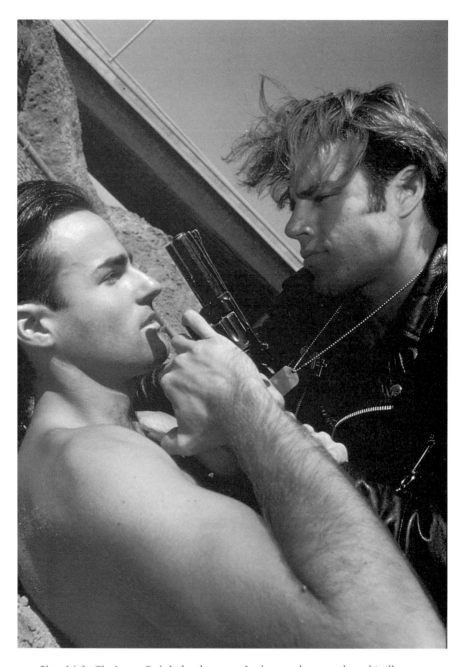

Plate 14.2   The Living End. Luke threatens Jon's complacency about his illness.
Courtesy of October Films.

Araki's genre-based interrogation of the *social* apparatuses of identity, including cultural systems such as cinema.[9]

The panic of AIDS triggers a paradoxical dynamic which Luke and Jon act out, shifting between the unraveling annihilation of the death drive and the self-preservation instinct of mastery. After their first night together, Luke tells Jon: "There's thousands, maybe millions, of us walking around with this thing inside of us, this time bomb making our futures finite. Suddenly I realize we've got nothing to lose, and we can say fuck work, fuck the system, fuck everything. Don't you get it? We're totally free. We can do whatever the fuck we want to." But the point is not really to do "whatever the fuck we want," since doing so could bring about the cessation of desire. Rather than reaching a goal, the object is to keep juggling fantasy scenarios in order to keep the sense of self alive. The challenge is to sustain psychic subjectivity and stability in spite of the diagnosis. The quintessential response to Luke's invitation to "do whatever the fuck we want" is Jon's dilatory question, "Like what?" Jon counters Luke's rage and aggression with delay as, together, they choreograph apotropaic dances of desire and keep satisfaction just out of arm's reach.

Endless repetition and aimless circulation are the machinery of fantasy. They explain the desultory itinerary of Luke and Jon's road trip and describe the means of regaining a sense of subjectivity after the shock of *objet a(ids)*. *The Living End* represents the perpetual motion of desire; it really doesn't matter if Jon and Luke are in Montana or Pluto, as long as they're moving, suspending quotidian concerns like paying the rent or getting sick. Slavoj Zizek notes: "It is precisely the role of fantasy to give the coordinates of the subject's desire, to specify its object, to locate the position the subject assumes in it. It is only through fantasy that the subject is constituted as desiring: *through fantasy, we learn how to desire*" (6; emphasis in original). Fantasy, even outlaw fantasy, links itself to patterns of expectation and, thus, to genre; it does not range completely free of anchor to cultural, societal, or familial moorings. Jon and Luke's journey is a rite of corporeal passage through the mise-en-scène of fantasy. The heroes re-pair the chaos brought on by the diagnosis by rediscovering and reinventing the landscapes of the road genre. They assert the primacy of cruising as a privileged, active response to the abject position into which they are cast by being afflicted by AIDS.

Brought together in desire by the *objet a(ids)*, Jon and Luke unleash the fear, anger, and rebellion against society that Luke previously expressed in spray-painting his accusations – "I blame society." Luke's reckless response is increasingly common in what we might call "AIDS noir" stories, which reject the hack narrative device of ending when the sick person dies, and instead create tales of social activism and collective aggression. For instance, some characters in James Robert Baker's novel *Tim and Pete* (1993) figure they might as well die as AIDS-terrorists as from the disease itself. Artist and activist David Wojnarowicz, who died from AIDS in 1992, perceived the close links between body, landscape, and social order that *The Living End* also explores. Writing about his reaction to being diagnosed as HIV-positive, Wojnarowicz said:

> It simply underlined what I knew existed anyway. Not just the disease but the sense of death in the American landscape. How when I was out west this summer standing in the mountains of a small city in New Mexico I got a sudden and intense feeling of rage looking at those postcard perfect slopes and clouds. . . . I couldn't buy the con of nature's beauty: all I could see was death. The rest of my life is being unwound and seen through a frame of death. My anger is more about this culture's refusal to deal with mortality. My rage is really about the fact that WHEN I WAS TOLD THAT I'D CONTRACTED THIS VIRUS IT DIDN'T TAKE ME LONG TO REALIZE THAT I'D CONTRACTED A DISEASED SOCIETY AS WELL.
>
> (emphasis in original: 106)

The idea of a sick culture imposing a death sentence on a rebellious type who is innocent in heart but never given a second chance is not new or unique to AIDS. Araki cites as one of his influences Fritz Lang's *You Only Live Once* (1937), in which Henry Fonda plays a troubled young man whose prison record prevents him from getting a clean break from society, even after he has paid his dues. If one is sentenced to death anyway, why not feel rage at the injustice of it all? Why *not* at least try to escape?[10]

AIDS is one type of historical event which alters what Kaja Silverman calls society's "dominant fictions." Silverman rereads Freud's writings on "war trauma" to show how history can sometimes "undo our imaginary relations to the symbolic order" (55). This dissolution, Silverman contends, encourages us to recognize an "*internal* response to an *external* danger" such as war – and, I would add, today's pressing threat of AIDS (56). She explains: "Since the kind of traumatic neurosis which is typified by war trauma can only be bound through repetition . . . [,] disintegration constantly haunts the subject's attempt to effect a psychic synthesis" (61). Silverman develops her ideas in relation to films from the mid-1940s to explain the postwar cinematic representation of male "lack" or void. But her theories illuminate the male-focused AIDS film as well. The traumas of the Second World War and of AIDS may both manifest themselves in cinema "as the compulsion to repeat experiences which are so threatening to the coherence of the male ego that they come close to exposing the void at the center of subjectivity" (63). In these terms, Luke acts out the compulsion of the death drive to violate all limits of the ego and its search for constancy, which Jon in turn represents with his stability. In *The Living End*, Luke's body – with its health, vitality, and sexuality – seems so at odds with his diagnosis that he cannot reconcile the two images even by cutting open his wrists to ponder his virus-carrying blood. As the destructive and irresponsible member of the duo, Luke embodies *thanatos*. He symbolizes a "radical unbinding . . . defined as the compulsion to repeat experiences of an overwhelming and incapacitating sort," in contrast to Jon's manifestations of the ego's mechanisms of "psychic bonding" (Silverman: 58).

The death of sexual desire is the silent worry of this film, not the death of cinema; *The Living End* becomes an argument to the gay community *not* to succumb to the AIDS crisis through aphanisis, the disappearance of sexual desire. Cruising detours a death drive with the continual search for sex and endless desire – the film's alternative to Luke's suicidal compulsion and Jon's equally acquiescent tendency to become the complacent HIV-positive victim. The film lets Luke play out his death drive to its violent but failed end, and it encourages Jon to shake free from his obeisant, self-blaming persona. While Jon is responsible compared to Luke, the film proudly proclaims its own irresponsibility and invests in seeing Luke corrupt Jon. A few days after Jon warns Luke to stop making sexual advances while he is at the wheel, Jon's caution turns to reckless joy at receiving a blow job from Luke while driving past a cop car. *The Living End* favors an outlaw reaction over a victim response to the epidemic, although it uses Jon and Luke to problematize both tendencies.

Araki writes the risks of desire and death into a dramatic crescendo in the film's final scene at the beach, where Luke has knocked out and tied up Jon, then rapes him as part of his plan to shoot himself at the moment of orgasm. By actually pulling the pistol trigger when he climaxes, Luke plays out this outlaw scenario to its illogical conclusion. Only the fact that he had already shot his last bullet at a bank's Automated Teller Machine prevents him from suicide. Only then does Luke abandon his compulsive attraction to violence and suicide. The thwarting of his death drive catalyses Luke to fall back through to the "other side of the mirror." Rejecting the aggression of *thanatos*, Luke flips into the productive energy of *eros*. He throws away the spent gun and unties Jon, who hits Luke in anger and walks away in disgust. Yet Jon returns, eventually resting his head on Luke's shoulder as the camera pulls back to the final frame: a long shot of the two alone on the horizon. Thus Araki transforms the beach scenarios of earlier gay films as site of Fire Island cruising (e.g., Warhol's *My Hustler*, 1966) or AIDS postmortem fantasy *topos* (e.g., *Longtime Companion*, 1990), as well as of (non-gay) French New Wave films, including Godard's final scene after failed love in *Pierrot le Fou*. *The Living End* closes with the same ambiguity of the famous escape to the beach in François Truffaut's *The 400 Blows* (1959). By revising the end of this death-inflected hybridized genre, *The Living End* appeals for the continuation of life and gay sexual desire in spite of AIDS and the nihilism the disease may create.

Narrative Imagination and Social Ills

Arguing that the AIDS epidemic has "*resolved* rather than *occasioned* a crisis in signification – the crisis that has always been gay sexuality itself," Paul Morrison explains the denouement of typical narrative by using Freud's normative readings of heterosexuality, whose pleasures are focused on "end-pleasure," or genital orgasm. Morrison writes: "Like the well-made narrative, moreover, normative sexual activity is end-haunted, all for its end. The perversions of adults . . . are thus intelligible only as 'the sickness of *uncompleted narratives*' . . . multiple narratives, endless narratives, nonnarratives [thus become] everything that our culture designates or denigrates as 'promiscuity'" (162; emphasis in original). Not only does *The Living End* enjoy its homosexual celebrations and endless narrative, but the film counters those homophobic cultural readings of AIDS that perpetuate the stereotype that "the perverse, the promiscuous, just want to die" (Morrison: 163). The persistence of apocalyptic outcomes in narratives of gay sexuality stresses the thin line between our own agency in telling stories and the power of genre to dictate stories "of" us. When genre takes us hostage without our awareness, we are at the highest risk of believing we imagine fresh endings that are, in fact, banal and highly ideological. For example, D. A. Miller accuses Susan Sontag, in his review of her *AIDS and Its Metaphors*, of falling prey to the homophobic cultural myth. Miller claims that Sontag's book falls victim to the very "end-of-the-world rhetoric" that she sets out to critique in her discussion of AIDS, because Sontag concludes that apocalyptic thinking may be "inevitable." Miller asks: "What sort of 'liberation' can be effected by an analysis whose terms make it thus consonant with 'the standard plague story . . . of inexorability, inescapability'? So thoroughly does that story come to take Sontag herself prisoner that by the end she gives up even pretending to be doing something besides retelling it" (99–100). The insight of Araki's film is to place a plague story in the road genre – thus doubling the apocalyptic narrative structure in order to punctuate his counter-generic response.

The Living End risks opening up a simultaneously irresponsible and utopic space by flouting the logic of death and endings, thus inviting taboo knowledge like that obtained in ancient Greek epic when heroes traveled through the underworld, land of the dead. The film's veneer of nihilism and its proclamation of irresponsibility can be unpacked to show how Araki creates an odyssey which traverses dangerous symbolic terrain only to defy the AIDS threat. "Responsible" means that which "can be charged with being the cause, agent, or source of something" (*Webster's Dictionary*). Thus the adjective and the personality trait it describes both refer to Jon's willingness to blame himself for his medical status, and simultaneously point to what Luke's "bad boy" energy rejects. In contrast, to be irresponsible is to refuse to answer for consequences, to be unable to

Plate 14.3 The Living End. The HIV-positive road outlaws with their wheels.
Courtesy of October Films.

render satisfaction, to be insolvent or unaccountable for another person's
debts (including, presumably, what Euripides calls death: "a debt we all must
pay") – all of which are issues in the film. On the road in *The Living End*, the
responsible and irresponsible circulate and eventually transform one another.

Instead of being distracted by the typical homophobic issues which harass gays,
Araki's film concerns itself with the equally menacing effect of the AIDS crisis on
the self-identifications of and within the gay community. *The Living End* refuses
subject positions that have traditionally repressed gays, as do other gay cultural and
political activist groups such as ACT UP, Queer Nation, and the queer film movement in general. In particular, the film rejects homophobia and the law. Rather
than "claiming as an ontology what is only a point of address" (Silverman: 61),
Luke knows that his life is not threatened by the menacing interpellations which
confront him. For instance, the lesbians who abduct Luke try to pinpoint a name
for the phallus/penis while holding him at gun point. They trill through an extensive repertoire of synonyms, stopping only on the term "love gun" to (mistakenly)
flaunt the superior power of their pistol. He remains aloof in the back seat as if
he recognizes that the surplus of signification, including the girls's gun, fails
to address his subject position. A later scene shows Luke controvert the name-
calling of three camped-up gay-bashers by killing them. The impotence of all
these bellicose hailings is stressed not only by their repeated failure, but by their
very excess within the film. The night he runs to Jon after "probably" killing a

cop, Luke literally rejects the commandment of the law, indicting its authority as irrelevant in comparison to his vengeful wrath at society. *The Living End* thus stages some of the scenarios through which gay men are daily, and dangerously, addressed, and fails to heed them because it wants to focus instead on the impact of being pronounced "HIV-positive."

As the cock of the walk, Luke refuses to cower before the threats intended to intimidate him. But Jon sways toward being harmfully interpellated by his HIV status, a response which could possibly make him more vulnerable to becoming ill via the disease. Jon's dilemma shows itself most clearly on the same day that he learns his HIV test results: when an unknown caller interested in phone sex gives Jon the chance to have an extreme version of safe sex, based on the exchange of words instead of bodily fluids. Any chance that Jon will be seduced by an auditory love-making disappears once he has experienced Luke and "his smell, his touch." Compared to the safe onanism of the phone partner, Luke seems alive. Although it took two calls from the mystery man for Jon definitively to refuse the phone sex invitation, what's important, within the value system of the film, is that Jon does not fall for the "sex in a plastic bag" mentality that "calls" to him after the diagnosis.

In contrast, Jon's straight female friend Darcy lives for the telephone calls that penetrate her isolation from the outer world. She acts as harbor to Jon's anchor, giving him a maternal clinginess against which he rebels and a home base from which he runs. Darcy is a painter who dresses funkily in retro-boheme punk clothes and lives with her boyfriend in an art studio. While the film privileges an irresponsible fantasy world for Jon as a fugitive on the lam and in "mad love," it paints Darcy as the risk to avoid. With her disproportionate concern over Jon's diagnosis, she becomes the film's straw man of how one should *not* react to the disease. Darcy's distress assaults male sexuality: she comes home from visiting Jon only to be surprised to find that her own boyfriend is "still up," and refuses all his sexual advances until he starts seeing someone else. After Jon embarks on his adventure with Luke on the road (and between the sheets), she pathetically sits at home waiting for Jon's collect calls, and rages when she misses one.

Luke tells Jon at the breakfast table after their first night together, "The generation before us had all the fun. And we get to pick up the tab," yet Darcy is the one constantly picking up the tab when Jon calls her collect from unknown locations. But the tab most in arrears is *The Living End*'s own debt to women. From the pistol-wielding lesbians, to the jealous wife who surreally murders her bisexual husband with a kitchen knife, to the supreme fag hag Darcy, the film feminizes its representations of caution and angry frustration with love relation-ships. Although each character in this film is flawed in some fashion, Darcy offers the most troubling portrait because it is the least farcical. Not only does Darcy mollycoddle him, but Jon wears a Jesus T-shirt in the beginning of the film that mirrors the Jesus bumper sticker on the lesbians' car. These symbols signal a distastefully prudent, blame-fraught, and effeminate response to the disease, from which Luke's heretical, macho madness rescues Jon.[11] Thanks to Luke's intervention, the religious signifiers shift from representing a female sphere of devotion to the alternate, more manly theme of resurrection. Since the heroes' names mirror the disciples Luke and John, authors of two of the Gospels (which were revisionary, utopic texts in themselves), the biblical references melt into a homoerotic fantasy of a righteous brotherhood which traverses the road (genre) to instill undying faith among the masses (of men).

Although the avowed devotee of Godard and a masculinist brand of alternative film-making, Araki owes some thanks to feminist cinema. Feminist film-making has a vital history as an avant-garde challenge to dominant ideology and aesthetic form – especially vis-à-vis issues of gender identity and sexual freedom (the "sex–gender system"). Feminist cinema helped open up the expressive opportunities and political edge enjoyed by Araki as both a film-maker and a gay man of color, even if acknowledging this particular predecessor seems to cause the "anxiety of influence" normally credited to one's forefathers. Teresa de Lauretis traces the early debates of feminist cinema in relation to Godard and the avant-garde theorists and film-makers of the 1960s to 1970s. Her account reminds us of the passion with which feminists first used metacinematic means to reject a narrative tradition which killed off the heroine as the tragic end to her attempt to rebel. Sally Potter's *Thriller* (1979), for instance, centers on "Mimi's suspicion that she has been murdered by the plot of Puccini's opera *Bohème*" (de Lauretis: 107). Since the dominant "sex–gender system" produces narratives which tend to be misogynistic and homophobic, dissidents like feminists, gays, and lesbians heighten their chances of survival when they ally together, rather than antagonize one another. *The Living End* may legitimately be more interested in surveying a separate gay space than a pluralistic queer or bi-gendered one. By casting its female characters unsympathetically, however, it fails to comprehend that any potent condemnation of hegemonic "sex–gender" practices must address the twin evils of misogyny and homophobia.

Certainly films should be entitled to express apprehension about the opposite sex. But adopting genre without interrogating how its deep structure affects gender relations causes questions about the vitality of cinema to resurface. We must demand the postmodern road film to refuse to fall subservient to an antinomy in which models of resistance, spontaneity, truth, independence, and mobility are masculinized, and passivity, acquiescence, fixity, and fatalism are feminized. Araki rejects frequent comparisons of *The Living End* with *Thelma and Louise* (1991), but *both* films try to subvert the road genre in their protest against the impossible, yet seemingly inescapable, confines of heterosexist patriarchy. Araki sees his own protagonists as political activists fighting against the system, but is cool toward *Thelma and Louise* because, he says, its heroines "act just as brainless and obnoxious as men. That's not exactly progress on the feminist front to me" (Kalmansohn: 41). Yet fantasies of anger and outlaw resistance are not the sole property of the gay male community. Indeed, it is thanks to the popularity of a box office hit like *Thelma and Louise* that (independent and studio) road films enjoy a renaissance in Hollywood and that "sex–gender" rebels began subverting the presumptions of the road genre and the privileges of its so-called "universal" hero.[12] Through the women's (short-lived) performance as outlaws, *Thelma and Louise* deconstructs the naturalized but masculinist codes and conventions at work in the road genre. But this couple, unlike Araki's, is not immune to the generic death sentence: although Thelma and Louise act as agents of contradiction and resistance, their fate becomes increasingly inseparable from the road film's prescriptive finale of death. Since heroines still find it harder than heroes to modify the destiny of the genre, we can glimpse the daunting conflict between a narrative's archaic deep structure and its contemporary re-vision.[13] Those interpretations which disallow the same agency to Thelma and Louise as afforded to male outlaws in road films show the difficulties in reading or constructing a feminist-subject position even within the genre of rebellion.

The Road as Familiar Landscape of Rebellion

The familiar landscape of rebellion offered by the road story serves a tale about an urgent present-day illness. As an "escape route," the road is ever ready at hand for the last-minute exit of people whom life has left nothing else to lose. The road story wields a big jackpot in identity re-vision, because it narrates resistance to the status quo. The road symbolizes an utopic (or sometimes dystopic) space in which one can escape from institutions such as the law, marriage, or capitalism. As a site of deviant discourse, the road offers a territory of enunciation that can be appropriated by cultural rebels who use film genre as a shared public "forum," a metaphoric commons or *polis*, from which to launch a critique of society. But the road story does not merely entertain with tension-releasing fantasies of rebellion. Its very familiarity can be the basis for a sneak cultural attack on the narrative and identificatory structures which shape one's private self-identity *and* one's willingness to protest publicly against structures which are homophobic (or, for that matter, racist or misogynistic). For this reason, Araki's choice of the road story enhances the political dimension of his fantasy of a living end.

Of course, simply using the road genre and its recent innovations to invoke a rebellious, liberatory, or transformative *topos* does not automatically make each road film progressive. Nor is the death of an HIV-positive protagonist at the end of a film necessarily homophobic or hackneyed. The road story brings with it a complex social history that informs our readings of these stories. In *The Living*

End, the unique junction and disjunction of these potent semiotic registers – how they can read against one another – are put in to play. These twists to generic expectations reawaken our utopic desires and offer a new perspective on our daily routines.

Until the 1990s, only a few road films had overtly destabilized the norms which install the male, white, heterosexual, middle class as the genre's central protagonist. This did not, however, prevent people of different subculture communities from using the outlaw genre to navigate the fantasy coordinates of their desires. We can enjoy road films in complex ways even when our identity group is not explicitly represented in its master-narrative. But film-making in the 1990s, especially genre revisionism, shows the return of what was repressed in dominant cinema: collective pride in "deviant" gender, sexuality, and ethnicity has surfaced to haunt, taunt, infect, and transform the narrative structures that once denied it representation. This genre of rebellion is increasingly used and altered by such groups to insert their "own kind" as the leading protagonist – not just antagonists – thereby feeding a group fantasy which celebrates its difference from the norm. The once-masculinist road story of the lone anarchist on the run is reborn when genre becomes a vehicle for the representation of "otherness" along the lines of marginalized class, race, sexuality, or gender. Alastair Fowler states that genre's function is to "mediate between the flux of history and the canons of art" (24). It is exactly that line between history and art which rebel subcultures work to change right now via genre re-vision. When part of a community cannot see itself in the historical record (because of failing to be represented by official power) or in mainstream culture, then genre is one highly normative place to begin to modify society's prescriptions of identity. Rather than see in genre an archive of hegemony, today's alternative film-makers envision the opportunity to revitalize, instead of reject, the canons. Meaning and transformation come from changing our structures of being and knowing, including genre. In this way, marginal communities create a radically different meaning out of a once recognizably hegemonic form – and, in this very specific but oblique way, artfully transform society and its standards.

Recent Gay and Women's Road Films

The increasing recognition of the myriad experience of sexuality and gender occurs not only among alternative film-makers and cultural critics, but also now in the general film marketplace. Two recent films with drag queens on the road give testimony to the popularity and mainstreaming of gay challenges to the "sex–gender" system. The 1994 Australian film, *The Adventures of Priscilla, Queen of the Desert*, and the 1995 feature film with Hollywood hit stars, *To Wong Foo, Thanks for Everything! Julie Newmar*, invite us to note how the road story consistently encourages this play with identity. Because these two films use the conventions of the romance and comedy to situate their road stories, they follow a far different trajectory from an adventure road film like *The Living End*: the comedies emphasize self-transformation, the reversal of obstacles, and the attainment of dreams. *Priscilla* envisions the formation of the happy queer family, complete with gay father in drag and lesbian mother, and features a straight gentleman willing to fall in love with a transsexual. But where the film makes headway in the favorable representation of drag queens, it unfortunately perpetuates ambivalent subject-positions for women in its portrayal of the Filipina immigrant, who bears the weight of the film's misogyny and racism.[14]

While women are not demonized in *To Wong Foo*, they suffer from unabashed condescension when the drag queens teach the female residents of a small town the true meaning of friendship among women and liberate them from boredom and spousal abuse. What rescues the film from smug paternalism is the transformation of the entire town, not just the road travelers. Change is available to the stationary characters as well as to the mobile, masculine heroes. In this way, *To Wong Foo* offers a counter-example to *The Living End*'s male characters, who regain psychic vitality while Darcy passively watches her life crumble. *To Wong Foo*'s spotlighting of racial difference as a trope, and its self-conscious play with the gender expectations of the road comedy, somewhat compensate for its high-heeled "faux pas." And, as far as I can trace, this is the first road feature film directed by a woman (unless one counts Kathryn Bigelow's 1987 *Near Dark*, in which vampires travel by van, or the 1994 short-run flop *Mad Love* by Antonia Bird).

There's also now a spate of "women's road films" of the comedy genre which seek to capitalize on the new market generated by *Thelma and Louise*, including: *Leaving Normal* (1992), *Bound and Gagged: A Love Story* (1993), and *Camilla* (1994). In particular, the 1995 film *Boys on the Side* is another road-HIV story which puts a trio on the lam, but these women are running with a whole gamut of issues: murder, flagging careers, infection with AIDS, lesbianism, motherhood, and marriage. Like *Thelma and Louise*, the road film's death sentence is obeyed in *Boys on the Side*: its HIV-positive heroine dies, causing the heartbroken lesbian to resume her arrested trip to the West. AIDS and lesbianism function in this film like fashion accessories that update an old wardrobe that no longer quite fits; thankfully, these novelties have the good style not to be homophobic, hence the lesbian is not fated to be the one who dies. As the recycling of a formula, genre films can easily succumb to becoming a banal commodity rather than an adroit way to shed perspective on the familiar aspects of life. Compared to these genre "knock-offs," *The Living End* takes bold steps to restructure the logic and thus the outcome of the road film.

Utopia: Perverting the Road Film's Limits

In *Utopics: Spatial Play*, Louis Marin focuses on the generative power of utopic discourse. He suggests that such discourse occupies the empty place of a historical resolution to a contradiction – neither one nor the other of contraries, but contradiction itself. Utopic rhetoric stages an imaginary or fictional solution to the contradiction, and thus engenders incongruous spaces which are not comprehensible via a totalizing philosophy. Marin defines u-topia, literally meaning no-place, as "the place of the limit on which depends the disjunction that founds knowledge" – a place we acknowledge via the play of spaces rather than something about which we directly know (xiv). Such spatial play sketches out "the empty places (topics) of the concepts social theory will eventually occupy," and, as such, "is an ideological critique of the dominant ideology" (xiv). Marin's theories enable us to see how Araki's genre-bender pushes the road film to the paradox or perversion of its limits. *The Living End* stresses life instead of death; overt homosexuality instead of an oblique subtext of erotic homosociality (as found in a road film like *Thunderbolt and Lightfoot*, 1974, for example); a productive utopia/dystopia rather than a representation of a particular space; and cinematic reversals and "winks" in place of slavish subjection to Hollywood or avant-garde formulas. When the ending is altered, the entire epistemology of *telos* is paradoxically, retroactively revisioned – which has obvious implications for the stories a society tells about a life-threatening disease. *The Living End*'s heroes break out of the genre's strictures, and although driven by AIDS, their end is living. The alchemy by which Araki transforms the road genre moves us from rigid conventionality into hoping that the progression of the virus's damage could be suspended just as miraculously as the road genre's predetermined endings. The road motif symbolizes the movement of gay bodies not only through the landscape, but especially metaphorically forwards into the future when there might be a cure to the disease.

The Living End's deviation from the road film launches viewers into negotiating the gap between our genre expectations and the revisions manifested in the plot. The film effectively taps the deep longing for rebellion or utopia that the road genre elicits, then uses it to comment on the problems faced by society's non-conforming groups, its "outlaws." In this way, the film creates for viewers a metamorphosis like that experienced on a road trip, by generating new scenarios for the audience's own fantasies and new coordinates for imagining desire. By frustrating the generic dead end, which might satiate our expectations but not stimulate new vision, the film encourages the endless circulation of desire which constitutes subjectivity. It simultaneously makes a political statement by showing the undying circulation of gay desire despite the AIDS crisis – despite homophobia specific to the *topic* of homosexuality and cultural master-narratives which fail to provide a *topos*, or place, for the marginal "other" marked by queerness, ethnicity, disease, etc. In its dialogue, *The Living End* targets everything from cultural products such as genre films to the Bush Administration's anti-gay policies, squeezing the symbolic structures we take for granted until they crack, requiring utopic resolutions to be imagined in the manner described by Marin. But, where it excels in challenging the homophobia of patriarchy, *The Living End* disappoints in its assent to misogyny. Fredric Jameson's comment that "ideological commitment is not first and foremost a matter of moral choice but of the taking of sides in a struggle between embattled groups" reminds us that attention to liberatory subject-positions based on gender as well as sexual freedom need be an important goal for the next generation of revisionary road films (290).

Although viewers never learn the medical, legal, or quotidian outcome of Jon and Luke, the film urges love despite the obvious problems. Closure of the story is irrelevant, because it is a new attitude of love that the film wants to stimulate in the audience. In the final scene, after the rape, Jon walks back to Luke and gently touches him in a gesture which signals he can see a part of Luke (and himself) that is bigger than the nihilistic response to being HIV-positive. This "bearing witness" quality of love shown by Jon toward the contradictory, violent, ambivalently endearing Luke models an acceptance which goes beyond the sentimental specifics of the relationship between the two anti-heroes to encourage a broader public tolerance of young gays or of the large, varied community of people who are HIV-positive. *The Living End* is not the "irresponsible" love story or *memento mori* its surreal excesses disguise it as being. Its play with the road genre never degenerates into a tragedy about moribund film-making, but instead becomes a generous, impassioned plea for a continuation of love, desire – and cinema – in spite of the social problems which plague us at the end of the century.

Acknowledgments

Thanks to Rick Bolton, Joseph Allen Boone, and Tania Modleski for their generous assistance on this essay.

Notes

1 Jameson says of generic discontinuties: what is at issue is "not so much an organic unity as a symbolic act that must reunite or harmonize heterogeneous narrative paradigms which have their own specific and contradictory ideological meaning" (144).
2 For instance, French New Wave director Jean-Luc Godard uses techniques of Brechtian distanciation, such as in *Weekend* when Roland states, "This film's crap. We're always meeting nut-cases" (Godard: 56). In contrast, Araki inserts "nut-cases" into the background of the action, but his characters never directly comment on them or on the film-making process *per se*.

3 "Catharsis," the Greek word for purification, connotes a contamination which requires moral cleansing.

4 In fact, Araki's colleague Gus Van Sant, also uses the same posture from *Blow Job* in a key scene in *My Own Private Idaho* (1991).

5 Neupert notes: "*Weekend*, with its fragmented narrative line, diverse intertitles, impossible characters, and political monologues, looks like a muddle of film modes and genres, not all of which fit easily within a unified concept of 'the fiction film'" (145).

6 Stallybrass and White define the domains of transgression in terms of these four inter-related arenas: body, geography, group identity, and subjectivity. Each functions as interconnected discursive sites where conflict may occur between "social classification and psychological processes." The conflicts between collective society and individual psyche are "where ideology and fantasy conjoin" (25).

7 The *objet a* is not an object, person, or goal which satisfies the drive, but that which gives the drive something to want, or someone toward whom desire can be focused. It creates an alibi for the drive by being a metonym of the greater cause of desire. Zizek notes: "The *objet a* is precisely that surplus, that elusive make-believe that drove the man to change his existence. In 'reality,' it is nothing at all, just an empty surface (his life after the break is the same as before), but because of it the break is none-theless well worth the trouble" (8). Lacan says: "The *petit a* [*objet a*] could be said to take a number of forms, with the qualification that in itself it has no form, but can only be thought of predominantly orally or shittily. The common factor of *a* is that of being bound to the orifices of the body" (164). Grosz adds: "Lacan asserts that the drives' source is always defined by the erotogenic rim, the orifice, or a cut on the body's surface that marks a threshold between its interior and its exterior, and thus also a site of exchange between the subject and the world" (75).

8 Bakhtin defines chronotope as the means for expressing time and space in a novel. Different chronotopes organize a novel's fundamental narrative events and pinpoint the places of narrative meaning. He discusses how the road chronotope represents both a place where the hero gains distance and perspective on everyday private life, where "space is filled with real, living meaning, and forms a crucial relationship with the hero and his fate" (120), and simultaneously signifies "a time of exceptional and unusual events, events determined by chance" (116).

9 We can guess that Araki is also making a joke about cinema being "the imaginary signifier," as theorized by Christian Metz. Metz says: "Film is like the mirror. . . . In the mirror the child perceives . . . its own image. This is where primary identification (the formation of the ego) gets certain of its main characteristics: the child sees itself as an other. . . . [In the cinema,] the fact that the spectator has already known the experience of the mirror (of the true mirror), and is thus able to constitute a world of objects without having first to recognize himself within it" (45–6). A link between the impact of AIDS and the death of cinema, such as that made by Araki, might be said to find support in Metz's observation: "Chain of many mirrors, the cinema is at once a weak and a robust mechanism: like the human body . . . like a social institution" (51).

10 Such a view, of course, opposes the idea of Original Sin and the need for redemption which colors the road stories of Southern author Flannery O'Connor. It furthermore emphasizes the extent to which Araki rejects the conservative stand that AIDS is divine retribution for the sin of homosexuality.

11 The word "heresy," which pinpoints Luke's "deviation from a dominant practice" as well as the film's unorthodox use of religious symbols, derives from the Sanskrit word *sarati*, meaning to run or flow, mirroring the fugitive theme of the road trip. Interestingly, *sarati* is also the root of the word "serum," that watery part of blood vital to healthy systemic circulation, to nurturing body cells, as well as to the transmission of HIV.

12 Araki began production on *The Living End* well before *Thelma and Louise* (1991) was released; however the end was rewritten after a screening at the Sundance Film Festival in 1992 (Ansen: 68) to revise the original script which ended with the death of both lovers (Araki's Production Notes).

13 While Thelma and Louise as characters remain loyal to the structure of the road genre with its predetermined outcome, Jon and Luke are more capable of acting as "actants" with the power to deviate from the genre's deep structural imperative to die. Although adventure road films routinely end with the deaths of paired men, e.g., *Easy Rider*, the switch to female (or gay or ethnic) protagonists alters the implications of the genre in significant ways. Revisionists can use generic expectations to their advantage, even without altering the deep structure, but should remain attentive to the full implications of their choices.

14 See my "Drag as Nation: Performing the Ab(ba)original Walkabout in 'Priscilla, Queen of the Desert'" in *Vanishing Point* (Stanford University Department of Comparative Literature) 2 (1996): 7–24.

Works Cited

Ansen, David. "Off the Beaten Track: Three Films Explore Love, Death and the Cosmos." *Newsweek* (August 31, 1992): 68.

Araki, Gregg. "Production Notes." Press Kit from October Films. *The Living End* is distributed by October Films, New York.

Baker, James Robert. *Tim and Pete*. New York: Penguin Books, 1993.

Bakhtin, M. M. *The Dialogic Imagination*, trans. Caryl Emerson and Michael Holquist, ed. Michael Holquist. Austin: University of Texas Press, 1981.

de Lauretis, Teresa. *Technologies of Gender: Essays on Theory, Film, and Fiction*. Bloomington, Indiana University Press, 1987.

Fowler, Alastair. *Kinds of Literature: An Introduction to the Theory of Genres and Modes*. Cambridge, MA: Harvard University Press, 1982. Cited in Ulrich Wicks, *Picaresque Narrative, Picaresque Fictions*. New York: Greenwood Press, 1989.

Godard, Jean-Luc. *Weekend and Wind From the East*, trans. Marianne Sinclair and Danielle Adkinson. Modern Film Scripts. New York: Simon & Schuster, 1972.

Grosz, Elizabeth. *Jacques Lacan: A Feminist Introduction*. London: Routledge, 1990.

Grundmann, Roy. "The Fantasies We Live By: Bad Boys in 'Swoon' and 'The Living End'." *Cinéaste* 19 (Fall 1992): 25–9.

Jameson, Fredric. *The Political Unconscious: Narrative as a Socially Symbolic Act*. Ithaca: Cornell University Press, 1981.

Kalmansohn, David. *Frontiers* (August 28, 1992): 41.

Lacan, Jacques. *Feminine Sexuality: Jacques Lacan and the École Freudienne*, trans. Jacqueline Rose, eds. Juliet Mitchell and Jacqueline Rose. New York: W. W. Norton, 1985.

Marin, Louis. *Utopics*, trans. Robert A. Vollrath. Atlantic Highlands, NJ: Humanities Press, 1984.

Metz, Christian. "The Imaginary Signifier." *The Imaginary Signifier: Psychoanalysis and the Cinema*, trans. Ben Brewster (1974). Bloomington: Indiana University Press, 1982. 1–87.

Miller, D. A. "Sontag's Urbanity." *October* 49 (1989): 91–101.

Morrison, Paul. "'End-Pleasure': Narrative in the Plague Years." *Narrative and Culture*, ed. Janice Carlisle and Daniel R. Schwarz. Athens: University of Georgia Press, 1994. 160–78.

Neupert, Richard. *The End: Narration and Closure in the Cinema*. Detroit: Wayne State University Press, 1995.

Powers, John. "Beetle in the Grass: Why Gregg Araki Doesn't Kill Himself." *LA Weekly* (August 21–7, 1992): cover, 18+.

Silverman, Kaja. *Male Subjectivity at the Margins*. New York: Routledge, 1992.

Stallybrass, Peter and Allon White. *The Politics and Poetics of Transgression*. Ithaca: Cornell University Press, 1986.

Webster's New World Dictionary. 3rd ed., eds. Victoria Neufeldt and David B. Guralnik. Cleveland: Prentice Hall, 1994.

Zizek, Slavoj. *Looking Awry: An Introduction to Jacques Lacan Through Popular Culture*. Cambridge: The MIT Press, 1991.

15

MY OWN PRIVATE IDAHO AND THE NEW QUEER ROAD MOVIES

Robert Lang

In 1990, writing in *The New York Times*, Caryn James announced unequivocally that, "Today's Yellow Brick Road Leads Straight to Hell." The film that prompted her to lament "how far film makers have come from the road to Oz," and that made her realize there was something that should be identified as "the new, subversive road movie," was David Lynch's *Wild at Heart* (1990). Unlike most film critics before her, James has a very definite notion of what the (classic) road movie is:

> Films like *The Wizard of Oz* [1939] and Preston Sturges' *Sullivan's Travels* [1941] defined the standard pattern for road movies: whether the hero was a scarecrow or a rich film director bumming cross-country during the Depression, characters traveled through danger and disillusionment to healthy self-knowledge and back to the safety of home. They followed an optimistic course as old as the American West and as deeply entrenched in our culture as Whitman's "Song of the Open Road"
>
> (1)

James believes that *The Wizard of Oz* has profoundly influenced the contemporary road movie, but that "The creators of today's road movies recognize that the road leads to the nightmarish wilds of society and of their characters' own hearts" (25). Using *Wild at Heart* and *Something Wild* (1986) as her primary examples, James noted that in the happy endings of such films, however, contemporary film-makers "fight for the persistent hope that the road still leads to a place where dreams come true" (25).

The road movie genre has taken yet another turn recently, with the appearance in the 1990s of a veritable wave of independently produced queer films – some of the more successful or critically interesting ones being Gus Van Sant's *My Own Private Idaho* (1991), Gregg Araki's *The Living End* (1992), and Steve McLean's *Postcards From America* (1994; adapted primarily from two of David Wojnarowicz's semi-autobiographical books, *Close to the Knives: A Memoir of Disintegration* and

Memories That Smell Like Gasoline). In the mainstream, too, gay-themed or queerly inflected road movies have appeared in the 1990s: *Boys on the Side* (1995), *The Adventures of Priscilla, Queen of the Desert* (1994), *To Wong Foo, Thanks For Everything! Julie Newmar* (1995), and *Total Eclipse* (1995). But it can hardly be said that the independently produced queer road movies end happily, even if there is a sense – implicit in the films' struggle against homophobia – that the road may yet lead to a place where dreams come true. For whatever reasons, the queer cinema of the 1990s has emerged as a distinct phenomenon and has drawn considerable attention in the mainstream press; and it is one of the aims of this essay to examine why this should be so.

Thomas Waugh has observed that the "same-sex imaginary" of the gay-authored narrative cinema from 1916 to 1990 has remained remarkably constant in its preservation, and even heightening, of "the structures of sexual difference inherent in Western (hetero)patriarchal culture," but that it "usually stops short of those structures' customary dissolution in narrative closure" (145). Since the 1980s, however, we have seen a new breed of young gay directors who are "very much plugged into their gay constituency" (154). Moreover, as Waugh notes, "the international circuit of gay festivals has begun to consolidate something like real gay genres, gay audiences, and gay authors, arguably for the first time in our history" (154).

And yet, what do we make of films – like *My Own Private Idaho* and *Postcards From America* – that could be interpreted as suggesting that homosexuality is caused by unhappy childhoods, or worse? When *Postcards From America* was screened at the 1994 New York Film Festival, Stephen Holden, blaming the film-maker, wrote in *The New York Times*: "Mr. McLean's film adaptation . . . makes a heavy-handed Freudian equation between the vicious beatings Wojnarowicz endured at the hands of his father and his cruising for rough trade at truck stops and on the road" (14). And of *My Own Private Idaho*, one critic observed that

> Inevitably . . . *Idaho* says many things about homosexuality, and the indirect message is troublesome in how it eerily recalls films from the 50s and 60s, when homosexuality tentatively emerged from the cinematic closet only to be embraced by (presumably straight) directors eager to reduce it to Freudian pathology.
>
> (Cheshire)

But the new queer film-makers have not felt under pressure to make propaganda films for the gay movement, especially as, with hindsight, some of them believe the "gay liberation criticism" of the post-Stonewall decade – with its simplistic eagerness to endorse "positive images" and condemn negative stereotypes – has largely failed us.[1] Gregg Araki, for example, subtitles *The Living End* "An Irresponsible Movie," which says, in effect: "Take it or leave it." Araki hopes his movies will also be seen by non-gay viewers, but he speaks and works as a gay film-maker with little interest in second-guessing the hypothetical non-gay audience.[2]

On the eve of *My Own Private Idaho*'s release, Araki expressed some curiosity about what sort of impact Van Sant's film would have on mainstream attitudes and markets. "I think [*My Own Private Idaho*] will be important as a test of Hollywood's acceptance of the concept of a young auteur who makes films with quasi-gay themes and big stars," he told the interviewer. But Araki made it clear that there is a price to pay for "Hollywood's acceptance," and it is not one he is willing to pay:

> There's a real danger in following the Hollywood "carrot": the worst thing in the world to me would be becoming one of those filmmakers who is perpetually "in development." I would rather make a cheap movie than talk to "D-girls" and lawyers for three years. But I guess that's just my bad attitude. . . . The freedom of [independent filmmaking] is that you can do whatever you want.
>
> (Araki quoted in Oliver: 28)[3]

Van Sant told *Elle* magazine the same thing: "If I'm going to do something without the muscle and money of Hollywood, I should be able to do something that they wouldn't do" (quoted in Elder: 132). Clearly, if the road movie as a genre has developed a new, queer variant, it is because of what the independent film in the 1990s makes possible. But what are the likes of Araki, Van Sant, and McLean saying in their films? How are those of us who are traditionally unrepresented, or underrepresented, or misrepresented by Hollywood in fact being represented in the new queer road movies?

There appear to be a number of affinities between the road movie genre and the contemporary homosexual imaginary. The symbolism of "the road" as the freedom from constraints (the freedom to travel, discover, forget, experiment, escape, *move* . . .) has a correspondence, first of all, in the gay affirmation of sexuality: of sexuality as a celebration of the body and the senses. Gay men now generally acknowledge the centrality of the erotic impulse in the gay imaginary, and the dominant patterns of gay male sex – accurately described by Segal, echoing Richard Dyer, as "a basic romanticism combined with an easy acceptance of promiscuity" (154) – appear in the narratives of the new queer road movies, just as they do in some of the narratives of male gay pornographic film. It is easy to see the attraction of gay film-makers to the road movie genre, with all the possibilities it provides characters who choose to live and love outside the institution of the monogamous heterosexual partnership and the conventional nuclear family. In the 1970s, gay cinema – when it mirrored the master narrative of the (hetero)patriarchal cinema built on the conjugal drive – would usually not show its gay protagonists coming together at the end. The reason "gay closures are seldom happy endings," Waugh writes of the cinema in the 1970s, is that "We don't establish families – we just wander off looking horny, solitary, sad, or dead" (145). Waugh's half-ironic remark, "We don't establish families," is also a gesture toward the liberating notion that as gay men and women we are free to invent our own narratives, take a different road, form new definitions of family, and make new rules for the partnerships we might wish to enter. The queer road movies of the 1990s, more often than not, don't have conventionally happy endings, but something has certainly changed, for they cannot be called *un*happy endings, either.

The Hustler

In what follows, I wish to examine in particular the figure of the hustler, who has been prominent in the cinematic and literary gay imaginary for quite some time, and who can be seen as emblematic of the queer road movie protagonist. Like his female counterpart a century ago, the male prostitute is a subversive figure. Mary Ann Doane notes the increased fascination in the literature and art of the late nineteenth century with the figure of the prostitute as emblematic of the new woman's relation to urban space – the prostitute as the epitome of the female *flâneur*. Doane also suggests that "the prostitute represents the collapse of sublimation as a concept and hence the downfall of the 'sublime' – the 'end of the aura and the decline of love'" (264). The concept of the sublime (the sublime as "the locus of non-exchangeability," in accordance with Kant's understanding of it as indissociable from an individual subjective experience) is "seriously threatened" when "the body becomes a form of property which is exchangeable, when subjectivity and sexuality themselves are perceived as being on the market" (264–5).

The figure of the contemporary hustler, thus, not only comprehends this scandal, he also threatens the very underpinnings of the patriarchy, in which men can never themselves serve as commodities on the market. (As Luce Irigaray observes, the patriarchal order – as an economy of desire – is a man's game, in which *women* are circulated among men [170–91].) Indeed, the frequent insistence on the element of exchange in so many homosexual encounters (among Arabs in North Africa, for example) can be seen as an attempt imaginatively to save the structural underpinnings of the patriarchy, as the very condition of desire. The hustler and his john play roles, which may or may not correspond to the real reasons that bring them together.

The complexities of hustler–john dynamics have been perceptively analyzed by Michael Moon, and they suggest the extent to which the erotic undercurrents of the road movie – whether or not a hustler figures in the plot; and always in buddy movies – are inscribed within a force field of homophobia:

The supposedly spoiled and stigmatized role of john may be recuperated for some johns by making a kind of imaginary straightness of his own depend on the performed straightness of the hustler: a john's not descending to (in his mind) the depths of being queer while continuing to have sex with young men may depend on his success at maintaining the pretense that he does not have sex with queer men or boys and is consequently "not really queer."

(30)

Almost every mainstream road movie in which two men travel together – whether it be *Road to Morocco* (1942) with Bing Crosby and Bob Hope, *Scarecrow* (1973) with Gene Hackman and Al Pacino, *Thunderbolt and Lightfoot* (1974) with Clint Eastwood and Jeff Bridges, *Les Valseuses/Going Places* (1974) with Gérard Depardieu and Patrick Dewaere, *Planes, Trains and Automobiles* (1987) with Steve Martin and John Candy, *Innerspace* (1987) with Dennis Quaid and Martin Short, or *Dumb and Dumber* (1994) with Jim Carrey and Jeff Daniels – contains at least one scene that turns on homosexual anxiety and the taboo of same-sex attraction. In *Road to Morocco*, for example, Bing Crosby and Bob Hope are shipwrecked and washed up onto a Moroccan beach. They make their way to a city and find a restaurant, where they eat an enormous meal for which, of course, they haven't the money to pay. As they're discussing their dilemma, a local man comes in and gestures to Hope. Hope is afraid to talk to the man, so Crosby goes over to him. The man offers to buy Hope (for the Princess Shalamar/Dorothy Lamour), and gives Crosby some money. When Hope realizes he has been bought, he panics; and in a very funny exchange of dialogue, asks his friend: "Why would a guy buy a guy?"[4] The pornographic basis of the fantasy (of the man who manages to capture another man for use as an unwilling sexual object) is thus explicitly acknowledged, and Hope's anxiety about it is the reason the scene plays for laughs.[5] In a sense, too, the scene is made possible because it occurs in a road movie, which puts the characters in a strange land where – we're told – the people are "peculiar" and will "buy anything."

A similar moment occurs in *My Own Private Idaho*, during a conversation in a coffee shop between the two hustler friends, Mike (River Phoenix) and Scott (Keanu Reeves). Mike falls into a narcoleptic fit while trying to evade a man he thinks is "a pervert" (Hans, played by Udo Kier). When Mike returns to consciousness, he finds himself with Scott, whom he now asks sarcastically, "So, how much do you make off me when I'm asleep?" Scott replies gravely: "What! You think I'd sell your body while you're asleep? No, Mike . . . I'm on your side." The scene does not play for laughs, not only because the film is not a comedy; but because it acknowledges the reality of male hustling and pimping in the lives of its characters; and the two men will acknowledge, later in the film, that their friendship is virtually indistinguishable from love (but defined, ultimately, by its non-genitality). Although Mike is saying, in effect (just as Bob Hope's character protests to his friend), "You can't sell me! You don't own me!" he does not ask why a guy would buy a guy. Fifty years after *Road to Morocco*, the road movie can explore some of the erotic complexity of male–male friendships, without prohibitive cultural anxieties and Production Code pressure making comedy the only genre in which such questions can be honestly addressed.

One of the reasons the hustler can be proposed as an emblematic road movie figure is that, like the nineteenth-century *flâneur*, every hustler can be seen as living his own daily road movie, whether on the open road or on the streets of the city. But, if the *flâneur* is a man of pleasure, the hustler is a worker, he is on the job. One must therefore make the crucial distinction between real hustlers and hustlers on the screen.

Cinematic hustlers are overdetermined figures, with a complicated relation to "reality," because, among other reasons, film-makers often seek to make even more ambiguous the already ambiguous question of the extent to which the hustler is hustling for money, or hustling for sex (under the guise of hustling for money). Where the reasons a young man will become a prostitute are sometimes – perhaps often – confused and obscure to him, the subjectivity of his cinematic representation is a rather different matter. The hustler on the screen is a figure of identification for a viewer, and need not be identified with literally. In other words, a hustler on the job more often than not just looks like a (gay) man cruising for sex. In movies, he is a hustler for narrative reasons: to give him an identity, to give him something to do, to make possible the sexual encounters that are part of the plot.

It was only a matter of time before the queer road movie proper would emerge as its own genre, and not surprising that so many of them should include scenes of male hustling. Whether in *Midnight Cowboy* (1969) or *Pee-wee's Big Adventure* (1985), a man on the road is a man looking for something, and who sooner or later finds himself pretending to be something he isn't, or thinks he isn't, or wishes he were, or doesn't realize he wishes he were. It is in the nature of movies as dream-texts to speak the characters' unconscious desires, or those of a narrator. Thus, we have the hustler – who may only be a hitch-hiker, like Sissy Hankshaw in Van Sant's *Even Cowgirls Get the Blues* (1993), who hustles rides. Regardless of the kind of ride the hustler is looking for, the road, as Pee-wee can attest, is a big adventure, where almost anything is possible.

"Quasi-gay Themes and Big Stars": *My Own Private Idaho*

There is no question that the new queer movies under discussion in this essay deal with the affective bonds between men in a way that is unprecedented in the

Plate 15.1   River Phoenix and Keanu Reeves as road hustlers in
My Own Private Idaho.

(quasi-mainstream) American cinema. But, as discourses on masculinity in contemporary American culture, these films demonstrate that the progression toward
a more frank treatment of homosexuality – of homosexual *desire* – does not
necessarily clarify the issues involved. Thus we're given to understand in *My Own
Private Idaho* that Mike is hopelessly in love with Scott; and that Scott (the "prince"
in the story) is going through a conventionally rebellious, experimental phase
– on his way, we might say, to resolving his Oedipus complex. But the film
does not identify Mike unambiguously, or unproblematically, as gay. And Scott's
willingness to have sex with men (albeit as a hustler) is offered simply as his
chosen method of upsetting his father. On the one hand, the film implies that
Mike's desire – which comes into focus as an unrequited love for Scott – has something to do with his tragic yearning for his lost mother, and is a function of
his incestuous family history; and, on the other hand, the film leaves Scott's
desire relatively unexamined, as if heterosexuality needed no analysis, and homosexuality were just a phase in a Freudian sequence leading to proper object-choice
(autoeroticism – narcissism – homosexual object-choice – heterosexual object-
choice).

Most reviews of the film imply that the bond between Mike and Scott can be
explained in fairly simple terms (i.e., they both just happen to be hustlers, but the
one is gay, the other not), and that they take to the road because Mike is looking

for his mother, and Scott wants to get away from his father. Interviewers, too, felt safe at this level of analysis, and the actors themselves responded accordingly. When, for example, Keanu Reeves and River Phoenix were asked by *Interview* magazine if, "in deciding to do this film," the theme of the search for home and family in *Idaho* was important to them, Reeves immediately replied: "Oh, not for me." Phoenix, on the other hand, said: "I have really strong feelings about the search for home and mother. I thought it was very, very touching" (Sikes and Powell: 88). The overtly homoerotic aspects of the movie are scarcely mentioned in the interview.[6] *Interview*'s readership would include members of that "hetero-sexual, alternative audience" that Araki believes his films are "in sync with" (quoted in Rea: H1), but such readers and their magazine are too "cool" to consider whether some young men who trade sex for money might do it not only for economic reasons, but for their own compelling psychological reasons as well.

Van Sant, at least, is honest and direct about why Mike is a hustler. He told Gary Indiana, in an interview for *The Village Voice*:

> You only get to see Mike having pleasure when he hugs the guy at the end . . . in that scene where he watches *The Simpsons*. He was supposed to hug the guy like it was something he lost that he needed very badly. He did only have it once, it's true, but it was one of the main ideas behind his hustling, that he needed to be held, and touched. He didn't necessarily need to have sex. But he needed to be close. It was one of the reasons he liked being a hustler. . . . [He needed] to be wanted, and he could be wanted by men who wanted him for slightly different reasons than he wanted them to want him. He was really after attention and affection. But still what he missed was basically from a man, and not from a woman. He didn't have a father.
>
> (62)

Keanu Reeves, rather less articulate than his director, told *US* magazine: "I don't think [my] part is risky; there's not a lot in the film about sucking dick and getting fucked. I think it's more about family and the lives out there. I mean, it's *more*" (quoted in Román: 318). There seems to be no holding back in his remark. Reeves seems to want to be candid. But there is a note of defensiveness in what he says; and he would appear to be trying to separate the film's subject matter from its meanings. If, as he implies, "family and the lives out there" have little or nothing to do with "sucking dick and getting fucked," then why, we may ask, have the main characters – who *are* searching for home and family, it is true – both chosen to be hustlers? We might ask what kind of "home" and "family" the characters are searching for; and how the film articulates the theme of their search. It is the "*more*" – whatever it is – that an analysis of the figure of the hustler ought to reveal.

Clearly – but no doubt for different reasons – Van Sant and his actors (and *Interview*) have a stake in a certain kind of mystification of the subjectivity of the hustlers in the film. Indeed, Van Sant told Lance Loud in *American Film* magazine that he didn't think that the characters are really gay: "They're . . . whatever street hustlers are" (35).[7] He complained to Gary Indiana that

> One thing I figure, a person's sexual identity is so much different than just one word, "gay." You never hear anyone referred to as just "hetero." If you're "hetero" that doesn't really say anything, and that's why people don't say it. If you're gay, that also isn't saying anything. You'd have to qualify it more. It's too broad a thing. There's something more to sexual identity than just a label like that.
>
> (57)

Film critic Amy Taubin would seem to be correct, then, in observing that, while Van Sant is "one of the few openly gay directors in Hollywood, [he] bridles at turning sexuality into a soundbite. He's attracted to the liminal, to barely perceptible thresholds between identification and desire" (28).

There has always been a certain ambiguity and "mystique" surrounding the figure of the hustler in gay cinema, which was given its most extended treatment in Warhol's *My Hustler* (1966), and in *Flesh* (1968), the Warhol-produced/Morrissey-directed feature-length movie starring Joe Dallesandro.[8] *Flesh* and *Idaho* differ, however, in the way they evoke this mystique: which perhaps tells us something about what has changed in the gay political climate in the twenty-three years between the two films. The question remains, however: How do these films speak to *my* (or your) desire? How am I interpellated or identified by these films? What fantasies do they mobilize? There is also the profound issue of empowerment, both individual and collective. Do the films ultimately, and by whatever means, "translate into a fantasy of general sexual empowerment in a hostile social setting" (Waugh: 151)?

For Van Sant, there is purportedly a political stake in maintaining the aura of ambiguity surrounding the hustler, which he suggests by letting us know that his actors are straight: "It's a political act to do a film like this. They're handling it very well for being obviously straight" (quoted in Loud: 35–6). But audiences never really know about an actor's real-life sexuality. We may sometimes think we know the "real" story, but the discourses that produce that (image of) sexuality are complex, ever shifting, and contradictory – resulting in a perception, or, more properly, a *fantasy*, that rarely has much to do with anything we could call the "truth." What does it mean to say that River Phoenix and Keanu Reeves are straight? Why are we even told this? Because, as Van Sant would like us to believe, it is politically more effective in the struggle against homophobia if the actors can be seen as endorsing tolerance towards homosexuals without being accused of having a personal reason for doing so. It may also sharpen the sexual edge of the film to have two well-known straight actors play gay. Still, there is the possibility – and it is disturbing to consider – that Van Sant's remarks are a 1990s variation on the closet: he is an openly gay director reassuring the public that his actors aren't "Other." There is, too, the complex matter of Van Sant's own erotic imaginary, which viewers perforce are asked to assimilate – an imaginary that is obviously engaged and even aroused by trade: the straight hustler who has sex with other men.

The Road from Oz

The hustling theme is announced early (and with great wit) in *My Own Private Idaho*. Not since *Flesh* has a feature-length film confronted the subject so directly. We see a man entering a porn shop, and as he passes a rack of magazines, the cover boys come to life and speak directly into the camera. Scott, bare-chested and wearing a cowboy hat, his magazine coverlines announcing that he is "Ready to Ride," or is a "Homo on the Range," speaks:

> *Scott*: I never thought I could make it as a real model. . . . It's all right so long as the photographer doesn't come on to you, and expect something for nothing. I'm trying to make a living. I like to have a professional attitude. Of course, if the guy can pay me – hell, yeah! – here I am for him. I sell my ass. Do it on the street occasionally for cash. Or I'll be on the cover of a book. It's when you start doing things for free, that you start to grow wings. Isn't that right, Mike?
> *Mike*: What? [Mike, on the cover of his magazine, appears in a loincloth, trussed up against a pillar, like St Sebastian.]
> *Scott*: Wings, Michael. You grow wings and become a fairy.
> *Mike*: What do you care about money? Shit, you got plenty of money. Why don't you just go ahead and just do whatever it is that you do – I can only imagine what that is – and do it for free?

All the boys on the covers of the other five magazines start talking at once. One of them looks over to where Scott is and says, "So, what are you doing on the cover of that magazine, slumming?" Scott ignores all their comments and questions. He simply looks into the camera, and says: "Actually, Mike is right. I am going to inherit money, a lot of money."

A danger in commercial narrative films is that the significance of such dialogue can often be overlooked, in the hungry demand for action and the unfolding of a plot. When Scott says he never thought he could make it as a real model, he could, paradoxically, be saying that he never thought he'd make it as a real man. But he then discovered that manliness is largely a matter of posing

– an image. The irony, of course, is that models are not quite the thing itself. A model provides an image (a model) of the thing. And so, what is it for which Scott proposes himself as the model? The cowboy as gay icon? Do we have, in this world, only models of men? What, then, does Scott mean when he talks about hoping to (appear to) be a *real model*? Like Joe in *Flesh*, getting paid for what he does makes all the difference to Scott (he likes to have "a professional attitude"). It gives him an *identity*. In our culture, it is traditionally masculine to conceive of identity as deriving from one's work. The center of the film's meanings, however, is condensed in Mike's mumbled, almost inaudible question: "*Why don't you just go ahead and just do whatever it is that you do – I can only imagine what that is – and do it for free?*"

As in most classic Hollywood movies, the first five minutes of *My Own Private Idaho* announce several of the film's main themes, inscribed in the oneiric logic of metaphor and hallucination. After a dictionary definition of narcolepsy – "a condition characterized by brief attacks of deep sleep" – a title card tells us we're in Idaho. Then: a shot of the road. Mike enters the frame, and in voice-over says: "I've always known where I am by the way the road looks. Like, I just know that I've been here before."[9] In road movies, of course, the road is never less than a hieroglyph containing many meanings, and Mike continues: "There's not another road anywhere that looks like this road, I mean, *exactly* like this road. . . . like someone's face . . . like a fucked-up face." As Mike stares intently at the road – which leads straight from the camera to the distant horizon of snowy mountains – he falls in a narcoleptic seizure.

The camera cuts to a strange, telephoto-close shot of the snow-capped mountain peak at the horizon, half obscured by swirling, white clouds; and then cuts to a shot of Mike with his head resting in his long-lost mother's lap. In this shot, like a representation of the Virgin Mary mourning over the dead body of Christ, she is dressed in white, and saying softly, as she runs her hand through his hair: "Don't worry, everything's going to be all right. I know, it's okay . . . I know." Then, as one critic describes it, the screen fills with a supremely ambiguous image: "an unpainted wood farmhouse, isolated against a hillside of empty fields – at once pure and bleak, alluring and abandoned-looking, home or a hollow shell" (Jameson: 2). The music on the soundtrack rises lyrically into song – " . . . the cowboy is singin' this lonesome cattle call." A star shoots across an evening sky; more shots of the road are intercut with a shot of a giant roadside effigy of a square-jawed cowboy, and shots of Mike getting a blow job from a john in a room in Seattle. Eddy Arnold continues to sing: "He rides in the sun, 'til his day's work is done, and he rounds up the cattle each fall. . . . " As Mike starts to come, we see an extraordinary, metallic-glittering shot of salmon leaping upriver at sunset. The song on the soundtrack ends; we get a shot of the lake where the salmon were spawned and where they have returned to propagate and die. Then, as Mike reaches orgasm – in a witty and shocking allusion to the tornado-borne vehicle in *The Wizard of Oz* that takes Dorothy from Kansas and lands her in Oz – the farm-house falls from the sky and crashes noisily into a million splinters on the Idaho road. The john, whose name turns out to be Walt, drops $20 on Mike's belly and walks out of the room. Mike asks him for two more dollars, and Walt says (in a line that actually explains why Mike is a hustler): "What's the matter, you can't get it from your dad?" Mike pleads: "My dad and I don't get along too well, you know that, Walt." Walt, who is fat, middle-aged, and ugly, replies teasingly: "I know, we don't get along too well now either, do we!" Mike continues to plead, and Walt gives him another $10.

My Own Private Idaho is essentially Mike's story, and as such it would seem at first to offer the viewer a depressing thesis about homosexuality. It is the viewer who gains some insight into the subjectivity of the main characters, but by the end of the film the main character is on the same road where he began, appearing to have gained no liberating insight into his desire and who he is. The lesson he learns – if that it be – is that the Oedipal scenario is immutable, damaging, and tragic; but, for all that, and for those forged under the pressure of its dire imperatives, it is perhaps better than nothing. The viewer, on the other hand, may learn a slightly different lesson: if the Oedipal scenario is damaging, it might be rejected altogether. While the ending of the movie is ambiguous – we do not know who it is that picks up Mike on the road after he has fallen into a narcoleptic sleep – the published screenplay indicates that it was Van Sant's original intention to have Scott pick up his friend (Van Sant: 186–7).

The most liberating thing about *My Own Private Idaho* is that it resists the notion that the Oedipal scenario, which is resolved in an image of home and family, is the inevitable, and only, happy one. The film ends on an image of the car disappear-ing down the road, followed by a shot of the deserted farmhouse, and finally a title card that reads: have a nice day. The film implies that the ego is the enemy of desire: though Scott settles on an identity – he internalizes the image of his father – Mike is still "on the road" at the end of the film. He is still desiring. While many gay viewers may see Mike as a sad, down-and-out gay man who just can't find his way home to gay happiness, I prefer to read the endings of both the published screenplay and the film itself as being radical, in that they refuse to offer an identity politics. This is what makes the film *queer* (as opposed to gay).[10]

Idaho's homages to *The Wizard of Oz* are very telling of the distance between the two films and of how utterly different the destinies of Mike and Dorothy must be in a (hetero)patriarchal world. Van Sant makes full use of the irony that – as a recently published humor book puts it – "[*The Wizard of Oz*] has been described as an allegory for gay men fleeing the drab (i.e., black-and-white) world to a Technicolor fantasyland over the rainbow" (DiLallo and Krumholtz: 157). The camp response to a hostile world, it would seem, is a difficult one to support in the 1990s (the success of the 1995 gay comedy *Jeffrey* notwithstanding), and one not much favored by gay independent film-makers (Araki "despises" *Torch Song Trilogy*, which, only a little less so than *The Birdcage*, 1996, appears to have been made by and for straight people). When Dorothy begs the good witch Glinda, "Oh, will you help me? Can you help me?" Glinda replies: "You don't need to be helped any longer. You've always had the power to go back to Kansas." The Scarecrow asks Glinda why she never told Dorothy this before, and Glinda tells him: "Because she wouldn't have believed me. She had to learn it for herself." Dorothy is instructed to tap her heels together three times, and think to herself: "There's no place like home!" After she does so, we get a shot of the farmhouse flying through the sky and coming down to land in Kansas. The lesson Dorothy has learned is that "If I ever go looking for my heart's desire again, I won't look any further than my own back yard, because if it isn't there, I never really lost it to begin with."

As a mainstream Hollywood movie made in 1939, *The Wizard of Oz* tries to end on an ideologically correct note ("There's no place like home"). But, as Salman Rushdie rightly protests, "The movie's Kansas is informed not only by the sadness of dirt-poverty, but also by the badness of would-be dog-murderers. And *this* is the home that 'there's no place like'? *This* is the lost Eden that we are asked to prefer (as Dorothy does) to Oz?" (17). The queer difference between a studio-era road movie like *The Wizard of Oz* and an independent one like *My Own Private Idaho*, obviously, is that the narratives of Hollywood, as they do to this day, can achieve closure only if they end on a hetero-patriarchal principle (family and home or heterosexual coming-together as *telos* of Hollywood narrative epistemology) (Allen: 609–34). While it may be true that many gay men and women see Dorothy's escape from Kansas as a potent fantasy that speaks to their own sense of entrapment in a homophobic society, the film, ultimately, is made for that mythically homogeneous heterosexual mainstream audience, the members of which may feel excluded or "different" in some way, but who want ultimately to belong to that mainstream, to take their rightful place in its familial ordering of affective ties and identities.

The new queer road movie may not take its protagonists to the Emerald City and leave them there, but it does not sell out in this way, either. It refuses categorically to endorse the "family values" that have done so much to make gay men and women miserable. Back home in black-and-white Kansas, Dorothy "begins her second revolt, fighting not only against the patronizing dismissals of her own folk but also against the scriptwriters, and the sentimental moralizing of the entire Hollywood studio system. *It wasn't a dream, it was a place*, she cries piteously. *A real, truly live place! Doesn't anyone believe me?*" (Rushdie: 57). The new queer road movie believes in the dream – in the sense that queer happiness is understood to be possible – which is why the new queer road movie eschews the "happy ending" of Hollywood cinema, a tacked-on coda that at best is ironic and at worst a reinstatement of the repressive structures the protagonist(s) sought to escape.

For Mike, there is no "home" to go to. There is no Uncle Henry and Auntie Em waiting anxiously for him to open his eyes when he returns from his dream or nightmare; and, when his farmhouse crash-lands, it is destroyed. If Mike has recognized anything new by the end of the film, it is that he is doomed – always to be alone and lonely; not even to have a dog to comfort him, as Toto is always there to comfort Dorothy. He will, in a sense, never find his mother, as Scott has done. And he does not have a father. He can never "come home," as Scott does. He can never take his place in a familial order, which is the *only* order understood by society. Mike's homosexuality is figured as an impossible identity. The fantasies in which love and identity are grounded are short-circuited by incest (Mike's father is his brother); and Mike cannot be inscribed within the Oedipal structure that makes it possible for others to live – makes it possible for them to sustain fantasies, or believe in illusions (which are perfectly real), of connection, arriving, and recognition. Mike's seizures are a metonymy and metaphor for this short-circuit of meaning. The Oedipal scenario, which Scott's story represents, does not comprehend Mike. Only in the fantasies made possible by hustling – as one of the gaps, or contradictions, in society's sexual system – can Mike have any identity at all. The only hope, perhaps, is that a good fairy will pick him up one day. This is the underlying fantasy of most road movies that are on some level about cruising, hustling, or hitch-hiking: that the next encounter will be the one that will take the protagonist "home."

The Search for an Obscure Object of Desire

While it has been noted frequently that the special resonance of the American road movie derives from "the ways freedom and social mobility have been linked to physical mobility as themes in North American culture, or at least that part of it which Hollywood has attempted to represent" (Eyerman and Löfgren: 54), we might say that the *queer* road movie has emerged as a development in the cultural and psychoanalytic crisis of gender (and genre) described by Timothy Corrigan in *A Cinema Without Walls*. Corrigan historicizes the road movie as a postwar phenomenon in which, "more and more, the family unit, that oedipal centerpiece of classical narrative, begins to break apart, preserved only as a memory or desire with less and less substance" (145). He suggests that the car "becomes the only promise of self in a culture of mechanical reproduction. As in the economic politics of most postwar societies, boundaries and borders disappear (at least temporarily) in a car and with them the sanctions, securities, and structures of a family tradition" (146). With the disruption and dismantling by the Second World War of the ideal represented by the family, "the most secure and likely replacement for that heterosexual unit is the male buddy-group left over from that war" (147). Not surprisingly, Corrigan insists that most road questers invariably want "an authentic home, a lost origin where what you see is what you are" (154).

The queer variant of the road movie is only that – a variant – but it is nevertheless interesting for its radical rejection of what we can call, with some irony, "family values." What distinguishes the queer road movie from all other Hollywood genres is the centrality of homosexual desire. But, considering that we live in a patriarchy, this is not, and cannot be, merely a matter of changing the gender of the protagonists in a (hetero)patriarchal narrative driven by the conjugal imperative. It is therefore worth quoting from an interview between Félix Guattari and George Stambolian, for the light it sheds on the radical potential of the queer road movie's conception of desire:

> F.G.: For me desire is always "outside"; it always belongs to a minority. For me there is no heterosexual sexuality. Once there's heterosexuality, in fact, once there's marriage, there's no more desire, no more sexuality. In all my twenty-five years of work in this field I've never seen a heterosexual married couple that functioned along a line of desire. Never. They don't exist. So don't say that I'm marginalizing sexuality with homosexuals, etc., because for me there is no heterosexuality possible.
>
> G.S.: Following the same logic there is no homosexuality possible.
>
> F.G.: In a sense yes, because in a sense homosexuality is counterdependent on heterosexuality. Part of the problem is the reduction of the body. It's the impossibility of becoming a totally sexed body. The sexed body is something that includes all perceptions, everything that occurs in the mind. The problem is how to sexualize the body, how to make bodies desire, vibrate – all aspects of the body.
>
> (68)

Guattari's remarks about the problem of how to "sexualize the body" are crucial to the implicit project of the queer road movie. The road movie protagonist, after all, is a body moving through space – functioning "along a line of desire" – and, although [Deleuze and] Guattari's concepts are not at all Freudian (indeed, they are specifically anti-Freudian), we might consider Freud's comment on "the dissatisfaction with home and family" that so often motivates the traveler. The queer road movie protagonist's specific dissatisfaction with home and family invariably has to do with the fact that the traditional family is a heterosexual/patriarchal structure which does not acknowledge (his) desire.[11] If to become a subject (to become a person) is to "learn one's place," the queer subject learns early that – with subjectivity necessarily and fundamentally a spatial achievement (Kirby) – he has no place in the traditional family. If he is to be a desiring subject, a sexed body, he must leave the spaces of home and family. The true queer road movie narrative thus never ends but remains conscious of and committed to what Guattari is attempting to articulate when he talks about sexualizing the body. As narratives without conventional closure, functioning along lines of desire, not moving toward marriage and the containment of sexuality, queer road movies are quintessentially postmodern, with implications that are liberating for some, and perhaps disorienting and disturbing for others. As Paul Schmidt very perceptively argues, "Homosexuality is an alienation introduced into the very root of the social order, into sex as procreation. We say usually that the opposite of homosexuality is heterosexuality, but that's not quite it. The opposite of homosexuality is marriage" (235). In this sense, we can see how the queer road movie is fundamentally opposed to marriage. Instead, as Schmidt puts it, the genre examines "the problem of trying to establish a relationship beyond the patterns of kinship, and within a state that is defined precisely by the denial of bonds and ties: by separateness, apartness, in-betweenness, individualization and reflexivity. And by vision, ultimately: the vision of Otherness" (242).

If the average queer road movie is not quite so ambitious in its vision, nor its protagonists so extreme in their attempts to establish a relationship "beyond the patterns of kinship," it shares at least some of this questing belief in happiness, in

Plate 15.2 My Own Private Idaho's heart-rending campfire scene.

a liberation of desire, in the totally sexed body, in the powerful reality of queer love. As Mike says to his friend, in *My Own Private Idaho*'s heart-rending campfire scene: "I could love someone even if I . . . you know, wasn't paid for it. I love you, and . . . you don't pay me. I really want to kiss you, man. Good night, man. I love you a lot. You know that. I do love you."

Acknowledgments

My thanks to Charles Silver for his gracious help with my road movie research at the Museum of Modern Art, and to the wise and witty Ed Sikov for his stimulating comments on an earlier draft of this essay. I dedicate the essay to Leslie Lang, my first hitch-hiking companion, with whom I traveled across southern Africa when we were 16.

Notes

1 Waugh's sympathetic and perceptive article "The Third Body," makes this point forcefully.
2 "Both in my life and in my films, gayness and sexuality have never really been an issue, something to 'come to terms with,' or overcome, or struggle with. It's just sort of there. In a way that's how I view race too. That it's just part of people's make-up" (Araki quoted in Oliver: 28).
3 Some of the dangers Araki alludes to appear to have plagued *Even Cowgirls Get the Blues*, the film Van Sant made after *Idaho*. The film is an interesting failure, and deserves an analysis – not possible here – of "what went wrong" when Van Sant followed the Hollywood "carrot."
4 In Van Sant's *Mala Noche* (1985), Walt offers Roberto $15 to sleep with Johnny. The pimping scenario, it would seem, preserves [the hustler's] dignity. The idea is that if the john cannot persuade the [boy] to sleep with him, his best friend can – he'd be doing it for his friend. The motive is doubly displaced (as if sleeping with the john for money were not enough of a motive).
5 In an essay he shared with me after I completed this essay, Steven Cohan explores the queer dynamics of the Hope and Crosby series; see "Queering the Deal: On the Road with Hope and Crosby," *Out Takes*, ed. Ellis Hanson (Durham, NC: Duke University Press, forthcoming 1997).
6 For further intertexts, especially in light of the references below to *Flesh*, consider that *Interview*'s publisher was Andy Warhol, who in a sense created Joe Dallesandro's ambiguous hustler image. It is not without relevance, either, that Van Sant had plans to make a long film about Warhol, and that Phoenix hoped to get the Warhol role.
7 There is an interesting intertext in having Lance Loud do the interview, as he did in the famous documentary *An American Family* (Craig Gilbert, 1973), which is not unlike certain Warhol films in the way it raises questions about authenticity, and the extent to which the presence of a camera will affect the subjects being filmed. In *An American Family*, Lance – who is seen to be undergoing a troubled adolescence – eventually comes out as gay.

8 Mainstream cinema, it's worth pointing out, when it treats the issue of hustling at all, prefers to figure the hustler as heterosexual – as in *Midnight Cowboy*, *American Gigolo* (1980), and *The Basketball Diaries* (1995) – but since *My Own Private Idaho* and *Postcards from America*, the independent cinema has returned to the theme of the gay hustler, with *Frisk* (1996), *Hustler White* (1996), and *johns* (1996).

9 "Love is home-sickness," wrote Freud, "and whenever a man dreams of a place or a country and says to himself, while he is still dreaming: 'this place is familiar to me. I've been here before,' one may interpret the place as being his mother's genital or her body" (245).

10 My reading of the end of the film is perhaps too optimistic. Consider Maurizia Natali's observation that "The scenic horizon always appears to designate a cultural terminus for the American imaginary, a limit continually fixed and displaced by a cinema that seeks to contain the society's lines of flight" (95). Where the classic Western, she notes, "fixes a map and a horizon which the heroes traverse before arriving at the tableau shots of the happy ending" (95), the road movie – a genre that came into its own after the collapse of classic cinema – puts into play "a regressive force, a desire for a *wilderness* that has historically disappeared in an era of highways and national parks. The desire for flight without a name" (95). The road movie hero, writes Natali, moves along a trajectory "toward a scenic terminus that reveals itself to be in reality an immobilising and catastrophic tableau, an indifferent space that is impossible to catch up to [*rejoindre*] without confronting death there, and which is really an emblem of the past, dangerously fooling the eye" (95) (my own translation).

11 As the reader will have noticed, I generally restrict my discussion of the queer road movie to its male variants, but my comments often apply equally to female queer road movies, like *Faster Pussycat! Kill! Kill!* (1965) or *Even Cowgirls Get the Blues*.

Works Cited

Allen, Dennis W. "Homosexuality and Narrative." *Modern Fiction Studies* 41.3–4 (Fall–Winter 1995): 609–34.

Cheshire, Godfrey. "*My Own Private Idaho*." *New York Press* (October 9–15, 1991).

Corrigan, Timothy. *A Cinema Without Walls: Movies and Culture after Vietnam*. New Brunswick, NJ: Rutgers University Press, 1991.

DiLallo, Kevin, and Jack Krumholtz. *The Unofficial Gay Manual: Living the Lifestyle (Or at Least Appearing To)*. New York: Doubleday, 1994.

Doane, Mary Ann. "Sublimation and the Psychoanalysis of the Aesthetic." *Femmes Fatales: Feminism, Film Theory, Psychoanalysis*. New York: Routledge, 1991. 249–67.

Elder, Sean. "Young Actors Go Wild With Gus Van Sant: A Search for Family and Freedom, from *Drugstore Cowboy* to *Idaho*." *Elle* (October, 1991): 130+ [3 pp.].

Eyerman, Ron and Löfgren, Orvar. "Romancing the Road: Road Movies and Images of Mobility." *Theory, Culture & Society* 12 (1995): 53–79.

Freud, Sigmund. "The Uncanny" (1919). *Standard Edition of the Complete Psychological Works of Sigmund Freud*, ed. James Strachey. London: Hogarth Press, 1953. Vol. 17, 219–52.

Guattari, Félix. "A Liberation of Desire" (an Interview by George Stambolian). In Stambolian and Marks. 56–69.

Holden, Stephen. "Outraged Autobiographies Make a Collage of Gay Life." *The New York Times* (October 8, 1994):14.

Indiana, Gary. "Saint Gus: From Portland to Hollywood, the Director and His Camera Remain Candid." *The Village Voice* (October 1, 1991): 57+ [3 pp.].

Irigaray, Luce. "Women on the Market." *This Sex Which Is Not One*. Ithaca: Cornell University Press, 1985. 170–91.

Jacobson, Harlan. "Gus Van Sant Travels His Own Uncomfortable Route." *The Boston Sunday Globe* (October 13, 1991): A11.

James, Caryn. "Today's Yellow Brick Road Leads Straight to Hell." *The New York Times* (August 19, 1990): section 2, 1+ [3 pp.].

Jameson, Richard T. "Gus Van Sant Country." Essay in Fine Line Features press kit (Clippings archive, Museum of Modern Art, New York).

Kirby, Kathleen M. *Indifferent Boundaries: Spatial Concepts of Human Subjectivity*. New York: The Guilford Press, 1996.

Loud, Lance. "Shakespeare in Black Leather." *American Film* (September/October, 1991): 32–7.

Moon, Michael. "Outlaw Sex and the 'Search for America': Representing Male Prostitution and Perverse Desire in Sixties Film (*My Hustler* and *Midnight Cowboy*)." *Quarterly Review of Film and Video* 15.1 (1993): 27–40.

Natali, Maurizia. *L'Image-paysage: Iconologie et cinéma*. Paris: Presses Universitaires de Vincennes, 1996.

Oliver, Bill. "L.A.'s Bad Boy Gregg Araki." *Off-Hollywood Report* (1992): 28.

Rea, Steven. "Gay Lovers on the Run from the Law and Illness." *The Philadelphia Inquirer* (September 6, 1992): H1.

Román, David. "Shakespeare Out in Portland: Gus Van Sant's *My Own Private Idaho*, Homoneurotics, and Boy Actors." *Eroticism and Containment: Notes From the Flood Plain*, eds. Carol Siegel and Ann Kibbey. New York: New York University Press, 1994. 311–33.

Rushdie, Salman. *The Wizard of Oz*. London: BFI, 1992.

Schmidt, Paul. "Visions of Violence: Rimbaud and Verlaine." In Stambolian and Marks. 228–42.

Segal, Lynne. *Slow Motion: Changing Masculinities, Changing Men*. New Brunswick, NJ: Rutgers University Press, 1990.

Sikes, Gini and Powell, Paige. "River Phoenix." *Interview* (November, 1991): 83+ [2 pp.].

Stambolian, George and Elaine Marks, eds. *Homosexualities and French Literature: Cultural Contexts/Critical Texts*. Ithaca: Cornell University Press, 1979.

Taubin, Amy. "Trials and Tribulations." *The Village Voice* (May 24, 1994): 28.

Van Sant, Gus. *Even Cowgirls Get the Blues & My Own Private Idaho*. London: Faber & Faber, 1993.

Waugh, Thomas. "The Third Body: Patterns in the Construction of the Subject in the Gay Male Narrative Film." *Queer Looks: Perspectives on Lesbian and Gay Film and Video*, eds. Martha Gever, John Greyson, and Pratibha Parmar. New York: Routledge, 1993. 141–61.

16

DISASSOCIATED MASCULINITIES AND GEOGRAPHIES OF THE ROAD

Stuart C. Aitken and Christopher Lee Lukinbeal

"Disassociation" . . . refers not only to the detachment of the subject from the world, but also to the deterioration of the internal ordering of subjectivity. . . . The internal–external relation breaks down, resulting in a degeneration of interior organization, and finally – one can imagine, in advanced stages – in a confusion of the external order too. Things begin to circulate, and no longer know their places. Foundations and frameworks crumble and things loop and circle and shift and spin: the inside flies to pieces and explodes outwards, the outside melts and fragments, and elements from both sides drift freely across an indifferent boundary. If the outside is unstable to such a degree that the subject becomes disengaged, who wouldn't want to induce the same confusion, in reality, so that inside and outside come once again into harmony?

(K. Kirby: 102)

It is not necessarily a slick, professional performance but the spectacle of Mitzi singing the drag cabaret classic "I've Been to Paradise, but I've Never Been to Me" is nonetheless a spellbinding opening to Stephan Elliott's road movie *The Adventures of Priscilla, Queen of the Desert* (1994). The song is an aphorism for the consequent road trip from Sydney to Alice Springs embarked upon by drag queens Mitzi and Felicia, and transsexual Bernadette so that they can perform their cabaret act in a club owned by Mitzi's estranged wife. Priscilla, a bus acquired for the trip, not only provides an eponym for the movie, it also embodies what Michel de Certeau calls a spatial story because it places a high value on the geographic coalescence of identity politics and mobility. The journey to Alice Springs is about how mobility, scale, and space "disassociate" Mitzi, Felicia, and Bernadette from their local roots in Sydney, but it is Priscilla that furnishes a haven from which the three friends can safely face issues of sexual identity, home, family, and community. The bus – replete with drag wardrobes, bar and vanity dressers – encapsulates a classifying frame within which the protagonists' gay identity is reified in contrast to the homophobic environment through which they pass. The vehicle is a safe haven because it is the embodiment of the protagonists' drag identity, but it also extends their bodies and enables them to disrupt the scale of the local. Before leaving, for example, Mitzi confides that he needs to "get some space." Speeding through the vastness of the Australian Outback enables him to unshackle the fetters of his home in urban Sydney. For Felicia, riding the vast open spaces in a giant slipper atop the bus with the wind blowing out fifty feet of silk behind him represents a transformation into Cinderella and Diva. The Outback seems to offer space for sensational self-affirmation. At the same time, Bernadette, Mitzi, and Felicia are visual spectacles agitating the cultural contrived meaning of Outback identity: strong heterosexual men and women up against an indomitable environment. Various conflicts and encounters during the road trip highlight important tensions between the social and the spatial. After Felicia gets beaten up by a group of drunken miners, Bernadette points out how space contrives boundaries that reify fears about difference: "It's funny, we all sit around mindlessly slagging off in that vile stink-hole of a city, but in some strange way it takes care of us. I don't know if that ugly wall of suburbia has been put there to stop them getting in or us getting out." The road trip to Alice Springs is an attempt to contest these contrived spaces of difference, but it is also about coming to terms with other hegemonic norms such as family and fatherhood. In Alice Springs, Mitzi is reunited with his son and his wife who is portrayed as a stereotypically strong and capable Outback woman. Issues of fatherhood, family, and belonging are highlighted against the full spectacle and fiasco of the cabaret act. *Priscilla* ends with Mitzi and his son returning with Felicia to the gay, drag community in Sydney. They leave Bernadette with her new-found lover in Alice Springs. The last scene of the movie is Mitzi's and Felicia's spectacular performance of an ABBA song to the applause of an enthusiastic Sydney audience.

This chapter is an exploration of the ways that masculinity is liberated through the space and scale of the road movie genre. As a classic road movie, *Priscilla* – the omnibus and omnipurpose – contests some of Western society's dominant narratives on sexuality, family, and home but, ultimately, we argue that it falls short of a liberatory masculinity. Kaja Silverman suggests that Western patriarchal logic requires an unwavering faith in the unity of the family and the adequacy of a male subject who is in place and taking responsibility. By ending with an affirmation of home and family, *Priscilla* seems to embrace the constraints of this patriarchal logic. We say this not to denigrate the importance of men taking on child-rearing responsibilities, but rather to highlight the fight against sedentariness that characterizes a large part of the patriarchal male myth.

To begin unraveling the ways that the patriarchal male myth is inscribed in road movies, we borrow Kathleen Kirby's inherently spatial notion of 'disassociation,' as it is defined in the epigraph. Disassociation is an intriguing starting point for analysis not only because it suggests the necessity of an imbalance between internal and external space but also because, in the context of the road movie, it highlights a juxtaposition between place-based sedentarism and disengaged mobility. On the one hand, we have Silverman's adequate home-based masculinity and, on the other, resistance to mere adequacy through travel and the road. The latter supplants place-identity with a personal geography that is based upon movement and mobility. We offer this essay, then, as a description of geographies of masculinity that are (dis)embodied through mobility and resistance and as an analysis of road movies that take these geographies as their main theme.[1]

In what follows, we first note the importance of understanding how space and scale are produced, and the role patriarchy plays in that production. To detail thoroughly the ways that the production of space and scale are part of a larger patriarchal project is well beyond the scope of this essay and, as such, the evolving discussion on these topics receives only brief accounting in the pages that follow. Instead, we focus on the concept of belonging and argue that it need not necessarily imply place-based identity. We suggest that there may be value in following the logic of disassociated spatial subjectivities. We then reflect upon the nature of masculinity and the 'hysteria' brought on by mobility. Disassociated masculinity is thus compared and contrasted to place-based masculinity. We consider as an example the hegemonic tensions running through Gus Van Sant's *My Own Private Idaho* (1991) and Wim Wenders's *Paris, Texas* (1984), and compare them with *Priscilla*. The point we want to make is that the patriarchal gaze and male hysteria are ingrained in many road movies, and that this voyeurism and neurosis emasculate *all* forms of human subjectivity.[2]

Unstable Geographies: Contrived Spaces and Scales

The apparent naturalness of our everyday geographies until very recently relegated our understanding of space to a mosaic that simply contained human activities. Human subjectivity was derived from activities and interpersonal relations, and was determined in part by how we identified with places. Place was a fixed locality, and space was an empty, Cartesian plane until it became colonized with people, their activities, and culture. It is now commonly accepted that space comprises multiple valences which influence its manipulation and reproduction. Space is assumed to be more than a passive stage upon which actors compromise, negotiate, and struggle because it constitutes, and is constituted by, power relations. It is not difficult to argue that social relations constitute, form, and manage space but, in a very real sense, space is more than an end-product of these processes, it is itself a process. It may follow, then, that the reproduction of space parallels the reproduction of other forms of identity.

If we agree that the language of geography contextualizes current critical discussions, then we begin to realize that a great danger lies in assuming an apparent stability and immutability of place and space. Neil Smith ("Homeless/ Global": 97) notes that the metaphorical uses of space are now so fashionable that there is a danger of losing sight of material conceptions of space. Notions of distanciation, grounding, displacement, subject positioning, and mobility may be used to describe the location of people in social systems, and ways of knowing may be described as marginal discourses, decentered hegemonic narratives, and so forth, but these spatial metaphors also work to reinforce the "deadness of space" and thereby deny us "the spatial concepts appropriate to analyzing the world" (Smith, *Uneven Development*: 169). This happens when metaphors lose sight of material conditions and everyday social practices, which is precisely the problem of the road movie genre and the apparent free mobility of its subject. The danger is that spatial metaphors of mobility combine to form an incontestable meta-narrative which, in the case of the road movie, may be simply another form of hegemonic masculinity. Before elaborating upon this more fully, we need to ask how understanding the production of space can help us with issues of political identity and sexual difference.

As a spatially produced set of categories, geographic scale may be viewed as a primary means through which differentiation, including sexual difference, takes place. Scale not only establishes boundaries but it can engender a metaphorical sense of hierarchy that empowers and disables political contestation. It follows, then, that aspirations for authority and territorial control and the establish-ment of real boundaries can be construed as a denial of difference. The creation of a space and a justice based upon this kind of logic and reason hinge upon an understanding of life that is essentialist, exclusive, and controlling. It is also a life that is sedentary and immobile because the boundaries metaphorically limit movement and the freedom to define political identity. Typically, these traditional versions of political identity involve either some hierarchical, scaled, and arbitrary valuation of difference or, less often, some uniform treatment of difference, that, while appearing more equitable, disguise the real and ongoing forms of domination that exist by upholding scale as "natural." Elsewhere, one of us argues that it is critical to understand more fully the relations between the production of space and the production of scale so that we can exorcise the power relations which contrive and constrain political and sexual identities and differences (Aitken). If we agree that masculinities and femininities must be simultaneously understood at multiple scales – from the physical scale of the ego and self, to the seemingly larger scales of patriarchy and capitalism – then we must also consider the evolution of a perceived naturalness of certain spatial and scalar arrangements, in particular the notion of place identity and sedentary belonging.

The ideas of spatiality and the production of scale are extended by several contemporary writers who suggest that our previously clear signs of belonging – of the relation between locality, participation and identity politics – are collapsing in favor of a *terra infirma* that establishes new "geographies" based upon the theme of a scale-less mobility (cf. Cresswell; Rogoff; Robertson et al.; Rapport). These writers argue that ideological "reality" is changing to embrace identities which no longer are about a form of being that is sedentary but, rather, focus upon becomings that infer movement and *jumping scales*. The notion of unfettered travel and mobile citizenship establishes a sense where being is replaced by becoming. Within this framework, an ironic contradiction arises in many Western cultures – notably, North America, Brazil, Argentina, and Australia – where mobility as a central colonizing theme of national (male) identity and control over large "empty spaces" is juxtaposed against mobility as a rebellion against authority and a hegemonic norm that requires men to "stay at home and take responsibility for their families." The enduring contradiction between emancipation and emasculation – from the myths of Daniel Boone, Davy Crockett, and Ned Kelly to those of contemporary road warriors – juxtaposes a supposed external flight to freedom and a call from a scale beyond the family with the more subtle forms of internal disfigurement seemingly acquired by staying at home.

The mobility represented in road movies establishes a sense of transcending the boundaries of scale. We argue that, with many road movies, this is only a sense; a psychic freedom that offers emancipation but, in actuality, practices emasculation. In order to unravel these concepts more fully, we need to understand how emancipation and emasculation are inculcated with the new mobile geographies of masculinity. We begin with a discussion of male hysteria as the basis of emasculation and then turn to the mobile gaze as a possible avenue for more liberatory masculinities. We tie the discussion throughout to the road movie as an allegory for mobile masculinities.

The Flight of the Phallus and the Mobile Gaze

Some feminists position hysteria as a bodily expression and reaction to oppression by patriarchal society and the social roles assigned to individuals. They suggest that hysteria, initially and in popular usage today, is a way to justify moral condemnation of the "other." Male hysteria, to be hysteria at all, has to be modeled after female hysteria. The diagnosis of hysteria for a man is often a sign of weakness, the labeling of a man as a non-man: "a castration in a word" (Lucien Israël quoted in Showalter: 291). According to Lynne Kirby, "what male hysteria shows us is not so much the coding of men as women, as the uncoding of men as men" (126). Male hysteria is about the emasculation that men experience when separated from scale-defined gender roles. It is also a disease that is "seen" (gazed upon) as deviant from a patriarchal norm. If male hysteria is mobility away from the status quo, the cure is a reinscription into hegemonic space and place. In other words, the remedy is to assimilate men back into the societal and sexual roles assigned to them by patriarchy and hegemonic masculinity – marriage, family, and *productive* employment.

Male hysteria is a disassociation from hegemonic masculinity, and its allegory, the road movie, is a spatial performance of the disenfranchised spirit. In road movies we see the flight of the phallus through motorized escape: castrated from hegemonic masculinity, mobile masculinity is the "other" to the extent that it is the rival with the father.[3] Tim Corrigan suggests that hysteria in the road movie points to a crisis in male subjectivity and a genre that emphasizes the demise of the family unit. The myth of the road movie combines the hysterical and the disassociated into a paradigm that celebrates a search for self through spatial angst and unstable family geographies. What, then, are the relations between hysteria, the gaze, and road movies, and in what ways can the gaze be reconceptualized to offer liberatory forms of sexual identity?

Despite conceptual problems and a certain amount of uncritical use in film studies, the gaze seems to hold out promise for describing the limits of road movie subjects, delimiting their boundaries and indicating possibilities for their reconstruction. Although some feminists and postmodernists argue that the gaze is now commodified, genderless, and mobile (cf. Kaplan; Friedberg), we follow Kathleen Kirby's suggestion that, even when reversed, the gaze is constituted within a patriarchally produced space. In order to overcome the patriarchal principles that underlie this production, we need to view space and scale as "unnatural" and, by so doing, we are able to construct a flexible boundary for the gaze in response to the pressures exerted by differently produced spaces and scales. Constituted as such, the gaze not only indicates the contours possessed by different sexual geographies, but it also becomes a fluid medium for one side to effect changes in the shape of other sides (K. Kirby: 128). Within this framework, Kirby suggests a model that positions the gaze as part of a field with flexible geographic boundaries which are delimited by the occupants of the field:

> To my mind, the gaze denotes not an instrument of the already powerful, nor a field open to infinite play, but instead a graphic illustration of what happens when the genders come together. It is an illustration of the complementary shapes drawn for their subjectivities by culture, an indication of the mutability of gender shaping, and a place to test, manipulate and attempt to reform both the form of the genders and the relation between them. In this depiction, the gaze appears as the middle area of a tripartite space, a flexible boundary taking shape in response to the pressures exerted

by either side. The gaze indicates the contours they already possess, but also can be a medium for one side to effect changes in the shape of the other.

(K. Kirby: 127)

Kirby suggests a geography of the gaze with inclusive and flexible boundaries. It maps a topography that disrupts the symmetry of the gaze while at the same time aligning it with various subject positions. We noted earlier our belief that sexual difference is stabilized through assuming that space and scale are natural and inviolable. Within the constraints of this assumed landscape, sexuality can be reified through a cadastral system that parcels and arranges difference *a priori*. If our premises begin with the unnaturalness of any *a priori* spatial and scalar arrangements for the gaze then we are better placed to understand its liberatory possibilities. Changing the effect of the gaze, Kirby concludes, cannot occur through reversals and reinscriptions, but only by reconfigurations of subjective space (K. Kirby: 141). This can be done most effectively by distorting the conventional composition of the viewing subject in relation to space.

Kirby's reconfiguration of the gaze with flexible and indifferent boundaries has important implications for understanding mobility and male hysteria. In a moment, we will show how important the conceptualization of subject boundaries is to understanding male hysteria, but for now we need to elaborate more fully on the mobile gaze. Guiliana Bruno and Anne Friedberg contextualize the mobilization of the gaze with the new phenomena of industrialized society. The experience of train travel, for example, helped establish cinema by providing a reference in which to situate cinema as a new form of "panoramic perception" that defied the scale of the local. Both trains and cinema restructured space and time by constructing a subject who was simultaneously still and in motion. Roland Barthes describes the paradoxical effect of "the illusion of immobility in the panic and pleasure of transplantation" as "transported immobility"(144). The contradictory feelings of panic and pleasure imparted by travel, he suggests, create a psychic stasis from which clarity may form. By annihilating the space lying between two points of travel, trains and cinema profoundly effect spatial perception and place-based belonging, heralding

> no less than a technological restructuration of the relation between the traveler/spectator, vision, and space . . . [they] fundamentally alter the terms of understanding of subjectivity and perception, effecting a crucial realignment of subject and image. . . . The classical cinema, through a regularization of vision and the subject's relation to the screen, reasserts and institutionalizes the despatialization of subjectivity.

(Doane: 43–4)

This new form of perception is attained at a price: the pleasures of despatialization and the thrill of being shot through space are counterbalanced by "the terror of collision, and its psychological effects, phobia, anxiety and, in many cases, hysteria" (L. Kirby: 116). Hysteria for the railroad passenger is the anticipation of de-railment. Hysteria for the film viewer is the assault on vision through discontinuous editing, rapid scale changes (extreme long shots to close-ups). As narrative cinema developed, invisible editing and montage absorbed the shock of the interrupted journey. With the improvement of both train travel and cinematic editing it can be argued that the hysteria produced by panoramic perception was reduced, but it can also be argued that it was psychologically hidden and became a repressed trauma for the viewer. The mobilization of the gaze made possible a new spatial subjectivity but it also generated the potential for repressed hysteria. Of course, as we argued earlier, hysteria is not necessarily a negative attribute if it encompasses a resistance to patriarchy. Thus, the paradox of simultaneous enlightenment and traumatization accompanies the mobilized gaze.

Anne Friedberg suggests that, through the mobilized gaze, the scale of the body with all its racial, gender and class pretensions becomes a much more fluid site for subjectivity: "a veritable depot for departure and return" (110). *Flânerie* was removed from the exclusive domain of men to anyone who had the capacity to consume, irrespective of age, gender, ethnicity, or race. Cinema, for example, allowed women to experience *flânerie* in the form of a mobilized virtual gaze. It allowed them to experience the "erotics of darkness and (urban) wandering denied to the female subject" (Bruno: 51). In this socio-sexual public space "different backgrounds, classes, venues, and genders are transgressively put in close touch, share intimacy in fleeting encounters" (Bruno: 52). In short, Friedberg and Bruno argue that the mobilized virtual gaze accommodates difference and liberates sexuality through the practice of transgressive spaces. These spaces offer indifferent boundaries where genders come together and change one another, which, in turn, allows the gaze to be reconstituted as a flexible medium. In what sense, then, do road movies construct transgressive spaces? Given the link between the mobile gaze and male hysteria, it is not difficult to argue that road movies symbolize a movement through the layers of repressed memories. This journey to being before self is upon a difficult road and so the road movie genre becomes entangled in its own sets of metaphors, myths, and vanishing points.

Sexuality may be liberated with the mobilized gaze and the creation of transgressive spaces but the vehicle of the road movie is often a powerful constraint on that liberation realizing its full potential. As Michel de Certeau asserts: "Only a rationalized cell travels. A bubble of panoptic and classifying power, a module of imprisonment that makes possible the production of an order, a closed and autonomous insularity – that is what can traverse space and make itself independent of local roots" (111). As a critical part of de Certeau's spatial stories, the vehicle may be thought of as critical ordering principles of everyday life, but it also embodies the rationality of Michel Foucault's panopticon. The mobility afforded by automobiles extends Foucault's and de Certeau's metaphors so that we simultaneously become jailers and prisoners within a moving panoptic cell. Michael Atkinson notes that "the structure of the car, designed both to conform to our bodies' shortcomings and powerfully extend them, has become how we regard the world". He likens the windscreen to a Panavision-shaped lens highlighting where we are going, and the rear-view mirror to a miniature movie within a movie that highlights where we have been. Our view from behind these Panavision-shaped lenses "is how we measure the width of continents (which have all become significantly smaller), how we both close ourselves up within our self-made universes and gain access to every corner of the globe" (16).

In what follows, we suggest that the *vehicle* as a rationalized panoptic cell and the *road* as a linear vanishing point provide spatial metaphors for the *journey* that constructs a political identity of maleness. This political identity constricts and emasculates while at the same time offering a subjectivity of mobility and freedom.

Geographies of the Road

In the preceding discussion, we established that new geographies are currently being theorized to highlight space and scale as important aspects of political and sexual identity. We suggest also that there are links between male hysteria and mobility that may be usefully probed by reinventing the notion of the gaze with an explicit consideration of transgressive spaces and mobile boundaries between subjects. In the balance of this chapter, we compare *My Own Private Idaho* and *Paris, Texas* with *Priscilla* to suggest that Stephan Elliott's movie bends back to and reifies rather than contests the "natural" patriarchal order of the gaze. Alternatively, the works of Van Sant and Wim Wenders, although not without problems, offer a more liberatory masculinity because they highlight the unnaturalness of spatial and scalar relations. Our arguments find focus in these three movies' representation of the *vehicle*, the *road*, and the *journey* as it relates to the spatial and scalar construction of masculinity.

We noted in the introduction that the bus in *Priscilla* embodies the three protagonists and provides a safe haven for their journey. It represents a mobile panoptic cell from which sexual and political identity are reified. One of the "adventures" of Priscilla is precipitated by a breakdown in the desert. This is the only time in the movie that Mitzi, Felicia, and Bernadette come close to hysteria. All of them, however, busy themselves with various activities so they do not think about the open space that threatens to engulf them. To "break down" like Priscilla in this open space would be a sign of weakness, a sign of defeat, a sign of hysteria. It is important to note that the only time the drag queens come close to losing confidence in themselves is during this breakdown. They are never hysterical, even in times of shock (Bernadette hearing about the death of a loved one, Felicia and Bernadette finding out about Mitzi's paternity, Felicia getting beaten up by the miners). Shock provides the possibility of crashing the panoptic cell and, by so doing, losing fixed subject identity to a multiplicity of personal, social, and spatial scales.

The hysteria of the road movie is the thrill of riding at the edge of self-identity, being simultaneously motionless (holding onto the scale of one's identity) and in motion (transcending social/spatial scales and annihilating space and time). The vehicle, however, locks us into an *a priori* spatiality that not only reifies identity but also fixes the gaze. From this position the gaze can only be projected or reversed, both of which are constituted within patriarchal logic. Mitzi, Felicia, and Bernadette may be spectacles in a homophobic landscape, but as they gaze upon that landscape they take power from its "otherness."

More often than not, the shock/thrill becomes the spectacle of identity, a glimpse of non-fixation, an existential moreness, to which we respond by being either ambivalent, happy/content, or hysterical in our situatedness. In *Priscilla*, shock reinforces the scalar fix provided by Sydney and, during the journey, by the bus itself. Rather than becoming hysterical about patriarchal subjugation, the thrill of the mobile adventure allows for the protagonists' return to place-based sedentarism. With the social disaster of the Alice Springs cabaret performance behind them, but with a new sense of belonging engendered by the reunion of Mitzi and his son, the three drag queens fulfill Felicia's fantasy by climbing King's Canyon in full costume: "a cock in a frock on a rock" times three. From the vantage point of King's Canyon, Bernadette looks out over the Australian bush and comments "It never ends, does it? All that space!" Felicia asks "So, what now?" to which Mitzi replies "I think I want to go home." In the penultimate scene, Felicia plays with Mitzi's son in the back of the bus as they drive back to Sydney; from the driver's seat a close-up of Mitzi's face suggests paternal pleasure.

Despite the liberatory potential of Mitzi's creation of home, family, and community, *Priscilla* does not offer a new model of masculinity and the gaze because it buys into the architecture of stable space, naturalized notions of scale, and a sedentary form of being. By encompassing their sexual and political identities within the bus and thereby creating a safe haven for the journey, there is never a possibility of contestation and the only moment of potential hysteria is when the bus breaks down. In one sense it is refreshing to view a movie that affirms gay identity and suggests the naturalness of same-sex parenthood. This notwithstanding, our contention is that the broader narrative of the movie, with its focus on family, community, and sedentarism is suffused with a seemingly incontestable patriarchal logic.

If the vehicle is a panoptic cell that offers subject stasis, the road offers a linear conduit to an infinity beyond the constraints of the body. A primary focus of *My Own Private Idaho* is the road as a rational, connecting mode of movement for the vehicle as it travels between locales. Gus Van Sant's movie opens with Mike standing in the middle of a road that traces linearly straight out in front of him to a vanishing point on the crest of an Idaho hill: "I always know where I am by the way the road looks. Like I just know that I've been here before. I just know that I've been stuck here. Like this one fucking time before. . . . There is not another road that looks like this road. It is one kind of place. One of a kind." Mike walks away from his duffel bag and into the middle of the road. The duffel bag slowly collapses to one side and then, Mike too, collapses to one side. Throughout the movie, Mike's narcolepsy "enables an eerie, yet exhilarating sense of dislocation and narrative slipperiness. It's often unclear whether we're inside or outside Mike's skull, in real time or dream space. Whenever Mike falls out, Van Sant's camera winks out of existence, too. Events unfold in jump cut. We recurrently awaken with Mike as if the world were newly invented, under clouded circumstances in obscure locales" (Greenberg: 24). With *My Own Private Idaho*, we get a sense of the liquefaction of internal space as Mike's external space degenerates. Most people who suffer narcolepsy have frightening hallucinations accompanied by cataplexy. Mike exhibits just the opposite symptoms: his external space is his frightening hallucination, whereas his internal space is a comfortable place of mother love and images of a serene Idaho landscape. Through the depiction of Mike's narcolepsy, Vant Sant subverts the distinction between internal and external space. This distinction permits space and scale to appear "natural." Time and space circulate, collapse, and are turned inside-out in Van Sant's deliberately deranged meditation on the search for love and family.

With its focus on the road, *My Own Private Idaho* beautifully contrasts contrived mobile resistance and male hysteria. Mike, the son of a dysfunctional family, sells his body and lives his life out on the road as a mobile hysteric in the sense that his subjectivity and the road meet in a powerless, disenfranchised blend. Mike's narcolepsy is related to a dependent-symbiotic relationship with his mother. His narcoleptic escape to the image of his mother's arms in the heartland of America seems to occur whenever he is stressed over a hustle. The rich imagery of the movies' initial sequence – country and western music, clouds billowing across the screen, giant plastic cowboys – ends with a little wooden cabin plummeting from the heavens on Mike's road. No longer in Idaho, he is awakening out of his rural fantasy as he climaxes for an unseen client.

Dependency is so strong in Mike that his narcolepsy becomes an expression of separation anxiety and hysteria.[4] Throughout the movie, he searches for mother love and nurturing on a road that symbolizes these securities but is unable to provide them. Mike wants to be part of a normal family. "What's normal?" asks his friend Scott. "A mom and dad, and shit like that" he replies. River Phoenix's portrayal of Mike as a lost innocent gained him critical acclaim and the beauty of Van Sant's direction is that it rises above the degradation and dysfunction of his life with a poetic faith that makes real the vision of innocence. Mike's neurological disorder enables Van Sant to muddle time, space, and place in a feeling that leaves us diverted from his neurosis and concerned about the person.

Perhaps it is Van Sant's unexpected mobilization of subject and space that is the ultimate promise of the vanishing point of the road. With his friend Scott, Mike steals a motorcycle to travel the heartland in search of his mother. The journey is a narrative device for Mike's search for self. The scenes with Scott and Mike on the road are some of the most affecting in the movie. They are two friends moving together in opposite directions and with different motives. Mike's battle is an attempt to find his way back to his mother, whereas Scott is intent upon embarrassing and tormenting his homophobic father, the mayor of Portland, by slumming with street people and prostituting himself. In the scene where we first meet Scott, he finds a safe resting place for a cataplexed Mike after they turn a trick for a rich Seattle woman:

> I grew up in a neighborhood like this with my Dad. He has more fucking righteous gall than all the people he lords over. And those he created, like me his son. But I almost get sick thinking I am a son to him. You know you have to be as good as him to keep up. You have to be able to lift as big a weight. You have to be able to throw that weight as far. Or make as much money. Or be as heartless. My Dad doesn't know that I'm just a kid. He thinks that I'm a threat.

Scott's mobile resistance is contrived because he is biding time until he receives an inheritance on his twenty-first birthday. His resistance is to the upper class lifestyle of patriarchy and hegemonic masculinity represented by his father. The metaphor of Scott as threat is played out in the first meeting of father and son when Scott almost causes his father to have a heart attack. By positioning himself as "threat," Scott solidifies his alter street persona. Resistance to the father is a disassociation from him and his ideals, and the acceptance of another mobile, street father/lover, Bob Pigeon, a Falstaff character to Scott's Prince Hal. Once distanced from the theatrics of Bob Pigeon's court, Scott confesses that he has always been planning to change his image back into the world of his father's hegemonic norm. His mobile resistance is just a mask, but the only "real" power he wields is the choice of when to turn back into hegemony's grasp. Even this decision is taken away from him when he falls in love with a woman in Italy as part of the search for Mike's mother. By precipitating his decision to return to the patriarchal realm of his real father, this new-found heterosexual love removes him from the road and, also, from Mike's unrequited homosexual love. When

Scott returns to Portland his view of the street (and Mike) is from the panoptic bubble of his limousine. Scott's final reinscription into his new role is a Shakespearian denunciation of his Falstaff father and the subsequent funerals of both of his fathers, symbolizing Scott's passage into masculinity. The funerals take place on the same day in the same cemetery with Mike and Scott watching each other from the other side of a newly created class and sexual boundary. Scott's ability to jump scale in this way highlights Mike as a lost innocent. Scott has learned to harness the powers of larger scales: he moves into the "natural" space of patriarchy but still leaves open the possibility of returning to the transgressive, mobile space of the street. Scott's resolution is to position his two lifestyles as mutually exclusive — he cannot combine them in a mutually coherent whole and consequently must occupy the "space" of one or the other.

Scott and Mike play out two forms of masculinity caricatured respectively by obsessive father hate and duplicity, and by mother love and lost innocence. It is Mike's spatial story, however, that carries the moral edge of movie. Mike's own private Idaho is where the road leads him internally — back to his mother and the solitude of the vast Idaho plains. This idyllic place can be reached only through narcolepsy. At the beginning of the movie, before his collapse, Mike squints at the vanishing point of the road comprising a hill's crest and two trees which combine into the unsettling semblance of a face: "This is . . . like someone's face . . . like a fucked-up face. I know that face." In essence, the "fucked-up" roadface leads him on an Oedipal journey and the horrors of mother separation that it encompasses. Idaho is the heartland of his psyche, it is the one earthly place which reminds him of an internal harmony that connects him with his mother. Consequently he is forced to return to her time and time again (represented symbolically by the salmon returning to spawn at the beginning and end of the movie). The Idaho road is the place where his internal and external world meet, where there is the possibility of unity and order without the mother.

Like *Idaho*, Wim Wenders's *Paris, Texas* revolves around the hopelessness of an American nomad's search for self and family in a landscape of unreflexive icons. Paris is a "real" place in Texas toward which Travis journeys, but he never arrives. It is simultaneously a nostalgic search for his past, a forward-looking embodiment of reckless frontier spirit and a need for the security of his nuclear family. Like Mike's journey to his own private Idaho, it can be argued that Travis is searching for his Oedipal origins. Early on in the movie we learn that Paris is where Travis's parents met and where he was conceived. We learn also that, when he and his wife Jane were still together, Travis bought a "piece of dirt" in Paris that he hoped would eventually become their home. *Paris, Texas* is about the impossibility of the nuclear family and the sedentary male in place and taking responsibility.

Paris, Texas begins with Travis's return as a mute from the desert to find water. The desert may be an allegory for male hysteria. He emerges from a deeply focused aerial shot of a bleak landscape wearing a red baseball cap and a double-breasted pin-stripe suit. The camera focuses uncomfortably on his wild staring eyes. His search for water takes him to a bar where he passes out after sucking on ice. His brother Walter arrives after receiving a call from a doctor who is called upon to treat Travis. Travis does not wait for his brother but instead walks off back into the desert. Walter later catches up with him on a country road, but Travis is reluctant to enter the car. If the car is a panoptic bubble, then perhaps for Travis it represents a beginning point which could lead him out of his vast mobile hysteria into the confines of patriarchy and family. Finally, Walter persuades Travis into the car and takes him to a hotel, bringing him further into society and out of the desert. Just when Travis appears to be "coming around" he sees his face in the mirror and takes off again.

In *Paris, Texas* mirrors metaphorically contextualize the identity crises of the male subject. The mute Travis is in crisis over his own image because he cannot recognize himself. These early scenes position Travis at the border between transgressive space with its indifferent boundaries and the logic of the patriarchal gaze with its natural spaces. His inability to come to a Lacanian "mirror stage" again

Plate 16.1 Paris, Texas. Travis (Harry Dean Stanton) re-emerges from the desert, an allegory for male hysteria.

sends him running back to the wilderness of the pre-Oedipal land.[5] Walter picks him up again, this time on a desert railway track: "Do you mind telling me where you're heading. There's nothing out there. Don't you trust me or something." Walter takes him back to the hotel, where, after having taken a bath, shaven and attired in new clothes, Travis again contemplates his reflection in the mirror. This time, he does not run from his image. Travis has returned from the pre-Oedipal and now must find his way back into society. It is a photo-booth snapshot of his family and the picture of the lot in Paris that provide a conduit back into society. On the drive to Los Angeles with his brother, Travis finally talks to Walter: "Paris, Paris, Paris . . . Did you ever go to Paris? Could we go there now?" As he articulates this first sentence he has spoken in four years, Travis's finger is on a map of Texas pointing to a place that is only a few miles from where they are currently driving. Walter, unaware of Travis's finger on the map, thinks he is talking about Paris, France.

Travis is reunited with his son Hunter in Walter's home in Los Angeles. Our assessment of the apparent harmony of Walter's nuclear family is kept in abeyance with the continual noise of cars on the freeway. When Travis offers to meet his son at school and walk him home, Hunter replies: "Nobody walks here." Thus begins Travis's assimilation back into society. In one scene, he is looking through magazines when the maid asks him, "What are you looking for?" Travis replies, "The father." After a brief discussion the maid understands that Travis wants to look like a "father." Travis is trying to relearn his masculine role as father for his son. The maid asks him if he wants to look like a rich or poor father, because, as she explains, there is no in-between. Travis wants to learn the image of the rich father, the image of hegemonic masculinity. The maid dresses him in a white linen suit accompanied with a hat, and explains that a rich father is "dignified" and "stiff."

In a remarkable scene in the middle of a bridge over an LA freeway, Travis stops to listen to a lone, and seemingly hysterical, prophet of doom:

> You will be caught . . . I make you this promise on my mother's head! For right here today, standing on the very head of my mother . . . they will pluck you right out of your fancy sports cars. There's nowhere. . . . There will be no safety zone. . . . You will all be expedited to the land of no return! It's a delegation to nowhere, and if you think that's going to be fun you got another thing coming! I may be a slime bucket, but I know what the hell I'm talking about. I'm not crazy and don't say I didn't warn you. I warned you!

As the ranting subsides Travis moves closer and puts his hand on the man's shoulder in a gesture that presages those used by the angels in Wenders's *Wings of Desire* (1988) as they quiet the panic and anxiety of those they watched over. In his discussion of *Paris, Texas*, Tim Corrigan suggests that this scene highlights the possibilities of road for exploring "other cultural and other gendered geographies" (160). To us, it seems to suggest also a moment of clarity and serenity for Travis as he begins a new journey both metaphorically and physically.

After his encounter with the hysterical prophet of doom, Travis sets out, now accompanied by Hunter, in search of his wife. Travis reveals to Hunter that his own father died in a car wreck having lost the ability to imagine reality: "My daddy had this idea in his head that was a kind of a sickness. He had this idea about her and he looked at her but he didn't see her, he saw his idea. And he told people she was from Paris. It was a big joke but after a while he believed it." This revelation presages our discovery of Travis's own feelings about Jane and why he fled into the desert. Once again Travis crosses the desert, this time in a old, battered Ford Ranchero. He is tipped off by Walter's wife that he can find Jane at a bank in Houston where she deposits money for Hunter on the fifteenth of every month. The landscape of the journey to Houston, according to film critic David Denby, is that of a self-conscious American myth replete with the "comic surrealism of plastic and neon out in the great Nowhere" (52). As they wait for Jane under the video-cameras of the bank in Houston, Travis and Hunter are surrounded by a landscape of chrome, glass, and steel which is topped by an American flag hanging on the end of a crane. Jane arrives and they follow her to the bordello where she works. A mural of the statue of liberty covers one side of the building. It is a scene that could have been lifted from the pages of Jean Baudrillard's *America*.

In the penultimate scene, Travis confronts his wife in a peep-show fantasy booth of the bordello. They are separated by a one-way mirror through which clients can see the women, but the women can only hear the clients on a telephone. Travis recounts the events that lead up to his hysteria in the form of a parable. He speaks of a man who had become obsessively transfixed upon his wife, so much so that he could not keep a job because he longed to be with her. Soon his obsession turns to jealousy, alcoholism, and the thoughts of her cheating. The wife becomes pregnant and, after giving birth to the child, begins feeling more and more oppressed by family binds:

> She accused him of holding her captive, of making her have the baby. She told him she dreamed of escaping. That was all she dreamed about. Escape. In the dream she saw herself at night running down a highway, running across fields, running down dry riverbeds, always running and always as she was just about to get away he would be there to stop her somehow. He would just appear and stop her somehow. And when she told him these dreams he would believe her. He knew she had to be stopped or she would leave him forever. Then he tied a cowbell to her ankle so that he could hear at night if she tried to get out of bed. But she learnt to stuff a sock in the

cowbell and inched her way off the bed and out into the night. He caught her one night when the sock fell out and he heard her trying to run in the highway. He dragged her back to the trailer and tied her to the stove. He just left her there and went back to bed and lay there listening to her scream. He listened to his son scream. He was surprised at himself because he didn't feel anything. All he wanted to do was sleep and for the first time he wished he were far away lost in some vast country where nobody knew him, somewhere without language or streets. And he dreamed about this place without knowing its name and when he woke up he was on fire. Blue flames burnt the sheets of his bed. He ran through the flames to the only two people that he loved but they were gone. . . . Then he ran. He never looked back at the fire. He just ran. He ran until the sun came up and he could not run anymore. Then the sun went down and he ran again. For five days he ran like this until every sign of man had disappeared.

Travis's hysteria was caused by his inability to give his wife freedom to be herself, the bounds created by having to do productive work for the family, and his inability to condone the actions of his own father. The hysteria took legs and transported him back to the pre-Oedipal plane, a place without language where the crisis with the father did not exist.

During the telling of this tale, Jane realizes that she is listening to Travis and, when he finishes, she asks to see him. In a remarkable image from Wenders's

Plate 16.2 Paris, Texas. Travis and Jane (Nastassja Kinski) struggle to communicate.

cinematic genius, she dims the light on her side of the booth as he raises his lamp to shine it upon his face. What we see in the mirror is Travis's face outlined by Jane's blonde hair and superimposed upon her frame. There are several ways that this scene can be interpreted. The peep-show is the epitome of the male gaze and so, at one level, Jane's request to see Travis is as a classic reversal of that gaze. At another level, the scene could imply the narcissistic dominance of the patriarchal male gaze over women because the reflection we see is of Travis's image enframed by Jane's hair. As Jane watches Travis, he can only stare back at himself: "I can't see you Jane." In yet another take on this scene, Tim Corrigan suggests that Travis sees Jane "only in the image of his failure to have any history but his own, again blindly in love with his own symptoms" (156).[6] Another interpretation, one we find more satisfying, suggests that Travis has given up the power of the gaze and, by so doing, he recognizes, in a truly Lacanian moment, himself in the figure of the (m)other. We feel that this interpretation fits best with Kirby's flexible geography of the gaze because it suggests a negotiation between two people over the indifferent boundaries of male and female. Thus, both Travis and Jane give up the power of the gaze and recognize the contours of each other's political identities. Their separation is different from that of Mike and Scott at the fathers' funeral in *Idaho*. In Van Sant's conclusion to the relationship of Mike and Scott, boundaries are sharply drawn by class and Scott's ability to jump scale. For Jane and Travis, separation is metaphorically represented by the peep-show mirror that prevents them from connecting physically. But they have connected emotionally, through Travis's articulation of his hysteria, and this is more important than buying into the myth of a sustained familial relationship. In true Baudrillardian style, they are separated by the mirrored layers of their own illusions of the American myth.

Conclusion

Most road movies contrive a mobility of resistance that is produced from, and produces, male hysteria. Hysteria is brought about by road movies precisely because hegemonic concepts of masculinity seem to become unhinged but, nonetheless, the gaze remains immobile and embedded within the logic of patriarchy. This paradox occurs because, at its simplest, the space of the road movie subject is internally constituted by a mobile vehicle that makes possible a particular kind of visual power for the occupant. At the same time, scale is usurped as local ties are uprooted, and the subject's relations with external space are destabilized by literal, metaphorical, and narrative speeds. The mobile male subject becomes hysterical because he is disassociated from a local scale and/or vehicle and, hence, his own adequacy. This adequacy is defined by a dominant "reality" that is patriarchal in nature. Disassociated masculinity is also about a reordering of external and internal space and subjectivity. This comes about when one space can no longer accept the order and functionality of the other space. In the case of male hysteria, the external ordering can no longer be accepted by the internal. As we gaze outward we capture a world that allows our subjectivity to grow. When gazed upon we are situated in place. The internal gaze allows for growth, while the external gaze reasserts boundaries of self. Negotiating the dialectics of the internal and external gaze constitutes and bounds the healthy self. Dominant hegemonic "reality" is maintained through viewing a strict boundary between the internal and external, between the self and other. This allows hegemonic reality to naturalize and control space and scale. However, there are no "natural" breaks between the internal and external space.

Although the conflicting myths of freedom, mobility, and sexuality in movies such as *Priscilla* celebrate the potential of a liberatory masculinity, this celebration is moribund because these movies are structured through a gaze that is not only patriarchal but also *immobile*. Despite its subject matter, there are no transgressive spaces in *Priscilla* through which the subject of hegemonic masculinity can be contested. Alternatively, *My Own Private Idaho* and *Paris, Texas* create transgressive spaces where the mirror-images of *the* mother and *the* father in the Oedipal myth can be played out and rebelled against.

In *Idaho*, Van Sant's portrayal of Mike as a lost, mobile innocent is juxtaposed against Scott's contrived mobility and ultimate capitulation to patriarchy. It contests hegemonic masculinity more fully and subtly than *Priscilla* because it highlights the Oedipal battle and, by so doing, dares to contest the spaces and scales that reify patriarchal logic. Aided by a poetic imagery that relies on startling narrative and stylistic shifts rather than interpretative dialogue or linear plot designs, the film jumbles space and time. It is Van Sant's ability to jump scale and treat space in terms of mythic imagery that highlights Scott's duplicity with patriarchy and Mike's dependency on Scott. In short, it is the contradictions between Scott and Mike that ultimately transcend the myth of the hegemonic masculinity. At the end of the movie, Mike once more stands alone on his Idaho road and from the soundtrack we hear a quirky rendition of "America" played on a musical saw. Mike contests hegemonic norms – the patriarchal capitalism, heterosexuality, and the naturalized spaces that Scott ultimately embraces – with an innocent mobile gaze: "I'm a connoisseur of roads. Been tasting roads all my life. This road will never end. . . . It probably goes all around the world." Mike collapses in a narcoleptic fit. A pickup stops long enough for its occupants to get out and steal his shoes and duffel bag. After a while, another car pulls up and an anonymous man gets out, inspects Mike's soporific form and then carefully picks him up and places him in the car. It is a wonderfully inconclusive ending that rebels against the norms of sedentarism and patriarchal logic in a wasteland of American myths.

In *Paris, Texas*, Wenders's representation of Travis as a man coming to terms with his own hysteria is emblematic of the giving up of the gaze. At the end of the movie, Travis reunites his son with his wife and drives off into the Houston night. In a tape-recorded message left for Hunter, he confides a spatial resolution to his hysteria: "The biggest thing I hoped for cannot come true. I know that now. You belong with your mother . . . I am afraid of what I might find but I'm even more afraid of not facing that fear." Travis's inability to return physically to Paris is also his inability to be with Jane physically and his inability to accept the American myth of the nuclear family. Nonetheless, he has found language and is able to relate his tale of hysteria. As such, Travis's return of Hunter to Jane symbolizes his own return to the mother/Paris so that he is not locked somewhere in the mythic in-betweeness of space – between the two mirrors of the mother and the father – nor is he locked within the Oedipal myth.

Paris, Texas and *Idaho* construct masculinities as subordinate gender variants lying on the edges of hysteria and disassociation. Each concludes with continued mobility and the serenity of the central character before yet another hysterical border between external and internal spaces. While mobile resistance as displayed in many road movies may be viewed as a jump across *geographic* scale, it harnesses no power to change the scale of larger social structures because patriarchy is often able to confine this mobile resistance to manageable, albeit moving, scales. Movies such as *Paris, Texas* and *Idaho* successfully contest hegemonic masculinity only by constructing space and scale as contrived and unnatural.

Notes

1 Of course, today's road movies are not necessarily constructed with white males as the central protagonists: girlfriends (*Thelma and Louise*, 1991), blacks (*Poetic Justice*, 1993), Native Americans (*Powwow Highway*, 1988), the mentally challenged (*Rain Man*, 1988) and even pets (*Homeward Bound*, 1993) now take to the road. But, as Michael Atkinson suggests, "Thelma and Louise could not exist without a tradition of macho-dominated interstate rambling to counteract" (17).

2 Our understanding of male sexuality comes from a deep suspicion of the essential and naturalized categories of male and female. Masculinity is a complicated and unstable structure. Our sexuality is not fixed although gender is reified and naturalized through hegemonic biological, sexual, and social norms. Men and women adopt various strategies in their efforts to conform to, or to contest, historically and geographically mediated ideas of femininity and masculinity. There is no essential male or female body or essence. Our focus on masculinity in this essay is not narrowly defined by the male body but, rather, it recognizes different masculinities and the power relations and alliances that comprise these masculinities.

3 Egyptians and Greeks first diagnosed hysteria as the flight of the uterus away from the female body. Alternatively, male hysteria is the flight of the phallus. As Elaine Showalter explains, "hysteria is no longer a question of the wandering womb; it is a question of the wandering story. . . . The stories of race and gender in hysteria still remain to be told" (335).

4 Narcolepsy is sometimes called idiopathic, meaning "not caused by any other disease" (Kellerman: 66). Early studies suggested that narcolepsy was a kind of hysteria in that it is a reaction to intense psychological and emotional tensions. In addition, it is often related to life transitions such as first leaving home when there are strong feelings of dependency.

5 Jacques Lacan suggests that our oppositions develop at the "mirror stage" through a process of subtraction similar to that found in Freud's pre-Oedipal stage. Lacan's subject has no identity, but is being created in the fissure of a radical split. The identity that seems to be that of the subject is in fact an image fashioned by the subject's perceptions of what others see it to be (Aitken and Zonn: 198). Importantly, mirror stage occurs with the beginnings of language acquisition.

6 We believe that Corrigan repeatedly misses the point of Travis's hysteria. Travis is not indulging in narcissism and egomania, just as the desert is not constituted as a separate "outer space." Rather, both desert and Travis are constituted by hysteria.

Works Cited

Aitken, Stuart C. *Family Fantasies and Community Space*. New Brunswick, NJ: Rutgers University Press, forthcoming, 1997.

Aitken, Stuart C. and Leo E. Zonn "Weir(d) Sex: Representation of Gender–Environment Relations in Peter Weir's *Picnic at Hanging Rock* and *Gallipoli*. *Environment and Planning D: Society and Space* 11 (1993): 191–212.

Atkinson, Michael. "Crossing the Frontiers: The Road Movie Found New Wheels?" *Sight and Sound* 4.1 (1994): 14–17.

Barthes, Roland. "Dining Car." *The Eiffel Tower and Other Mythologies*, trans. Richard Howard. New York: Hill & Wang, 1984.

Baudrillard, Jean. *America*. London: Verso, 1989.

Bruno, Guiliana. 1993. *Street Walking on a Ruined Map: Cultural Theory and the City Films of Elvira Notari*. Princeton: Princeton University Press, 1993.

Corrigan, Tim. *A Cinema Without Walls: Movies and Culture after Vietnam*. New Brunswick, NJ: Rutgers University Press, 1991.

Cresswell, Tim. "Mobility as Resistance: A Geographic Reading of Kerouac's 'On the Road'." *Transactions, Institute of British Geographers: New Series*, 18.2 (1993): 249–62.

de Certeau, Michel. *The Practice of Everyday Life*, trans. Steven F. Rendall. Berkeley: University of California Press, 1994.

Denby, David. Rev. of *Paris, Texas*. *New York Times* (October 19, 1984): 52.

Doane, Mary Anne. "' . . . when the direction of the force acting on the body is changed.': The Moving Image." *Wide Angle* 7.1–2 (1985): 42–57.

Foucault, Michel. *Discipline and Punishment*. New York: Vintage Books, 1977.

Friedberg, Anne. *Window Shopping: Cinema and the Postmodern*. Berkeley: University of California Press, 1993.

Greenberg, Harvey R. Rev. of *My Own Private Idaho*. *Film Quarterly* (Fall 1992): 23–5.

Israël, Lucien. *L'hystérique, le sexe, et le médeoin*. Paris: Masson, 1983.

Kaplan, Anne E. "Is the Gaze Male?" *Powers of Desire: The Politics of Sexuality*, eds. Ann Snitow, Christine Stansell and Sharon Thompson. New York: Monthly Review Press. 309–27.

Kellerman, Henry. *Sleep Disorders: Insomnia and Narcolepsy*. New York: Brunner/Mazel Publishers, 1981.

Kirby, Kathleen. *Indifferent Boundaries: Spatial Concepts of Human Subjectivity*. New York: The Guilford Press, 1996.

Kirby, Lynne. "Male Hysteria and Early Cinema." *Camera Obscura* 17 (1988): 112–31.

Lacan, Jacques "Ecrits." trans. A. Sheridan. New York: W. W. Norton, 1977.

Rapport, Nigel. "Migrant Selves and Stereotypes: Personal Context in a Postmodern World." *Mapping the Subject: Geographies of Cultural Transformation*, eds. Steve Pile and Nigel Thrift. New York: Routledge. 267–88.

Robertson, G., Mash, M., Tickner, L., Bird, J., Curtis, B., Putman T., eds. *Travelers' Tales: Narratives of Home and Displacement*. New York: Routledge, 1994.

Rogoff, Irit. "Terra Infirma: Geographies, Positionalities, Identities." *Camera Austria* 42 (1993): 70–9.

Showalter, Elaine. "Hysteria, Feminism, and Gender." *Hysteria Beyond Freud*, eds. Sander Gilman, Helen King, Roy Porter, G. S. Rousseau, and Elaine Showalter. Berkeley: University of California Press. 286–344.

Silverman, Kaja. *Male Subjectivity at the Margins*. Routledge: New York, 1992.

Smith, Neil. *Uneven Development*, 2nd ed. Oxford: Basil Blackwell, 1990.

—— "Homeless/Global: Scaling Places." *Mapping the Futures: Local Cultures, Global Change*, eds J. Bird, B. Curtis, T. Putman, G. Robertson and L. Tickner. London: Routledge, 1993. 87–119.

INDEX OF FILMS

GENERAL INDEX